Church, Politics
and Society:
Scotland 1408-1929

Church, Politics and Society:
Scotland 1408-1929

Edited by
NORMAN MACDOUGALL
Department of Scottish History
University of St Andrews

JOHN DONALD PUBLISHERS LTD
EDINBURGH

ISBN 0 85976 094 4

Exclusive distribution in the United States of America and Canada by Humanities Press Inc., Atlantic Highlands, NJ 07716, USA.

Phototypeset by Burns & Harris Limited, Dundee.
Printed in Great Britain by Bell & Bain Ltd., Glasgow.

Preface

THIS volume grew out of a two-year seminar programme organised jointly by the Departments of Ecclesiastical History and Scottish History at the University of St. Andrews, and held in St. John's House, the Centre for Advanced Historical Studies in the university, throughout sessions 1980-1982. Speakers with specialist interests were invited to contribute papers on the broad theme of 'Church and Society', and as a result of the interest generated by what they had to say, it was thought desirable to make all the papers available in book form. The present volume is the result, covering an enormous timespan from the birth of Bishop Kennedy around 1408 to the reunion of the Church of Scotland with most of the United Free Church in 1929. No effort has been made to produce a comprehensive survey of the development of the Scottish Church and the institutions associated with it; rather this volume is concerned with the careers of prominent individuals within the Church and with the response of the Scots to the challenge of the vast ecclesiastical changes in the five centuries under review. If its publication helps not only to stimulate interest, but also further research on the subject, then this book of essays will have served its purpose admirably.

The editor would like to thank all the contributors for their patience and cheerfulness in meeting the demands of converting the spoken into the written word within a fixed time limit; Professors J. K. Cameron and T. C. Smout for their skill, enthusiasm, and work in the planning and carrying through of the series; and the latter also for his generous assistance throughout the editing of this book.

Norman Macdougall
St. Andrews, 1983

Contents

Contributors

Norman Macdougall is Lecturer in Scottish History, University of St. Andrews

Leslie Macfarlane has recently retired as Reader in Medieval History, University of Aberdeen

Roderick Lyall is Lecturer in Scottish Literature, University of Glasgow

Jenny Wormald is British Academy Reader in the Humanities and Lecturer in Scottish History, University of Glasgow

Michael Lynch is Lecturer in Scottish History, University of Edinburgh

Roger Mason is the Glenfiddich Research Fellow in Scottish History, University of St. Andrews

James Kirk is Lecturer in Scottish History, University of Glasgow

Walter Makey is Edinburgh City Archivist

Julia Buckroyd is Director of the Hollins College London programme

Henry Sefton is Master of Christ's College, Aberdeen, and Lecturer in Church History, University of Aberdeen

Richard Sher is Special Lecturer in History and Humanities at New Jersey Institute of Technology

Alexander Murdoch is the author of 'The People Above': Politics and Administration in Mid-Eighteenth Century Scotland (1980)

Ian Machin is Reader in Modern History, University of Dundee

1

Bishop James Kennedy of St. Andrews: a reassessment of his political career

Norman Macdougall

JAMES KENNEDY was a major figure in the Scotland of his day. His virtues as a scholar, as a prominent papalist during the schism of the 1430s and 1440s, and perhaps above all as the energetic creator of St. Salvator's College in St. Andrews, have been covered at length, and very ably, by modern writers, above all Dr. R. G. Cant[1] and the late Dr. Annie Dunlop.[2] From their work emerges the picture of a man who combined scholarship and piety with efficient organisation of his diocese and his new college, a cosmopolitan figure of considerable significance. The bishop's achievements at St. Andrews have rightly earned him pride of place as the most outstanding man of his time in the burgh and the diocese over which he presided for a quarter of a century; and his reputation, in Fife at least, is secure.

Yet uncritical adulation of any public figure, however great his virtues, inevitably does truth a disservice, and in the century following Kennedy's death there grew up a distorted view of the bishop as a statesman of incomparable ability whose saintliness inevitably led him to the right decisions, and whose qualities in the political sphere are beyond dispute. This area — the political arena in which Kennedy played a part in three reigns — requires closer examination; for it would appear that the bishop's role in national politics was not nearly as significant as he himself would have wished, nor was his political career as successful, or indeed commendable, as later writers have suggested.

Such a view is not, perhaps, wholly original. In 1974 Dr. Ranald Nicholson took a few side-swipes at Kennedy, especially at the bishop's acceptance of an English pension towards the end of his life.[3] On the whole, however, modern writers — including Nicholson — have viewed the Bishop of St. Andrews favourably, setting him on a pedestal at least as high as the other great fifteenth-century ecclesiastical statesman, William Elphinstone of Aberdeen. Understandably the best press of all for Kennedy comes from his biographer, Dr. Annie Dunlop, whose *Life and Times of James Kennedy* is a formidable work of scholarship, quite indispensable to anyone working on fifteenth-

1

century Scottish history. But Dr. Dunlop's book is much more a 'Times' than a 'Life' of Kennedy, indeed in parts of the work she loses sight of the bishop altogether and plunges into an extremely detailed description of the political events of the reign of James II. When her bishop does emerge he is often thrust into the forefront of political life simply because his biographer felt that he should have been there. How far can this wishful thinking be justified by the available evidence?

Here we encounter an immediate problem, namely that Kennedy — like many other major fifteenth-century figures — lacks a contemporary biographer, so that his reputation is based largely on the narratives of sixteenth-century chroniclers — John Major, Bishop John Lesley, Robert Lindsay of Pitscottie, and George Buchanan. For the reign of James II, and the early years of the minority of James III — the 'essential' Kennedy period — there exists only one contemporary narrative, the so-called 'Auchinleck Chronicle', some fifteen folios of the Asloan manuscript, which sketchily covers the period 1420 to 1461 in at least two separate series of entries. Entitled 'ane schort memorial of the Scottis corniklis for addicoune' — presumably for addition to the Scotichronicon — these curious fragments, frequently separated by gaps and incomplete at the end, nevertheless provide an extended treatment of the political events of James II's reign, and a precise detailing — including the keeperships of the principal royal castles — of those who held power during the early minority of his son.[4] Yet in the entire 'chronicle' there is only a single reference to Bishop Kennedy. Under the date 1445, the writer describes 'ane richt gret herschipe' made in Kennedy's Fife lands by the Earl of Crawford, James Livingston, and the Ogilvies, and goes on to say: 'Incontinent eftir, bischope James Kennedy cursit solempnitlie with myter and staf, buke and candill contynually a yere and Interdytit all the placis quhar thir personis ware'. The curse was apparently effective, for within a year Crawford was mortally wounded in a fight with Huntly at Arbroath, and he died within eight days. After Crawford's death, the chronicler continues, no-one could risk burying him because of the bishop's curse, and the earl's body lay for four days until Kennedy sent the prior of St. Andrews to lift the interdict.[5]

Thus in the entire contemporary historical literature of the period — admittedly very scanty[6] — Kennedy is remembered only for the power of his curse. This is slender evidence on which to build a career for the man who would eventually be remembered as the greatest ecclesiastical statesman of his day, the wise counsellor of James II who played a vital part in crushing the Black Douglases in the 1450s and was the natural choice as head of the government in the early 1460s. For it is not until the early sixteenth century that Kennedy's supposed key role in Scottish politics of the 'fifties and 'sixties is given extended treatment.

The starting point for any discussion of this sixteenth-century legend must be John Major's *History of Greater Britain*, published in 1521.[7] Although Scottish events are not Major's main concern, he has a great deal to say about the Bishop of St. Andrews. He mentions St. Andrews university and Kennedy as its first real benefactor, founding a college 'small indeed, but fair to look at and of good endowment'.[8] He describes Kennedy's translation from Dunkeld to St. Andrews in 1440, and then moves on to the events of the 'fifties and 'sixties. In the crisis following James II's murder of William, eighth earl of Douglas, at Stirling, Kennedy plays a vital role. According to Major, 'by the wise measures of James Kennedy, Archbishop (sic) of St. Andrews, who was cousin to the King, the King was victorious . . . for Scotland, as I see, the earl of Douglas was too powerful: he had thirty or forty thousand fighting men ever ready to answer his call . . . It is related by many that from the beginning of his reign James the Second felt the burden of the Douglas power so strongly that he had it in mind to desert his kingdom of Scotland; but by the wise counsel of James Kennedy and the active help of this prelate he was enabled to form a loftier purpose. Kennedy so carried things that the earl of Angus, a Douglas by name, and his brother on the mother's side, and most of the other brothers of earl Douglas, were brought over to the side of the King'.[9]

Thereafter Major passes on at once to further moralising on the perils of exalting great houses like the Black Douglases; but he has already said enough to establish Kennedy's position as James II's right-hand man, winning over the opposition and so helping to crush the Earl of Douglas. The assumption throughout is that the Douglases posed a vital threat to the king and were at one stage stronger than him in the armed support which they could muster. In the interests of accuracy, it should be said at once that Kennedy was not archbishop, that the Earl of Angus needed no winning over to the royal side as he was a royal supporter throughout, and that Kennedy certainly did not bring over to the king the other brothers of Douglas, one of whom was killed in battle against the royal forces, and two of whom were executed. The conclusion must be that Major had little detailed information about the events or the personalities of the 1450s, and that he was following a tradition established some time between that period and his own — a point to which we must return.

After the death of James II, according to Major, 'the king was a child, and the whole government of Scotland was then in the hands of James Kennedy, archbishop of St. Andrews'.[10] As we shall see, this statement is untrue; Kennedy was not head of the new government, but abroad when it was formed. Major's remark, however, reflects a tradition of the bishop's importance in his last years, a tradition also to be found in his obituary of Kennedy, which is worth quoting at length: 'In the year one thousand four hundred and sixty-six died James Kennedy, and he was buried in that college of St. Salvator at St. Andrews which he himself had reared and richly endowed. I have found among our fellow-countrymen no man who rendered more signal public service than this prelate. It was by the wise means of his devising and the skill with which he put them into practice that earl Douglas, the most powerful of our Scottish nobles, was brought to nought. In his time, too, the whole kingdom enjoyed tranquillity, and the truce with the English king was kept inviolate. Besides St. Andrews he held no benefice — unless it was that of Pittenweem, which amounted to no more than 80 pieces of gold. Yet did he build at his own charges, and richly endow it, a college at St. Andrews . . . In addition, he built a huge and very powerful ship, and likewise for himself he prepared a splendid tomb, so that many men are apt to put the question on which of those three things he had spent the most. Two points in this man's conduct I cannot bring myself to praise: to wit, that along with such a bishopric he should have held a benefice in commendam, even though it was a slender one; nor do I approve of the costliness of his tomb'.[11]

There are two separate strands in this obituary — Kennedy at St. Andrews, his college, ship, tomb, and commend, about which Major has broadly accurate information, and Kennedy as a national figure, about which he clearly knows very little at all. However, his aim was not primarily to describe accurately the events of James II's overthrow of the Black Douglases, but to point a moral about the dangers of the overmighty subject. For Major, writing between 1517 and 1521 and dedicating his history to the young James V, the Black Douglases were the classic fifteenth-century case of a noble family with so much power that the crown's position was menaced, a family moreover which, although crushed by 1455, forfeited and exiled, continued to support English intrigues against Scotland for the next thirty years. Furthermore, as Major was writing during the protracted and uncertain minority of James V, the theme of the overmighty subject was a very relevant one. He makes oblique references to the dynastic ambitions of the Governor, John, duke of Albany;[12] and he was no doubt impressed by the unstable personal and political career of the queen mother, Margaret Tudor. There was a natural tendency for Major's work to reflect the problems of his own time, and this is nowhere more apparent than when he discusses the 1460s in Scotland. This period, viewed with more than half-a-century of hindsight, had apparently all the political elements which would be familiar to Scots during James V's youth — a royal minority, faction at court, and a dubious queen mother, Mary of Gueldres.

This last element — the role of Mary of Gueldres in the early 1460s — provides us with a clue to the motivation behind at least some of the Kennedy legend. Queen mothers have rarely been popular historical figures, and in terms of propaganda which can be mounted against them, they are exceedingly vulnerable simply because of their sex. Thus Major, who was clearly aware of Kennedy's control of the young James III at the end of the bishop's life, and who knew that Kennedy and Mary of Gueldres had been rivals in the early 1460s, also absorbed a tradition, nowhere enshrined in writing until the late fifteenth century in the annals of William Worcester,[13] that the queen mother had taken lovers after her husband's death. As Major describes it, Mary of Gueldres had 'dealt lewdly' with Adam Hepburn of Hailes, a married man, and he was quick to point the moral: 'Now, I say that this woman was herein exceeding careless, for she should rather have taken a lord who had no wife, or the heir of some lord; and she thus acted more wickedly than did the wife of James the First'.[14] It seems probable that the sixteenth-century chroniclers, drawing on oral tradition for their information about the activities of queen mothers following their husbands' deaths, confused the two women. Joan Beaufort, daughter of the Earl of Somerset, died in Dunbar castle, the keeper of which was Adam Hepburn of Hailes, in 1445; Mary of Gueldres died only eighteen years later, and later rumours named her *lovers* as the Duke of Somerset and Adam Hepburn of Hailes, at Dunbar castle.[15] If such a confusion did exist, and the chroniclers' censures are directed against the wrong queen mother, then the claims that Mary of Gueldres was a wilful woman endangering the minority government by her low amours, restrained only by the good Bishop Kennedy, cannot be sustained, and the modern historian requires to look very closely, not at the queen mother, but at the political motives of the bishop.[16] In the early sixteenth century, John Major had no such problems; and the good — and indeed justified — opinions of Kennedy which had come down to him because of the bishop's work at St. Andrews were merely reinforced by the apparent instability of the queen mother, a situation with which Major was very familiar in his own day. What Major therefore established, or at least confirmed, in his *History* was the legend of Kennedy as the principal supporter of James II against the Black Douglases, and as the upholder of good government committed to him after the death of that king because of the vagaries of the queen mother, Mary of Gueldres.

Once established, the Kennedy legend grew at some speed during the sixteenth century. In his vernacular history, completed by about 1568,[17] Bishop John Lesley enlarges on Major's theme of the dangers of the overmighty subject, and makes much of the struggle between James II and the Black Douglases in the early 1450s. He claims that after the assassination of the eighth earl by the king in February 1452, the Black Douglas opposition was so strong that the king 'wes determinit to haif left the realme, and to haif passit in Fraunce by sey, were not that bischop James Kennedy of St. Androis causit him to tarrye, upoun the hoip he had of the assistance of the Erle of Huntlye principallie, quhome he had persuadit to convene ane army furthe of the northe partis, and com forduart to the south for the Kingis relief'. There duly followed the battle of Brechin in May 1452, when Huntly as the royalist general defeated Crawford, the ally of the Black Douglases. But Lesley then turns immediately to describe the final confrontation between James II and the new earl of Douglas and his supporters, whom he credits with an army of 30,000, greatly outnumbering the royal force. King James, however, did not despair but, 'encouraged be the prudent and wise counsell of the bischop of Sainct Androis, sent a herrald to the Erle of Douglas, and required him to scale his army and submit himself to the King, or ellis that he wald gif him battell the nixt daye.'[18] There follows Lesley's description of the defection to the royal faction of the principal Douglas supporters, and praise of James II for avoiding civil war — a remarkable verdict on a man who started it no less than three times in five years.[19] Lesley's final comment on the fall of the Douglases once again stresses Kennedy's involvement. 'The King,' he writes, 'using the advice of his kinsman James Kennedy' — at this point upgraded to archbishop — 'compassed his purpose in the ende, dispatching out of the waie all theis as he any waies mistrusted; of quhilk nomber namely war the Douglas, whose puissance and auctorite (not without cause) he ever suspected'. Lesley concludes by repeating almost verbatim Major's words on the subject of James II's desire to flee the realm, his being restrained by Kennedy, and Kennedy's bringing over to the royal side the Earl of Angus; and he follows Major exactly in passing on to a homily on the dangers of the overmighty subject.[20]

However, when he moves on to consider the opening of the reign of James III, Lesley has some new information, for instead of simply accepting Kennedy as head of the government, he claims that there was a council of regency which included, apart from Kennedy himself, the queen mother, the Bishop of Glasgow, and the Earls of Angus, Huntly, Argyll, and Orkney. He is, however, quick to assert Kennedy's supremacy within this group by remarking that 'during the tyme that B. James Kennedy leivit, [the council] aggreit weill on the governement of the realme, bot nocht so weill eftir his deceis'.[21] Lesley's obituary of Kennedy follows, with the bishop dying about a year late on 10 May 1466, and described as 'noble, wise, and godly'. By Kennedy's advice, in this account, James II had 'subduit the Erle of Douglas and his faction, and keipit guide peace with Ingland'. Lesley concludes with conventional praise of Kennedy's college, his ship, and his tomb, and speculation as to which of the three cost the most.[22]

Thus Lesley's account, though fuller than that of Major — as might be expected of a man who had access not only to printed parliamentary records but also consulted diplomatic material and monastic cartularies — does not substantially extend the Kennedy legend. The two additions to it are his claim that Kennedy was responsible for bringing the Earl of Huntly over to James II's side in 1452, and the statement that the bishop kept a firm peace with England.

When we turn to the *Historie* of Robert Lindsay of Pitscottie, completed in 1579, we find that the author lives up to his reputation as the most colourful and least accurate of the sixteenth-century chroniclers.[23] Naming John Major as one of his sources, Pitscottie provides us with two already familiar themes, namely Kennedy's vital assistance to James II during the Black Douglas crisis of the 1450s, and his heading of the government in the early 1460s. In the former case, he describes a large rebel army, far larger indeed than the king's, confronting James II 'to caus him ather to fecht or flie out of Scotland . . .' The king in despair sailed to St. Andrews to ask for Kennedy's counsel, and the bishop, whom Pitscottie assures us was 'ane wyss and godlie man', suggested that James II should have dinner while he went off to his oratory to pray for the king 'and the common weill of this cuntrie'.[24] James II ate and Kennedy prayed, and then the king himself was set to praying for victory over the Earl of Douglas, 'lykas he had done befoir of him and his predecessouris quhan thay oppressit the common weill of the cuntrie' — a reference no doubt to God's assistance in James II's assassination of the eighth earl in 1452.[25] Some of the Pitscottie manuscripts[26] here interpolate the tale of the sheath of arrows.

Kennedy took the king to his study where James's bow and arrows were conveniently lying, handed him a number of arrows strongly bound together and invited him to break them over his knee. When the king protested that this was impossible, Kennedy took the arrows one by one, proceeded to break each of them separately, then pointed out the obvious moral — that James II could not break his enemies when they were gathered together in strength, but might well do so if he tackled them one at a time. In practical terms, Kennedy's advice to the king in Pitscottie's account was to grant remissions to all those in arms against him if they would come over to his side. The bishop's contribution to this enterprise was to bring over James Hamilton, described as 'principall captaine to the Erle of Douglas at this time'.[27] Thus another small strand was added to the Kennedy legend. In Major's account, the bishop was responsible for bringing over the Earl of Angus to the royal side; in Lesley, it was Huntly *and* Angus; and in Pitscottie it becomes Hamilton.

When he comes to deal with the minority of James III, Pitscottie dispenses with the complexities of Lesley's councils of regency, and simply tells us: 'In this time Bischope James Kennedie hes the gyding of the king and his consall in good wnitie and peace quhairbe the common weill florischit greatlie'. He also credits Kennedy with organising a fifteen years' truce with England, though as he remarks with refreshing candour, 'the speitall cause of tranquilietie and peace in Scotland was because the Inglischemen had civell weiris amang thame selffis'.[28] Thereafter it remains only for Pitscottie to follow the Major-Lesley line in describing Kennedy's three main achievements — his college, his ship, and his tomb — and to throw in a tentative cost of at least £10,000 sterling for each, before passing on to the bishop's obituary. His virtues are extolled at length; he was godly and wise, and learned in many sciences; he made quarterly visitations of every parish kirk in his diocese; he insisted on a large proportion of church resources being used for relief of the poor; and he kept parsons and vicars in their churches, preaching and ministering to the sick.[29] Thus Pitscottie, inventing his ideal churchman in the late sixteenth century, allots all his virtues to Bishop Kennedy, and turns a man whose concern for, and work in, his diocese is well known, into a kind of ecclesiastical superman.

George Buchanan's *Rerum Scoticarum Historia*, published in 1582, provides us with the final sixteenth-century flowering of the Kennedy legend.[30] In contrast with earlier writers, Buchanan is not at all concerned about the problem of the Douglases in the 1450s, and his remarks about the period are vague in the extreme. To solve the difficulty that 'the royal power was too weak to oppose the conspiracies of the wicked', Kennedy is credited with suggesting to James II that he should summon an assembly of the estates to Edinburgh. Shortly afterwards Buchanan describes the touching scene in which the Earl of Crawford, Douglas's ally, donned penitential garb, and in tears begged forgiveness of Kennedy and the king for his rebellion.[31] Apart from this set piece, there is no further reference to the Black Douglas crisis and Kennedy's supposed major role in supporting the king throughout. Instead Buchanan passes quickly on to the minority of James III, during which we are informed that 'James Kennedy, archbishop of St. Andrews . . . then surpassed all others in Scotland, both in authority and reputation'.[32] Having made this claim, Buchanan almost immediately denies it by indicating that Kennedy was in fact a leader of faction in the first parliament of the new reign. Edinburgh's Royal Mile apparently divided the opposing parties, with Kennedy and his supporters in Holyrood and the queen mother, Mary of Gueldres, in Edinburgh castle. According to Buchanan, on the third day of the dispute the queen mother emerged from the castle with her followers and had herself publicly proclaimed tutoress to the king and regent of the kingdom. Kennedy then appeared from Holyrood and made a speech at the market cross condemning the queen's faction, whereupon a fight between the two parties ensued, with the Bishops of Galloway, Glasgow and Dunblane finally intervening to plead for a month's truce.[33]

Buchanan's version of events was treated with contempt as early as the late eighteenth century, when Pinkerton remarked that many of his tales about the period were pure fabrication. But the great humanist continued to have his defenders, and as late as 1827 Aikman could still say that Buchanan's 'stern, unbending integrity' invariably inspired him to write the truth.[34] The remainder of the story, however, makes it clear that this was not Buchanan's purpose at all, and indeed supplies us with his motivation. The month's truce between the factions having expired, according to Buchanan there followed a public debate in which Mary of Gueldres briefly put her case for retaining control of her son, whereupon Kennedy delivered himself of an enormous oration, the main purport of which was to condemn the government of women. We may be fairly sure that, although Mary of Gueldres is named, Mary Queen of Scots was Buchanan's target, and he puts into Kennedy's mouth the argument that government by women was against nature and the ancient law, citing such unlikely precedents as the crimes of the Saxon queen Ethelburgh to prove his point. Those who support a woman as head of state, according to Kennedy/Buchanan, threaten 'to destroy the whole frame of our government, established on the best laws and institutions when they desire us to approve of female rule, for which our ancestors had not even a name'.[35]

In spite of pages of similar inflated rhetoric, Kennedy did not apparently make his point, for the outcome of the crisis, according to Buchanan, was the establishment of a council of regency of which the queen mother was a member.[36] Buchanan adds to this catalogue of contradictions and political infighting by going on to claim that 'the affairs of Scotland were administered with so much justice and tranquillity, that the oldest man alive never recollected any time of greater security, or more settled peace, chiefly owing to the wisdom and prudence of James Kennedy, who then ruled the court'.[37] Not surprisingly, the bishop receives a marvellous press from Buchanan in his obituary. The nation had lost 'a public parent', who 'exceeded in liberality all the bishops who have gone before, and all who have succeeded him, even to this day, although he possessed no great ecclesiastical revenue'. He is indeed praised for not collecting benefices to increase his wealth, 'that what was basely grasped by avarice, might be more vilely spent in luxury'. Somewhat inconsistently Buchanan then extols Kennedy for his magnificent and costly tomb, and ends by pointing a moral — that 'after he, who was the constant censor of morals, was removed, public discipline began to decay by degrees, and becoming corrupted, dragged nearly all that was virtuous along with it'.[38]

It is abundantly clear from all this that Buchanan, in spite of his lavish praise of Kennedy's virtues, had very little detailed information about the bishop. He says next to nothing about the Black Douglas crisis, does not know the name of Kennedy's St. Andrews foundation, and does not mention his ship. It follows that he did not draw directly on the earlier sixteenth-century histories of Major and Lesley, but was concerned above all to inveigh against the government of women in his own day. Thus, early in the century John Major had used Kennedy as an illustration of the forces of good battling against the misgovernment of queen mothers and the power of the overmighty subject; but by 1582 Buchanan had reduced the bishop's stature to the extent that Kennedy became little more than a vehicle for the condemnation of Mary Queen of Scots.

Herein lies the major difficulty in studying the political career of Bishop Kennedy. If we accept any of the sixteenth-century chroniclers' accounts at their face value, we are left with little more than an accumulation of half-truths, misconceptions, and colourful inventions; but if we ignore these later eulogies, all that survives is the contemporary 'Auchinleck' story of Kennedy's curse in 1445. Any estimate of Kennedy's true political significance, therefore, must be based on official records of the time — the Great Seal Register, Exchequer Rolls, acts of parliament — and on charters in private and foreign archives. Cross-reference between these and — where appropriate — the contemporary 'Auchinleck' fragments enables us to build up a sketchy picture of the political events of the time, and of Kennedy's place in them.[39]

The third son of a much married mother and a father who was probably killed shortly before the future bishop's birth, James Kennedy was born about 1408.[40] His mother, Mary Stewart, was the sister of King James I, and her first marriage had been to George Douglas, earl of Angus. The Kennedy children might therefore expect influential support and rapid advancement, and James Kennedy, who as the third son seems to have opted for an ecclesiastical career at an early stage, entered St. Andrews university about 1426. His expenses during his three years' Master's course were provided by the revenues of the canonry and prebend of Ayr, later replaced by the more valuable subdeanery of Glasgow; and for further endowment while at university he was granted a pension from the customs of Cupar. His benefactors were Bishop Cameron of Glasgow and his uncle James I.[41]

So far, so good. Kennedy took his Master's degree in 1429 and was holding academic office at St. Andrews the following year.[42] But then, possibly because his eldest brother had been imprisoned — together with the Earl of Douglas — by James I, and the Kennedys had fallen into disfavour, James Kennedy lost his Cupar pension, and went abroad to the new University of

Louvain, where he matriculated in the Faculty of Law and emerged as Bachelor of Decreets sometime before the end of January 1433.[43] However, if Kennedy had in fact lost favour with James I, he soon recovered it, as he was provided anew to the subdeanery of Glasgow in the spring of 1433.[44] But the real break-through in his career came almost four years later. In January 1437, disregarding the wishes both of the Dunkeld chapter and Pope Eugenius IV, James I thrust Kennedy into the bishopric of Dunkeld.[45] One can only speculate as to Kennedy's character at this time, but in career terms he may well have felt that, at the age of twenty-nine and after a difficult period when he had been forced to study at Louvain without even an academic post, he had now safely 'arrived'. Yet within a month of Kennedy's provision to Dunkeld, his uncle James I was assassinated and the new bishop was faced not only with hostility at home and abroad — the Dunkeld chapter and the pope — but with the political perils which were bound to follow the accession of the new king, who was only six.

Kennedy solved this immediate career problem in two ways; first, he gave his support to the new minority government of James II, and especially to the widowed queen Joan Beaufort,[46] to the extent that when the bishopric of St. Andrews fell vacant in 1440, it was through the queen mother's supplications that Kennedy was provided to the see. Secondly, he pacified — indeed gained the support of — the pope, who, absorbed by the problems created by his struggle with the Basel conciliarists,[47] was prepared to accept Kennedy as bishop of Dunkeld — in spite of papal reservation of the see — in return for the new bishop's loyalty.

He received it unreservedly. In under two years, Kennedy had emerged as the leader of the papalist party in Scotland, and reaped substantial rewards from a grateful pontiff — the abbey of Scone, to be held in commendam, from September 1439, and a rapid translation to St. Andrews on the death of Bishop Wardlaw the following year.[48] Most remarkable of all, when Kennedy proved incapable of raising the 3,300 gold florins 'common services' payable on entry to the see of St. Andrews — a failure for which he should have incurred the penalties of excommunication — he was rapidly absolved and allowed to remit only half the fixed sum.[49] But such positive commitment to Eugenius IV brought Kennedy into considerable danger at home, for many influential Scots supported the conciliarist pope — or anti-pope — Felix V. This group included not only the Black Douglases — by far the most powerful magnate family in Scotland — but also their allies the Livingstons, whose many offices included the vital custodianship of the young James II. Not only did the Douglases have clerical ambitions — Earl James the Gross's second son James was made Bishop of Aberdeen by Felix V in 1441 — but the Livingstons were kinsmen of the famous conciliarist Thomas Livingston, abbot of Dundrennan, who received Kennedy's old bishopric of Dunkeld at about the same time.[50] Thus from the start of the 1440s, Kennedy was struggling to survive and, apart from a brief period in 1444-5, he played no major part in political life throughout the decade.

Lack of reliable contemporary evidence for the events of 1443-4 makes any final judgment on the political struggles of these years impossible. What is undeniable is that a Black Douglas-Livingston alliance to control James II, and possibly also to thrust Sir William Crichton out of the Chancellorship, emerged in the late summer of 1443. Kennedy may originally have joined this faction, indeed one later source suggests that he acquired the vacant Chancellorship.[51] If so, he cannot have retained it for long, as James Bruce, bishop of Dunkeld, had been appointed Chancellor by the late summer of 1444.[52] Whatever the exact circumstances, Kennedy clearly felt that his political future lay in aligning himself with the opponents of Douglas-Livingston control of the young James II — that is, the queen mother, Joan Beaufort, her second husband Sir James Stewart, the 'Black Knight' of Lorne, the Earl of Angus and ex-Chancellor Crichton.[53]

The bishop had backed the wrong horse. In the civil war which followed, the Douglas-Livingston faction were clear winners almost from the start. They had possession of the king, and on his fourteenth birthday on 16 October 1444 they shrewdly declared him of age, so that not only could the queen mother no longer claim tutelage of her son, but also all opponents, including Kennedy, could be declared rebels guilty of treason.[54] By the summer of 1445 Angus and the wily Crichton had made terms with the new regime, the queen mother was dead, her husband had fled into exile,[55] and Kennedy's political future looked extremely bleak. If he had been moved to oppose the Douglases and Livingstons by fear that he might lose his commend of Scone, much more was at stake in the parliament of June 1445, when the victors seem to have considered depriving him of his bishopric of St. Andrews. A precedent for such action existed within living memory, for in 1425 Bishop Finlay of Argyll had been deprived for his part in the Albany rebellion against James I.[56] In the event, Kennedy did not suffer a similar fate, possibly because of his influence with the pope; but he paid the penalty for supporting the losing side in 1444-5 by failing to acquire any major office of state; and he had no chance whatever to influence the policies of the government for the next four-and-a-half years. His frustration is most clearly illustrated by his solemn cursing of the Earl of Crawford for harrying Kennedy lands in Fife. This action not only achieved the desired result — Crawford was killed at Arbroath in January 1446 — but earned the bishop his only reference in contemporary narratives.[57]

Kennedy's position remained uncertain as long as the adolescent James II was in the keeping of the Livingstons and their Black Douglas allies. But the emergence of King James as an adult sovereign in 1449 completely altered the situation, for the king speedily overthrew the Livingstons, forfeiting those in key offices, and executing two of them after a parliamentary trial in January 1450;[58] and with hardly a pause, James II went on to attack the Black Douglases, thus precipitating a further civil war which ended only with the total overthrow of the family in 1455. As we have seen, the sixteenth-century chroniclers, for a variety of reasons, turned history on its head at this point and suggested that James II was threatened by a formidable combination of feudal magnates whose armed might on occasions far exceeded his own; therefore assistance was desperately needed to prop up King James's shaky throne, and Kennedy provided it. But the truth seems to have been that the Black Douglases, although a most powerful family which had acquired for itself three out of the eight Scottish earldoms by 1449, constituted a threat only in the king's mind. Indeed, no clear evidence of treason on their part can be found until after the king attacked them; and throughout the crisis they were no match for James II's duplicity and ruthlessness.

What was Kennedy's role in all this? He was of course a supporter of the king, and no doubt hoped to repair his damaged fortunes in that way. Thus he sat in the parliament of January 1450 which condemned the Livingstons, and he joined Chancellor Crichton, William, eighth earl of Douglas, and the merchants of Edinburgh in making sizeable loans to James II — for all of them a means of emphasising their loyalty after the recent Livingston purge.[59] Thereafter his role was far more limited than later writers suggest, for three reasons — first and most obvious, he was not in Scotland during the early stages of the ensuing crisis; second, even if he had been, he would not have been James II's principal counsellor; and third, the king's desperate position in relation to the Douglases is largely fiction.

After his emergence from relative obscurity in the January parliament of 1450, Kennedy spent no more than eight months in Scotland; he held no office of state, but he frequently witnessed royal charters at Edinburgh, and he was present at a general council held at Perth in May.[60] Thereafter both he and his rival the Earl of Douglas went on pilgrimage to Rome to take part in the jubilee celebrations of 1450. Thus, between 28 August 1450 and 18 April 1452, Kennedy appears to have spent much, if not all, of his time abroad; he was certainly in Rome in January 1451 and at Bruges four months later.[61] It was during his absence and that of his fellow pilgrim Douglas, in the summer of 1451, that James II attacked the Black Douglas lands; and probably Kennedy was still abroad when, in February 1452, King James murdered Douglas at Stirling.

Even had the bishop of St. Andrews been in Scotland, he would not have played the major role ascribed to him by the later chroniclers; for the king looked elsewhere amongst the higher clergy for his political advisers. During the minority, between 1444 and 1447, his Chancellor had been James Bruce, successively bishop of Dunkeld and Glasgow;[62] and far more striking, William Turnbull, who succeeded Bruce at Glasgow, was Privy Seal for twenty years and quite overshadowed Kennedy as an influential royalist in the late 'forties and early 'fifties. Turnbull's influence was based partly on long service — apart from being Privy Seal, he had acted as royal secretary for a time, was a constant royal charter witness from 1428, and was employed as a diplomat as early as the 1430s — and partly on intimacy with the king. Thus James II thought highly enough of Turnbull to raise a loan from Scottish merchants in Aberdeen, Dundee, and Edinburgh to pay for the delivery of the bishop's Glasgow bulls; and Turnbull was first among the witnesses to King James's marriage contract in June 1449, at a time when Bishop Kennedy's fortunes were still in eclipse.[63] Apart from Turnbull, the dominant court group in 1450-1 seems to have included Chancellor Crichton and his brother George, the Admiral; and it appears to have been this triumvirate which incited James II to attack the Earl of Douglas.[64]

Finally, it would appear that in spite of subsequent royal propaganda designed to stress the menace of the Black Douglases — the classic 'overmighty subject' theme upon which John Major was to fasten — the Douglases were in fact the victims of sustained royal attacks designed to destroy them. As Drs. Nicholson and Brown convincingly show, it was James II, *not* the Douglases, who initiated the conflicts of 1451, 1452, and 1455.[65] Far from considering fleeing the kingdom, and frantically appealing to the absent Kennedy for assistance, as Lesley suggests, the king was so far in control of the situation that he could murder the eighth Earl of Douglas in February 1452 and have his action publicly accepted by the three estates in June. Even the circumstances of the murder itself suggest premeditation — a powerful earl who was nevertheless so frightened of his king that he demanded a safe-conduct before coming to a conference with James II at Stirling; a king who delivered the safe-conduct via one of Douglas's forfeited friends, William Lauder of Hatton; and who brought the earl to two days of talks, on the second of which Douglas had to confer not only with the king, but with a group of courtiers, most of whom stood to gain politically and territorially by Douglas's death, and who were quick to ingratiate themselves with the king by stabbing the earl twenty-six times.[66]

In spite of the murder, or perhaps partly because of it, James II received continued and increasing support throughout the spring. He himself was able to conduct a successful siege of Hatton Castle in Midlothian late in March or early in April; and on 18 May the royalist Earl of Huntly beat Douglas's ally Crawford for the king at Brechin.[67] The records make quite clear the extent of royal support at this time; apart from Huntly, James II could count on the Crichtons, the Earls of Angus and Orkney, and Bishop Turnbull of Glasgow, who lent the king 800 marks from the proceeds of the 1450 jubilee indulgence.[68] What of Bishop Kennedy? Probably some time during the spring, and certainly before 18 April 1452, he returned to Scotland and lent the king a modest £50.[69] His real contribution to the royal cause was to allow the queen, Mary of Gueldres, to complete her third pregnancy in St. Andrews, safe from the fighting taking place in Angus and the south and west. The future James III was born, presumably in the episcopal castle, towards the end of May, and the king's relief and gratitude to Kennedy are alike demonstrated in the 'Golden' Charter of 1 June 1452, confirming all the lands which the bishop had formerly received in regality from the crown, with immunity from tolls and levies and the right of minting money.[70]

Thus, fifteen years after James I had thrust Kennedy into high office, the bishop had safely 'arrived' and could be assured of royal support. In the remaining eight years of James II's reign, we find Kennedy as a fairly frequent witness to royal charters, a member of the first estate in the parliaments of 1452 and 1454, and an auditor of exchequer in 1452, 1455, and 1456.[71] He appears, however, to have played no major part in the final Black Douglas crisis of 1455, when in any case the king did not require his assistance, as the Douglas empire collapsed like a house of cards and Earl James's three surviving brothers were easily defeated by a handful of southern lairds at Arkinholm.[72] Kennedy may however have lent the king money over and above the initial £50 in 1452, for in 1456 we find him receiving a remission of custom on wool from his sheep pastured at Wedale, while in 1457 he was in receipt of the fermes of Ballincrieff in Perthshire, the latter grant expressly contrary to the Act of Annexation passed in the parliament of 1455.[73]

In spite of these signal marks of royal favour, Kennedy cannot be seen as the elder statesman of James II's last years, the wise ecclesiastic on whom the king relied for guidance and counsel. He did not receive any office of state; when King James required specific services for which rewards of government offices were appropriate, he turned to others. Thus George Schoriswood, bishop of Brechin, helped the king to filch the earldom of Mar from the Erskine claimant, and was made Chancellor for his pains;[74] while John Winchester, bishop of Moray, already a royal charter witness, ambassador, and parliamentarian, in high favour with King James since 1451, was made one of four royal commissioners to revise the rentals of the earldom of Moray when James II seized it in 1457.[75] At the very end of the reign, in the early summer of 1460, when the king found it expedient to change Chancellors yet again, he turned not to Kennedy but to Andrew Stewart, Lord Avandale, whose practical support for the crown during the Douglas crisis of 1452 had apparently extended to thrusting his dagger into the body of the eighth earl of Douglas.[76] Kennedy's support had understandably been of a less dramatic kind; and his rewards from the king were proportionately modest.

The accidental death of James II, aged only twenty-nine, during the siege of Roxburgh in August 1460 might substantially have altered the bishop's political fortunes. The new king, James III, was only eight, a long minority was inevitable, and Kennedy might have been expected to play an important role in the new government. But for the second time within a decade, Kennedy was abroad when major changes were underway at home. He had started out for Bourges by 17 June 1460, to take part in negotiations for a Danish marriage treaty and settlement of outstanding disputes between Scotland and Denmark, for which Charles VII of France had offered his services as a mediator. But Kennedy fell ill at Bruges, failing to reach France, and some time in 1460 Charles VII wrote exhorting the bishop to return to Scotland as soon as he recovered his health, in order to persuade the Scottish council to support the Franco-Lancastrian axis in foreign policy.[77]

The French king probably overrated Kennedy's political influence in Scotland; and in any case the bishop was too late. The first parliament of the new reign, which Kennedy does not appear to have attended, was held in February 1461, and the three estates placed the young James III in the care of his mother, Mary of Gueldres, and the lords of her council.[78] Kennedy's absence may be explained by his still being abroad — there is in fact no evidence of his return to Scotland before 2 May 1461[79] — and so he lost whatever chance he might have had of acquiring high office in the new regime. Thus Major's and Lesley's much later statements that the bishop had charge of the entire government of Scotland are simply untrue. The queen mother, a capable and determined politician, made a number of new appointments early in 1461 — for example she put her own men in as keepers of Edinburgh, Stirling, and Dunbar castles at the conclusion of the February parliament, and she chose James Lindsay, provost of Lincluden, as Privy Seal[80] — but she was largely content to rely on her late husband's leading ministers. Official records leave us in no doubt as to who these men were, and indeed provide evidence of remarkable stability and continuity of service in the higher echelons of government. Thus Andrew Stewart, Lord Avandale, made Chancellor by James II in 1460, held the post for no less than twenty-two years; Colin Campbell, earl of Argyll, the most active politician amongst all the nobility, was regularly at court in James II's latter years, a constant parliamentarian for twenty years, royal counsellor, Master of the Household from 1465, and an auditor of exchequer in July 1462.[81] Archibald Whitelaw, humanist, diplomat, and tutor to James III, was royal secretary for over thirty years from 1462;[82] while David Guthrie of Kincaldrum, later Sir David Guthrie of that ilk, was successively Treasurer, Comptroller, Clerk Register, and Captain of the royal guard over a period of thirteen years from 1461.[83] To these names may perhaps be added that of William Sinclair, Earl of Orkney and Caithness, who in June 1461 had the guardianship of the young James III, apparently with the approval of parliament.[84] These men, together with Privy Seal Lindsay, were the key personalities in the government of Mary of Gueldres; and four of the six were to continue in office for many years under her son. Their control of the major offices of state and royal household in the early 1460s is a salutary reminder that much of the political history of James III's minority can be written without reference to Bishop Kennedy at all.

Thus the later chroniclers, in describing the bishop's political career in the 1460s, were at least correct in stating that Kennedy was a leader of faction and an opponent of Mary of Gueldres; and it seems likely that the divisions between them were not so much matters of policy as of personality. Kennedy's exclusion from government following his late return to Scotland in the spring of 1461 no doubt helped to foster in him a sharp jealousy of the queen mother; and though the story of her misappropriation of royal funds is based on a much later misconception,[85] and tales of her adultery are quite unfounded,[86] Kennedy's struggle with Mary of Gueldres during the period 1461-3 is attested by the bishop himself in a despatch to the King of France, in which he fulminates about the great division in the country 'caused by the Queen, whom God pardon'.[87] We can only speculate as to what Kennedy hoped to achieve by setting himself up against the royal council and the three estates; possibly, mindful of the struggle for possession of the adolescent James II twenty years before, he saw history repeating itself and hoped to repair his own, and his family's, political fortunes by obtaining control of James III. The boy had after all been born in St. Andrews, and the bishop may well have felt that this fact, together with his unbroken record of loyalty to the crown before 1460, merited Kennedy guardianship of the king at this stage.

Whatever his hopes, Kennedy appears to have been unsuccessful, at least until the last months of Mary of Gueldres' life. Only very rarely is he to be found as a charter witness before September 1463; he had missed the parliament of February 1461 and does not appear to have been present at that of October 1462; he was not appointed as an auditor of exchequer until 1464, by which time the queen mother was dead; and he was not made an officer of state. As Bishop of St. Andrews, and a man with powerful kin in the west of Scotland, Kennedy was not of course politically impotent; but his contribution to the running of the kingdom before the autumn of 1463 seems to have been limited to joining the Bishop of Glasgow in an unproductive interview with the rebel Earl of Ross on the Isle of Bute in June 1461,[88] a visit which was probably prompted largely by fears for the safety of the nearby Kennedy lands in Ayrshire.

In the autumn of 1463, however, Bishop Kennedy's political fortunes underwent a dramatic change. From 13 September he is to be found constantly with the court, at Edinburgh and elsewhere, the first witness to all registered Great Seal charters.[89] The bishop's emergence from relative obscurity may perhaps be related to a sudden deterioration in the queen mother's health; for Mary of Gueldres died on 1 December 1463.[90] Since her husband's death her achievements, especially in foreign policy, had been considerable. Without striking a blow, she had recovered Berwick for Scotland from the fugitive Lancastrian king and queen, and had skilfully abandoned Lancaster for York when it was clear that the Lancastrian cause in England was doomed.[91] Kennedy's stubborn adherence to the unpopular Franco-Lancastrian axis long after it made any political sense finally collapsed in the face of the facts, and in 1464 a long truce with Yorkist England had to be negotiated. The bishop, who had been involved in a number of diplomatic missions throughout his career, took no part in this one; the fifteen years' truce arranged at York was the work of others.[92] Kennedy was however prepared to swallow his pride and accept a pension from Edward IV, presumably granted on condition that he used his influence to ensure that the Scots gave no further assistance to the house of Lancaster.[93] He may well have acquiesced in this with an ill grace; and only his death the following year really eased the path towards better relations between Scotland and England.

With Mary of Gueldres' influence permanently removed, what was Kennedy's political role in the last eighteen months of his life? Undoubtedly he acquired some of the power which he had been seeking for so long. The three estates, meeting early in 1464,[94] gave Kennedy custody of the young James III; he was one of the auditors of exchequer in May 1464; and he is to be found both in parliament and privy council. As custodian of the king he travelled north on the royal progress of summer 1464, a three-month-long journey which included visits to Dundee, Aberdeen, Elgin, and Inverness.[95]

Yet even in this last period of his life, Kennedy is unlikely to have had control of policy making. Dr. Dunlop remarks that 'it is significant that he changed none of the great officers of state';[96] but surely the truth is that Kennedy was in no position to do anything of the kind. His fellow travellers on the progress of 1464 — Chancellor Avandale, Colin, earl of Argyll and Master of the Royal Household, Secretary Whitelaw and Treasurer Guthrie — had all served Mary of Gueldres at a time when Kennedy had sought to undermine her position in pursuit of unpopular and inoperable foreign policies. Now the bishop had tardily obtained custody of the young king; but it was surely the 'great officers of state', rather than Kennedy, who dictated the direction of foreign and domestic policy. There is nothing in contemporary evidence to suggest that Kennedy had a pre-eminent position in the state in 1464-5; indeed, the fact that he was not involved in the York negotiations might lead us to believe that his role was limited to his guardianship of James III.

However, nothing became Bishop Kennedy so well in his life as his leaving of it. He died — appropriately enough at St. Andrews — on 24 May 1465, surrounded by the entire court, kin and rivals alike, and the young king for whose arrival in the world the bishop had provided the refuge in which he himself was now dying.[97] Present at Kennedy's deathbed was his brother Gilbert, first Lord Kennedy, keeper of Stirling castle, to whom the bishop had already entrusted the custody of the king;[98] and Kennedy's nephew Patrick Graham, whom he had helped obtain the bishopric of Brechin in 1463,[99] would succeed his uncle at St. Andrews. Viewing this belated advancement of his family and kin, Kennedy had some reason to die a contented man. But if, in his last hours, the bishop reviewed his own political career, he must have felt less cause for satisfaction. His search for high office was understandable; he was the son of Robert III's daughter, the nephew of James I, he had obtained a bishopric before he was thirty, and a brilliant career seemed in prospect. But almost immediately he had been dogged by misfortunes which stretched over a generation — the assassination of James I, the 'Little Schism' caused by the activists at the Council of Basel, and absences abroad in the crucial years 1450-52 and 1460-61. Successful men are generally luckier than Kennedy; but he also contrived to make trouble for himself by political blunders, such as backing the wrong side in the civil war of 1444-5, and by intransigence, most clearly illustrated in his efforts to impose a Franco-Lancastrian alliance on Scotland in spite of the opposition of queen mother and privy council. Indeed, it is likely that, but for the deaths of Bishop Turnbull in 1454 and Mary of Gueldres in 1463, Kennedy would not even have obtained the governmental position which he made his own at the end, that of custodian of the king.

Thus in 1521, when John Major praised Kennedy for his creation and erection of St. Salvator's College at St. Andrews, he had hit upon the bishop's lasting legacy. It has been no part of this essay to remember Kennedy for his artistic and educational endowments, and inevitably his role in government reveals only part of a many-sided man, a man who was far more than a mere political bishop. But the evidence would also seem to suggest that he was rather less than a saint.

NOTES

1. R. G. Cant, *The University of St. Andrews: A Short History* (Edinburgh and London, 1946), especially 22-7.

2. Annie I. Dunlop, *The Life and Times of James Kennedy, Bishop of St. Andrews* (Edinburgh, 1950).

3. R. G. Nicholson, *Scotland: The Later Middle Ages* (Edinburgh, 1974), 406.

4. The 'Auchinleck Chronicle' is printed in the Scottish Text Society's edition of the Asloan Manuscript (*The Asloan Manuscript*, ed. W. A. Craigie, Edinburgh and London, 1923, vol. i, 215-244). The original is NLS MS. Acc. 4233. Thomas Thomson, in a well-meaning effort to impose some sort of order on the text, printed it some time before 1819 in two forms — first with the entries in the order of the original MS., and then rearranged in what Thomson believed to be chronological order and given the arbitrary title 'A short chronicle of James the Second, King of Scots'. The result has not been clarification but further confusion, for Thomson's rearrangement is in many places highly questionable and in some instances clearly incorrect. Nevertheless his edition was issued in 1877 by T. G. Stevenson, who added a preface and a title 'The Auchinleck Chronicle' (because the MS. came from the library of Alexander Boswell of Auchinleck), but otherwise followed Thomson exactly. In my assessment of these fragments I have benefited greatly from Dr. R. J. Lyall's study of watermarks and the gatherings in the original MS. Dr. Lyall's findings will soon appear in print. In the meantime, it is salutary to remember that the 'Auchinleck Chronicle' was not written in Auchinleck and that it is not a chronicle.

5. *Asloan MS.*, i, 220.

6. Another possible source, a chronicle fragment appended to the earliest manuscripts of Wyntoun's *Orygynale Cronikil* and covering the history of Scotland from its legendary beginnings down to 1482 (B.M. Royal MS. 17 DXX, ff. 299r-308r.) does not mention Kennedy at all.

7. John Major, *A History of Greater Britain* (S.H.S., 1892).

8. Major, *History*, 28.

9. *Ibid.*, 383.

10. *Ibid.*, 387.

11. *Ibid.*, 388-9.

12. *Ibid.*, 218-9.

13. The best survey of Worcester's annals is K. B. MacFarlane, *William Worcester: A Preliminary Survey*, in *Studies presented to Sir Hilary Jenkinson*, ed. J. Conway Davies (Oxford, 1957), 196-221.

14. Major, *History*, 388.

15. This argument is more fully developed in Norman Macdougall, *James III: A Political Study* (Edinburgh, 1982), 54-7.

16. The other principal charge brought against Mary of Gueldres by later writers — that she was using her control of James III in the early 1460s to misappropriate crown

revenues — is based on a misreading of the Asloan MS., where the statement that the queen mother 'suld nocht Intromet with his [the king's] profettis bot allanerlie with his person' relates chronologically *not* to what has gone before — a section dealing with the parliament of 1461 and the depredations of the Lord of the Isles — but follows a gap in the MS. and should be considered together with the *next* entries, dated 1420, 1436, 1438 and 1440 (*Aslóan MS.*, i, 232-233). Although the identity of the queen mother is not revealed in the Auchinleck fragment, it seems probable that Joan Beaufort, *not* Mary of Gueldres, is intended. On James I's death in 1437, Joan Beaufort was granted £4,000 by the estates for the maintenance of her son James II, and was forced to give this up following her marriage to the Black Knight of Lorne in 1439. Modern writers (including Macdougall, *op. cit.*, 54) have failed to notice this discrepancy; and I am indebted to Dr. R. J. Lyall for confirming my recent suspicions about the chronology of the original MS.

17. John Lesley, *The History of Scotland from the Death of King James I, in the Year 1436 to the Year 1561* (Bannatyne Club, 1830).

18. Lesley, *History*, 23-4.

19. See Nicholson, *op. cit.*, 354-5, 359, 369-71.

20. Lesley, *History*, 25-6.

21. *Ibid.*, 33-4.

22. *Ibid.*, 37.

23. Robert Lindsay of Pitscottie, *The Historie and Cronicles of Scotland* (ed. A. J. G. Mackay, S.T.S., 1899-1911), vol. i.

24. Pitscottie, *Historie*, i, 116-7.

25. *Ibid.*, 117.

26. *Ibid.*, cl, 117-8.

27. This was a case of wishful thinking, based on the later power of the Hamiltons in Pitscottie's own time; and he gives the game away by crediting Hamilton with having mustered 300 foot and 300 horse, only a tiny fraction of the enormous Douglas army of 40,000 which he describes: Pitscottie, *Historie*, i, 118.

28. *Ibid.*, 153.

29. *Ibid.*, 159-161.

30. George Buchanan, *Rerum Scoticarum Historia* (translated Aikman, 4 vols., Glasgow and Edinburgh, 1827), vol. ii, books xi, xii. All references below are to Aikman's edition.

31. Buchanan, *History*, ii, 140, 156, 158.

32. *Ibid.*, 170.

33. *Ibid.*, 172-3.

34. *Ibid.*, 176.

35. *Ibid.*, 175-83.

36. *Ibid.*, 183-4. The names of the councillors — William Graham (Patrick Graham?), Robert Boyd, 'then Chancellor', Robert earl of Orkney, John Kennedy (Gilbert, Lord Kennedy?), and the Bishops of Glasgow and Dunkeld — reveal that Buchanan had very little information as to the personalities in power in the late 1460s.

37. *Ibid.*, 186.

38. *Ibid.*, 189.

39. The notes below will make clear my indebtedness to the late Dr. Annie Dunlop. One of the great strengths of her biography of Kennedy was her uncovering of information about the bishop's early career, and I have inevitably drawn heavily on this.

40. James Kennedy, the bishop's father, was the second husband of Mary Stewart. She married five times (probably), and came close to outliving her son, as she was still alive in February 1462: Dunlop, *Bishop Kennedy*, 2-3. James Kennedy (the father) was killed by his natural brother sometime before 8 November 1408: *Ibid.*, 2.

41. Vatican Registers of Supplications 249, f. 199v., cited in Dunlop, *op.cit.* (for canonry and prebend of Ayr); *Registrum Episcopatus Glasguensis* (Bannatyne and Maitland Clubs, 1843), ii, 615 (for Glasgow subdeanery); *The Exchequer Rolls of Scotland*, ed. J. Stuart and others (Edinburgh, 1878-1908), iv, 440, 468 (for Cupar pension).

42. *St. Andrews Acta* (SHS, 1964), i, 24, 30.

43. Dunlop, *op. cit.*, 7.

44. *Ibid.*, 12.

45. A. Myln, *Vitae Dunkeldensis Ecclesiae Episcoporum* (Bannatyne Club, 1831), 17; *Calendar of Entries in the Papal Registers relating to Great Britain and Ireland: Papal Letters* (London, 1893-   ), viii, 653.

46. *The Acts of the Parliaments of Scotland*, ed. T. Thomson and C. Innes (Edinburgh, 1814-75), ii, 31, 54; Dunlop, *op. cit.*, 23.

47. For an excellent elaboration of the problems posed for Scotland by the Council of Basel, see J. H. Burns, 'The Conciliarist Tradition in Scotland', *SHR*, xlii, 89-104.

48. Dunlop, *op. cit.*, 38, 39-41. Kennedy, whose career was dogged by his inability to be in the right place at the right time, was probably at the papal court in Florence when Bishop Wardlaw of St. Andrews died (9 April 1440). The conciliarist anti-pope Felix V provided James Ogilvy, vicar of Markinch, to St. Andrews, so that Eugenius IV's support for Kennedy had to be convincing if the latter was to prevail. Kennedy had returned to Scotland by 26 May 1441, but it was not until 30 September 1442 that he celebrated his first mass at St. Andrews: *Registrum Magni Sigilli Regum Scotorum*, ed. J. M. Thomson and others (Edinburgh, 1882-1914), ii, Nos. 266, 267; Dunlop, *op. cit.*, 40.

49. *Ibid.*, 40 n.8; and see n. 48 above.

50. Dunlop, *op. cit.*, 41-5; Nicholson, *op. cit.*, 332-8, for the details of the Scottish ecclesiastical contest during the 'Little Schism'.

51. G. Crawford, *The Lives and Characters of the Officers of the Crown and of the State in Scotland* (Edinburgh, 1726), 29, 32; Dunlop, *op. cit.*, 59-60, 59 n. 6; Nicholson, *op. cit.*, 339-340. It is possible that Crawfurd confused the offices of Chancellor of the kingdom and Chancellor of the University of St. Andrews in Kennedy's case. Significantly, Kennedy's first activity in the latter post occurred in 1444: Cant, *op. cit.*, 22.

52. *RMS*, ii, No. 273.

53. Nicholson, *op. cit.*, 341; Macdougall, *op. cit.*, 12; Dunlop, *op. cit.*, 64-76.

54. *Reports of the Royal Commission on Historical Manuscripts* (HMC), (London 1870-   ), Report xii, pt. viii, 114-5.

55. *APS*, ii, 59-60; W. Fraser, *The Douglas Book* (Edinburgh, 1885), ii, 39; iii, 427 (for Angus); Dunlop, *op. cit.*, 63; *ER*, v, 180, 221 (for Crichton); *Asloan MS*, i, 219; *ER*, v, 196 (for the queen); *APS*, ii, 59-60 (for Stewart of Lorne).

56. *Registrum Episcopatus Brechinensis* (Bannatyne Club, 1856), i, 100-102; Nicholson, *op. cit.*, 343.

57. *Asloan MS.*, i, 220.

58. *APS*, ii, 33, 35, 36; *Asloan MS.*, i, 235. For details *see* Nicholson, *op. cit.*, 350-351.

59. *APS*, ii, 37; *Glasgow Registrum*, ii, 373-4; *ER*, v, 393.

60. *RMS*, ii, Nos. 309-389 *passim*; *APS*, ii, 66.

61. Dunlop, *op. cit.*, 119, 433.

62. *Fasti Ecclesiae Scoticanae Medii Aevi* (2nd draft, St. Andrews, 1969), 98; John Dowden, *The Bishops of Scotland* (Glasgow, 1912), 322.

63. For Turnbull as Privy Seal and Secretary, see *RMS*, ii, Nos., 116-128; as diplomat, *see* Dunlop, *op. cit.*, 12, 166n. A succinct modern biography of Turnbull is John Durkan, 'William Turnbull, Bishop of Glasgow', *Innes Review*, ii, (1951).

64. The involvement of Turnbull and the two Crichtons in encouraging James II to attack Douglas is suggested in Law's MS. abridgement and continuation of the Scotichronicon (De cronicis Scotorum brevia (1521) and Continuatio (1524), Edinburgh University Library, Dc. 7. 63, f. 128 v.). John Law, canon of St. Andrews, was a contemporary of John Major, that is three generations removed from the events of the 1450s. But his isolated statement about James II's counsellors must be taken seriously because it is supported by available contemporary record evidence: *RMS*, ii, 403-416; and see *ER*, v, Pref., xxxvii, lxxxv-lxxxvi.

65. Nicholson, *op. cit.*, 355-6, 358-9, 369-372; J. M. Brown (now Wormald), 'Taming the Magnates?', in *The Scottish Nation* (ed. G. Menzies, London, 1972), 53; and in some more detail, the same author's 'The Exercise of Power', in *Scottish Society in the Fifteenth Century* (ed. J. M. Brown (now Wormald), London, 1977), 48-50.

66. *Asloan MS.*, i, 239-241; Dunlop, *op. cit.*, 132-3; Macdougall, *op. cit.*, 21-3.

67. *Accounts of the Lord High Treasurer of Scotland*, ed. T. Dickson and Sir J. Balfour Paul (Edinburgh, 1877-1916), i, ccxvii; *Asloan MS.*, i, 238.

68. *RMS*, ii, Nos. 533-551; *Ibid.*, No. 542 (for gift of 800 marks).

69. *Ibid.*, No. 544; *ER*, v, 604.

70. *RMS*, ii, No. 1444.

71. See Dunlop, *op. cit.*, 433-5 (Kennedy Itinerary).

72. Nicholson, *op. cit.*, 370.

73. *ER*, vi, 119, 359; *APS*, ii, 42.

74. *Spalding Club Miscellany*, v, 275-6; Dunlop, *op. cit.*, 185.

75. Dowden, *Bishops of Scotland*, 159-60; Dunlop, *op. cit.*, 178.

76. *ER*, vi, 617 (Avandale was already Chancellor by 19 June 1460, the date of the annual audit of exchequer); *Asloan MS.*, i, 240-241 (for his involvement in the Douglas murder).

77. Dunlop, *op. cit.*, 199-200 (for Bourges and Kennedy's failure to arrive); *Ibid.*, 435 (Kennedy Itinerary); Kennedy's despatch, in Jehan de Waurin, *Anchiennes Cronicques d'Engleterre* (ed. Dupont, Société de l'histoire de France, 1863), iii, 166.

78. *Asloan MS.*, i, 232.

79. Dunlop, *op. cit.*, 435.

80. *Asloan MS.*, i, 232.

81. For Argyll's career, see A. L. Brown, 'The Scottish 'Establishment' in the later 15th century', *Juridical Review*, 1978, pt. 2, 96; *ER*, vii, 107 (for Argyll as auditor of exchequer).

82. *Handbook of British Chronology, passim*.

83. *Ibid.*, and *RMS*, ii, Nos. 1132-1175 (for Guthrie as captain of the royal guard).

84. *Records of the Earldom of Orkney* (SHS, 1914), 54.

85. See above, n.16.

86. Macdougall, *op. cit.*, 54-7.

87. Waurin, *op. cit.*, iii, 166 (discussed in Dunlop, *op. cit.*, 219-220, where a different view of the bishop's actions is offered).

88. *RMS*, ii, No. 1196.

89. *Ibid.*, Nos. 758-831.

90. *ER*, vii, 389.

91. Macdougall, *op. cit.*, 57-61; and for a different view, Nicholson, *op. cit.*, 399-406.

92. *Rotuli Scotiae in Turri Londinensi et in Domo Capitulari Westmonasteriensi Asservati*, ed. D. Macpherson and others (1814-19), ii, 410-12; *Calendar of Documents relating to Scotland*, ed. J. Bain (Edinburgh, 1881-8), iv, No. 1341. The seven Scots commissioners nominated in the spring of 1464 were Andrew Muirhead, bishop of Glasgow; Archibald Crawford, abbot of Holyrood; James Lindsay, provost of Lincluden and Privy Seal; Colin Campbell, earl of Argyll; Robert Lord Boyd; William Lord Borthwick; Sir Alexander Boyd of Drumcoll. It may be significant that Kennedy's name was on the original list of commissioners drawn up on 5 December 1463 (*Rot. Scot.*, ii, 409).

93. *Cal. Docs. Scot.*, iv, No. 1360.

94. It seems likely that Kennedy acquired custody of James III in the Edinburgh parliament of January 1464, at which he was present (*APS*, xii, 29). Dunlop (*op. cit.*, 241 n. 6) remarks that 'there is no reference to this Parliament or General Council in the printed Acts', and this statement is followed by Macdougall, *op. cit.*, 68 n. 48. But later Dr. Dunlop corrects herself and takes account of the Edinburgh parliament ('Kennedy Itinerary' in Dunlop, *op.cit.*, 435). For James III's much later statement that Bishop Kennedy acquired custody of the king at this stage, see C. A. J. Armstrong, 'A letter of James III to the Duke of Burgundy', *SHS Miscellany viii*, 19-32.

95. *ER*, vii, 229; *RMS*, ii, Nos. 796-810; *HMC Rep. xv*, App. viii, 37.

96. Dunlop, *op. cit.*, 254.

97. The court was at St. Andrews from at least 14 March to 5 June: *RMS*, ii, Nos. 828-833. After the summer progress of 1464, the autumn had been spent in Edinburgh and St. Andrews, Christmas and New Year 1465 at Stirling, and on the court's return to St. Andrews by mid-March, presumably Kennedy fell fatally ill and the royal stay was unduly protracted as a result.

98. *RMS*, ii, Nos. 831-2; *ER*, vii, 346, 392; SRO Ailsa Charters No. 96.

99. Dunlop, *op. cit.*, 251-2.

2

Was the Scottish Church reformable by 1513?

Leslie Macfarlane

UNTIL comparatively recently, historians of the late medieval Scottish Church were seriously disadvantaged by the limited amount of source material known or available to them, and by their seeming inability or reluctance to place the Scottish Church squarely within its European setting, where it belonged. At the provincial level they had long been able to take into account the relevant legislation to be found in D. Wilkins' *Concilia Magnae Britanniae et Hiberniae*, in A. Friedberg's great edition of the *Corpus Iuris Canonici*, Thomas Thomson's *The Acts of the Parliaments of Scotland* II, and the conciliar *acta* collected in Joseph Robertson's *Statuta Ecclesiae Scoticanae*; while at the diocesan level there were volumes VI-XII (1404-1471) of the *Calendars of entries in the Papal Registers relating to Great Britain and Ireland*, Augustinus Theiner's *Vetera Monumenta Hibernorum et Scotorum*, a few printed episcopal registers, monastic chartularies, some protocol books, burgh records and the muniments of the three ancient Scottish universities to help them along. But anyone who has worked for long in continental archives, or who has taken a close look at Dorothy Owen's analysis of the holdings in English ecclesiastical archives,[1] soon becomes aware of the comparative scarcity of late medieval Scottish ecclesiastical records and of the difficulty which faced earlier generations of scholars when trying to present an authentic picture of the Scottish Church at work in the fifteenth century. For example, given the fact that no medieval commentaries on Scottish provincial legislation have survived comparable to Lyndwood's *Provinciale*,[2] it has never been easy to follow the workings of the late medieval Scottish Church courts; or given that we possess no Scottish priests' manuals comparable to William of Pagula's *Oculus Sacerdotis*,[3] it has not been possible to assess pastoral efficiency other than in terms of the threats and warnings to be found in Scottish provincial and synodal legislation. Nor can our few episcopal registers and monastic chartularies tell us much about the spiritual health of the Church in fifteenth-century Scotland. Indeed, their fragmentary nature is such as to lead one of our foremost historians to wonder if medieval Scottish bishops and their chancellors ever seriously kept proper registers at all.[4] As for placing their source material squarely within its fifteenth-century European setting, it is true that an earlier generation of Scottish ecclesiastical historians knew what appropriations, pluralism and non-residence meant in the thirteenth and four-teenth centuries, although they were less well aware as to how crown, papal and lay patronage came to be applied. But given their own understanding of the Reformation, their concentration on the loss of spiritual leadership at the top and on the disordered state of the mid-sixteenth century Scottish clergy, many of them attempted to explain the condition of the fifteenth-century Scottish Church in terms of its state in 1560, when it had already been captured by the Scottish crown and nobility. Hence they attributed an irreformability to the fifteenth-century Scottish Church which they were not really entitled to claim for it.[5]

The remarkable renaissance in late medieval Scottish ecclesiastical studies in the past twenty years has considerably modified those views. The first two major works to herald its approach were Gordon Donaldson's The Scottish Reformation and David McRoberts' Essays on the Scottish Reformation, but since then a series of invaluable reference works and a number of excellent articles and books have appeared to bring about a decisive shift in our presuppositions on the late medieval Scottish Church.[6] Of the wide range of intensive research accompanying this renaissance, however, one of the most significant projects has been the work steadily being carried out over the years by a number of scholars on the Chancery, Datary, Cameral and Rota records of the papal Curia to be found in the Vatican Archives;[7] work modelled on and inspired by that great Scottish historian Dr. Annie Dunlop (née Cameron), the value of whose Cameral and Supplicationary studies in those Archives[8] popes Pius XI and Pius XII were themselves among the first to acclaim.

Now anyone who has worked for weeks, months or even years in the Vatican Archives, and who has refused to be intimidated by their vast late medieval collections, will know that it is crucial to interpret them within the context of that violent and restless age itself. For unless he has fought his way through the bafflingly complex temporal problems of the later medieval papacy, any scholar working there will soon be asking himself the sort of question which Henry VII of England, Charles VIII of France or James III of Scotland never asked themselves, namely, what on earth was the papacy doing having temporal states at all? Or unless he has studied late medieval papal finance, how can any ecclesiastical historian begin to understand that until Renaissance popes could resume their temporal states, they were quite unable to reduce their spiritualia and remain solvent at the same time, as all the fifteenth-century conciliarists and reformers insisted that they should; a dilemma which has often prompted the forthright question that if selling ecclesiastical offices cash down to the highest bidder wasn't simony, what was? On the other hand, any secular monarch or Renaissance pope of the day would simply have demanded to know what patronage was all about, if offices at one's disposal couldn't either be sold or given to one's trusted friends or relations. Or again, scholars checking through the expenses incurred by Nicholas V and later Renaissance popes in tearing down the old Constantinian basilica of St. Peter's and bringing in architects like Bernardo Rossellino and, later, Bramante and Michelangelo, to rebuild it, might well question the necessity for these costly and flamboyant gestures. But in doing so they would fail to understand the deep need the Romans of the day had for urban stability after centuries of pillage and vandalism, and their need to recover their self-respect as their new city took shape under their eyes. Or lastly, unless late medieval historians understand those doctrines of sovereignty current in fifteenth-century Europe: of the prince as legislator, of the civilists' formula *Rex est imperator in regno suo*, and what these meant to monarchs like James III, Edward IV or Louis XI, what can they possibly make of their ruthless political bargaining and double dealing with the papacy?

In order to understand the diminishing options of the late medieval papacy, then, it is essential to place these administrative papal records firmly within their historical context. Only then can it be seen that fifteenth-century European monarchs expected the papacy to resume its estates and live of its own, just as they were being forced to do by their subjects; and if it couldn't do so, that was its problem, not theirs; they had troubles enough of their own, trying to remain solvent. Hence their protective antipapal legislation, their systematic exploitation of episcopal and abbatial vacancies, their manipulation of crown patronage, and in James IV's case his flagrant abuse of the primatial office between 1497 and 1513. These difficulties, grave enough in themselves for the Renaissance papacy, were heightened by Charles VIII's intrusion into Italy in 1494, which not only posed a serious threat to the stability of the papal states themselves, but also compelled Alexander VI himself to assume the leadership of the opposition to the French occupation of southern Italy, since it was clear that the Italian dukes, through whose territory Charles VIII's armies had already marched their way, were neither organised nor united enough to offer any resistance to them. On their part, it must be said, popes like Julius II and Leo X matched the aggressive nationalism of the more powerful secular monarchs of their age with a strong counter-argument of their own; namely, their conviction that they alone wielded universal jurisdiction. This they regarded as the essence of their office. But humanists like Lorenzo Valla, church reformers like Nicholas of Cusa, and most ordinary folk, too, still judged the papacy by special standards of their own, according to which popes from Boniface VIII onwards had simply run down a blind alley and had led the Church astray. It was this dialectic which gave the period its inner tension, and it is only when we see the struggle within this framework that we begin to understand why its solution required the restructuring of late medieval society, which neither the papacy nor the secular rulers of Europe were prepared to initiate. As they saw it, their task was to support that society, not subvert it.

Given this situation, what chance did any bishop stand in a far-off periphery of Christendom who was deeply committed to spiritual reform and the genuine well-being of his diocese? If he had paid even one *ad limina* visit to Rome in the course of his episcopate, or even if he had come out on an official visit as the king's orator, he would have been in turn intimidated, humiliated and almost certainly disillusioned before he returned home to his diocese or king. Certainly a number of Scottish bishops were, as anyone who has worked his way through the *Distributiones Bullarum* series in the *Archivio di Stato di Roma*, now in the Vatican Archives, will know. What would have depressed him would have been the sheer amount of money required to do anything or get anything done. There were charges for notaries, abbreviators, secretaries and sealers of documents at every stage in the Departments of the Chancery, the Datary, the Camera and the Roman Rota; the procedures of the Curia could be rigid and inexorable. But then, this is exactly what obtained at the court of his king at home. Even so, no Scottish bishop could have gone to Rome at this time and not have been profoundly impressed in other ways: by the Curia's efficiency, by the Rota's scrupulous regard for equity; and as for Rome itself, by the sheer elegance of the city. To have been to Rome and returned to Scotland must have been a scarring and unforgettable experience for Scottish ecclesiastics in the later fifteenth century.

One such visitor was William Elphinstone, bishop of Ross between 1481 and 1483 and then of Aberdeen from 1483 until his death in 1514. His own predicament was typical enough. Denied access to the bishopric of Ross because he refused to pay the common services of his predecessor,[9] and then excluded from Aberdeen for a further five years for opposing the papal Camera's sum of 14,300 gold florins which he and the bishop of Glasgow together owed for their common services, he was eventually forced to meet his share, by instalments,[10] from a poverty-stricken diocese, the episcopal revenues of which the crown had been quietly pocketing during those five years, when the See was technically vacant and a number of its parish clergy already on the breadline. Not surprisingly, when Elphinstone was finally consecrated, he found the diocese in poor shape. His dean, chancellor and archdeacon may not have been resident, since their offices had been challenged, and the diocese lacked its Official.[11] It had been forty years since a bishop had promulgated any constitutional reforms, and doubtless a realistic appraisal of the conditions under which the parish clergy lived would soon have to call for firm remedial measures. His Cathedral was unfinished with only the nave and the north transept complete. Of the hundred parishes in the diocese, forty-two had been appropriated to religious orders, while the Cathedral itself drew on the revenues of fifty-four others to support its twenty-nine prebendary canons, its twelve vicars choral and the bishop himself.[12] As for the ecclesiastical lands of the diocese, Elphinstone had no precise information on their state on his arrival, but his experience as a commissioner of crown lands would have reminded him that unless landowners were vigilant, a number of their rents, grassums and entry fines could never reach them. He could hardly have begun his pontificate under worse conditions.

Elphinstone was a realist. He was very well aware of the weaknesses inherent in the late medieval church, and he knew that a system which was underpinned by patronage, pluralism, non-residence and appropriations was bound to erode his spiritual jurisdiction, to limit his opportunities to choose, educate and reform his clergy, and to instruct and edify his laity. His first task was to shake off the metropolitan and primatial jurisdiction of the archbishop of St. Andrews, to which at that time, in 1483, all Scottish bishops were subject. In Elphinstone's view the primacy had come too late, had been ill-conceived, and could block his path to Rome.[13] There is no doubt that he foresaw the implications of metropolitan jurisdiction more clearly than most of his episcopal colleagues. As an ex-Official of Lothian and one of the most experienced ecclesiastical judges in the kingdom, with an intimate knowledge of the procedures and judgements of the Roman Rota, he recognised that the Rota offered more to a Scottish ordinary than did the appellate court of his metropolitan. Hence we find Elphinstone appealing successfully to Innocent VIII to exempt him from Archbishop Scheves' jurisdiction in 1490,[14] after which records are singularly free from any appellate litigation between the two men. And there is this to be said for Elphinstone's integrity of principle in this matter. When he was himself nominated as Archbishop of St. Andrews and primate in 1513, he immediately exempted from his jurisdiction Andrew Stewart, the bishop of Caithness, who had been nominated to take his place in Aberdeen.[15]

The disposal of patronage in the later Middle Ages was an exercise which demanded considerable prudence if bishops were to avoid walking into legal minefields. They had first to contend with the king, the most powerful ecclesiastical patron in the realm, who not only held the advowsons of crown livings, but also the patronage of those belonging to tenants-in-chief then in ward to him as minors; and in addition, since 1450, the crown held the patronage of every living belonging to the bishopric during the vacancy of the See, whether technical or otherwise.[16] Wherever they turned in the later Middle Ages, in fact, bishops found the crown challenging their patronage. Two or three examples must suffice to show how Elphinstone dealt with this problem. No sooner had he been consecrated at Aberdeen in the spring of 1488, when he wrung from the papacy his right, based on a Conciliar edict of 1419, to collate, provide, present, elect or dispose of all prebends in his gift for six out of the twelve months of each year,[17] which enabled him to fight off all comers, including the king, in order to choose his own men; a right he renewed on 18 January 1495.[18] In consequence, when James IV tried to foist Thomas Halkerston on him as archdeacon of Aberdeen in 1508, Elphinstone successfully blocked his nomination, knowing that he would have been an absentee pluralist, even though the king was actively supporting Elphinstone in his University project at the time, and probably expected something in the nature of a *quid pro quo* from him. A further example concerned Elphinstone's institution of Andrew Bisset as vicar of Inverurie in 1490, which both the king, the abbot of Lindores as patron of the church — and the pope himself — had tried to block with an expectative grace, but which Elphinstone defended on his 1488 mandate and won.[19]

In these and other ways — and the Vatican records are sprinkled in this period with such patronage disputes in the diocese of Aberdeen — Elphinstone fought off pluralists and barrators, whether they came from the pope, lay patrons or the king. Of course he didn't always win. His dean, James Brown, for instance, had purchased his office at the Roman Curia in 1483, before Elphinstone could gain entrance to his See, probably through the influence of his kinsman George Brown, the bishop of Dunkeld who was a friend of cardinal Roderigo Borgia, soon to become Alexander VI. James Brown was wealthy, a pluralist, and almost certainly the father of two children, and the nature of his appointment was an offence to those reforms Elphinstone had set his heart upon introducing into his diocese. Some twelve years later we find Elphinstone still opposing what he considered to be an illegal appointment in the first place, and asserting his own rights as the diocese's lawful bishop in 1483, a matter which he appears to have regularised when he visited the Roman Curia in January and February 1495;[20] and Brown did in fact become one of Elphinstone's most loyal supporters in his University project. By virtue, then, of his tenacity, patience and clearmindedness, Elphinstone managed to recruit a first-rate team of diocesan administrators to help him carry out the much needed reforms in his diocese: John Fletcher, his chancellor; Alexander Galloway, rector of Kinkell, designer of sacrament houses, and later Rector of the University and Official of the diocese — one of Elphinstone's earliest and most gifted protégés; Thomas Myrton, treasurer and then an excellent arch-deacon of the diocese; and Henry Babington, his dean on the death of James Brown, a theologian and, significantly, a Cistercian, one of those rare appointments of a regular to this office in the whole country at this period.[21]

The creation of the University of Aberdeen also afforded Elphinstone an opportunity to absorb into his diocese some of the University's most dis-tinguished teachers, since the two foundation bulls of the 1495 and 1505 gave him the right to appoint its first officers. In this way William Strachan, John Lindsay and Henry Spittal all became rectors of the Snow Kirk (S. Maria ad Nives), the parish church of Old Aberdeen, on their successive appointments as reader in canon law.[22] Again, Thomas Strachan, the grammarian, became canon of Tullynessle, Alexander Vaus, another grammarian, was canon and rector of Turriff, while some of the University's earliest graduates like Alexander Hay were also given prebends when vacancies occurred, and were similarly absorbed into the life of the diocese.[23] In addition to this University group, the bishop also nominated other graduates like Henry Allan, rector of Ruthven, and three of his own kinsmen, Arthur Elphinstone, rector of Inver-boyndie, Adam Elphinstone, rector of Invernochtie, and William Elphinstone, rector of Clatt. And although the diocesan records tell us little about perpetual or stipendiary vicars with care of souls other than their names, the fact that some of them like Edward Cunningham of Cushnie, John Lumsden of Tarves, Bernard Gargil of Inverboyndie and John Garioch of Kemnay were graduates inducted during Elphinstone's pontificate would seem to suggest that the bishop was not only concerned with the educational qualifications of his Cathedral administrators, but that when the opportunity presented itself he urged patrons to offer him curates with masters' degrees;[24] while the additional fact that the records sometimes omit to prefix a graduate vicar's name with his master's title may give us pause to question whether the educational level of this grass-root class of parish priest was as abysmally low as has often been supposed. Certainly it is evident that there were a number of graduates working as parish priests in the diocese by 1502, and it is reasonable to argue that after the foundation of the University their number gradually rose.[25]

The roll call of Elphinstones listed above, who were clearly brought into the diocese only because they were the bishop's kinsmen, raises the issue of nepotism in its most acute form, since such a system of family preferences must have been unjust at times, and was clearly abused both by the Church and the crown. And yet to condemn this practice out of hand would be fundamentally to misunderstand the nature of late medieval feudal society. The truth is that the bond of kinship was the strongest binding force in fifteenth-century Scottish society, whether clerical or lay. The Scottish feudal barony, for instance, was still basically a closely knit family affair, bonds of alliance being merely one of its outward military and legal manifestations.[26] In such a society, trust was the requirement, loyalty the key. And even though the higher clergy were not faced with inheritance problems as were their feudal counterparts, it is evident that as far as their appointments to positions of trust were concerned, blood was thicker than water, and the loyalty of the known better than that of the unknown. This would appear to be the explanation for Elphinstone's appointments of his kinsmen to positions of trust within his programme of diocesan reform, such as that of Adam Elphinstone in 1490 as archdeacon (the bishop's eye), and upon Adam's death in 1499, of Robert Elphinstone.[27] Their loyalty was assured and had no need to be bought.

The problems of non-residence, pluralism and appropriations also have to be understood within their late medieval context, and seen for what they were: political, legal and financial compromises, and the result of difficult centuries-long clashes of principle between Church and State. As with nepotism, to condemn these practices as unmitigated disasters is merely to pass gratuitous judgement on the fabric of that society, or to say that the Church should not have developed in this way. That is as may be, but as all ecclesiastical historians know, there were perfectly legitimate reasons why it did develop in this way, and corrective legislation was available when the system was abused. The constitutions of the diocese of Aberdeen, for example, forbade non-residence of canons, under pain of heavy fines, without a legitimate reason, like their studying at a University. The problem here, however, was that local Ordinaries were often caught in the cross fire between the claims of rival patrons, thus leaving the dignities unfilled and making non-residence inevitable while litigation dragged on between the parties concerned. The problem was compounded by the increase in the number of universities being founded in the later Middle Ages, which, with their system of benefice rolls, gave graduates an edge, or was thought to give them an edge, when seeking employment. But in Scotland, at any rate, there were too few consistorial benefices available for the increasing number of highly skilled graduates trained to fill them. The crown was perfectly happy, of course, to cream off and employ a number of them as civil servants, provided the Church paid for them, since, lacking an educated laity to govern the country and administer its judicial system, it needed to make full use of its educated clergy. And understandably, graduates who had spent extra years reading law or theology at the universities were reluctant to lower their sights and take up parochial duties, and were ready to scramble for higher livings wherever they could be found. It is apparent, therefore, not that there were too many graduates in the country, but too many clerical graduates for the amount of ecclesiastical funds and benefices available to them, a situation which could only further the cause of pluralism and non-residence, and widen the gap between the higher and lower clergy.

The fact that the system of appropriations was more widely spread in the late medieval Scottish church than in most parts of Europe also has to be seen against the background of its relative poverty and its own peculiarly divisive regional structure and lack of unity. The development of appropriations in Scotland has been well told elsewhere.[28] The system was defended by the bishops on the grounds that they needed money for cathedral building projects, maintaining church fabric, providing adequate stipends for their administrators and vicars choral, and for the institution and maintenance of the hospitals and almshouses in the diocese. Equally, religious corporations argued that they needed considerable revenues not only to maintain their buildings, but also to offset deterioration in rents, ruinous harvests, the fall in the value of the Scottish pound, and to pay the expenses of their lawsuits at the papal or royal curia. Clearly they saw nothing wrong in taking away a proportion of the revenues of those parishes of which they were patrons, pooling it with their other resources, and redistributing it across the board. The system, however, could not fail to weaken the parochial structure itself, and to lay itself open too easily to abuse; and although episcopal registers and monastic chartularies provide examples of bishops being able to improve the rights of curates by instituting them as vicars perpetual, thereby making them irremovable at another's will, there is equal evidence to show that they were often forced to litigate on their behalf to have their stipends raised.[29]

Given, then, that non-residence, pluralism and the annexation of parish revenues to cathedral chapters, religious corporations or secular colleges were endemic features of the late medieval Scottish Church, it is not surprising that specialists in this field, recognising these defects as ineradicable, have come to believe that the task of reform was beyond its resources or capabilities.[30] The case history of the diocese of Aberdeen between 1488 and 1513, however, would suggest otherwise. True, Elphinstone was only able to accomplish his reforms by taking on either the pope or the crown singly, and rarely both at the same time, as his supplicatory correspondence in the Vatican Archives shows. And yet, by stabilising and redistributing his Chapter's funds, and maintaining good relations with James IV, the burgh of Aberdeen and the religious orders within the diocese, he was able to initiate a campaign of liturgical, spiritual and educational reform which continued well into the sixteenth century and left its permanent mark on the North-East. It is instructive to see how he accomplished this.

His first act was to make the Cathedral canons corporately responsible for the stipends of all the *ministri inferiores* by placing an annual levy on each of the twenty-nine prebendaries varying in proportion with the value of their prebend. This amounted to £169 and was to be set aside for the vicars choral and chaplains. He then pooled the moneys accruing from all the chaplaincy benefactions, and by placing a variable levy on each of the Cathedral chaplains according to the value of their benefaction, he was able to set aside a further annual sum of £86.15.8. This total of £255.15.8 he divided among his twenty vicars choral, two deacons, two subdeacons, two acolytes and six choirboys, the sum varying according to their responsibilities, with an extra honorarium for the master of the 'Sang Schule'. The remaining annual sum of £42.14.4 from the chaplaincy benefactions was earmarked for the non-resident chaplains saying their anniversary masses elsewhere. An additional £26, paid out of the Chapter Common fund, was apportioned to the sacrist and eleven choirboys. In this way a sum of £328.9.0 was taken from the common fund for the stipends of all the *ministri inferiores*, yet no canon suffered a financial loss, no vicar choral or chaplain received less than £10 annually, the choirboys were paid a fair stipend, and all were paid regularly.[31]

Elphinstone partially achieved this by augmenting the Chapter common fund with cash benefactions, in the form of annual rents on tenements or property which he persuaded the local burgesses of Aberdeen and local members of the nobility to gift to the Cathedral and to the parish church of St. Nicholas. But it is clear from the large sums he paid out for his massive building programme at the Cathedral that, leaving aside the monies he received in his capacity as keeper of the Privy Seal and one of the Lords Auditors, much of which he fed into his various reform projects, he must have drawn the extra money from the Chapter lands themselves, namely, from their forty-two prebendal, eleven common and his own mensal church lands which made up the total of the fifty-four parishes appropriated to the Cathedral. Yet each of his curates out in the landward parishes was guaranteed a minimum stipend of £10, and where possible the bishop strove to inaugurate them as vicars perpetual, just as he had already solemnly inducted his vicars choral as such at the Cathedral. His success here, however, undoubtedly came from his close examination, at the outset of his episcopate, of the Chapter's rental books and the Cathedral charters and inventories, in order to discover the extent of his lands and the conditions under which these and other benefactions were held. This was particularly important to Elphinstone, since the

See had been technically vacant between 1480 and 1488, and it soon became obvious to him that a number of these lands or their revenues had been dissipated during that period or even further back in time, and they would only be recovered by litigation. Hence we find him engaged throughout the first ten years of his office in protracted lawsuits both at the papal and royal curia, some of which he was able to settle only when he visited Rome himself in 1495.[32]

As one of the most experienced civil lawyers in Scotland, however, the bishop was in a strong position to recognise when brieves of diligence, wrongeous intromission or perambulation could be raised, when arbitration was called for, or whatever other form of action might be required to win back the lost temporalities of these Chapter lands, and from 1488 onwards we can trace his successful actions against Alexander Chalmer and his heirs over the lands of Murthill, Alexander McPherson for the wrongeous occupation of the bishop's lands at Mortlach and Dalmeath, and other causes involving the wrongful uptaking of rents and customs.[33] Such newly won lands and revenues considerably augmented the Chapter's common fund. But undoubtedly his most profitable litigation was his successful pursual and recovery, in 1492,[34] of David I's gift of the second teinds to the bishopric in 1136, which the crown had resumed and gifted out again to others. In this way, once having established the rights of the bishops of Aberdeen to these teinds, Elphinstone was able to recover those of Drummanour and Fordyce from Lord Forbes,[35] those of Philorth from Lord Errol,[36] and the second teinds of other Chapter lands from a number of other lairds, to the extent of hundreds of pounds Scots. And even if the bishop was not able to recover all the cash owed to him and his Chapter, at least an important right had been reclaimed. The Aberdeen *Rentale* of 1511, fragmentary though it is, tells us that by that year the second tenth within the diocese amounted to £83.5.4 annually, while those from the diocese of Moray brought in a further £5.6.8. Even without the second tenths, the annual rentals for the bishop's and the Chapter's lands in 1511 amounted to £682.17.8[37] in cash alone, leaving aside the large amounts of food sent in kind.

Elphinstone's recovery of some of the temporalities lost to the bishopric of Aberdeen during its technical vacancy between 1480 and 1488 was surely not an exceptional exercise, given that other bishoprics frequently suffered the same fate during this period. We may well ask ourselves, then, whether others of his episcopal colleagues were not also stabilising and redistributing their Chapter funds on similar lines, and whether, therefore, the effect of appropriations was as disastrous on the parish clergy as has often been supposed. Certainly in Elphinstone's case the system did not shipwreck the parochial establishment, and clearly the bishop did not ignore the needs of the poorer vicars in his diocese; on the contrary, he used the system to improve their lot. Only the lack of so many episcopal registers of dioceses other than Aberdeen prevents us from showing whether this may not also have been true elsewhere. In much of all this litigation to reclaim his rights, Elphinstone pursued the crown. Moreover, by having remained loyal to James III in the crisis of 1488, the bishop had not endeared himself to those who had surrounded the young king at the commencement of his reign. Prudence and loyalty to the crown, however, demanded that Elphinstone should not lose the confidence which James IV was prepared to place in him both as an administrator and a judge, and it is a distinguishing feature of their relationship that in spite of the bishop's relentless pursual of the crown in matters concerning his rights, and James IV's equally ruthless exploitation of those rights on occasion, the two men respected each other and remained friends. Thus James IV, although almost destroying the confidence of the entire Scottish hierarchy by his scandalous successive nominations of his brother and then his illegitimate son to the archbishopric of St. Andrews in 1497 and 1504, was nevertheless fully and practically supportive of Elphinstone's own diocesan reforms; while on his part, while disapproving of much of James IV's antipapal legislation, the bishop remained one of the king's most active members of his parliaments and Councils. In the overall cause of the Church, Elphinstone had long since realised that friendships like these had to be worked at.

The same was also true of his relations with the burgh of Aberdeen and with the religious orders of his diocese. When Elphinstone arrived in Aberdeen in the spring of 1488, relations between the See and the burgh could hardly have been more strained. Since 1442 its burgesses had been generously contributing towards the cost of building a new choir for their parish church of St. Nicholas, encouraged, from 1477 onwards, by Bishop Spens's annual gift of the second teinds of Aberdeen. On Spens's death in 1480, however, the new bishop, Robert Blacader, withheld this gift, which had thereupon been lost to the project. Immediately upon his arrival, Elphinstone decided not only to continue the annual payment of the teinds, but also to take over the responsibility for the whole work itself, organising its labour force and encouraging further gifts for its completion.[38] It was sufficiently far advanced to be dedicated by Elphinstone in 1498,[39] and was finally completed in 1513, making it then the largest parish church in the country, and one of the most beautiful. His commitment to building a permanent bridge over the river Dee made him still more popular with the Aberdonians. Such a project had been discussed earlier in the century, and letters in the Vatican Archives record that the pope had been petitioned twice, in 1427 and 1436, to grant indulgences which would allow the whole community to subscribe towards its construction.[40] But the project had advanced little by 1489, the amount of money required in wages and materials seemingly having defeated them all. Upon Elphinstone's taking up the project, large quantities of stone, rubble and timber were collected, and a master mason was appointed to complete the task.[41] In the event, the bridge was not completed until 1529, but Elphinstone left a considerable amount of money in his will for the fabric of the bridge,[42] and had persuaded others to set sums aside for its maintenance. His building projects at the Cathedral and King's College, too, brought considerably increased employment and trade to the city. In these and other practical ways, like his finding a mediciner for the burgh in 1503 in order to combat recurring visits of the plague, and his inviting the king to visit Aberdeen on a number of occasions, and Queen Margaret in 1511, Elphinstone consciously involved himself in its affairs, and steadily built up the confidence between the burgh and the bishopric which was to endure up to the Reformation and beyond.

Although Elphinstone had no direct control over the religious orders within his diocese, it was important for him to establish and maintain good relations with them, since they not only worked alongside the secular clergy, but often did work which the latter were unable to do. Thus the Trinitarian friars worked on the Aberdeen waterfront, looking after the needs of foreign seamen, especially the sick and the dying or those in prison in the Tolbooth gaol.[43] The Dominicans had established themselves on Schoolhill in the thirteenth century[44] and, because of their rigorous intellectual training, had long been used by the bishops of Aberdeen as itinerant preachers throughout their scattered diocese. Elphinstone was particularly friendly towards them, and once his University project had got underway in 1495, the Order was the first to send students to it, four of them applying to read theology there from the moment teaching began, and their Provincial John Adamson being the first to become a doctor of theology at Aberdeen.[45] Clearly Elphinstone looked to the Order to spearhead his reforms throughout the diocese, and in his will he left both their Aberdeen and St. Andrews houses of studies money for improvements and enlargement. To a lesser extent, though no less positively, Elphinstone drew the Aberdeen Carmelite friars into his programme of intellectual and spiritual reform, their orthodoxy and adoption of the *devotio moderna* having, as Boece tells us, a special appeal to him.[46] We find one of them, for example, employed as a scribe copying out the lectures of the Sub-Principal of King's College for the use of the theology students there.[47] As for the Franciscans, Elphinstone and the Burgh Council enjoyed excellent relations with them, as is evident not only from the money the bishop left them in his will, but also from the gifts of the bishop's relations and the large number of benefactions they received from the Aberdonians themselves, a number of whom joined the Order as craftsmen, while others became scribes and preachers. All of them believed in the apostolate of work within a framework of conventual life of spartan simplicity, and it is significant that when the Reformers came to Aberdeen in 1559 and 1560, the townsfolk of Aberdeen refused to allow them to desecrate Franciscan property.[48]

Elphinstone's relations with the three monastic communities in his diocese, the Augustinian priory at Monymusk, the Cistercian abbey at Deer, and the Tironensian house at Fyvie, were more formal; and since his jurisdiction over them was strictly laid down by canon law, he was unable to impose any of his diocesan reforms unilaterally upon them. Nevertheless, the parish church of Monymusk, as distinct from the priory, had been erected into a prebend of St. Machar's Cathedral in 1445, so that Elphinstone was able to, and did, exercise some control over its revenues and curates, even though the archbishops of St. Andrews were its patrons.[49] In consequence, we find Elphinstone in 1506 increasing the amount to be paid by the rector of Monymusk to his vicar choral at St. Machar's, but at the same time ensuring that the curacy stipend at Monymusk never fell below £10.[50] Moreover, the two curates appointed to Monymusk during Elphinstone's episcopate were both Aberdeenshire men: Richard Strachan, who afterwards became the prior, and Thomas Scherer, a graduate and later dean of Christianity at Strathdon. Since both these excellent appointments occurred during the minorities of their archbishops, it seems most likely that, though crown nominees, they were really appointed on Elphinstone's advice. The same kind of manoeuvre appears to have happened at the parish church of Deer, which had also been appropriated to St. Machar's Cathedral.[51] This prebend, too, came under Elphinstone's reforms of 1506, when he appointed master William Boece to the rector of Deer's stall in the Cathedral, and made sure that the stipends of both the vicar choral and the curate of the parish church did not fall below £10 per annum.[52] The parish church of Fyvie also came under his scrutiny in 1506, the abbey of Arbroath, its patron, having its tax increased to safeguard the income of the parish curate.[53] Elphinstone may even have had some say in the appointment of Alexander Lichton as vicar pensionary of Fyvie parish church in 1489, since, although presented by the abbot of Arbroath, he was an Aberdeenshire priest.[54] The bishop was aware of the fundamental weaknesses of the monastic economy in the late fifteenth century, more especially because as a Lord of Council he frequently heard causes of spoliation of monastic lands and of failure to pay teinds, debts or rents to monks. He was aware that the number of Augustinian canons at Monymusk and monks at Deer was very low, and that Fyvie was no longer viable as an independent house. But he was unable to present them with any programme of spiritual reform, and he could not prevent the crown from appointing non-effective commendators. All he could do here was to keep a watching brief on their lands and act as constructively as he could on their behalf. Basically, their reform was beyond him.

The reform of his own diocesan clergy, however, was by no means beyond him, and there is ample evidence in the Vatican archives to show that he took on this task early in his episcopate and was still working at it on his death twenty-six years later in 1514. We have already seen how he improved the stipends of his vicars choral, chaplains and parish curates, and had striven, where possible, to make their positions permanent. He had also had some success in the selection of his Cathedral officers. The rationale behind all this activity, social justice apart, was his conviction that since man was created in order to love and serve God, it was incumbent upon bishops to protect and educate their clergy, to instruct and edify their people, and to beautify the house of God. As far as the public worship of God was concerned, his liturgical programme of reform included the enlargement of his body of vicars choral at the Cathedral to twenty, the introduction of a skilled musician, John Malison, as master of the 'Sang Schule', a musical examination for both the vicars choral and choir boys on entry, and a revision of the Divine Office to both simplify it and give it a more Scottish character. One reason for this revision was that, by the end of the fifteenth century, a number of new religious feasts had been inaugurated, like the Name of Jesus, the Iconia, the Five Wounds and the Compassion of the Blessed Virgin which needed to be incorporated into Scottish breviaries.[55] Again, with the rapid spread of printing on the Continent, it was apparent to Elphinstone — as indeed it must have been to all his episcopal colleagues — that unless the Scottish church soon had a printed Use of its own, their market would be flooded with service books of the Roman or Sarum rite. And thirdly, given the growing interest in Scottish history among the clergy and laity, and the encouragement then being given to the cultivation of devotion to local saints by bishops and abbots throughout the land, Elphinstone recognised that it would be opportune to produce a Calendar in a revised Breviary which could include more Scottish saints.

All the essential ingredients for a major revision of Scottish service books were present, then, by 1500, and sometime between 1494 and the end of the century Elphinstone gathered a team around him to produce, first, a Scottish Martyrology,[56] and then the Aberdeen Breviary itself.[57] It is doubtful whether the project, which took several years to complete and was one of the first set of books to be run off Chepman and Myllar's printing press at Edinburgh in 1510, would ever have got off the ground, however, without the king's support. Quite clearly, James IV saw all this religious patriotism as the ecclesiastical counterpart of his own political struggle to unify the country, and for this reason alone had backed Elphinstone's project through the press. And certainly it would never have been accepted by his fellow bishops as the Scottish use, in spite of its careful inclusion of the patron saints of each of the Scottish dioceses, plus a number of other regional saints, without the royal backing. Yet liturgically it made sense, since here for the first time was a national Breviary which gave prominence to national saints like St. Andrew and St. Margaret, took regional differences into account, but at the same time avoided inter-diocesan friction by ensuring that diocesan patronal saints were major feasts for their own particular diocese, and for no other. As such, it enjoyed a modicum of success, was adopted as the Scottish use by the diocese of Moray, and deserved to have been more widely accepted. The fact that it had no second edition, however, was not so much due to the death of James IV soon after its publication, and the national crisis which the tragedy caused, but to the appearance, rather, of the revised Quiñones Breviary in 1535, which excised many of its earlier uncritical historical lessons and restored much of its earlier scriptural content, thereby rendering much of Elphinstone's Breviary obsolete.[58]

Nevertheless, with all its limitations, the Aberdeen Breviary was a step in the right direction in the liturgical reform of the Scottish Church. This needs to be said because it is often argued that the pietistic trends which breviaries like Elphinstone's reflected — the sufferings of Christ, the Compassion of the Virgin at the foot of the Cross, and the like — were morbid and ran counter to the tide of optimistic humanism then sweeping through Europe. It is said that they could only have made their readers even more introspective, superstitious and over-credulous. Moreover, the argument continues, the self-conscious nationalism which service books like these induced in their readers could only have provoked further aggressive outbursts and prolonged the chauvinism which had too long afflicted the Scottish nobility and clergy. But the point has already been made that these trends have to be seen in their contemporary European setting, not only in their political context, but also within their intellectual, cultural and religious framework. And the truth is that late medieval Europe saw, not a decline, but an increase in pietistic religious devotion among its peoples. Whether literate or not, men and women of that period had an intense devotion to the Eucharist. Love and compassion, too, in their violent and insecure age, had important compensatory parts to play. In this sense, therefore, Elphinstone's Breviary was certainly no anachronism. The importance to Elphinstone of national saints like Andrew and Margaret, Ninian and Columba, then, lay not in their ability to rally the forces behind the saltire, as Blind Hary's *Wallace* was intended to do, but rather to help his fellow Scots to discover their real past, which took in a number of cultures and traditions; while, at the same time, saints like Machar or Drostan, for example, enabled the peoples of the diocese of Aberdeen to identify themselves with their own particular locality.

Another assumption — the supposedly low moral and educational standards of the Scottish parish clergy in the later Middle Ages — deserves closer critical analysis. The general statutes and *synodalia* of the period are missing, and in any case would only have provided us with the punitive legislation for would-be transgressors. A surer ground for proof that the level of their education was rising rather than falling at this time can be sought, rather, in the increase in the number of burgh grammar schools being founded throughout the fifteenth century, in the steady flow of clergy attending the three Scottish universities, in the inventories of Cathedral and university libraries of the period, and in the theological and philosophical books owned by individual clergy throughout the land. We are robbed of the kind of evidence which English episcopal and chapter *acta* can provide on the training of their clergy, but if we look through the Vatican records, the Aberdeen episcopal registers, and among Elphinstone's own library books, a number of further clues emerge which throw even graver doubt on blanket generalisations about the ignorance and worthlessness of the late medieval Scottish parochial clergy. There was, first, the care which Elphinstone took to control the appointments of his diocesan chancellors who were responsible for the training of his *ordinandi*, and those of his archdeacons who visited the clergy in their parishes and reported back to the bishop on the state of each parish and its curate. Secondly, we know that he could call on a number of his graduate prebendaries at the Cathedral to provide some of the intellectual training required of his *ordinandi*. There is also the fact that in Elphinstone's own personal library at the time were to be found a manual for parish priests and a treatise on the moral aspects of confessional practice, together with five other pastoral books, all of which dealt specifically with problems affecting the pastoral life;[59] and although no actual priest's manual of that period seems to have survived their destruction at the Reformation, it is difficult to believe that those responsible for the training of the clergy at St. Machar's Cathedral school did not also possess books of instruction similar to those to be found in Elphinstone's library.[60] If this is so, then the majority of parish priests in the diocese would have received instruction on their pastoral duties, the administration of the sacraments, on the ecclesiastical calendar, fast days and other regulations affecting the daily life of themselves and their parishioners, besides more detailed advice on the celebration of the Mass. As for the practical instruction required for their anointing the sick or burying the dead, there is ample proof that the diocese was well served at the time with *rituale*, as can be seen, for example, in the Rathen Manual.[61] There is plenty of evidence also available to show that parish life itself was vigorous and active, particularly in the burghs.[62]

Nevertheless, it remains to be asked whether the reforms attempted by Elphinstone in the diocese of Aberdeen between 1488 and 1514 were in some way exceptional; or indeed, whether in spite of his tenacity he was merely tinkering with weaknesses within the structures of the late medieval Church which were already ineradicable. As to the first, an analysis of the careers of the twenty-seven bishops and archbishops who filled the thirteen Scottish Sees during this period reveals that at least sixteen were graduates, most of them having taken further degrees abroad in law, and one in medicine. As a body they were able, experienced men in both Church and State affairs, conscientious, and rarely absent from their dioceses for long periods; and it is difficult to believe that a number of these did not also have their battles with the crown and at the Roman curia to nominate their own diocesan officials and clergy, or stabilise and redistribute their chapter funds, or attempt to raise the level of education among their clergy, or build hospitals and almshouses for the sick and elderly. And if it has been possible to discuss Elphinstone's work at Aberdeen in more detail than that of his episcopal colleagues, this is simply because there are more records extant about him: Boece's intimate biography,[63] the early records of Aberdeen University,[64] the excellent series of Burgh Council Registers at Aberdeen,[65] the administrative and legal records of the central government,[66] and the fortuitous survival of a number of the registers and inventories of St. Machar's Cathedral.[67] But what records we have of Scheves' work at St. Andrews, and Blacader's activities in Glasgow, suggest that their contribution to the welfare of their archdioceses was also positive and continuous; and had we the missing registers of some of the other bishops, we might also discover that their record, too, was by no means as dismal as has often been inferred. Indeed, the excellent work now being carried out in the Vatican Archives on the Rota, Cameral and Datary records of the papal curia, together with the ongoing work on *The Calendars of Entries in the Papal Registers relating to Great Britain and Ireland* for the pontificates of Innocent VIII, Alexander VI and Julius II,[68] is likely to confirm their doggedness and tenacity in the face of considerable papal and royal opposition.

This is not to deny that the papacy was by now exhibiting serious juridical and fiscal weaknesses, some of its own making, some not, which could only rigidify its structures still further, and over-bureaucratise it as an institution.[69] Within the national churches themselves, the gap between the higher and lower clergy was too wide. There were too many clerics in society doing work which should have been done by the laity. There was a considerable amount of anti-clericalism, and much ignorance and superstition about the saving truths of the Christian faith. It was easier to recognise these weaknesses than to cure them. Understandably the papacy did not wish to hand over the total control of the national churches to secular monarchs, although a number of kings, including James IV, Henry VIII and Louis XII had by now almost reached that position. As for the imbalance between the clerical population and the laity, this is certainly true if we look at a diocese like Aberdeen. From the diocesan registers we can estimate that there were about 150 secular priests working in the diocese by 1513, to which must be added a further 60-80 members of religious Orders; and given that the population of the diocese at the time was about 8,000, this produces a figure of one cleric to 32 lay people — a very high ratio indeed. When we come to break this down in terms of their employment, however, we find that less than half of them had the cure of souls, the remainder being engaged on administrative, teaching and social tasks which could equally have been done by qualified laymen; but these were simply not then available in sufficient numbers, in spite of the 1496 'Education' Act,[70] although the balance was then gradually tipping towards the laity in terms of their employment as Lords of Council and other central government officials. Yet all these clerics were supported by ecclesiastical endowments of one kind or another which neither the papacy nor the secular powers could suddenly have dismantled without providing alternative sources of income in their place; and this they were either unable or unwilling to do. As for anti-clericalism, this was a permanent feature of medieval feudal society, where the clergy as a class were built into the establishment; and much of the lay hostility was directed not so much against them as against a system which operated tacks and teinds capable of being abused.[71] As for the ignorance and superstition which permeated their Christian world, the conservatism of the national hierarchies which prevented them from providing vernacular translations of the Bible was regrettable, but their failure to do so was not because they were against vernacular translations as such, but because they objected to unauthorised vernacular translations, which they feared could lead to heresy. As for heresy itself at the turn of the century, apart from the Lollards of Kyle, it would seem that Lollardy had little hold in Scotland. Rather we might reflect on the increasing number of books of devotion to be found in Scottish secular households during this period. In spite of its flawed performance, then, the Scottish Church was still reformable by 1513; indeed, its people still looked for its reform from within, even in 1560.

D

NOTES

1. Dorothy M. Owen, *The Records of the Established Church in England* (British Records Association, 1970).

2. For which see C. R. Cheney, 'William Lyndwood's Provinciale', *The Jurist* xxi (1961), 405-434.

3. L. E. Boyle, 'The Oculus Sacerdotis and some other works of William of Pagula', *TRHS* 5 (1955), 81-110.

4. G. Donaldson, 'Church Records', *The Scottish Genealogist* ii, 3 (1955), 14.

5. See, for example, the preface to D. Patrick's edition of *The Statutes of the Scottish Church* (SHS, Edinburgh 1907), D. Hay Fleming, *The Reformation in Scotland* (Edinburgh 1910), or A. R. MacEwen, *A History of the Church in Scotland*, 2 vols (London 1913-18).

6. Among the reference works must be noted J. Durkan and A. Ross, *Early Scottish Libraries* (Glasgow 1961), a significant and invaluable study of the libraries of late medieval Scottish churchmen; I. B. Cowan, *The Parishes of Medieval Scotland* (SRS, Edinburgh 1967); D. E. R. Watt, *Fasti Ecclesiae Scoticanae Medii Aevi* (St. Andrews 1969); P. McNeill and R. Nicholson, *An Historical Atlas of Scotland c400-c1600* (St. Andrews 1975); I. B. Cowan and D. E. Easson, *Medieval Religious Houses in Scotland* (London 1976). Important revision articles now include I. B. Cowan, 'Church and Society', in *Scottish Society in the Fifteenth Century*, ed. Jennifer M. Brown (London 1977), and Jenny Wormald's racy and informative chapter on the pre-Reformation Scottish church in her *Court, Kirk and Community: Scotland 1470-1625* (London 1981).

7. Held on microfilm in the Department of Scottish History, University of Glasgow, and carried out under the auspices of the Ross Fund directed by A. A. M. Duncan and I. B. Cowan, the project makes available a rich new source of evidence for Scottish ecclesiastical and legal historians, as can be seen from I. B. Cowan's 'Church and Society' article noted above, and from J. J. Robertson's essay on 'The development of the law', in *Scottish Society in the Fifteenth Century*, ed. Jennifer M. Brown (London 1977).

8. E.g. A. I. Cameron, *The Apostolic Camera and Scottish Benefices, 1418-1488* (London 1934); *Calendar of Scottish Supplications to Rome, 1418-1422*, ed. E. R. Lindsay and A. I. Cameron (Edinburgh 1934); *Calendar of Scottish Supplications to Rome, 1423-1428* (Edinburgh 1956); *Calendar of Scottish Supplications to Rome, 1428-1432*, ed. A. I. Dunlop and I. B. Cowan (Edinburgh 1970); *Calendar of Papal Letters to Scotland of Clement VII of Avignon 1378-1394*, ed. Charles Burns (Edinburgh 1976).

9. *Calendar of Entries in the Papal Registers relating to Gt. Britain and Ireland*, [CPR] vol xiii ed. J. A. Twemlow (London 1955), 738.

10. *Ibid.*, vol xiv, 152-156.

11. D. E. R. Watt, *Fasti Ecclesiae Scoticanae Medii Aevi* (St. Andrews 1969), 8-9, 13, 20, 24.

12. Shown in map form by L. J. Macfarlane in *An Historical Atlas of Scotland c400-c1600*, ed. P. McNeill and R. Nicholson (St. Andrews 1975), 190-191.

13. For this attitude, shared by most of the Scottish hierarchy at that time, see L. J. Macfarlane, 'The Primacy of the Scottish Church 1472-1521', *Innes Review* xx (1969), 111-129.

14. *CPR* xv, ed. M. J. Haren (Dublin 1978), no. 377, 184-85.

15. *The Letters of James V*, ed. D. Hay (Edinburgh 1954), 4.

16. *APS* ii, 37-38 and G. Donaldson, 'The rights of the Scottish crown in episcopal vacancies', *SHR* xlv (1966), 27-35.

17. *Vatican Archives*, Reg. Supp. 882, f. 113.

18. *Ibid.*, Reg. Supp. 998, f. 296.

19. *CPR* xv, ed. M. J. Haren (Dublin 1978), no. 686, 361-62.

20. *Vatican Archives*, Reg. Supp. 999, f. 43.

21. For these appointments, see Watt's *Fasti*, 13, 24, 16, 20 and 9.

22. *Fasti Aberdonenses*, ed. C. Innes (Edinburgh 1854), lxxx, 21-31.

23. Hector Boece, *Murthlacensium et Aberdonensium Episcoporum Vitae*, ed. J. Moir (Aberdeen 1894), 90-92.

24. *Collections for a History of the Shires of Aberdeen and Banff*, ed. J. Robertson (Aberdeen 1843), 335, and *Illustrations of the Topography and Antiquities of the Shires of Aberdeen and Banff* ii, ed. J. Robertson (Aberdeen 1847), 126-27; iii (Aberdeen 1857), 583 and 480.

25. Some 20% of the Aberdeen clergy were graduates even in the fourteenth century, for which see D. E. R. Watt, 'University Graduates in Scottish Benefices before 1410', *RSCHS*, xv (1966), 82.

26. Kinship, bonds of alliance and manrent, and the blood feud have been magisterially discussed by Jenny Wormald in 'Bloodfeud, Kindred and Government in early modern Scotland', *Past and Present* 87 (1980), and in 'The Local Community', Ch. 2 of *Court, Kirk and Community: Scotland 1470-1625* (London 1981).

27. D. E. R. Watt, *Fasti Ecclesiae Scoticanae Medii Aevi* (St. Andrews 1969), 16, 20.

28. I. B. Cowan, 'Some aspects of the appropriations of parish churches in medieval Scotland', *RSCHS* xiii (1959), 203-222; and the same author, 'The religious and the cure of souls in medieval Scotland', *RSCHS* xiv (1963), 215-30, and 'The organisation of Scottish secular cathedral chapters', *RSCHS* xiv (1963), 19-47.

29. An example is given in the *Chartulary of the Abbey of Lindores 1195-1479*, ed. J. Dowden (Edinburgh 1903), 124-128.

30. *Cf.* the conclusions drawn by I. B. Cowan in 'Vicarages and the Care of Souls in Medieval Scotland', *RSCHS* xvi (1969), 111-127, and the same author, 'Some Aspects of the Appropriation of Parish Churches in Medieval Scotland', *RSCHS* xiii (1959), 203-222.

31. For all these details see *Registrum Episcopatus Aberdonensis* [*REA*] ii, ed. C. Innes (Edinburgh 1845), 93-100.

32. E.g. his retrieval of thirteen prebendal lands, including his own mensal lands, for which see Vatican Archives, *Reg. Supp.* 999 f. 249.

33. *REA* i, 319-20; 205-06; *The Acts of the Lords Auditors of Causes and Complaints* [*ADA*] *1466-1494* (1839), 121.

34. *REA* i, 330.

35. *ADA*, 148, 153-54; *REA* i, 326.

36. *The Acts of the Lords of Council in Civil Causes* [*ADC*] *1478-1495*, i (1839), 280.

37. *REA* i, 379.

38. Numerous references occur in *Extracts from the Council Register of the Burgh of Aberdeen 1398-1570*, ed. J. Stuart (Aberdeen 1844), 48-51; 78-80; 85-86.

39. F. C. Eeles, 'Notes on a missal formerly used in St. Nicholas, Aberdeen', *PSAS* xxxiii (1899), 440-460; *Chartularium Ecclesiae Sancti Nicholai Aberdonensis*, ii, ed. J. Cooper (Aberdeen 1892), xxxi.

40. *Reg. Supp.* 215 ff. 191v-192; *Reg. Supp. 320*, f. 187v.

41. Hector Boece, *Murthlacensium et Aberdonensium Episcoporum Vitae*, ed. J. Moir (Aberdeen 1894), 98.

42. *ADC* (Public Affairs), 28-29, 505.

43. P. J. Anderson, *Aberdeen Friars* (Aberdeen 1909), *passim*, and *Medieval Religious Houses: Scotland*, 2nd ed., I. B. Cowan, D. E. Easson and R. N. Hadcock (London 1976), 107-108.

44. P. J. Anderson, *Aberdeen Friars*, 12.

45. Boece, *Vitae*, 92-93, and *Officers and Graduates of the University and King's College*, ed. P. J. Anderson (Aberdeen 1893), 97.

46. Boece, *Vitae*, 100; but see also *Medieval Religious Houses: Scotland* (2nd edition), 135, and P. J. Anderson, *Aberdeen Friars*, 51, 55, 60, 62.

47. J. C. Barry, *William Hay's Lectures on Marriage* (Edinburgh 1967), ix-xlviii.

48. W. M. Bryce, *The Scottish Greyfriars*, ii (Edinburgh 1909), 229-234.

49. *REA* ii 65, 152, 253.

50. *Ibid.*, 97-98.

51. *Ibid.*, 40, 252.

52. *Ibid.*, 94, 97.

53. *REA* i, 224-25; ii, 66, 95, 97.

54. *Liber S. Thome de Aberbrothoc*, ii, ed. C. Innes (Edinburgh 1856), Nos. 320, 402.

55. For these new feasts see R. W. Pfaff, *New Liturgical Feasts in later Medieval England* (Oxford 1970). A number of them were gradually appearing in Scottish service books, like the Arbuthnott missal, but there was no uniform practice in Scotland at the time, for which see D. McRoberts, *Catalogue of Scottish medieval liturgical books and fragments* (Glasgow 1953), and the same author, 'The medieval Scottish liturgy illustrated by surviving documents', *Transactions of the Scottish Ecclesiological Society* (1957), 24-40.

56. The sole copy of this Martyrology is to be found in Edinburgh University Library ms D.b.1.8.

57. The Aberdeen Breviary has been fully and magisterially analysed by J. D. Galbraith, *The Sources of the Aberdeen Breviary* (Aberdeen University M.Litt. thesis, 1970), to whom the author is deeply indebted.

58. I. A. Muirhead, 'A Quignonez Breviary', *Innes Review*, xiv (1963), 74-75; D. McRoberts, 'Some 16th century Scottish Breviaries', *Innes Review*, iii (1952), 33-48.

59. Leslie Macfarlane, 'William Elphinstone's Library', *Aberdeen University Review* xxxvii (1958), 253-71, especially at 267-269; and *Catalogue of the Incunabula in Aberdeen University Library*, compiled by W. S. Mitchell (Edinburgh 1968), esp. INC 34, 190, at 13, 71.

60. An inventory of the scriptural, pastoral and moral works to be found in St. Machar's Cathedral Library in 1469 is listed by M. R. James, *A Catalogue of the Medieval Manuscripts in the University Library, Aberdeen* (Cambridge 1932), 77-83 (AUL ms 249).

61. D. Macgregor, 'The Rathen Manual', *Transactions of the Aberdeen Ecclesiological Society* iv, (Aberdeen 1905), 1-83. See also D. McRoberts, *Catalogue of Scottish medieval liturgical books*, *passim*.

62. In general *cf* D. McKay, 'Parish Life in Scotland 1500-1560', in *Essays on the Scottish Reformation*, ed. D. McRoberts (Glasgow 1962), 82-115; I. B. Cowan, 'Church and Society', in *Scottish Society in the Fifteenth Century*, ed. Jennifer M. Brown (London 1977), esp. 118-119; but for Aberdeen, see *Extracts from the Council*

Register of the Burgh of Aberdeen 1398-1570, ed. J. Stuart (Aberdeen 1844), *passim*.

63. *Hectoris Boetii Murthlacensium et Aberdonensium Episcoporum Vitae*, ed. J. Moir (Aberdeen 1894), 57-114.

64. *Fasti Aberdonensis*, ed. C. Innes (Aberdeen 1854).

65. Aberdeen City Archives, *Council Registers* vols. 6-9 (1466-1517).

66. These include *APS* ii (1424-1567); *RMS* ii (1424-1513); *RSS* i (1488-1529); *ADA* (1466-1494); *ADC* (civil) (1478-1495); *ADC* ii (1501-1503); *ER* vols. 7-13; and *Accounts LHTS* (1473-1513), 4 vols.

67. Esp. mss 248-250, now in Aberdeen University Library, for which see M. R. James, *A Catalogue of the Manuscripts in the University Library, Aberdeen* (Cambridge 1932), 76-86, and *Registrum Episcopatus Aberdonensis*, 2 vols., ed. C. Innes (Edinburgh 1845).

68. Vol. xv, ed. M. J. Haren (Dublin 1978); vol. xvi, ed. A. P. Fuller (Alexander VI, in progress); vol. xviii, ed. M. J. Haren (Julius II, in progress).

69. Note, for example, the introductions provided by L. E. Boyle, 'The Papal Chancery at the end of the Fifteenth Century', and M. J. Haren on papal diplomatic in *CPR* xv, ed. M. J. Haren (Dublin 1978), xv-cxxi, as evidence of the papal curia's sophistication at this time.

70. *APS* ii, 238, clause 3.

71. See M. H. B. Sanderson, 'The Feuars of kirklands', *SHR* lii (1973), 117- 136, and the same author, 'Some aspects of the Church in Scottish society in the era of the Reformation', *Records of the Scottish Church History Society*, 17 (1972), 81-98.

3

Complaint, Satire and Invective in Middle Scots Literature

Roderick Lyall

THE marches between literary criticism and historiography are as wild, as forbidding, and as treacherous as the more literal Marches which played such an important role in the political and social history of medieval Scotland. There are few reliable maps; morasses and bogs await the unwary; and anyone from either side who ventures into these debatable lands in pursuit of escaped ideas is likely to find himself ambushed by specialists from across the border. To reside in such territory is to invite the suspicion of both sides. That is to say, abandoning the metaphor, that there is an area between the critical discussion of literary texts for their own sake and historiography in which specialists of neither kind feel really at home, and sometimes are not at home when they believe themselves to be. Historians are sometimes apt to leave literary evidence out of account altogether; and when they do consider it, the literary critic is perhaps inclined to find discussion insufficiently subtle in its treatment of strictly literary considerations, such as convention, the exploitation of rhetorical *topoi*, and the modulation of tone. Literary critics, on the other hand, frequently upset historians by assuming that historical situations were less complex than the extant evidence actually shows them to have been, or by relating literary texts to their social or political contexts in an over-simple way.

Yet the problem cannot be ignored. Much of the literature of any age comments upon political events or social forces either explicitly or by implication, and neither the historian nor literary critic can afford to ignore this difficult interrelationship. I am therefore attempting in this essay to examine one area of particular difficulty, as far as I am competent to do, from both sides; and in undertaking this task, I must begin with some literary distinctions. The three terms of my title, *complaint, satire* and *invective*, both indicate the range of my interest and raise terminological issues which require some clarification. *Satire*, of course, is a familiar term, although it is notoriously difficult to define. We understand by it writing which is critical of an individual or a class, which condemns a form of behaviour or a set of

44

values, and which employs some kind of rhetorical ploy or narrative device to persuade us to the author's point of view.[1] It can be applied to a literary genre, the 'formal satire' practised by Horace and Juvenal, by Hall and Marston, and by countless eighteenth-century poets, or more generally to a rhetorical mode, or even to a particular tone, found in many works which are not themselves formal satires. At this point, rather obviously, the neatness and exclusiveness of the definition have already begun to break down: critics are frequently disinclined to agree about the distinctive tone of a given work or passage, and the perception of satire can be as subjective as the perception of irony, its near relative, or of allegory. The edges of the category, then, are blurred and uncertain, and it is therefore useful to consider other modes which resemble satire but which can fairly readily be distinguished from it.

To one side of satire we find *invective*, which is sometimes regarded as a type of satire, or as one of its weapons;[2] where it occurs in isolation, however, it appears to me to be distinctly different. Fortunately for my argument, there is a tradition of Scottish poetry in which invective does occur in almost complete isolation: the flyting. Here name-calling is part of a game, a courtly entertainment, as in Dunbar's attack on Walter Kennedy:

> Mauch muttoun, byt buttoun, peilit gluttoun, air to Hilhous,
>> Rank beggar, ostir dregar, foule fleggar in the flet,
> Chittirlilling, ruch rilling, lik schilling in the milhous,
>> Baird rehator, theif of nator, fals tratour, feyindis gett,
>> Filling of tauch, rak sauch — cry crauch, thow art oursett;
> Muttoun dryver, girnall ryver, yadswyvar — Fowll fell the;
>> Herretyk, lunatyk, purspyk, carlingis pet,
> Rottin crok, dirtin dok — cry cok, or I sall quell the.   (241-8)[3]

The epithets are not intended literally, of course, and in a case like this it is the cumulative abusive effect which is the poet's real interest. The rules are the rules of a strange game, and there is no obvious way in which the details of Dunbar's characterisation of Kennedy correspond to reality. Elsewhere in this flyting, the position is a little more complicated. Earlier in the same round, Dunbar turns to Kennedy's poetic skills:

> Forworthin fule, of all the warld reffuse,
>> Quhat ferly is, thocht thow rejoys to flyte?
> Sic eloquence as thay in Erschry use,
>> In sic is sett thy thraward appetyte.
>> Thow hes full littill feill of fair indyte:
> I tak on me, ane pair of Lowthiane hippis
>> Sall fairar Inglis mak, and mair parfyte,
> Than thow can blabbar with thy Carrick lippis.   (105-12)

Again we should not take Dunbar's charges too much at face value: Kennedy was himself a noted poet in Scots (as Dunbar himself implicitly acknowledegs in 'Timor mortis conturbat me'),[4] and the demands of the flyting require that every possible source of abuse should be tapped without too much regard to truth or fairness. But the attack on Kennedy's Carrick origins and his links with 'Erschry', mirrored by Kennedy's subsequent suggestion that Dunbar, like his ancestors, is Anglophile to the point of treason, seems to reflect tensions within Scottish society which were real enough.[5] To the extent that Dunbar and Kennedy are here raising wider issues of cultural significance, then, they are moving away from 'pure' invective towards something which is more properly regarded as satire; but as long as the central preoccupation remains abuse of an individual, I suggest, and no fictional or rhetorical device is introduced to distance the poet from his target, as is the case throughout *The Flyting of Dunbar and Kennedie* and indeed throughout the genre of flyting, it is wiser to regard the result as invective.

If invective differs from satire partly in its concentration upon the individual, its refusal to deal seriously with broader moral or social issues, *complaint* is evidently at the opposite pole. The term gives rise to some difficulty. John Peter's theory that a clear-cut distinction could be made between complaint and satire, and that the latter was moreover virtually unknown in the Middle Ages, has not been widely accepted, and requires that much genuinely satirical medieval writing be ignored.[6] Yet to react by denying any validity in the distinction between the two concepts seems to me to err on the other side, since there clearly *was* medieval literature of 'reproof' which cannot properly be regarded as satire. I am not sure, however, that the distinction is really a generic one: I think it is rather a question of differing rhetorical modes, and there are many poems which seem to combine elements of both. At its most general, the mode of complaint is marked by straightforward *contemptus mundi*:

> Quhat is this lyfe bot ane straught way to deid,
>   Quhilk hes a tyme to pas and nane to duell;
> A slyding quheill us lent to seik remeid,
>   A fre chois gevin to paradice or hell,
>   A pray to deid, quhome vane is to repell;
>   A schoirt torment for infineit glaidnes —
> Als schort ane joy for lestand hevynes.[7]

Dunbar frequently strikes this note, but this is perhaps its most concentrated and clearly formed expression. The other-worldliness of his preoccupation here is an important guide to the nature of complaint, for it is this conviction that the things of this world are by their nature transitory, illusory in their attractiveness and a snare for man which often disposes the medieval poet towards complaint rather than satire. It is paralleled by the general view of man himself as fallen, since it is to the Fall that both sin and the misery of the human condition are to be attributed. Even when Dunbar is concerned with specific vices, therefore, he is inclined to focus upon the moral causes of abuse in a rather general way, and seldom attempts any analysis of social conditions in their own right:

Honest yemen in every toun
War wont to weir baith reid and broun,
Ar now arrayit in raggis with lyce;
And all for cause of cuvetyce.

And lairdis in silk harlis to the heill
For quhilk thair tennents sald somer meill
And levis on rutis undir the ryce;
And all for caus of cuvetyce.   (25-32)[8]

Any social comment in this passage is undermined by the banality of the refrain, and it would be a foolhardy scholar who used Dunbar's words as evidence of a decline in living standards at the turn of the sixteenth century. Such sumptuary complaint, if we may so term it, is a medieval commonplace,[9] and the allegation of exploitation in the second of these stanzas, while no doubt justified in a general way, is not sufficiently specific to indicate that Dunbar was aware of particular abuses characteristic of his own society. The problem, as perceived by Dunbar, lies not in the structure of late medieval feudalism, or — as in a remarkable passage in More's *Utopia*[10] — in enclosures, or even in the character of the king and his magnates, but rather in human nature itself, and in the prevalence of 'cuvetyce'. This could hardly be clearer than in the final stanza, in which Dunbar indicates the remedy for the social ills he has been describing:

Man, pleis thy makar and be mirry,
And sett not by this warld a chirry;
Wirk for the place of paradyce,
For thairin ringis na cuvettyce.   (41-4)

The framework of complaint, then, is not ultimately secular at all: abuses observed in this world are an inherent consequence of man's fallen condition, and the remedy lies less in immediate social reform than in a determination to transcend this world's vicissitudes.

Medieval satirists seem not to have had a clear generic conception of satire as such. They had at their disposal a range of satirical targets, many of them highly traditional, and an array of well-tried rhetorical devices. Some of the latter lead towards invective on the one hand (where direct denunciation of the individual or a small group takes over from a concentration on the correction of abuses) or towards complaint on the other (where the poet begins to deal in such broad terms with sin and the human condition that the particularity of social circumstances and individuals does not emerge). Both invective and complaint, it should be observed, are rhetorically straightforward, often amounting to little more than a catalogue of faults, while satire for the most part involves a more complex rhetorical structure, a fictional device or other persuasive weapon. Satire in this sense did not cease to exist in the Middle Ages, but its links with complaint were always a significant influence upon its character.

There can be no doubting the specific nature of the abuses which Dunbar sets out to condemn in his poem addressed to the merchants of Edinburgh. These stanzas are pervaded by the stench of fish in narrow streets, the arguments of street-traders and the importunings of beggars, and many of the details of the poet's description reveal close familiarity with the burgh which is his subject:

> Your stinkand scull that standis dirk
> Haldis the lycht fra your parroche kirk;
> Your foirstair makis your housis mirk
> Lyk na cuntry bot heir at hame . . .   (15-18)[11]

Even a quick comparison of the way in which Dunbar handles the theme of covetice in the poem I was discussing above with his methods here demonstrates something of the difference between complaint and satire: there, such details as there were were essentially conventional, even formulaic ('levis on rutis undir the ryce'), and the sequence of the poem was organised around a catalogue of the effects of a particular sin, while here the focus is much more narrowly upon the state of Edinburgh as Dunbar and his contemporaries knew it. All the rhetoric of the first eight stanzas is concentrated upon heightening the immediacy of the portrayal of the town, and upon using these details, in conjunction with the judgment embodied in the refrain, to build a case against the actual behaviour of the Edinburgh burgesses. In the last three stanzas, however, Dunbar moves on from this essentially satirical blend of description and condemnation. First, he resorts to a threat:

> Sen for the Court and the Sessioun,
> The great repair of this regioun
> Is in your burgh, thairfoir be boun
> To mend all faultis that ar to blame,
>   And eschew schame;
> Gif thai pas to ane uther toun
> Ye will decay, and your great name!   (57-63)

This rhetorical ploy has considerable relevance to the conditions of about 1500: the predominance of Edinburgh over, for example, Perth and Stirling as a royal, political and judicial centre was a phenomenon of the later fifteenth century,[12] and it was therefore presumably far from unimaginable that it might lose its position if it did not become more salubrious. The threat is given point by the following stanza, in which Dunbar exhorts the merchants of the burgh to abandon their extortionate practices, which he portrays as a considerable imposition upon visitors. Although the poet's rhetorical posture is a little different in each of these stanzas, I think it is still possible to regard them as satirical, since they are directed towards quite specific points of public policy. The final stanza is of a quite different rhetorical kind:

> Singular proffeit so dois yow blind,
> The common proffeit gois behind:

I pray that Lord remeid to fynd,
That deit into Jerusalem,
    And gar yow schame!
That sum tyme ressoun may you bind
For to [win bak to] yow guid name.   (71-7)[13]

Dunbar has mentioned 'profit' before in the poem, in line 50; but here it introduces a different order of argument. The focus now is less upon the abuses committed by the burgesses (profiteering, neglect of the town and of the needy) than upon the underlying moral causes and upon a solution which goes far beyond any practical changes in policy: since the root of the problem is cupidity, the remedy can only lie in *moral* reform, which can only come about through the intervention of Christ. To a modern audience, perhaps, this final stanza dilutes the strong satirical flavour of what has preceded it, but it seems to me that this widening of the argument from satire to complaint is an essential part of Dunbar's purpose. His framework, after all, is divine rather than secular, and the reform he seeks is of the most radical kind. This shift is well captured by the short fifth line of each stanza: for the first eight stanzas it is cast in the form of a rhetorical question ('Think ye not schame?'), but this is abandoned in the last three stanzas in favour of more positive variations, and in the final stanza it is used (through the active verb *gar*) to make it clear that the conscience which has been absent from the burgesses throughout the rest of the poem — for the implied answer to Dunbar's repeated question is of course 'No'! — will have to be the result of a divinely inspired moral revolution.

The twist at the end of this poem depends upon an analytical distinction of some importance, between satire proper and complaint. Elsewhere, to miss the point can lead to rather serious misinterpretation. I believe that some critics of Henryson's *Morall Fabillis*, for example, have been thus misled by a confusion of satire and complaint. I have discussed this question before,[14] but it is sufficiently important to justify some further attention in the present context. Scholars as diverse as M. W. Stearns, John MacQueen, Ian Jamieson, Ranald Nicholson and, most recently and extensively, Robert L. Kindrick have detected in the *Fabillis* a variety of topical allusions, and have therefore been inclined to view this collection as in some sense satirical.[15] I do not intend to repeat the detailed arguments which I believe refute the suggestion that *The Lyoun and the Mous*, for example, is essentially a topical poem about the unsuccessful coup of 1482; but I should perhaps say a little about the new identifications proposed by Professor Kindrick. According to his account of the political allegory in the *Fabillis*, James III is represented not only by the Lion in *The Lyoun and the Mous*, but also by Gib the cat in *The Taill of the Uponlandis Mous and the Burges Mous*, by the Lion in *The Parliament of Fourfuttit Beistis*, and by the shepherd in the *The Wolf and the Wedder*: Such readings, of course, require a wholesale setting aside of the sense of the fables as enunciated by Henryson himself. Gib the cat, it is clear, represents a more substantial threat to the welfare of the mice than the king's economic depredations:

O wantoun man that vsis for to feid
Thy wambe, and makis it a god to be;
Luke to thy self, I warne the weill on deid.
The cat cummis and to the mous hes ee;
Quhat is avale thy feist and royaltie,
With dreidfull hart and tribulatioun?   (381-6)[16]

It is surely perverse to read into this an attack on 'heavy tariffs, a debased coinage, and the grants to James' familiars'.[17] The whole point of the fable is that material prosperity and social position are transitory and not worth pursuing; and the near-capture of the mice by 'Gib Hunter, our jolie cat' — which, even covertly, would be an extraordinary way for Henryson to allude to the king! — illustrates the physical and spiritual dangers undergone by those who seek to rise above their lot in search of material comfort. It can scarcely at the same time represent an attack by the king on the material well being of his subjects. I do not mean to suggest that this fable is altogether lacking in satirical intent, but the object is rather different from that proposed by Professor Kindrick. The contrast between the two mice, who 'lay baith within ane wame' (214), is developed by Henryson to emphasise the contrast between the honest poverty of the 'rurall mous' and the social climbing of her sister:

The vther mouse, that in the burgh can byde,
Was gild brother and made ane fre burges,
Toll-fre als, but custum mair or les,
And fredome had to ga quhair euer scho list
Amange the cheis and meill, in ark and kist.   (171-5)

The snobbishness with which the burgess mouse treats her sister's hospitality is evidently not intended to redound to her credit, and the fable ends with the Uponlandis Mous' return to the security of her Spartan existence,

In quyet and eis withoutin ony dreid.   (363)

But such social satire as Henryson introduces is not really central to the fable: its theme of the superiority of 'small possessioun' over worldly goods belongs to the mode of complaint rather than that of satire.

If the application of *The Taill of the Uponlandis Mous and the Burges Mous* suggested by Professor Kindrick involves a distortion of the natural sense of the fable, the same is even more true of the more specific political references he claims for the other fables. There is no textual evidence whatever to justify the identification of the Wolf in *The Parliament of Fourfuttit Beistis* with William Scheves, or to provide a basis for reading the fable as an allegory of Church-State relations. Henryson's *moralitas* makes it clear that his allegory concerns the proper response of asceticism to the attractions of the world: the Lion symbolises not James but the World, the Wolf not Archbishop Scheves but Sensualitie, and it is not enough to dismiss such clear guidance with the self-fulfilling argument that it is 'a disclaimer which is to be expected in a poem such as this'.[18] Nor are we given any hint in either narrative or *moralitas* that the comic fable of *The Wolf and the Wedder* covertly refers to the assassination of the king's favourites at Lauder Bridge. Like *The Taill of the Uponlandis Mous and the Burges Mous*, *The Wolf and the Wedder* condemns social pretension, this time in relation to dress. Its theme is a highly conventional one, and could hardly be expressed by Henryson in more general terms than his exhortation to

> men of eurilk stait
> To knaw thame self, and quhome thay suld forbeir . . .   (2609-10)

Once again, its links are with complaint, and in the absence of a single shred of firm textual evidence, any topical allusion must be regarded as fanciful.

Social themes are clearly of some importance in the *Morall Fabillis*, but they are not on the whole treated in a satirical manner. This fact helps to illuminate the relationship between these social themes and the wider moral argument of the collection as a whole, for the technical and thematic variety of the *Fabillis* actually disguises an underlying unity of purpose. In diverse ways, Henryson's fables illustrate the moral perspective enunciated in the Prologue:

> Na meruell is, ane man be lyke ane beist,
> Quhilk lufis ay carnall and foull delyte,
> That schame can not him renye nor arreist,
> Bot takis all the lust and appetyte,
> Quhilk throw custum and the daylie ryte
> Syne in the mynd sa fast is radicate
> That he in brutal beist is transformate.   (50-6)

The appropriateness of the fable form lies in its association of human behaviour with animal characters, and the point of its attack is the bestial nature of man's devotion to the things of this world. This is exemplified by the stupid materialism of the Wolf in *The Taill of the Foxe that begylit the Wolf in the Schadow of the Mone* and elsewhere, and of the Mouse in *The Paddok and the Mous*, as well as by the social climbing of the Burges Mous. Even a fable with a *sentence* as immediate and as pointed as *The Scheip and the Doig*, with its condemnation of injustice and judicial corruption, attributes the social abuses it describes to the rule of 'Covetice', and concludes with a sweeping denunciation of prevailing conditions which transcends the evils of any particular regime in complaining of the entire misery of the human condition:

> Seis thow not, lord, this warld ouerturnit is,
> As quha wald change gude gold in leid or tyn?
> The pure is peillit, the lord may do na mis,
> And simonie is haldin for na syn.
> Now is he blyith with okker maist may wyn;
> Gentrice is slane, and pietie is ago.
> Allace, gude lord, quhy tholis thow it so?

> Thow tholis this euin for our grit offence;
> Thow sendis vs troubill and plaigis soir,
> As hunger, derth, grit weir, or pestilence;
> Bot few amendis now thair lyfe thairfoir.
> We pure pepill as now may do no moir
> Bot pray to the: sen that we ar opprest
> In to this eirth, grant vs in heuin gude rest.   (1307-20)[19]

The 'now' of line 1311 and elsewhere is deceptive, for Henryson is not in fact pointing to peculiarities of his own age, any more than the anonymous thirteenth-century poet was when he lamented that

> Fides hodie sopitur,
>   vigilatque pravitas

We come closest to genuine satire, perhaps, in the *moralitas* of *The Wolf and the Lamb*, where Henryson develops his source by attacking 'thre kynd of wolfis' who oppress the poor (corrupt lawyers, the greedy rich, and grasping landlords) — familiar targets of medieval satirists[20] — and in passages which are incidental to the main line of the moral argument: the characterisation of the Burges Mous, the mendicant Freir Wolff Waitskaith, the hypocritical, lascivious and sanctimonious hens of *Schir Chantecleir and the Foxe*. But overall, the mode of the *Morall Fabillis* is manifestly complaint, and the social problems identified by Henryson are due to man's fallen nature rather than to the specific faults of individuals or of a particular system.

Let us now return to the boundary between satire and invective. The personal, abusive element in Dunbar's poetry is well known, and we have already seen him at work in the 'pure' form of the flyting; but Dunbar is capable of striking a variety of abusive notes. He can be playful, as in his attack on James Doig, the keeper of Queen Margaret's wardrobe:

> Quhen that I speik till him freindlyk
> He barkis lyk ane midding tyk,
> War chassand cattell throu a bog:
>   Madam, ye heff a dangerous Dog!   (13-16)

He can turn his offensiveness against a larger group, as in his description of the tournament between a tailor and a soutar:

> Quhen on the telyour he did luke,
> His hairt a littill dwamyng tuke,
> He mycht nocht rycht upsitt;
> In to his stommok wes sic ane steir,
> Off all his dennar, quhilk he coft deir,
> His breist held deill a bit.
> To comfort him, or he raid forder,
> The Devill off knychtheid gaif him order,
> For sair syne he did spitt,
> And he about the Devillis nek

Did spew aganne ane quart of blek,
Thus knychtly he him quitt.   (49-60)

This last poem, however, raises a frequent difficulty with Dunbar: that is, the direction of his attack. That the burlesque tournament was intended as an unfavourable comment on the two groups of craftsmen is indicated both by the poet's subsequent, backhanded 'apology' and by the existence of other works, admittedly later than Dunbar's, making fun of tailors and soutars.[21] But it is also clear that other burlesque tournaments were composed in the later Middle Ages, and it is possible to read 'Nixt that a turnament wes tryid' as, in part at least, a satire on chivalric ceremonial. A similar intention is evident in Dunbar's poem about Sir Thomas Norny, a burlesque romance in the manner of Chaucer's *Sir Thopas*.[22]

The problem of the balance between invective and satirical comment on wider themes poses itself elsewhere in Dunbar's poems, most notably perhaps in those which concern the career of John Damian, 'The fenyeit freir of Tongland'.[23] That Dunbar, whom we know from other poems to have been a perennial seeker of benefices from James IV, should have been jealous of this foreign favourite is hardly surprising; and there is a good deal of evidence that Damian, 'the Franch leich', established himself as a prominent member of the king's household between 1501 and 1507, the year of his ill-advised attempt to fly from Stirling Castle to Paris with a pair of home-made wings.[24] He was made abbot of the Premonstratensian house of Tungland in 1504, and received substantial grants to support his efforts at distilling the 'quint-essence', of which whisky appears to have been an important constituent.[25] It is easy, therefore, to see Dunbar's two poems on the subject of Damian's brief flight as mere spite, as invective in the narrowest and least elevated sense. But I do not believe that this is altogether fair to Dunbar. In the first place, he does exercise considerable wit in constructing the fictional framework of his poems, and in the process he widens his focus from Damian himself. The central motif of 'As yung Aurora with cristall haile' is the attack on the flying abbot by a horde of birds, and the way in which their reactions are described emphasises the unnaturalness of Damian's attempt:

And quhen that he did mont on hie,
All fowill ferleit quhat he sowld be,
    That evir did on him luke.
Sum held he had bene Dedalus,
Sum the Menatair marvelus,
Sum Martis blaksmyth Vulcanus,
    And sum Saturnus kuke.   (62-8)

Perhaps this is just hyperbolic rhetoric, but it does link Damian with the world of slightly menacing mythology, in a manner repeated in 'Lucina schynnyng in silence of the nicht':

Under Saturnus fyrie regioun
Symone Magus sall meit him, and Mahoun,
And Merlyne at the mone sall him be bydand,
And Jonet the weido on ane bussome rydand,
Off wichis with ane windir garesoun.   (31-5)

Indeed, this is just one aspect of Dunbar's presentation of Damian as a figure of monstrous depravity: in 'As yung Aurora with cristall haile', he is portrayed as a 'Turk of Tartary', the murderer of a priest in Lombardy, and a dangerous quack. He is, moreover, a pseudo-priest, a charge not entirely without foundation in view of Damian's *in commendam* abbacy. Much of this, of course, can be dismissed as flyting-like exaggeration, as part of a skilfully constructed piece of invective; but at times Dunbar strikes a genuine note of moral outrage:

Unto no mes pressit this prelat,
For sound of sacring bell nor skellat;
As blaksmyth bruikit was his pallatt
   For battering at the study.
Thocht he come hame a new maid channoun,
He had dispensit with matynnis cannoun,
On him come nowther stole nor fannoun
   For smowking of the smydy.   (49-56)

Beside Dunbar's (no doubt self-interested) distaste at Damian's neglect of his ecclesiastical responsibilities here, there is contempt for the pursuits of the alchemist, which are, Dunbar implies, as improper and as unnatural, especially in a cleric, as the attempt at flying which is the occasion of the poem. What we see, then, is an attack on the proto-scientific world of alchemy, a theme which is not uncommon among medieval moralists, and is related to the suspicion regarding astrology which finds expression in Henryson's *Orpheus and Erudices*.[26] Although the personal motive of invective is of great importance in both this poem and its companion piece, therefore, it is accompanied by elements of a broader, more satirical approach; and it is worth considering the possibility that Dunbar was here responding to an interest in scientific matters which originated with the king himself.[27]

    In the period we have been discussing so far, up to about the end of the reign of James IV, the satirical portrayal of certain types and social groups can be seen shading off into complaint on the one hand and into invective on the other. Dunbar, clearly, employed all three modes at different times, frequently combining two of them as he combined other types of rhetorical convention: dream-allegory, formal dialogue, beast-fable, liturgical parody, and so on. Henryson, too, weaves some satirical material into his *Moral Fabillis*. We could doubtless find other examples, although there are relatively few genuinely satirical works in Middle Scots. The satirical elements in *The Thre Prestis of Peblis* are subordinated to more straightforwardly moral themes;[28] and even *The Buke of the Howlat*, written by Richard Holland about 1450,[29] which could be seen as a satire on social climbing and incidentally on the Papal court, combines whatever satirical purpose it has with many other interests: allegorical catalogues, panegyric of the Douglases, and high moral sententiousness. There is, however, a significant change of tone in the course of the sixteenth century. This is due, I think, not to the influence of classical models, for there is no vogue of formal satire in Scotland to parallel that which occurred in Elizabethan England, but rather it is a function of the development of parties which took place during the religious and political crises of the Reformation. Factions, of course, played an important part in the politics of fifteenth-century Scotland, especially during minorities and in such periods as the crisis of 1482, but (the doubtful case of Holland's *Howlat* apart) no satirical poetry survives as a record of them.[30] One important difference between the two centuries is the emergence of the printing press, and it is no doubt relevant that most of the controversial literature of the Reformation period survives in the form of broadsides, which were a vital part of the process of propaganda.[31] But the divisions in society by 1550 were deeper and more permanent than those which had existed in 1480 or 1500, and this change certainly left its mark on the writing of satire.

The change is reflected in the poetry of Sir David Lindsay, whose career extends from the last years of James IV until 1555. His earliest extant work, *The Dreme*, was written about 1528, and has much in common with the tradition of complaint: its account of the state of contemporary Scotland is set against the wider context of Heaven and Hell, and for all Lindsay's introduction of Jhone the Comoun-weill as his spokesman, and his positioning of the passage about Scotland at the climax of the poem, the problem is again seen, as it was by Henryson, as arising from the fundamental nature of the human condition. The balance is already different in *The Testament and Complaynt of the Papyngo* (1530), which combines in its first part sober advice to the king with anti-curial satire of a kind relatively uncommon in Scotland but familiar in England through the poems of Skelton, Alexander Barclay and, latterly, Wyatt, while Lindsay shifts in the second part to a much more scathing satirical account of the failings of the contemporary Church, presented under the allegorical fiction of a dialogue between the Papyngo and three clerical birds, the Pye (a canon regular), the Raven (a Benedictine) and the Gled (a friar). The attack on ecclesiastical abuses is both more explicit and more specific in the *The Tragedie of the Cardinale* (1547), in which Lindsay adopts a favourite satirical device of making the assassinated Cardinal Beaton confess his own crimes as he appears to the poet in a dream. Although the immediate object of the criticism here is Beaton, both the indirectness contributed to the poem by Lindsay's skilful use of a confessional persona and the tendency to generalisation of the argument, pointing to the universal force of mutability and applying the lessons of Beaton's fate to 'all proude Prelatis' (271), takes the *Tragedie* beyond the level of mere personal invective, and the poem ends with a call from Beaton himself for sweeping reform:

E

Quharefor I counsayle euerylk christinit kyng
Within his realme mak Reformatioun,
And suffer no mo Rebaldis for to ryng
Abufe Christis trew Congregatioun:
Failyeying thareof, I mak Narratioun
That ye Prencis and Prelatis, all at onis,
Sall bureit be in hell, Saule, blude, and bonis.   (421-7)[32]

The satiric force of this appeal is all the stronger because of the fiction that it is
made by Beaton, of all people, from beyond the grave, and there can be no
doubt that by this time Lindsay was firmly in the camp of the Reformers, in
political terms if not in theological ones. The programme of reform enunciated
at the end of *Ane Satyre of the Thrie Estaitis* (1552) provides for profound
changes in the government of the Church, short (but only just) of a formal
break with the Papacy; but it is important to recognise that here too Lindsay
blends political, religious and social satire with a broader moral statement
about the consequences for the human soul of a surrender to the seductive
appeal of Sensualitie, a double purpose which is well conveyed by the name of
the protagonist, King Humanitie.[33]

The complexity of Lindsay's satirical posture is due partly to his interest in
wider moral themes, characteristic of the complaint mode, partly to the uncertainty of his relationship to the eventual leaders of the Reformation. No
such caveats need be entered about the authors of *The Gude and Godlie
Ballatis*, whose Lutheran attachments are plain enough.[34] Although the earliest
extant edition of this collection was probably printed in 1566, it is very likely
that it existed in something like its present form by 1546: there is ample
seventeenth-century evidence that it was principally the work of John Wedder-
burn, who fled Scotland in that year.[35] Among the adaptations of secular
songs which are included in the *Ballatis* along with psalm translations and
Lutheran hymns are several which denounce in uncompromising terms contemporary ecclesiastical vices. The rhetoric of such pieces is of the simplest
kind; the effect derives from the accumulation of a catalogue of abuses, and
from a contrast between the subject matter and the tune on which it is hung,
but hardly from any striking poetic invention:

Of Scotland-well the Freiris of Faill
The lymmerie lang hes lestit;
The Monkis of Melrose maid gude kaill
On Frydayis quhen thay fastit,
The sillie Nunnis caist up thair bunnis
And heisit thair hippis on hie:
    Hay trix, tryme go trix, vnder the grene wod tre.   (57-63)[36]

Although these lines are unusually specific, they point to a recurring preoccupation of the Reforming poets, the laxity and low moral standards of the
clergy, especially the regular clergy. In taking up such themes, of course, they

were adopting conventions long popular among medieval satirists, but there is no doubt that the criticism has acquired a new edge:

> The Bischop of Hely brak his neck,
> Dishereist of his benefice,
> Cause he the priestis wald not correct,
> Curruptand Goddis Sacrifice;
> Sen our Hely, in his office,
> Is lyke in preuaricatioun,
> He sall ressaif sic lyke justice,
> Mak he nocht reformatioun.   (1-8)[37]

Such poems make up in vehemence for what they lack in rhetorical sophistication, although the reference to the fate of Eli the priest (1 Samuel 2-4) which forms the basis of this poem is neatly managed to provide an awful warning, apparently to Beaton.

After the crisis of 1560, controversial verse acquired a new significance; and the sectarian poems collected by James Cranstoun (covering the period mainly from 1567 to 1573) illustrate the effect on satirical writing of the sharper divisions and heightened passions of the mid-sixteenth century. Unlike the authors of *The Gude and Godlie Ballatis*, Robert Sempill and his contemporaries employed many of the devices of the medieval satirist, but to new purposes and through a new medium. There is a marked preference for the dramatic complaint, either in the mouth of a deceased political figure on the model of Lindsay's *Tragedie of the Cardinale*, such as *The Testament and Tragedie of vmquhile King Henrie Stewart* (printed by Lekprevik in 1567) and *The Bischoppis Lyfe and Testament* (1571), a scurrilous mock confession 'by' John Hamilton, archbishop of St. Andrews, or reporting the words of an allegorical figure of authority, as in *Ane Ballat declaring the Nobill and Gude Inclinatioun of our King* (1567) or the versified *Complaint of Scotland* (1570).[38] Although the argument of these pieces is frequently of the most explicit kind, it is evident that such medieval conventions as the allegorical dream or dialogue continued to provide a framework for post-Reformation satirists. Among the most interesting rhetorical devices are satirical personae, such as Maddie, 'Priores of the Caill mercat', employed by the Protestant satirist Robert Sempill, and Tom Truth. Such rhetorical disguises are the lineal descendants of Piers Plowman and Jack Upland, plain-speakers whose satirical power derives from the supposedly popular view they express.[39] That Sempill at least did not use his Maddie-persona as a genuine disguise is apparent from the challenge which he throws down at the end of his abusive poem attacking 'the Sklanderaris that blasphemis the Regent and the rest of the Lordis':

> Luik the first letter of euerie werss,
> Hangman! gif thow can reherss,
> Mark weill my name & set ane day:
> In fechting war thow neuir so ferss,
> Thow salbe marrowit and I may.   (56-60)[40]

The acrostic to which he points, 'ROBART SEMPIL', leaves no doubt that we are not intended to take too seriously (except as a manifest fiction) the authorship indicated in the colophon:

> Finis, quod Maddie, gar mak the boun
> To all the papistis of this toun.   (61-2)

She is perhaps used here to balance some rival persona, since the figure of Tom Truth was certainly employed by at least one of Moray's opponents,[41] but Sempill made use of her voice on later occasions as well, as in two poems written to lament the Regent's assassination. The rhetorical value of the persona is made explicit in one of these:

> For I, a wyfe, with sempill lyfe,
> Dois wyn my meit ilk day,
> For small auaill, ay selling caill,
> The best fassoun I may.
> Besyde the Throne I wait vpone
> My mercat by delay;
> Gif men thair walk, I heir thair talk,
> And beiris it weill away.
>
> In felloun feir at me thay speir,
> Quhat tythands in this land?
> Quhy sit I dum and dar not mum?
> Oft tymes thay do demand.
> To thame agane I answer plane,
> Quhair thay beside me stand:
> Na thing is heir bot mortall weir,
> Wrocht be ane bailfull hand.   (16-32)[42]

As an authoritative spokesman, Maddie has much in common with Lady Scotland or Lindsay's Jhone the Comoun-weill, but she is not an allegorical figure as they are. She represents, we are asked to believe, the opinion of the ordinary, sensible citizens of Edinburgh, an observer of events and a commentator upon them. If she looks back to the conventions of medieval satirical allegory, she also looks forward to the conventions of journalism.

A little later, Sempill found another role for Maddie, in an attack on Secretary Lethington. Attacked by Sempill's Marian opponent Tom Truth in 1568 as 'traitor Lethington' and 'this false Machivilian',[43] William Maitland of Lethington was sufficiently pro-Marian by 1570 to draw Sempill's own fire. The resulting poem is built around a metaphor which seems to owe much to Lindsay's *Papyngo*:

> A bailfull bird that wantis wingis to fle,
> Nureist in a nest richt craftie wylis to hatche,
> For fault of feit borne in ane ark of tre,
> In craftines to Sinon worthie matche . . .   (1-4)[44]

The bird is, of course, Maitland himself, and the occasion of the poem seems to have been his lodging in Edinburgh Castle with Sir William Kirkcaldy of Grange, who had been Maitland's custodian since his arrest in September 1569:

> This bailfull bird richt beinly can vpbeild,
> In castellis strang, hir noysum nest to byde;
> The feildis plane can not fra schame hir scheild.
> Quha heichest clymmis the soner may thay slyde:
> In wardly wit (by God) quha dois confyde
> Will be bet doun be duilfull destanie,
> And end thair lyfe with wretchit miserie.   (43-9)

The topical allusion is here followed immediately by a generalisation which is a commonplace of medieval complaint, and which echoes Lindsay's proverbial introduction of his Papyngo's fall:

> Quha clymmis to hycht, perforce his feit mon faill.   (73)

That it was Lindsay's poem, rather than any of the other possible sources, which was in Sempill's mind is confirmed by the following stanza, in which the 'monstrous bird' is warned against the possible onslaught of gleddis, ravinnis or the pyet (the same three birds which dismembered the Papyngo). Sempill links his bird metaphor with other familiar satirical devices, citing several Old Testament *exempla* of treachery, as well as the Trojan Sinon and Charlemagne's Ganelon, invoking proverbial lore to Lethington's discredit, and again associating him with the notorious Machiavelli ('A Scuruie Schollar of Machivellus lair' — line 8). Colloquial as the rhyme royal stanzas of the poem itself frequently are, there is a marked contrast between them and the eight-line stanzas of the Envoy:

> Jak in the bokis, for all thy mokis
> A vengence mot the fall!
> Thy subteltie and palyardrie
>   Our fredome bringis in thrall.
> Thy fair fals toung dois still impung
> Our Crown Imperiall,
> Lyke wauering thane, thy proces vane
>   Will brew the bitter gall.   (78-85)

The internal rhymes lend a vivacity to these lines which is characteristic of the Maddie persona, and Sempill here abandons his metaphor in favour of outright condemnation, shifting from the indirection of satire to the more straightforward mode of invective.

The relationship between satire and invective is here given a new twist. Like Dunbar's attack on Damian, the rhetorical indirectness of the poet's approach takes much of this piece away from the direct denunciation of invective; yet it is clear that there is little behind the poem other than the animosities of faction, and there is nothing to suggest that Sempill's eye is on any target other than the hated Lethington. There is an interesting parallel in George Buchanan's prose attack, *Chamaeleon,* which was written a little later than Sempill's poem.[45] Again, a single central metaphor is used to convey Lethington's nature, the various changes in his policy being compared, in unequivocally pejorative terms, to the changes of colour of the legendary chamaeleon. The structure of the attack is narrative, each stage of Lethington's career being described in some detail, always to his discredit and with frequent references to the central metaphor. Buchanan manages this rather simple rhetorical structure with considerable skill, and not without a certain wit; linking Moray's death with Lethington's captivity in Edinburgh Castle, he says:

> This not obtenit he obtenit aganis all the said regentis freindis will, to be send to ward in the castell of Edinburgh quhair he wrocht aganis the nature of the Chamaeleon, for he changeit the greater part of thame of the castell to his colour sa weill, that the conspiracy of the regentis deid lang afoir consavit wes than brocht to effect.[46]

For all his partisan hatred of Lethington, Buchanan adopts the sober pose of the historian in recording his career; but it is scarcely likely that even his contemporaries were unaware of the propagandist purpose underlying his pamphlet, and the concern of the authorities is evident in the raid on Lekprevik's house made on 14th April 1571, when it was believed that Buchanan's work had been put into print.[47]

In these attacks on Maitland of Lethington, who seems to have attracted the animosity of his contemporaries in a way that few other sixteenth-century politicians did, we see in an extreme form the effect upon satirical writing of Reformation politics. The targets of medieval satire were, as we have seen, mostly types: particular professional groups, some classes of clerics, women.[48] Much of the satirical writing of the fifteenth and earlier centuries shades off into complaint, as poets move away from particular abuses to the underlying moral causes. While retaining many of the conventions and rhetorical devices of medieval satire, the Reformers became more specific in their attacks, more aware of the possibility of immediate and particular change and less compromising in their denunciation of opponents who barred the way. Lindsay is a transitional figure in more senses than one, for the poems in which we can see his evolution from a fairly traditional provider of advice to a young king to a supporter of thoroughgoing reform of the Church also balance the moral themes of complaint with ecclesiastical satire of a new order of determined specificity; and they provided rhetorical models for Sempill and his contemporaries. In the controversial poetry of the decades after 1560, satire and invective are delicately balanced; there were, certainly, poets like Lethington's father Sir Richard Maitland and Alexander Arbuthnot, who continued to practise the tradition of complaint, but their poems are generally far from the world of satire and, interestingly, rhetorically less effective than the vigorous works of Sempill.[49] How far the traditions had diverged can be seen from two final quotations, the first from Maitland's poem on the civil wars,

'At morning in ane gardein grein', the second from Sempill's *Regentis Tragedie*:

O lord quhair ar thais zelous men
That in this land hes bene oft syis
That quhen they could persaue or ken
Ane trowble in the countrie ryis
 With wisdome and foirsicht
 Thay wald set all thair micht
Be greit travell and wordis wyse
Ane remedie wald sone devyise
And set all thingis aricht.[50]

Now Lordis & Lairdis assemblit in this place,
Ouer lang we talk of Tragedeis, allace!
Away with cair, with confort now conclude;
As gude in paper as speik it in your face:
Gif murtherars for geir get ony grace,
Ye will be schent: think on, I say, for gude;
Sen art and part ar gyltie of his blude,
Quhy suld ye feir or fauour thame for fleiching?
Ye hard your self quhat Knox spak at the preiching.[51]

NOTES

1. On definitions of satire, see David Worcester, *The Art of Satire* (Cambridge, Mass. 1940); Alvin Kernan, *The Cankered Muse* (New Haven 1959), 1-36; and A. R. Heiserman, *Skelton and Satire* (Chicago 1961), 291-312. An old-fashioned but still useful historical survey is S. M. Tucker's *Verse Satire in England before the Reformation* (New York 1908), esp. 1-34.

2. Cf. Worcester, *op. cit.*, 13-38.

3. 'The Flyting of Dunbar and Kennedie', *The Poems of William Dunbar*, ed. James Kinsley (Oxford 1979), 76-95; all quotations from Dunbar's poems are based on this edition.

4. Lines 89-90, *Poems*, ed. Kinsley, 178-81.

5. G. W. S. Barrow has argued for the absence of a significant Highland/Lowland division in the fourteenth and fifteenth centuries: cf. *The Kingdom of the Scots* (London 1973), 362-83. Perhaps attitudes to England were a more important issue (as they would appear to have been when Hary composed the opening lines of his *Wallace*), but sixteenth-century prejudices are reflected in Montgomerie's 'How the first Helandman of God was maid/Of ane horss turd in Argylle' (*Poems*, ed. James Cranstoun [STS, Edinburgh 1887], 280-1) and in Dunbar's own 'Off Februar the fyiftene nycht' (*Poems*, ed. Kinsley, 150-3).

6. John Peter, *Complaint and Satire in Early English Literature* (Oxford 1956). For a useful short critique, see Heiserman, *op. cit.*, 292-3.

7. *Poems*, ed. Kinsley, 173.

8. *Ibid.*, 189-91.

9. Cf. G. R. Owst, *Literature and Pulpit in Medieval England* (2nd edn, Oxford

1961); and Jill Mann, *Chaucer and Medieval Estates Satire* (Cambridge 1973), 118-9.

10. Sir Thomas More, *Utopia*, ed. Edward Surtz SJ and J. H. Hexter (New Haven 1965), 60-71.

11. 'To the Merchantis of Edinburgh', *Poems*, ed. Kinsley, 201-3.

12. Edinburgh had increasingly become an important royal centre; its predominance is most evident in its choice as venue for meetings of the Estates, which generally took place at Perth under James I, were shared between Stirling and Edinburgh (and, to a lesser extent, Perth) under James II, and which almost without exception took place in Edinburgh from the accession of James III. It is very rare for charters over the Great Seal to be issued outside Edinburgh after 1469, while Exchequer audits seem to have been settled there from the latter part of the reign of James II.

13. The reading 'win bak to' is conjectural, since there is a gap in the only manuscript at this point; see *Poems*, ed. Kinsley, 368.

14. See my article, 'Politics and Poetry in Fifteenth and Sixteenth Century Scotland,' *Scottish Literary Journal [SL]* 3(2) (December 1976), 5-29, at 5-11.

15. M. W. Stearns, *Robert Henryson* (New York 1949), 15-25; John MacQueen, *Robert Henryson: A Study of the Major Narrative Poems* (Oxford 1967), 170-3; I. W. A. Jamieson, 'The Poetry of Robert Henryson' (unpubl, Ph.D. diss., Edinburgh, 1964); Ranald Nicholson, *Scotland: The Later Middle Ages* (Edinburgh 1974), 500-9; Robert L. Kindrick, 'Lion or Cat? Henryson's Characterization of James III', *Studies in Scottish Literature [SSL]* 14 (1979), 123-31, and *Robert Henryson* (Boston 1979), *passim*.

16. *The Poems of Robert Henryson*, ed. Denton Fox (Oxford 1981), 19; all quotations from Henryson's poems are based on this edition.

17. Kindrick, 'Lion or Cat?', 125.

18. *Ibid.*, 128.

19. It is important to observe that these lines are almost certainly part of the Scheip's lament and thus fall within the fiction of the fable: see *Poems*, ed. Fox, 262, and Jamieson, 'The Poetry of Robert Henryson', 104.

20. On lawyers, see Mann, *op. cit.*, 86-91 and Owst, *op. cit.*, 339-49; on landowners and the nobility, Owst, *op. cit.*, 319-31.

21. See, for example, *The Bannatyne Manuscript*, ed W. Tod Ritchie (STS, 4 vols, Edinburgh 1927-33), iii, 22-6, 37; and Sir David Lindsay, *Ane Satyre of the Thrie Estaitis*, 11, 1280-1387, *Works*, ed. D. Hamer (STS, 4 vols, Edinburgh 1929-34), ii, 39-49.

22. *Poems*, ed. Kinsley, 98-9; cf. J. H. Eddy, 'Sir Thopas and Sir Thomas Norny', *Review of English Studies [RES]* n.s. 22 (1971), 401-9.

23. Since Tungland was a Premonstratensian house, there is no justification at all for the description of Damian as a 'freir': perhaps Dunbar chose the term (which is supported by both the surviving manuscripts) for its alliterative force, and there was a well-established satiric genre of the 'fenyeit freir' (cf. A. G. Rigg, 'William Dunbar, 'The Fenyeit Freir'', *RES* n.s. 14 (1963), 269-73).

24. On the career of Damian, see John Read, 'Alchemy under James IV of Scotland', *Ambix* 2 (1938-46), 60-7. There is an account of his abortive flight in Leslie's *Historie of Scotland*, ed. E. G. Cody OSB and W. Murison (STS, 2 vols, Edinburgh 1888-95), ii, 124-6.

25. To be strictly precise, we know only that Damian was provided on several occasions with 'aqua vite to the quinta essencia', and we do not know in what form the distillation of alcohol was available. But he was given two gallons on 18 October 1507, and was in need of another six quarts a month later (*T.A.* iv, 77, 80); other contri-

butions included 'a punschioun of wyne' (*ibid.*, iv, 79) and a barrel of vinegar (*ibid.*, iv, 108).

26. *Poems*, ed. Fox., 151-2.

27. Cf. the story recorded by Pitscottie concerning James IV's attempt to ascertain the original language of mankind (*Historie*, ed. A. J. G. Mackay [STS, 3 vols, Edinburgh 1899-1911], i, 237).

28. See my article, 'The Sources of *The Thre Prestis of Peblis* and their Significance', *RES* n.s. 31 (1980), 257-70, at 269.

29. No firm date has been established for Holland's poem. Matthew P. McDiarmid, 'Richard Holland's *Buke of the Howlat*', *Medium Aevum* 38 (1969), 277-90, argues for 1446, whereas Nicholson (*op. cit.*, 367) accepts the traditional date 1453-54. Marion Stewart, 'Holland's "Howlat" and the Fall of the Livingstones', *Innes Review* 26 (1975), 67-79, agrees with MacDiarmid's reasons for rejecting such a late date, but presents cogent arguments for 1450 on the basis of topical references she finds in the poem.

30. For McDiarmid, the *Howlat* comments upon the 'dangerous ascendancy' of the Earl of Douglas and his kin, while Stewart reads the poem as praise of the Douglases and criticism of the Livingstones. Another poem which comments on contemporary political issues, but which does not deal with factional differences and is in no sense satirical, is the anonymous 'Rycht as stryngis ar rewlyt in a harpe': the various texts of this work are conveniently compared in *The Maitland Folio Manuscript*, ed. W. A. Craigie (STS, 2 vols, Edinburgh 1919-27).

31. Cf. the comment by H. E. Rollins in an English context that 'throughout the history of the black-letter ballad no subject has called forth so many rhymes as the struggle between Protestants and Catholics', *Old English Ballads, 1553-1625* (Cambridge 1920), ix; the emergence of broadside ballads in England is well surveyed in this introduction, and in Rollins' 'The Black-letter Broadside Ballad', *PLMA* 34 (1919), 258-339. See also Leslie Shepard, *The Broadside Ballad: A Study in Origins and Meaning* (London 1962), 48-56.

32. Lindsay, *Works*, ed. Hamer, i, 143; all quotations are based on this edition.

33. Cf. J. S. Kantrowitz, *Dramatic Allegory: Lindsay's 'Ane Satyre of the Thrie Estaitis'* (Lincoln, Nebraska 1975), 61-77.

34. The Lutheran sources of the Psalm translations and other pieces in the collection were noted by A. F. Mitchell in his edition of *The Gude and Godlie Ballatis* (STS, Edinburgh 1897), xli-lvii; cf. Brian Murdoch, 'The Hymns of Martin Luther in the *Gude and Godlie Ballatis*', *SSL* 12 (1974-5), 92-109.

35. David Calderwood, *The History of the Kirk of Scotland*, ed. T. Thomson (Wodrow Society, 8 vols, Edinburgh, 1842), i, 141; cf. the sources cited by Mitchell, *ed. cit.*, xciii.

36. *Ibid.*, 206.

37. *Ibid.*, 180.

38. *Satirical Poems of the Time of the Reformation*, ed. J. Cranstoun (STS, 2 vols, Edinburgh 1891-3), i, 39-45, 193-200, 31-8, 95-9.

39. Cf. Kernan, *op. cit.*, 43-5; the earlier background is discussed by Helen C. White, *Social Criticism in Popular Religious Literature of the Sixteenth Century* (New York 1944), chap. I.

40. *Satirical Poems*, i, 67.

41. 'A Rhime in defence of the Queen of Scots against the Earl of Murray', *ibid.*, i, 68-81.

42. 'Maddeis Proclamatioun', *ibid.*, i, 149-55.

43. *Ibid.*, i, 73.

44. 'The Bird in the Cage', *ibid.*, i, 160-4.

45. Sempill's attack can be dated May 1570 (*ibid.*, ii, 106); *Chamaeleon* seems to have been written later the same year.

46. *The Vernacular Writings of George Buchanan*, ed. P. Hume Brown (STS, Edinburgh 1892), 52.

47. See Richard Bannatyne, *Memorials of transactions in Scotland 1569-1573*, ed. R. Pitcairn (Bannatyne Club, Edinburgh 1836), 110.

48. Mann, *op. cit*; Peter, *op. cit.*, 80-99.

49. The best texts of Maitland's poems are in *The Maitland Folio Manuscript, ed. cit.*, and in *The Maitland Quarto Manuscript*, ed. W. A. Craigie (STS, Edinburgh 1920). Arbuthnot's complaints are in *The Maitland Folio Manuscript, ed. cit.*, i, 49-61; other poems of his can be found in the *Maitland Quarto*.

50. *Ibid.*, i, 306.

51. *Satirical Poems*, i, 103.

4

'Princes' and the regions in the Scottish Reformation

Jenny Wormald

'IF you do think that the Reformation of religion, and defence of the afflicted, doth not appertain to you, because you are no Kings, but Nobils and Estates of a Realme . . . you are deceaved . . . you therefore be Judges and Princes, as no man can deny you to be, then by the playn wordes of David you are charged to be learned, to serve and fear God, which you can not do, if you despise the reformation of his religion . . . Your dutie is to hear the voyce of the Eternal your God.'[1] Thus did Knox demand of the Scottish nobility an acceptance of their role in God's tremendous plan for the renewal of his church on earth, in his *Appellation to the nobility and estates of Scotland*, written in Geneva in 1558. The immense power of the language of this appeal, and of its follow-up, the *Letter addressed to the Commonalty of Scotland*, surely owes something to Knox's frustration at being kept out of the Reformation movement by the very nobles whom he addressed; shortly before five leading Protestants had taken the courageous step of subscribing the First Band of the Lords of the Congregation in December 1557, Knox's return to Scotland had been stopped, almost certainly because the situation there was as yet too delicate to be shattered by the clarion call of uncompromising certainty.[2] The natural leader — for so Knox saw himself — was left to watch impotently from abroad, while events at home hung fire. What else could he do but transmit the 'voyce of the Eternal your God' to a nobility whose ears seemed so much more open to the voices of the world?

Knox was not, of course, alone in seeing that aristocratic commitment was vital. Throughout Europe those who sought Reformation or Counter-Reformation knew very well how crucial was the support of the secular leaders of society; Calvin and Beza never doubted the value of the conversion of even a single noble. How much was Protestant reform advanced when, in the 1550s and 1560s, 'all across Europe, from Scotland to Poland, nobles and gentry were openly rallying to the Protestant cause'?[3] Conversely, how much was it halted when the Catholics learned from the Protestants and cultivated the nobility of Europe? It was a policy which undoubtedly contributed to the shrinking of the 'Protestant share of Europe' from one-half in 1590 to one-fifth in 1650, a policy which had notable success in Poland where the aristocracy were wooed by such assurances as the fact that Polish was spoken in paradise, and the promise that even in hell, should any of them ever actually get there, they would be treated as a superior caste.[4]

Knox's appeal, therefore, was the appeal of the European Calvinist to the European nobility. But Knox was also a Scot — enough of a Scot to be beguiled by pride of kin to write with amazing moderation, even approval, of the notorious James Hepburn, earl of Bothwell, third husband of Mary queen of Scots, because Knox's family had been dependants of the house of Hepburn; 'this', he said, 'is part of the obligation of our Scottish kindness'.[5] His Scottishness was a double-edged weapon. Even more than the English Christopher Goodman, whose treatise *How Superior Powers Ought to be Obeyed* more explicitly acknowledged that if kings and nobles failed to advance God's work, then it was licit to look beyond them to the common people, Knox could invoke support from, and threaten, his Scottish princes with particular point because of their peculiar, perhaps, unique, role.[6] They were not 'princes' such as the German princes were. But neither were they simply an aristocracy under a king. They were the great men of what was, by contemporary standards, a remarkably decentralised state. Scottish government was by no means so politically weak as is often suggested, but it was certainly institutionally underdeveloped, and it made comparatively few of the kind of demands, for money or for war, which brought centre and locality into close contact. Individual lords, the main link between centre and locality, had therefore a more critically important position in their locality than, for example, their English counterparts.[7] This was the case even when there was an adult king on the throne. It was even more the case in the Reformation period itself, for after the death of James V in 1542, there was to be no effective ruler again for some forty years, when James VI came of age; the inconsistent posturings of Mary only added a mercifully brief period of unnecessary melodrama to an already tense and traumatic time of political, diplomatic and religious upheaval.

So not just Knox's rhetoric, but long social tradition and immediate political circumstances made the Scottish nobility, be it Calvinist or Catholic, 'princes' in a very real sense. Reformation Scotland thus offers in microcosm the chance to analyse the gradual establishment of the reformed church in a series of regions whose links with one another and with the centre could be very loose indeed, so loose that it was arguably the new Kirk, with its effective organisation overriding local boundaries, which did more to unify the non-highland area of Scotland than any government had ever done. Such analysis is, however, not yet possible, for local reformation studies have scarcely begun in Scotland.[8] Moreover, one important source — the large collection of bonds of manrent, maintenance and friendship, through which the magnates and lairds formalised their local alliances — in this context produces the astonishing fact that it is possible to read through the several hundreds of these bonds which survive from this period, and only occasionally be made aware that there was a Reformation at all.[9] This is not, therefore, a detailed study of the Reformation in the regions. It is, rather, an attempt to raise general questions about the extent to which aristocratic power might influence the course of the Reformation.

These questions are asked against the background of the persistent survival of that long-lived monster of Scottish historiography, the cardboard figure of a uniquely appalling aristocracy. If aristocratic motives in the Reformation period were very mixed, who was quite so cynical, even irreligious, as the aristocracy of Scotland which used Knox only when the time was ripe to achieve its political revolution in 1559-60?[10] If, in general, the nobilities of Europe were difficult, overmighty people, who was more difficult and overmighty than the lawless crew of Scotland?[11] It is a belief which goes back a long way. An anonymous English description of Scotland, written in the early 1580s, began by explaining the evils which beset the Scottish kingdom in terms of the excessive number of excessively powerful nobles. Criticism of the number was a fair point for an English observer, for there were as many Scottish as English peers (between 50 and 60) in a population no more than one-fifth of that of England; alarm at their power shows only the contempt and lack of understanding of the comparatively centralised for the comparatively decentralised state.[12] The English government was certainly concerned about the activities of the Scottish aristocracy, when it commissioned a series of reports on those who were 'well-affected' — that is, pro-English and Protestant — and those who were not.[13] In Scotland, the Kirk added its endorsement of the theoretic position of the magnates; no ordinary sinner, as we shall see, ever enjoyed the gentle perseverance meted out to the great Catholic nobles. Knox himself significantly contributed to the concept of supreme magnate power. Historians have tended to look at the problem from Knox's point of view, not surprisingly, for he said a great deal more about it than individual nobles said about theirs; aristocratic lack of single-mindedness does very easily look like a failure of commitment, particularly if the apparent power of the aristocracy was a reality. But it might be profitable to ask a different question: was it possible for any noble to emulate the single-mindedness of a Knox or a Calvin? Could any noble have done so? Indeed, given his social and political status and responsibility, *should* any noble have done so?

It is, of course, not necessary to look for absolute commitment to assume that, in this heavily localised society, controlled by magnates with the degree of power traditionally ascribed to them, the principle 'cuius regio, eius religio' — even if it was never said at Augsburg — would find particular expression. It is possible to identify areas like Kyle in Ayrshire, or Angus and the Mearns, where Protestantism was strong, or Aberdeenshire, where Catholicism survived, and link this to the presence of a powerful reforming earl like Glencairn, or laird like Erskine of Dun, or the great Catholic lords of the north, the earls of Huntly and Erroll. But even these areas turn out to be less than clear-cut examples. Ayrshire also contained two Catholic earls, Eglinton and Cassillis; it was the scene of the only organised attempt to hold public Catholic services, when John Hamilton, archbishop of St. Andrews, celebrated mass at Kirkoswald and Maybole at Easter 1563, under the protection of Kennedy lairds and their armed followers.[14] In Angus and the Mearns, the gentle Erskine of Dun, one of the heroes of Knox's *History of the Reformation*, found himself, as superintendent of Angus, an early victim of the censure of the General Assembly in December 1562; his only answer to a string of charges about failure to achieve more for the Kirk, the lack of standards in admitting readers and ministers, the presence of popish priests, the disgraceful fact that some ministers turned up late for Sunday preaching, was to enter a complaint in turn about Cumming, schoolmaster of Arbroath, who infected the youth with idolatry.[15] The problems facing the Kirk in Angus and the Mearns were further increased, in the 1580s, by the defection of David earl of Crawford, already 'in religion unsettled' by 1583 and a Catholic by 1589; his literary younger son, Walter Lindsay of Balgavies, wrote an account of the state of Catholicism in 1594, which explained the reason for his immunity as a Catholic in terms which give a remarkable twist to Knox's 'Scottish kindness', for he described kinship as 'invented by Satan to shed innocent blood', but acknowledged that, insofar as it protected powerful Catholics like himself, 'God has deigned to convert the poison into a remedy.'[16] On the other hand, although northern recusants were reasonably secure because of the presence of a number of Catholic magnates and lairds, it was still possible for the burgh of Aberdeen to recover the reforming zeal which had been evident as early as the 1520s, and successfully rid itself of the domination of the Catholic family of Menzies, the dependants of the earls of Huntly whose protection the burgh had long enjoyed.[17]

These are regions where there is at least a case for linking 'Princes' with the progress of the Reformation, or lack of it. Elsewhere it is even more difficult to establish such a link. In regional terms, the power and influence of the nobility were both more complex and more limited than might at first sight appear. One important and immediate limitation was that the magnates lacked a weapon of great effectiveness, the weapon of patronage. The Kirk endlessly exhorted the aristocracy to plant kirks and pay stipends. Indeed, it took a severely practical view of the matter when it received the great sinners, the leading Catholic nobles, to its bosom, making it a strict condition that absolution depended as much on the undertaking to do these things as on penitence and spiritual renewal; in the 1594 Assembly, for example, Alexander lord Hume had to accept and sign conditions which included the repair of ruinous kirks within the priory of Coldingham and all his bounds, the provision of livings for pastors, and the payment of stipends to ministers of three named churches, and only then would the Kirk absolve him.[18] It is clear enough why the Kirk put such a premium on this. Dr. Clair Cross, in her study of Henry earl of Huntingdon, has shown how far an earl of particular religious persuasions and sufficient standing could influence the region under his control by installing like-minded preachers. Huntingdon, powerful member of a puritan group, used his eight advowsons in Leicestershire and ten in Devon and Somerset to create 'moderate puritan uniformity', and went on to use his position as President of the North to make significant inroads, between 1572 and 1595, into the strong Catholicism that existed in the area when he took office; in all, he placed some forty-four pastors.[19] That is a notable example, and one which the Kirk itself would not perhaps have regarded as a model to be followed, for its preference was for more controlled help from the laity, but it indicates why the support of the leaders of secular society in maintaining right-minded ministers was so strongly sought. In any event, it had little chance to seek the co-operation of would-be Scottish Huntingdons; for the crown, by insisting on its right to the patronage of the religious institutions, to which 86% of the parish churches were appropriated, kept the lion's share of patronage in its own hands in the early years after the Reformation. In 1562, the queen provided to the first appropriated church which fell vacant, a church appropriated to Holyrood; the claims of the commendator, Robert Stewart, were set aside, and that created the pattern for the future. After the Act of Conformity of 1573, more patronage came to the crown, and although it lost some of it in the 1580s, with the beginnings of the erection of temporal lordships from the abbatial lands and the Act of Annexation of 1587, the impact of lay patronage was never great. This also militated against the Catholics. In the first few years of the Reformation, there are a few isolated examples of a Catholic magnate using his patronage to retain a Catholic priest, as the earl of Eglinton did at the church of Eaglesham in Renfrewshire.[20] But the acts of 1567 and 1573 enjoined on Catholic patrons the obligation to appoint Protestants, and within the limited context of lay patronage, that is what they did, usually appointing Protestant kinsmen, and thus satisfying at least a social if not a religious commitment.[21]

What the nobility could have done was to give the Kirk greater financial support, thus enabling the Kirk to establish an adequate number of ministers — a desperate problem in the early years — as well as implementing its vision of proper care for the poor and education for all. The principle that a minister's stipend should be the first charge on the teinds was eventually admitted in Lindsay of Balcarres' 'constant platt' of 1596, but not sufficiently put into practice, partly because of the sheer difficulty of disentangling the teinds from other sources of revenue, and partly because of the equal difficulty of persuading people, especially in an inflationary age, to reduce their incomes. In theory, the Catholic magnates had an obvious source of obstruction; in 1597, provision of a minister to Cruden in Aberdeenshire was blocked by the earl of Erroll's refusal to pay the stipend of the presbytery's nominee.[22] In practice, that was less of a problem than the general reluctance of Protestants as well as Catholics to pay up in all regions. This is an emotive subject, the real death-knell of the aristocracy's spiritual reputation in the eyes of the Kirk and its historians. It is therefore worth emphasising that it was not the case that nothing was done. The problem was that efforts tended to be piecemeal; even so, after the first decade of the new church's existence, ministers did have at least adequate stipends, and in some cases considerably more;[23] there were no cases of the really appalling hardship endured by the pre-Reformation parish clergy such as the wretched vicar of Alva in Banffshire with his pittance of 15 merks per annum.

Patronage and generosity to the Kirk, while of major importance to the religious leaders of Reformation Scotland, only scratched the surface of the problem facing its secular leaders. The furtherance of God's new Word, or the defence of his old, was not necessarily something which sustained, far less enhanced, what was of crucial importance to them: their power in their localities. In regional terms, that power derived not so much from land as from personal strength: that is, strength of personality, backed up by the extent and cohesion of their followings. Contemporary accounts give pride of place to that following in assessing individual aristocratic power.[24] And when power is personal rather than territorial, then of course the introduction of religious conflict can drive a coach and horses through hitherto unchallenged strength. In his brilliant article 'English Politics and the "Concept of Honour"', M. E. James, citing the Percy and Hastings families as examples, shows that having a foot in both religious camps might help to preserve rather than weaken a powerful family.[25] The general force of his argument is clear enough, but it is perhaps more relevant to the kaleidoscopic shifts in religion of mid-century England. In Scotland, at least the doctrinal course of reform, from a Catholic to a Calvinist church, was much more straightforward, for there was no monarch with the strength or inclination to wrench it from its path; the choice between what was an acceptable religious position and what was not did not fluctuate after the initial step had been taken in 1559-60. A new and dangerous ideological consideration was now added to those more practical local matters which might threaten the solidarity of magnate affinities. The theoretically vast power of the Hamiltons, reinforced by a chain of estates stretching from Ayrshire in the west up to Arbroath in the north-east was to avail them little when their dependants and tenants could look upwards only to the confusion created by the leaders of the kin: the duke of Châtelherault, whose misfortunes included a discredited regency, a congenital inability to make up his mind, and an heir who was a declared lunatic; and the other most prominent Hamilton, Châtelherault's bastard half-brother and an undoubted Catholic where Châtelherault was a doubtful Protestant, John archbishop of St. Andrews.

Because this family was so close to the throne, its collapse was spectacular. Less sensational, but equally important in the context of local power, was the effect of religious commitment on other magnate families. It is at least possible to speculate about the extent to which a change of religion from father to son, or the uncertainties which surrounded religious divisions within the regions, could undermine the prestige and influence of the great families; as traditional ties and habits of dependence, carefully built up over generations, were shaken by religious dissent, so one effect of the Reformation could be the contraction of power from the family to the individual. The Campbells suffered a major setback, despite the immense strength of the earls of Argyll, when three strongly Protestant earls were succeeded by a man who, for all his forceful personality — hitherto a crucial consideration — created a power vacuum when he removed himself first to London and then, as a zealous Catholic convert, to the Continent, where he entered the service of the king of Spain. Religious division at last provided Aberdeen with the lever to rid itself of the dominant Catholic family of Menzies, dependants of the Catholic earls of Huntly. And although the 'normal' political and social tensions in the north-east may certainly be adduced to explain the great feud between the earls of Huntly and Moray in the late 1580s and early 1590s, it is impossible to ignore the consequences of the desire of George, 6th earl of Huntly, and his grand-father, killed as a rebel at Corrichie thirty years earlier, to act as a spearhead of Counter-Reformation in Scotland. For there is little in the pre-Reformation history of this dominant family to suggest the possibility of such a widespread coalition of two earls and a considerable number of lairds as gathered round Moray to challenge Huntly, had not Catholicism and its accompanying evils, rebellion and treason, been added to envy of supreme power. In the long run, the fates of two massively important families, Campbells and Gordons, were settled by the individuals who succeeded the Catholic earls. Huntly's successor again took the wrong religious side in the mid-seventeenth century, with his refusal to join the Covenanters; the Gordons never wholly recovered from the damage done in the late sixteenth and seventeenth centuries. Argyll was succeeded by the colossal personality of Archibald 1st Marquis, who re-established control of his locality and went on to dominate Covenanting Scotland.

The real problem, which lay behind the immediate limitations of magnate influence on the Reformation itself, and the effects of religious divisions, was that the aristocracy had never enjoyed the vast and untrammelled power attributed to it; the overmighty Scottish magnate is an oversubscribed myth. They did not start from a position of total control. In telling them what they must do, to the glory of God, Knox asked for more than they could give; in threatening to drive a wedge between them and their followers if they did not do it, he was saying something which they could not ignore, because it was much more realistic, and very dangerous. When the English diplomat Killigrew made his much-quoted judgement in 1572 that 'I see the nobleman's great credit decay . . . and the barons, burghs and such-like take more upon them',[26] he was by no means wrong in the immediate context, and unintention-ally right in describing a situation which had existed at least since the fifteenth century, and no doubt earlier. The balance of power between the wealthier lairds and the earls in the localities was a very delicate matter. One reason for the making of secular alliances in large numbers from the mid-fifteenth century was that the rise of a number of families — Gordons, Hays, Hamiltons, Campbells and others, the major protagonists of the sixteenth century — brought to the top men who were not marked out, in terms of wealth and prestige, from other lairds, and who therefore had to construct, by means of

F

formal written agreements, followings for themselves, recognition of their new pre-eminence. The Gordons and Campbells did this with outstanding success, but even they could be vulnerable in the uncertain world of the Reformation. Other families, like the Hays and the Leslies, never created positions of such local dominance. The relationship between the Hays, earls of Erroll, and the powerful local family of Cheyne of Essilmont, for example, was reasonably good; but that did not mean Cheyne subservience, as Patrick Cheyne reminded Andrew master of Erroll in 1567, when he refused to ride with him to Edinburgh despite the invocation of the bonds of manrent made by the Cheynes to the earls of Erroll, and the affair ended with a written acknowledgement by the earl himself that Patrick owed service to him only, and not to his heirs.[27]

This is only to make the very general point which could apply to any pre-industrial society: the service of men was not given for lordship. It was given for good lordship; and it had to be earned. The followers of the great lords were themselves men of substance, heads of lesser kindreds and smaller followings; they were not servants. Moreover, in exactly the period when the 'new men' who were ennobled in the mid-fifteenth century, along with a subsequent group in the early sixteenth, were building up their personal positions in their localities, the change in the pattern of landholding — the feuing movement — was working to the advantage of the lairds, and indeed of many who had not formerly been proprietors of land at all.[28] The full effects of this were not realised until the seventeenth century;[29] but already by the time of the Reformation a further strain had been put on the theoretically static and ordained hierarchical society, making the balance of power between greater and lesser even more delicate. This means, for example, that although we do not know how that extraordinary body packed with lairds, the Reformation parliament of 1560, voted — for the accounts of Knox and Randolph agree only that few spoke out against its acts, but differ on who the few were — it cannot simply be assumed that those dependants of the earls of Huntly and Erroll who turned up spoke with their masters' voice. They may have remained silent; equally, they may have concurred with the Protestant majority.[30] More specifically, the important point about the bond made by the nobles and gentry of Kyle, Carrick and Cunningham for maintenance of the true religion in 1562 was not, as the author of the *History of the Reformation* suggested, that one John Knox turned up in the area, but that between them the two copies of this bond were signed in Ayr on 4 September by some 170 people. The first signature on one of the copies was the Catholic earl of Eglinton's, which would indicate that under pressure this earl was wavering, as even Huntly had wavered in the early months of 1560; the 170 signatures show why Glencairn could maintain, as his father with his own Protestant circle had done, a sturdy Protestantism.[31] Equally, it was the presence of a number of powerful Catholic families in the north — Cheynes, Hays, Menzies, various Gordons and others — which made it possible for the earls of Huntly and Erroll to hold out for so long; it was not the presence of two Catholic earls which forced a lingering Catholicism on their dependants.

If men did not simply follow the religious dictates of their lords, neither was doctrinal commitment the decisive factor in local relationships. It is both understandable and ironic that the very local, individual alliances between magnates and lairds which give so little hint of the Reformation should have been the model for the great religious covenants, beginning with the First Band of the Lords of the Congregation in December 1557, and reaching their greatest heights with the Covenants of the mid-seventeenth century.[32] For these bonds are a powerful reminder that religious divisions were not the whole story; the reason why there exist hundreds of agreements which conceal the great religious upheaval of the age is that secular pressures on Catholic and Protestant princes went on regardless, and were all the more compelling precisely because of the restrictions on princely power. Good lordship still had to be earned. The magnates still had their traditional social role, had to content their followers and dependants and act for their kinsmen, sorting out their criminal and civil disputes, whether they were dealing with men of the same faith or not. The Catholic earl of Eglinton was not deterred by religious issues from making a bond of friendship with the Protestant lord Boyd in 1563, as the last act in the settlement of feud between Montgomeries and Boyds. Private justice in Scotland involved not only private courts, but also the right and duty of the great lords to arbitrate and impose settlements on their followers; compensation to the victim, not retribution to the state, was a fundamental principle of Scottish justice, and it was in this area that good lordship, to Catholic and Protestant alike, found very practical expression.[33]

That expression was made more difficult by the Kirk, with its very different ideas which took no account of earthly expectations of traditional lordship. In its eyes, the magnates were the greatest opponents to its view of crime; for injury to the human which secular leaders sought to avenge was nothing compared to the sin against the Lord for which atonement was due. It was an ideological conflict which exercised the minds of the General Assembly; in 1596 it turned the full force of its rhetoric against 'Ane universall coldness and decay of zeale in all estates . . . Ane flood of bloodscheds and deadly feuds aryseing therupone, and universall assisting of bloodscheds for eluding of lawes . . . Universall neglect of justice both in civill and criminall causes; — as, namely, in granting of remissions and respites for blood, — adulteries and incests — no execution of good lawes made against vyces, or in favour of the Kirk and in civill matters . . .'[34] The Kirk failed to persuade the secular powers, and continued to fail until the mid-seventeenth century. For it was also a practical conflict, between reformers wholly inspired by the spiritual needs of the state, and the lords and heads of kingroups, dealing, in a long-established and effective way, with the secular problem of order in the localities. New pressures from the Kirk were not yet enough to offset much older pressures from powerful dependants; but they posed a massive ideological threat to the exercise of good lordship by the men whose survival as the dominant force in the state, both local and national, depended on it.

The way in which good lordship was understood in the highly personalised local societies which made up the kingdom of Scotland is central to the problem of aristocratic motivation in the crisis years 1559-60. One of the conceptual inconsistencies about the general thesis of overmighty magnates, long accustomed to defy the crown with impunity, is that they should have seen any particular advantage in a political revolution; why bother, when their power was already so great? But was there a political revolution at all? Was there not, rather, a religious revolution, led by reformers who were all too willing to encourage the secular powers to make that revolution possible by defying established authority? If the question is put that way round, then the lack of commitment about which the reformers complained can be seen not as worldly and self-seeking cynicism, but as something which had an ideology of its own. By and large, one must suppose, the magnates were not men who shared the theological knowledge and certainties of Knox and his fellow-preachers. Their perceptions were very different. Knox saw what had to be done, to the glory of God. They saw the dangers, if they followed Knox's road. Writing of the fourteenth century, Sir Richard Southern points out that 'the ecclesiastical hierarchy could not be seriously attacked without a threat to the whole social order . . . King and aristocracy became the chief supporters of conservatism in the church'.[35] Like so many of Southern's comments, that tells us something which is relevant to more than the period immediately discussed. There was no king in Scotland after 1542; but there were magnates who were asked to break free from their conservatism, to threaten the whole social order. How real that threat was can be seen in the gradual and inexorable undermining of the social order in the century following the Reformation, a process in which the Kirk, though not the sole agent, was certainly a major one. Of course the magnates of the mid-sixteenth century did not foresee the events of the mid-seventeenth; but it is impossible to believe that they were wholly unaware that the reformers wished to cast them in a role which would indeed mean revolution — a revolution against the order to which they belonged, as their fathers and ancestors had belonged.

In Scotland, the nature of political power itself was such that an act of rebellion was intensely difficult to engineer. The *laisser-faire*, supervisory role of the crown, and, in addition, the lengthy periods when there was no adult ruler at all, meant that in general the monarchy was remarkably unoppressive. Its demands were very much less than the demands of its allies, the monarchies of England and France; it still stood for personal lordship rather than threatening rule. It is perhaps easier to revolt against established authority when that authority by its own actions forces other considerations into second place, than to do so in a country which had no tradition of strong involvement by the government which might create a milieu in which present policies would outweigh the longer-term awareness that the noble who rebels against his lord the king may encourage his own dependants to do likewise. This is not a clear-cut issue; by 1559, Mary of Guise could be regarded as a ruler whose actions made challenge necessary — though that challenge was very far from revolution against authority as such — and it was not only the Scottish nobility who were alive to the ideological dangers of rebellion. But the unusual degree of local autonomy in sixteenth-century Scotland, and the particular nature of the lordship which was both expected and given, heightened the awareness of the dangers.

Knox himself is an excellent source for the uncertainties and fears which beset the minds of men fearful not only of risking their future in the next world by the religious choice they made, but of risking stability and order in this. Lord Ruthven, Protestant provost of Perth, 'a man godly and stout', lost his courage in May 1559 at the very moment when insurrection had begun, and fled to the regent, 'a great discouragement to the hearts of many', even if the discouragement lasted for only a few days before Ruthven returned to the Protestants.[36] There were many Ruthvens, torn between hatred of the French and fear of what rebellion would bring. The burgh of Aberdeen offered its support to the Lords of the Congregation only if they did not 'interpryss ony purpos against the autorite', at the very time when that great Catholic lord of the north-east, Huntly, was apparently considering whether the solution to the disturbances shaking society might be to join the Protestants.[37] On March 19, 1560 lords Erskine and Hume, showing the same indecision, wrote to lord James Stewart, as his 'friends and kinsmen', asking him to meet them, to help them to resolve their fears that the appearance of English troops would only add to present troubles, and begging even now for negotiations with Mary of Guise; they can hardly have been comforted by the answer, which praised their compassion for present miseries, but held out no hope of agreement with Mary.[38] Erskine had wavered for almost a year before moving into the reforming camp at the end of April. Knox had no sympathy for such doubts; in what is the classic prescription for the politically minded noble who would not support the church, Erskine was written off as 'the chief great man that had professed Christ Jesus and refused to subscribe the Book of Discipline'.[39] It is a comment which tells us a great deal more about Knox than about the men whose support he desperately needed, but would not seek in the temperate tones of understanding rather than the strident ones of absolute certainty.

It is surely both a moving and a profoundly thought-provoking comment on the attitude of those who joined their secular power to the spiritual voice of the reformers that at the deathbed of Knox's monster of craft and dissimulation, the queen regent, were the leading Protestant nobles, Argyll and lord James Stewart. Knox's gloating over the illness and death of that attractive personality is unpleasant to read, especially to a modern taste which looks for charity as an attribute of Christian leadership, but Knox was right to fear the regent, whose ability was so much greater than that of the queen her daughter. But the presence of Argyll and Stewart at her deathbed is as important to the understanding of the Scottish Reformation as Knox's perception that here lay the real enemy of the Protestant cause. Equally important is the appeal of the Lords of the Congregation to the nobility and commonalty of Scotland: 'if religion be not persuaded unto you, yet cast ye not away the care ye ought to have over your commonwealth, which ye see manifestly and violently ruined before your eyes. If this will not move you, remember your dear wives, children and posterity, your ancient heritages and houses; and think well these strangers will regard no more your right thereunto . . . whenever occasion will serve'.[40] The appeal to God, country and family was not the preserve of sixteenth-century Scotsmen, nor was it the language of Knox. It is the voice of the layman, whose responsibility for the lives rather than the souls of men must always sound more tarnished and yet should not be dismissed. The emphasis on defence, not attack, and on the things defended, provides a far better insight into the reasons both for support of the Reformation and the limitations on that support than explanations which seek to divorce political aristocrats from religious reformers.

The purpose of this essay has been to suggest two things: first, that the exercise of magnate power was a complex matter, very far from absolute, and genuinely contractual; and second, that the actions of those who found themselves on the national, and international, stage in 1559-60 may be better understood if their position in their localities, the base from which they came, is made the basis of understanding. It does not turn them into the soldiers of Christ for whom Knox looked, but does suggest that the historical tradition which can be traced back to Knox has overestimated their freedom of action, by leaving out of the reckoning the simple fact that the Reformation movement may have disturbed, but did not cast into a void, the normal social pressures and responsibilities of the great men of the localities. That in turn helps to explain two of the puzzles about Reformation Scotland: the extensive but ineffective survival of Catholicism and the lack of religious persecution.

The strength of Catholicism after 1560 is astonishing, not only in the north, but in Ayrshire, Galloway, Lothian, Perthshire, and in the highest circles of court and government; it did not help the Octavians in 1596-7 — already in difficulties because James VI had little appreciation for their efficient management of his finances — that a number of them were suspected of popery. Estimates of the number of Catholics vary considerably, but as late as 1602 one report put it as high as one-third of the nobility.[41] It is entirely understandable that assembly after assembly thundered out its fears of Jesuits and papists, particularly when these fears were reinforced by rumours which brought Alva to Scotland in 1570 and Spanish troops in the late 1580s and early 1590s.[42] The possibility of Counter-Reformation undoubtedly existed for half a century after the Reformation. It was never realised, as powerful Catholics failed to give any lead to those who, either from habit, conviction or confusion of mind and soul, clung to the old practices, often in very touching circumstances.[43] The reason for this is surely grounded in the localised nature of Scottish society. The long tradition of lack of involvement with the centre produced the extraordinary situation that its leaders thought in local and European terms; but there was a gaping hole between the local and the international.[44] It can hardly be overstated how exceptional it was for men to unite in anything approaching a common cause in Scotland, for reasons which ranged from ingrained habit to the weather;[45] from the late fourteenth to the mid-seventeenth century, the only completely clear examples are the battle of Flodden and the Protestant Reformation itself. So Ayrshire Catholics were protected by Kennedies and Montgomeries; Aberdeenshire Catholics by Gordons and Hays; in the borders, by the Maxwells. But these were local groups who remained in their localities. There was a brief moment in 1561 when more might have happened; for Huntly offered to lead a Catholic revival from the north, but was given no support, not only by the Catholic Mary, but also by the Catholic earl of Atholl, who, according to Knox, was a dissident voice in the Reformation parliament, and whose geographic position gave him the chance to unite with Huntly and crush the intervening Protestants of Angus. The opportunity was lost. Thirty years later, the brave letters of Huntly and his associates, assuring Philip II and the duke of Parma of the strength of Catholicism in Scotland, brought howls of anguish and fury from the Kirk; they did not upset the hard-headed realist who sat on the throne, who knew how empty these promises were. Catholicism remained regional, apart from the occasional contacts with Spain and France by a few individuals, satisfying their European self-image, but achieving nothing. So it remained weak.

On the other hand, the highly personalised nature of local society, the strength of non-religious considerations, made the lack of persecution more understandable. In 1610, for example, the Protestant bishop of Moray wrote a very moving little letter to king James, pleading that the Catholic laird of Gight should be left in peace, because he was ill and a trouble to no-one: so 'I wad humbly craiff your Hieness that he might keep his health in sum uder church', for the papists 'I perceive are not universally of ane corrupt disposition'.[46] It was unfortunate for the bishop that the laird recovered his health and within a few years was a considerable trouble to the Kirk, the privy council and the north-east, with his following of thugs, the 'band of Boys'. But the general point stands. James himself took a highly personal line on the subject of persecution, when he dismissed the bishop of the Isles' appeal for action against the Jesuits in Argyll, on the grounds that if anyone could civilise the highlanders, they were welcome to do so, even if they were papists;[47] he too had considerations other than the confessional.

Survival of social contacts between religious opponents did encourage an otherwise very tough Kirk to show astonishing tolerance towards the recalcitrant — if they were of high rank. In the 1570s, for example, the General Assembly was much exercised with the problem of the Catholic earl of Atholl. But its real victim was the Protestant bishop of Dunkeld, the front-line man told to go and excommunicate the local magnate, and denounced for failure by four successive Assemblies. The earl got very different treatment. When he refused the offer of learned and godly men to sit up throughout the night with him in an effort to resolve his doubts, on the grounds that he preferred a night's sleep and a longer period for contemplation, the Kirk rushed to comply; and when, at the end of the agreed period, he had still not conformed, it offered him an extension. But it suspended the unfortunate bishop.[48]

The Kirk never gave up, even with so hopeless a case as the earl of Huntly, three times reconciled to the church, once absolved by the archbishop of Canterbury, and buried a good Catholic. Huntly's second reconciliation in 1597 admirably illustrates what it was after. Two days of fast and sermons were followed by a day-long party in the burgh of Aberdeen. It was a party enjoyed not only by the repentant sinner and his ally, that other sinner the earl of Erroll, and by the town council, but also by the local ministers who flocked into the burgh for the occasion; and the day ended with food, wine and innumerable broken glasses (and presumably bodies as well) littering the pavements.[49] What lay behind this remarkable orgy was the desire of the Kirk to demonstrate with as much publicity as possible its victory over a great Catholic earl within his own area of influence; it exactly paralleled the publicity and ceremony which accompanied the resolution of a secular feud, for the very fact of publicity offered a safeguard for the future. If the Kirk would join with God in rejoicing over the return of any sinner, it would certainly do so with the maximum of noise when the sinner was quite such a catch; and it followed this up with relentless pressure on the earl to worship publicly, despite his insistence that it was unbecoming for the magnate, with his private chapel as his ancestors had had, to consort with the vulgar in the parish church.[50] Another form of pressure on Huntly and other Catholic lords was maintained by the simple expedient of sending godly men to live in their households; and although the Catholics could sometimes hit back, by equally simple expedients such as having to depart for Edinburgh on the king's business just as the godly man arrived on the doorstep, nevertheless polite but firm persistence put them in the weak position of being on the defensive, stalling for time instead of throwing off the bugbear.[51] In purely practical terms, the Kirk was well aware that the reconciliation of an earl of Huntly was unlikely to bring them the financial help they demanded, although it might lessen the chances of north-eastern ministers being beaten up by Gordon hangers-on. It was still, because of his personal prestige and position as the focal point of his locality, a notable triumph. Even more than specific actions, it was the public example of the great man of his region being reconciled to the Kirk which was, in the Kirk's eyes, the crucial factor.

Once the Reformation was an established fact, it was not only the Catholic magnates who were threatened by that astonishingly dynamic body, the Kirk. To the problems which the reformers' demands had imposed on the Protestant nobles at the time of the Reformation were added two new ones. They were offered the role of godly magistrate by a Kirk which interpreted that role very strictly in terms of assistance, and especially in practice financial assistance, rather than any kind of control; and they were told to submit themselves to ecclesiastical discipline, a discipline meted out by their social inferiors.[52] Their response to this massive challenge to their pre-eminent power, which had never been threatened before, was increasingly to stand aloof, leaving lay participation in the new church to the lairds. It was, in the long run, an attitude which did much to undermine their position in the regions; but they were in fact in an impossible dilemma, for participation on the Kirk's terms equally undermined that position.[53] For this reason, it would be much more appropriate to use the word 'revolution', not of the politics of 1559-60, but of the society so profoundly affected by the remarkable success of the Kirk. Yet it would be unsatisfactory to leave on quite such a negative note the part played by the most important people in Scotland in a movement whose small beginnings in the 1520s gave rise to a church of such immense self-confidence by the end of the century. To the magnates who gave it their support, the Kirk offered something which the Catholic nobility significantly lacked: a new and inspiring image of themselves. Precisely because their power was not absolute, the assertion that in their hands — they, the princes and judges — lay the reformation of religion and defence of the afflicted could have great appeal. Precisely because they, like their predecessors, knew that the interests of the world did not naturally turn to Scotland and that only by going out to meet the world would they be recognised, they could respond to the vision of a church which saw itself as one of the leading parts of the church universal through which God's word would be revealed. The nobility themselves were comparatively inarticulate about their role, although some of their contracts were beginning to show that to their traditional role of the king's greatest counsellors and the leaders of local society they added the concept of themselves as the principal servants of God.[54] But if they said little, there were others to say it for them. Descriptions of Catholic magnates, survivors of a weakened and increasingly discredited church, contrast sharply with the account given by James Melville, summoned to give spiritual comfort to the exiled Ruthven Raiders, the temporarily ousted group of Protestant lords associated with the presbyterian reformers in the early 1580s.[55] Melville's programme for them filled up their weeks with sermons, prayers, readings, conferences and meditations, with one week's fast each month. There was little time here for the traditional pursuits of the nobility, although concentration on the Old Testament had its own appeal for a military aristocracy, as did Melville's exhortation that they should return to their native country and fight off their political opponents 'as becomes valiant warriors and capteanes of the Lord's armie', as ideological a demand for armed rebellion as it is possible to imagine. One may doubt whether they were as grateful for his programme as Melville claimed, or whether they stuck it out in every detail when he left them after three months. But if he exaggerated their response, he did not invent it. For in concentrated form this was the theory advanced by Assembly after Assembly translated into practice: the magnate as the man of godly life, the inspiration and example to those over whom he had control. In social terms, the balance between Catholic and Protestant princes in the regions was almost equal; in religious and ideological terms, the advantages lay with the Protestants. But even that is a comment on what the Kirk did for the princes, not what the princes did for the Kirk.[56]

NOTES

1. *The Works of John Knox*, ed. D. Laing (Edinburgh, 1864), iv, 494-5. This essay examines in greater detail themes outlined in my book *Court, Kirk and Community: Scotland, 1470-1625* (London, 1981), chapters 7 and 8. On Knox's political thought, I have found very helpful R. A. Mason, 'Knox, Resistance and the Moral Imperative', *History of Political Thought* i (1980), 411-36.

2. Knox, *Works*, iv, 469-520 (Appellation); 521-38 (Letter). *John Knox's History of the Reformation in Scotland*, ed. W. C. Dickinson (Edinburgh, 1949), i, 136-7 (First Band).

3. J. H. Elliott, *Europe Divided, 1559-1598* (London, 1968), 95; for discussion of the importance of the nobility, 95-9, and the problems of the reformers' demands, 107-11. For understanding of the fact that the Scottish nobles and reformers were part of a European phenomenon, and not just involved in a purely Scottish situation, this book and H. G. Koenigsberger, *Estates and Revolutions* (Ithaca, 1971), especially chapter 9, are indispensable. Two important detailed studies are R. R. Harding, *Anatomy of a Power Elite: The Provincial Governors of Early Modern France* (New Haven, 1978), 37-67, and J. B. Wood, *The Nobility of the Election of Bayeux, 1463-1666* (Princeton, 1980), chapter 7. A very interesting case study of a prince is Owen Chadwick's 'The Making of a Reforming Prince: Frederick III, Elector Palatine', in *Reformation, Conformity and Dissent: Essays in honour of Geoffrey Nuttall*, ed. R. Buick Knox (London, 1977), 44-69.

4. G. Parker, *Europe in Crisis, 1598-1648* (London, 1979), 51-4.

5. *Knox's History*, ed. Dickinson, ii, 38; 'kindness' denotes 'kinship'.

6. C. Goodman, *How Superior Powers Ought to be Obeyed*, ed. C. H. McIlwain (New York, 1931). Knox was more negative; but his reiterated insistence that the common people could not escape the consequences of their own failure to act by hiding behind their princes' failure made the point clearly enough: Knox, *Works*, iv, 526-37.

7. This comment is less self-evident now than it would have been in the past; the localism of English society and the importance of local leaders have been given much emphasis in the exciting new work on the English localities by T. G. Barnes, Alan Everitt, J. S. Morrill and others; see also the very interesting discussion of power within the Tudor state in P. Williams, *The Tudor Regime* (Oxford, 1979), part III. This has narrowed the gulf which apparently existed between centrally-governed England and relatively ungoverned Scotland; but political circumstances still left the Scottish aristocracy more powerful, and the localities more 'local'.

8. The first step in this direction was taken by I. B. Cowan, *Regional Aspects of the Scottish Reformation* (Historical Association Pamphlet, 1978), and followed up by the same author: I. B. Cowan, *The Scottish Reformation: Church and Society in 16th Century Scotland* (London, 1982); the first Scottish burgh has received proper attention in M. Lynch, *Edinburgh and the Reformation* (Edinburgh, 1981); both whet the appetite for more work of this kind. The value of such studies is admirably demonstrated by C. Haigh, *Reformation and Resistance in Tudor Lancashire* (Cambridge, 1975), whose analysis of a remote and self-contained community has much to offer the historian of the self-contained Scottish localities; and for the subject discussed in this article, M. E. James's work on the magnates of the north of England is essential reading: especially *A Tudor Magnate and the Tudor State: Henry 5th Earl of Northumberland* (Borthwick Paper 30, York, 1966), 'The first earl of Cumberland and the decline of northern feudalism', *Northern History* i (1966), and also 'Obedience and

Dissent in Henrician England: The Lincolnshire Rebellion, 1536', *Past and Present*, 48 (August 1970).

9. Jennifer M. Brown, 'Bonds of Manrent in Scotland before 1603' (Glasgow Ph.D., 1974).

10. See, for example, Cowan, *Regional Aspects*, 5.

11. This idea is now challenged by recent work on fifteenth- and sixteenth-century Scotland, but it has held the field for a considerable time, and naturally influenced other scholars dependent on older histories of Scotland; overmighty magnates stalk the pages of D. H. Willson, *King James VI and I* (London, 1956), and turn up in, for example, J. R. Lander, *Crown and Nobility, 1450-1509* (London, 1976) and C. D. Ross, *Edward IV* (London, 1974). For the challenge, see the articles by J. Brown (now Wormald), 'Taming the Magnates?', in *The Scottish Nation*, ed. G. Menzies (London, 1972), 'Scottish Politics, 1567-1625', in *The Reign of James VI and I*, ed. A. G. R. Smith (London, 1973) and 'The Exercise of Power', in *Scottish Society in the Fifteenth Century*, ed. Jennifer M. Brown (London, 1977); and by A. Grant, 'Earls and Earldoms in late medieval Scotland, c.1310-1460', in *Essays Presented to Michael Roberts*, ed. J. Bossy and P. Jupp (Belfast, 1976) and 'The development of the Scottish Peerage', *Scottish Historical Review* lvii (1978); and the new magisterial study by Norman Macdougall, *James III* (Edinburgh, 1982).

12. British Library Additional MS. 35,844, ff. 195v-198r.

13. *Estimates of the Scottish Nobility during the Minority of James VI*, ed. C. Rogers (Grampian Club, 1873), 29-80.

14. Margaret H. B. Sanderson, 'Catholic Recusancy in Scotland in the Sixteenth Century', *Innes Review* xxi (1970), 97, 105; I owe a lot to this important article.

15. *The Booke of the Universall Kirk, Acts and Proceedings of the General Assemblies of the Kirk of Scotland*, ed. T. Thomson (Bannatyne and Maitland Clubs, 1839-45), i, 25-6.

16. *Narratives of Scottish Catholics under Mary Stuart and James VI*, ed. W. Forbes-Leith (Edinburgh, 1885), 351-60.

17. Brown, 'Bonds of Manrent', 327-33; B. McLennan, 'The Reformation in the Burgh of Aberdeen', *Northern Scotland* 2 (1976-7), 131ff.

18. *BUK* iii, 835-6, 839-42.

19. Claire Cross, 'Noble Patronage in the Elizabethan Church', *Historical Journal* iii (1960), 1-16.

20. Sanderson, 'Catholic Recusancy', 98.

21. I am indebted to my colleague Dr. James Kirk for this point, and for his patience in explaining this thorny subject.

22. Sanderson, 'Catholic Recusancy', 98-9.

23. W. Rowland Foster, 'A Constant Platt Achieved: Provision for the Ministry, 1600-38', in *Reformation and Revolution*, ed. D. Shaw (Edinburgh, 1967), 124-40.

24. *Estimate of the Scottish Nobility*, 7-28: 'The Scottish Nobility in An. Dom. 1577' by Alexander Park of Hay, 29-41; 'A Brief Opinion of the State, Faction, Religion and Power of the Severall Noblemen in Scotland . . . AD 1583'.

25. M. E. James, 'English Politics and the Concept of Honour', *Past and Present Supplement* 3 (1978), 17 and n.75.

26. *CSP Scot* iv, 432; G. Donaldson, *Scotland: James V-VII* (Edinburgh, 1965), 167.

27. *Illustrations of the Topography and Antiquities of the Shires of Aberdeen and Banff* (Spalding Club, 1847-69), iii, 21-2; Erroll Charters, 'Bonds of Manrent', 36.

28. Margaret H. B. Sanderson, *Scottish Rural Society in the Sixteenth Century*

(Edinburgh, 1982), especially 77ff.

29. W. Makey, *The Church of the Covenant, 1637-1651* (Edinburgh, 1979), chapter 1.

30. *Acts of the Parliaments of Scotland*, ed. T. Thomson and C. Innes (Edinburgh, 1830), ii, 525-6 (list of people present); *Knox's History*, ed. Dickinson, i, 338-9; *CSP Scot*, i, 466-7.

31. *Knox's History*, ed. Dickinson, ii, 55-6; W. Fraser, *Memorials of the Montgomeries, Earls of Eglinton* (Edinburgh, 1859), ii, 192-3; Eglinton's name appears on this version.

32. S. A. Burrell, 'The Covenant Idea as a Revolutionary Symbol: Scotland, 1596-1637', *Church History* xxvii (1958), 338-50.

33. Jenny Wormald, 'Bloodfeud, Kindred and Government in Early Modern Scotland', *Past and Present* 87 (May, 1980), 54-97.

34. *BUK* iii, 874-5. Adultery, like feud, is a good example of the frustration suffered by the Kirk because of the state's refusal to treat it purely as a major sin. It had begun well enough, making it a capital crime in 1563 in the parliament which passed a number of acts on behalf of the church; this was a distinct improvement on the 1551 parliament, which had similarly legislated to bolster up the pre-Reformation church's moral credibility, but which had made the penalty for adultery only putting to the horn: *APS* ii, 486 (1551) and 539 (1563). The 1563 act was followed up in 1567 and 1581: *ibid.*, iii, 38 and 213. Subsequently, however, state enactments, though acknowledging the religious offence, showed far more interest in dealing with problems of property which adultery might create: *ibid.*, iii, 543-4 (1592) and iv, 233 (1600). Not until the legislation of the 1640s and 1650 did the Kirk's attitude once again dominate. See the very interesting article by Keith Thomas, 'The Puritans and Adultery: the Act of 1650 reconsidered', in *Puritans and Revolutionaries: Essays in Seventeenth Century History presented to Christopher Hill*, ed. D. Pennington and Keith Thomas (Oxford, 1978), 257-82.

35. R. W. Southern, *Western Society and the Church in the Middle Ages* (London, 1971), 50 and 52.

36. *Knox's History*, ed. Dickinson, i, 172, 180.

37. *Extracts from the Council Register of the Burgh of Aberdeen* (Spalding Club, 1844-8), i, 322 (11 March, 1560); for Huntly, *CSP Scot* i, 323, 329, 332-4; by 17 April, however, it was reported that he was 'cold': *ibid.*, i, 364. Donaldson, *James V-VII*, 101-2. The leading Protestants Argyll and lord James Stewart put the problem very precisely when they wrote to Sir James Croft on August 1559, regretting that they were 'judged slow negligent and cold in our proceedings' and pointing out 'how difficult it is to persuade a multitude to revolt of established authority': *CSP Scot* i, 240.

38. *Ibid.*, i, 339.

39. *Knox's History*, ed. Dickinson, i, 201, 231-2, 261-2, 264, 275, 320-1, 344.

40. *Ibid.*, i, 225.

41. *Estimate of the Scottish Nobility*, 77-80.

42. *CSP Scot* ii, 323, 334; David Calderwood, *The True History of the Church of Scotland* (Wodrow Society, 1842-9), iv, 692-6; v, 192ff; *The Historie and Life of King James the Saxt* (Bannatyne Club, 1825), 257-9.

43. Letters by Jesuits in Scotland reporting on the state of the Catholics to their General in the early years after 1560 already give a strong impression of fear and demoralisation, attributing this very largely to the earl of Moray's power and the queen's weakness: *Narratives of Scottish Catholics*, ed. Forbes-Leith, 63-81.

44. I have much benefited from discussion with my research student Mr. Keith

Brown, who has made a detailed analysis of Lord Maxwell's career in the course of his work on Jacobean feuding which amply illustrates this point.

45. In January 1569, Huntly wrote an encouraging letter to Queen Mary which plunged to the depressing note in its final sentence that 'the wedder hes bene sa ewill heir this tuentie dayis past that it wes nocht possible till ane to trawell': *Registrum Honoris de Morton* (Bannatyne Club, 1853), i, 39-40.

46. *Miscellany of the Spalding Club* (Spalding Club, 1841-52), ii, 155-6.

47. Cathaldus Giblin, *Irish Franciscan Mission to Scotland, 1619-1646* (Dublin, 1964), 45-7; I am indebted to Dr. I. B. Cowan for this reference.

48. *BUK* i, 270, 287, 300, 309, 314-7, 331-2, 341. Atholl does seem to have conformed in the end, although the Kirk maintained a very watchful eye on him, even sending men to check up on his funeral rites in 1579; their report produced the decision from the Kirk that it 'thoght the crosse (on the mortcloth) and the stroupes super-stitious and ethnick lyke, and desyrit thame to remove the same', which was duly done: *ibid*, ii, 431. As was often the case, the wife was a more intractable problem than the husband, and the Kirk continued to agonise about Lady Atholl after the death of the earl, to no avail.

49. This is described in a marvellous letter from an Aberdeen lawyer, Thomas Mollison, to an Edinburgh friend, 28 June 1597: *Spalding Miscellany*, ii, lx-lxii.

50. *BUK*, iii, 980-1.

51. *Ibid.*, iii, 966-7, 980-6.

52. J. Kirk, *The Second Book of Discipline* (Edinburgh, 1980), 57-65, 117-20; 'The Development of the Melvillian Movement in Late Sixteenth Century Scotland' (Edinburgh Ph.D., 1972), Appendix IV. See the discussion of the godly magistracy, both royal and noble, in G. Donaldson, *The Scottish Reformation* (Cambridge, 1960), chapter 6.

53. The importance of the lairds is discussed by I. B. Cowan, 'Church and Society in Post-Reformation Scotland', *Records of the Scottish Church History Society* xvii (1971), 185-201. By the beginning of the early seventeenth century, there are signs of a myth growing up about the decline of aristocratic commitment since the Reformation period itself; in 1606, Andrew Melville, summoned before the Scottish councillors in London, turned on them, 'telling thame flatly, that they knew not quhat they did, and wer degenerat from the antiant nobilitie of Scotland, quho wer wont to give thair landis and lyffes for the fridom of the kingdome and Gospel, and they wer bewraying and ovirturneing the same!': *The Autobiography and Diary of Mr. James Melville* (Wodrow Society, 1842), 666. How astonished Knox would have been by this description of his tarnished princes and judges! In general, we need more individual studies of magnates and lairds such as exist in England: for example, S. L. Adams, 'The godly magistrate in action: the religious policy of Robert Dudley, earl of Leicester', a paper given to the Colloquium for Local Reformation Studies, Oxford, 1982; P. Collinson, 'Magistracy and Ministry: A Suffolk Miniature', in *Reformation, Conformity and Dissent*, ed. Knox, 70-91; R. Cust and P. G. Lake, 'Sir Richard Grosvenor and the rhetoric of magistracy', *Bulletin of the Institute of Historical Research* liv (1980), 40-53.

54. For example, at the height of the crisis in 1560, on 31 May, a bond was made by the duke of Châtelherault and the earl of Morton, in which Morton promised to support the duke 'nocht onlie in this commone caus to sett forwart the gloir of God and putting of this oure native cuntre to libertie fra bondage of strangearis, bot als in all utheris thair actionis, caussis . . .'; God, the French, and the fact that the Hamiltons

had renounced all possible claim to Morton's earldom and lordship of Dalkeith, were all considerations which lay behind this agreement: Hamilton Muniments, box 102. Other examples in which political groups stated their intention to maintain the true religion are given in Calderwood, *History*, iii, 644-6; iv, 26-7; v, 233-5 and 773-5. This last shows very clearly the point made earlier in this essay, that affinities included men of different faiths; it was made in March 1592 by the king, the duke of Lennox, a number of earls and lords and 154 others, to resist the authors of treasonable conspiracies, especially Huntly and his associates, and Jesuits, seminary priests and papists; the 154 included many families dependent on the house of Huntly. An example of the more usual agreement, made between two people, which included the promise of support in advancing God's true religion, is the bond between the earls of Morton and Argyll, made probably in 1578: Argyll MSS, vol 5/140.

55. Melville, *Diary*, 171-213.

56. I am grateful for the help I have had from the scholars of the Scottish Reformation, Dr. I. B. Cowan and Dr. J. Kirk, and from a scholar of a much earlier aristocratic society, Mr. C. P. Wormald.

5

From privy kirk to burgh church: an alternative view of the process of Protestantisation

Michael Lynch

ON 15 November 1572 John Knox lay on his deathbed. He had not long returned to Edinburgh to resume his ministry after spending fourteen months in exile in St. Andrews as the forces of the king's and queen's parties had fought for control of the capital in the final stages of the civil war. Although the king's men had recaptured the burgh, Edinburgh remained in a state of siege as the Marians held the Castle and still had hopes of aid from Alva in the Netherlands. On this day Knox was delighted by a surprise visit from an old and trusted friend, Archibald Stewart, a prominent Edinburgh merchant and member of the king's party town council which had just re-secured power after spending more than a year in exile at Leith. Stewart had since then been promoted a bailie; he would rise still further to become provost in 1578. It was an intimate re-union, important enough for Knox to rouse himself from his bed and order the breaking open of a fresh cask of wine. What Knox did not know was that this pillar of the burgh's Protestant establishment was lending money to the other side.[1]

It has been said that a civil war often helps to draw back the veil which usually covers society to reveal its innermost secrets.[2] This is undoubtedly true of the civil war which was waged intermittently between the deposition of Queen Mary in 1567 and the fall of Edinburgh Castle in May 1573, although this period has perversely been one of the most seriously neglected in sixteenth-century Scottish history. For Archibald Stewart was certainly not alone. Professor Donaldson has already found seventy-four Edinburgh burgesses who supported the queen in the early part of the war and rightly called this evidence startling. Yet if the whole of the war is taken into account, more than six times this number found themselves in the ranks of the queen's men.[3] Amongst them were the town clerk, the clerk of the kirk session, the master of the grammar school, the burgh's two procurators fiscal in the 1560s, its two surviving burgess provosts, its wealthiest craftsman and maltman.

Almost exactly half of the Edinburgh establishment — the top one hundred merchants — chose to support Mary. And the strength of Marianism was still more marked amongst the smaller merchants and craftsmen. The fact that more than half of Knox's own congregation in St. Giles chose not to follow him into exile in 1571 is an awkward statistic for those who try to describe the first ten years of the new reformed church in terms of the onward and rapid march of committed Protestantism.

Marianism was not, of course, synonymous with Catholicism. A wide variety of possible stances existed between the two poles of radical Protestantism and determined Catholic recusancy, and many who roved somewhere in between in the course of the 1560s found common cause in Marianism at the end of the decade. Their motives were often mixed, complex or even shifting. Yet it is important to realise that many of the factors which played upon them also influenced the growth and shape of the reformed church after 1560. The Reformation had come swiftly and, in many of the burghs, almost by accident in 1559-60. The Reformation settlement took much longer. Its progress varied considerably from burgh to burgh, but in each of them it is likely that the force of kin, the restraints imposed by the law and the very habits of burgh life and government were as important determinants as religious conviction. Compromise and conciliation were required as well as Protestantisation.

The Reformation carried the promise of a spiritual revolution; it was not clear whether it would bring about a social revolution as well. Yet there were portents. Knox had forecast in his tract, *A Letter addressed to the Commonalty of Scotland*, written in 1558, that there would be no distinction made between rich and poor in the new godly society to come.[4] This must have seemed a real possibility to the Protestant enthusiasts who made up the 'privy kirks' which formed in a number of burghs in the second half of the 1550s. Their composition is known only in Edinburgh, which was a more status-conscious society than most, but even there the elected elders and deacons ranged from the predictable professional men or wealthy merchants to ordinary master craftsmen or booth-owners and even, remarkably, to journeymen or apprentices. The *Letter to the Commonalty* has conventionally been seen as a manifesto for a future revolution; much of it should be seen rather as an attempt to justify what had already taken place in the privy kirks.[5]

The privy kirk, as it grew up in the 1550s, was an astonishingly broad church, albeit a small one. What remained to be seen was how it would fit into a minutely defined hierarchical society once it became established as the burgh church. There were already signs of internal divisions within the privy kirk of Edinburgh before the Reformation crisis. Some of its more respectable members had drawn back from the popular iconoclasm which had manifested itself in September 1558 in a riot during which the statue of the town's patron saint had been carried off.[6] The course of the crisis of 1559-60 must also have caused alarm. When the Lords of the Congregation deposed the sitting town council in October 1559, they had chosen some odd-looking replacements — among them a humble seed seller, the lowliest burgess to serve on Edinburgh's town council in the sixteenth century.[7] This must have been an embarrass-ment to the Protestant lords, one of whose justifications for deposing Mary of Guise as regent was to restore government into the hands of the well-born. After the Congregation retook the town in April 1560, its nominees went one step further in undermining the conventions of burgh government in an attempt to levy forced taxation on the town. It was customary that the stent-masters, appointed to assess individual taxation, be composed of well-respected men, drawn for the most part from the burgh establishment. The new regime turned, understandably, to Protestant loyalists, many of them from a fairly humble background.[8] In a number of ways the Reformation, although it had not set out deliberately to change the face of burgh society, threatened to do precisely that because Protestantism was still as yet a minority movement, forced to rely on what support it had.

Burgh society and government in Scotland was a complex mechanism, which varied in some of its details from burgh to burgh. It is one of the peculiarities of Scottish historiography that, although many historians have made passing references to the Reformation in the burghs, there has been little systematic study of the urban Reformation in Scotland, in marked contrast to the detailed work done, for example, on the Swiss and German imperial cities. The explosion of studies of the Reformation in the German cities did, however, build on a solid tradition of work in local history. It is difficult to say the same of Scotland, despite the work done by the Scottish Burgh Records Society in the nineteenth century. Not only has the Reformation in the Scottish burghs been neglected but so, more fundamentally, has the sixteenth-century Scottish burgh itself. This neglect has resulted, at times, in an imperfect understanding of how burgh government actually worked. It is usually thought, for example, that the burgh was governed by a town council which was virtually a closed oligarchy, able to re-elect itself from year to year.[9] It has been argued, as a con-sequence, that the closed doors of the council chamber were a significant aid to the rapid spread of Protestantism or, some would prefer, to the wholesale repression of Catholics.[10] Yet both of these arguments probably exaggerate the actual power available to burgh magistrates or councillors. A town council held authority only in so far as it represented the views of the burgh establish-ment and it protected the cherished privileges which held burgh life together. A burgh oligarchy usually rested not on flagrant nepotism or machine politics but on consent — perhaps not the consent of all the burgesses but certainly that of the wealthy and more privileged among them. It was only to be expected that elections would endorse those who enjoyed the respect and con-fidence of the burgh community. Where the common good of the burgh was tampered with or the election procedures abused, there was liable to be vociferous protest — as happened in Cupar in 1567 and with regularity in Aberdeen until the 'race of Menzies', a cadet branch of the Gordon family, earls of Huntly, was finally displaced in 1593.[11] Consensus was the key feature of burgh life since it drew together the three other guiding principles — custom, privilege and a sense of community. It was vital to the successful

G

establishment of burgh Protestantism.

The progress of the Reformation in the four largest Scottish towns was vitally affected by the search for consensus or the lack of it. In Perth the town council, which had suffered a purge by order of the regent in October 1559, was careful to use the traditional medium of a Head Court to test opinion in the burgh; more than two hundred burgesses turned up in the summer of 1560 to elect the burgh's commissioners to the Reformation parliament.[12] Consensus might also be produced by widespread confidence in a leading figure in the community; this seems to have been the case in Dundee, where James Haliburton, who had been provost of the burgh since 1553, enjoyed un-challenged support. This was probably the most important of the factors which combined to make Dundee's Reformation a more straightforward affair than most.[13] There was, by contrast, a good deal of friction within the burgh establishment in Aberdeen, and this seems to have produced a number of internal disagreements over how to react to the crisis in which the burgh found itself in the last months of 1559, when the Congregation reached the town. The ruling Menzies family had to resort to having a series of formal legal protests minuted in the council register, and its critics were particularly unhappy to trust the town's prized collection of religious valuables to its hands. These do, however, appear to have been isolated rumblings of discontent and did not mark either the crystallisation of an organised anti-Menzies faction or the emergence of an avowedly Protestant party in a burgh which remained over-whelmingly Catholic in its sympathies. It took fifteen, perhaps twenty, years for even the former to develop.[14] A Protestant town council was imposed upon Edinburgh by the Congregation not once but twice — in October 1559 and again in April 1560.[15] Nonetheless, Edinburgh's Reformation continued to be a stop-go affair even after the military victory of the Congregation in 1560 — because the new regime lacked consent.

The striking difference between the course of the Reformation settlement in Perth and Edinburgh is illustrated by the different way the Head Court was used in the capital. In Edinburgh, perhaps because of its greater size, the Head Court did not, by the middle of the sixteenth century, have the same symbolic significance, as it did in most Scottish burghs, of the burgh community meeting to settle matters relating to the common good. It was used primarily to allow each newly elected council to reissue municipal statutes and ordinances, most of them relating to food prices. Yet it was used in October 1561 to give greater force to two ordinances which the previous two town councils had issued, in June 1560 and March 1561, to banish stubborn Catholic clergy from the town.[16] Here was a determinedly Protestant town council, anxious to resecure the initiative after the return of Queen Mary two months before, manipulating the Head Court to bolster its position, which still, fully a year after the Reformation parliament, remained that of a minority party.

By November 1562, when the Edinburgh kirk session drew up a subscription list of 'the faithful brethren of Edinburgh', the Protestant regime in the capital had come halfway towards gaining a broad consensus of support for its programme: the list contained the names of exactly half of both the mercantile and legal establishments.[17] But a high price had been paid in the meantime. The first concession had come within a month of the regime's restoration to power in April 1560. The forced loan which it had tried to levy on the burgh met with stiff opposition and fell short of the target. The protests raised against its stentmasters forced the regime to change its tactics and appoint more widely respected figures to audit the tax and consider individual objections to the assessments which had been made. The first of the compromises forced upon Edinburgh's Protestant regime was not in obviously religious issues, such as the disposal of the town's religious relics or vestments, which proceeded apace in the autumn of 1560, but in a basic constitutional issue — the business of tax assessment and audit, which had to be seen to continue in a manner which enjoyed the confidence of the whole burgh community. It meant, in effect, that auditors and stentmasters must be drawn from Catholics or lukewarm Protestants as well as the godly.[18]

The same process of re-opening the corridors of power to those formerly accustomed to walk in them also took place, to a great extent, within the council chamber itself. Here there was no sudden change. It took place gradually over the course of the first half of the 1560s and it was marked by the fact that every annual election between 1561 and 1567 was a genuine contest, even within the restrictive practices which by statute governed procedure in burgh elections. Each of these elections resulted in a shift, in one direction or another, in a struggle for influence between the committed Protestants brought to power in 1560 and more moderate-minded men. By 1566 the slippage of power away from the original Protestant caucus of 1560 had gone far enough to tempt a number of them into violent conspiracy to help restore their position on the town council. Twenty-one Edinburgh burgesses were involved in the murky events which took place on the night of the Riccio murder.[19] Yet the position of Edinburgh's Protestant radicals was not secure, even after the revolution of 1567. Both the burgh establishment and the burgh community remained starkly divided in their loyalties — as the civil war at the end of the 1560s made clear. It was not until the end of that war that significant dissent was finally removed. By then, of course, John Knox was dead.

Dissent took a number of forms. From 1561 onwards men who were Protestants but fell short of being enthusiasts began to slip on to the council. One such man was John Marjoribanks, who by 1562 had reached the status of bailie. He was a leading figure in the council which decided in 1562 to dismiss the Catholic master of the grammar school, William Roberton, who had persistently refused to take communion under the new rite or even to attend the sermon. Roberton unexpectedly appeared in the council chamber with twenty-two character witnesses, among them a substantial representation from the burgh's professional men; also among them was Marjoribanks. Here was a Protestant magistrate publicly defending a Catholic recusant or, more precisely, his contract.[20] The Roberton case demonstrated the breadth and force of moderate Protestant opinion, which, if combined with vested interest, was strong enough to block the blanket implementation of a religious test on office-holders. One of Marjoribanks' colleagues on the council of 1562-3 was James Watson. He was a Protestant of a different stamp, a man who had been willing to take the risk of accepting office in the council appointed by the Congregation in 1559 and who would be suspected of involvement in the murder of Riccio. Yet Watson had a Catholic wife. She was one of the twenty-seven Edinburgh inhabitants brought before the Court of Justiciary in October 1563 for illegally attending a Catholic mass in the chapel royal at Holyrood, and her husband, a Protestant town councillor, had to appear to act as surety for her. In an agnatic society an outwardly resolute Protestant household might conceal a second household, resolutely Catholic, within it.[21] The split between Protestant pragmatist and Protestant radical did take on the form of a political struggle between two factions for control of the council. It also often took the form of a split in the Protestant mind — such as that of James Watson, where the pull of a wife's kin clashed with party policy, traditional habits might at times come into conflict with the new ideas, or the course of safety might appeal more than what Thomas Randolph, the English ambassador in Edinburgh, called 'running the violent course'.

A combination of factors combined to blunt the force and direction of Edinburgh's Reformation. The moral certainties of 1560 gave way to a series of practical considerations. When the council attempted at the end of 1560 to dismiss a craft deacon for committing adultery, it provoked a craft riot. Future sexual offenders who happened to be office-holders escaped with a fine.[22] Despite the fact that, as the council complained, some of the old clergy continued to hold a large section of the populace 'in blindness and error', it could not pursue too vigorous a campaign against them. When an ex-chaplain of St. Giles was caught saying mass in a private house in 1565, his manhandling after his trial triggered off a serious Catholic riot.[23] There was not a Protestant mob to turn to in the 1560s but there was a potential Catholic mob to provoke. It was unlikely, in any case, that a town council, many of whom had Catholic relations or clients, would agree to a policy of systematic victimisation of Catholics. Although there were some early attempts to banish unco-operative Catholic clergy, as the Catholic controversialist, Ninian Winzet, alleged, there is no record of any Catholic burgesses being banished from the town before 1569. Penal taxation of Catholics, which was another of Winzet's claims, also seems unlikely after Catholics were allowed back into the processes of tax assessment and audit in 1560. There is, on the contrary, a good deal of evidence to suggest that known Catholic recusants continued to trade and enjoy their other rights as burgesses.[24] It took some time before the process of Protestantisation was allowed to interfere with burgh privilege. Even after a determined hardline regime was restored to the council chamber as a result of the revolution of 1567, it found other barriers in its way. It brushed aside the combination of vested interest and natural conservatism which had protected the position of the Catholic master of the grammar school and dismissed him. Yet Roberton took his case to the Court of Session, the council's disingenuous pleas of his incompetence were swept aside and he secured his reinstatement.[25] Even when radicals had control of a burgh, the civil law might act as a check on their ambitions.

The most practical consideration of all was money. The finances of the reformed church in the burghs remain largely unexplored territory. Most burgh ministers were paid through the thirds of benefices, but the minister's stipend was only one of a number of new expenses and the rest had to be met out of the burgh's own resources. This burden became particularly onerous when a larger burgh took on a second charge, as Edinburgh did in 1562 and Dundee in 1569.[26] Burgh finances were gathered in by a bewildering number of indirect means — Edinburgh had almost thirty such sources[27] — and these varied in their details from burgh to burgh. The series of grants eventually made to the burghs in 1567 by Queen Mary of the lands and revenues of the old church lying within burghs varied significantly in their generosity. Edinburgh did rather poorly out of its grant; the collegiate church of Trinity College lay just outside the town walls and was excluded, but so was the Kirk o' Field although it lay just inside the walls.[28] The question of how the new burgh church was to be financed had to find different answers in different burghs. But in very few of the burghs does it seem that the reformed church was able to escape the problem which it faced elsewhere in Scotland — the serious lack of finance which stemmed from the failure to have accepted the full proposals made in the First Book of Discipline.

Edinburgh's answer to this problem was a drastic one. Knox in his *Letter to the Commonalty* of 1558 had forecast that in the new godly society to come rich and poor would have to contribute equally to it. Five years later the full consequences of this promise became clear in Knox's own burgh: the town council imposed a compulsory household tax of four shillings a year on all inhabitants. This broke a number of time-hallowed practices: direct taxation was occasionally resorted to for national purposes, but not for local; when national taxation was levied, it was generally confined to burgesses; merchants were assessed individually, according to their means, and craftsmen paid corporately through their craft guild; lawyers and the poor escaped altogether. The household tax of 1563 tried to establish not one new precedent but three — to make taxation for the new church direct, universal and flat-rate. The attempt was a disastrous failure; when the first instalment fell due in April 1564, the council met with such resistance that it was forced to convene all communicants to demand what each would 'freely grant' to the ministry. The forced tax of 1563 and the voluntary contribution which replaced it in 1564 were only two of a series of eight different schemes devised in Edinburgh in the course of the 1560s to help finance the responsibilities of its new burgh church. They all failed.[29] Historians of the Scottish Reformation need to come to terms with the fact that the full-scale establishment of Protestantism in the burghs required money, but money there, as elsewhere, was not readily forthcoming.

The reluctance to accept forced taxation applied, in Edinburgh, to poor relief as well as to paying its ministers. A number of the schemes devised in the

1560s had tried to yoke the two together. The burgh community preferred to deal with its poor by a combination of a traditional cheap food policy, by which the price of basic foodstuffs such as bread was kept artificially low, and a system, which had evolved after 1560, of voluntary collections at the doors of St. Giles each Sunday. The records of the kirk session solemnly record each week's contributions.[30] Ironically, the compulsory poor rate set up after the passing by parliament in 1574 of the 'Act anent the poor' seems to have raised less than the old voluntary system. The shortcomings of the new system led to serious friction between town council and kirk session in the area where, it might be expected, their co-operation should have been at its most fruitful. The council finally abandoned the scheme in 1576, grumbling that the burgh was not willing to be taxed, even to support its own poor.[31] It has been pointed out that the act of 1574 was modelled on the parliamentary legislation passed in England in 1572.[32] Yet there was a vital difference. The legislation of Elizabethan parliaments on poor relief built on successful measures which had already been taken in certain towns; London had established a compulsory poor rate in 1547 and Norwich had set up elaborate machinery designed to rationalise the treatment of its poor in 1571.[33] In England parliamentary legislation sought to extend a system which was already in existence. In Scotland the act of 1574, which allowed burghs and rural parishes to stent their inhabitants, was legislation designed to give added force to a system which had already been tried a number of times in Edinburgh and been rejected. The unwillingness of the burghs to meet the bill for the new godly society envisaged in the First Book of Disipline was probably the most lasting of the stumbling blocks in the way of its realisation.

It has recently been argued that Scotland saw a rapid progress towards a radical Reformation, far more so in the course of the 1560s than in England. In Scotland, saints' days were abolished, along with the use of the organ and the sign of the cross; ordinary bread was used at communion.[34] Most of this, and much else, was effected in most, although not all, of the burghs early in the 1560s. Yet, if the issues of money or patronage are examined, it is possible to see that the English towns were often moving more quickly than those in Scotland. Ipswich and Coventry had already evolved satisfactory means of paying their Protestant clergy in 1560, and this pattern was repeated in a number of market towns which acted as patrons of Protestant clergy, more radical in their inclinations than the general tenor of the Elizabethan settlement. The English borough corporations were significant early patrons of Puritan clergy as well as noble patrons like Leicester or Warwick.[35] Although the influence of the lairds was undoubtedly a vital factor in the conversion of many of the Scottish burghs to Protestantism, their influence was political rather than financial. The lairds, and even the Scottish nobility, were only very rarely Protestant patrons in terms of finance.[36] Town councils were left to their own devices, which were very limited; they lacked both tax-raising powers and a tradition of large-scale merchant charity, which was, by contrast, so marked in England.[37]

Perhaps the most strikingly radical feature of the privy kirks of the 1550s had been the role played in them by men who came from humble origins. Yet this was not fully continued after the Reformation had actually established Protestantism in 1560. Edinburgh's kirk session records are not available until 1574, but the lesser men who had been so prominent in the town council of 1559-60 and had guided the burgh through the Reformation crisis slipped back to their former obscurity once the crisis was over. The same pattern seems to have asserted itself once the privy kirk had to evolve into both a burgh church and a kirk session. The subscription list of 1562 demonstrated how much influence within the faithful had tipped towards the burgh establishment. It is true, to a certain extent, that the kirk session did give a new outlet to both craftsmen and smaller merchants, though not to apprentices or journeymen, who had held office in the privy kirk, or to more menial crafts, like candle-makers or bonnetmakers. The smaller men, in any case, usually had to content themselves with being deacons. The exact composition of town councils varied from burgh to burgh, and it was only to be expected that kirk sessions, which in many ways imitated the practices of town councils, should follow suit. It is a subject which requires further investigation. In Edinburgh, lawyers were not permitted to sit on the council, and if any group was given a new outlet in the kirk session for its influence, it was the burgh's legal profession. In the election of 1574 it was a lawyer who topped the poll, and lawyers filled five of the twelve elders' seats. The privy kirk, in taking on a 'public face', as Knox put it, had taken on respectability as well.[38]

There was thus a central paradox in the progress of the Reformation after 1560. It was indeed radical. Knox himself claimed in the Preface to Book IV of his *History:*

> As touching the doctrine taught by our ministers and . . . the administration of Sacraments used in our Churches, we are bold to affirm that there is no realm this day upon the face of the earth that hath them . . . in the like purity.[39]

He was writing about the period before the return of Queen Mary in August 1561. But this was a radical Reformation in a strictly limited sense — of liturgy and, to a lesser degree perhaps, of doctrine. How many converts did it have? At Easter 1561, eight months after the close of the Reformation parliament and four months before the return of Mary, only 1300 took communion by the new rite in Edinburgh.[40] They represented rather less than a fifth of the burgh's adult population. There was a radical new church but there was not a magical mass conversion to it in 1560 or immediately after.

In its wider social ramifications, also, beyond the questions of liturgy and doctrine, the Reformation should be seen as a radical movement trying to find acceptance in what was by instinct a conservative society. It proved compara-tively easy to be rid of Catholic relics or ritual; disposing of the contracts of Catholic office-holders or persuading the establishment into other radical courses proved more difficult. There were two potential brakes on the pace of the urban Reformation in Scotland. One was the very structure of burgh society and its customs. The other proved to be the men who held power — or seemed to — in each of the burghs. Power was not a divine right to be enjoyed, either by a burgh oligarchy or a local laird. The lairds around Peebles declared for the Congregation in the autumn of 1559 but the burgh refused to follow them.[41] The squabbles in Aberdeen in 1559-60 stemmed from a lack of confidence in the family which monopolised most of the burgh's offices. Both in promoting Protestantism and in defending Catholicism, lairds could only go so far. The force of the kin group, however extensive, was not enough in itself to guarantee holding sway over a burgh — as the case of the 'race of Menzies' in Aberdeen demonstrated. It had to be buttressed by force of personality and a reasonable amount of good government. Lord Seton, by the time he resorted to threats to visit Edinburgh with his 'kin friends' in June 1559, had lost most of his natural authority as provost — and with it the potential influence he had as a local Catholic magnate.[42] In much the same way, the authority of burgh magistrates was not enough in itself; it had to reflect a consensus of opinion within the burgh. Even where what appears to have been a Protestant oligarchy was in power, there were often divisions within it. Moderates, such as John Marjoribanks, or even ultra-Protestants, such as James Watson, with other things on their minds, were not the godly magistrates for whom the First Book of Discipline hoped. The history of the Reformation in the Scottish burghs could well be written in terms of exactly how much each burgh Reformation had to 'tarry for the magistrate' or for consensus to emerge from within the burgh community.[43]

The result was that there was no one Scottish Reformation but a series of local Reformations, each proceeding at its own pace and with its own distinctive set of features and problems. It seems easier to trace early popular support for Protestantism amongst Perth's craftsmen rather than in Dundee. Both Perth and Edinburgh had experienced a purge of their councils by Mary of Guise in 1559, but with seemingly different results, whereas Dundee had not. Aberdeen had its own distinctive brand of burgh politics but lacked a privy kirk; the coming of the Reformation in 1559 seems only to have added another, but still minor, issue to existing frictions. The coming of the Reformation to the burghs had proved to be a stop-go process. The Reformation settlement, which was set in motion after 1560, followed much the same pattern.

NOTES

1. M. Lynch, *Edinburgh and the Reformation* (Edinburgh, 1981), 147, 355-6.

2. A. Everitt, *The Community of Kent and the Great Rebellion* (Leicester, 1966), 13.

3. G. Donaldson, *Mary, Queen of Scots* (London, 1974), 135; Lynch, *Edinburgh*, 312-62.

4. D. Laing (ed.), *The Works of John Knox* (Edinburgh, 1844-64), iv, 528-30.

5. Lynch, *Edinburgh*, 38, 83, 276-80; see J. Ridley, *John Knox* (Oxford, 1968), 276-

8, and E. J. Cowan, *Montrose* (London, 1977), 24-5, for fairly representative views of the *Letter to the Commonalty*.

6. Lynch, *Edinburgh*, 85-6.

7. *Ibid.*, 80, 233.

8. *Ibid.*, 31, 79.

9. W. C. Dickinson and A. A. M. Duncan, *Scotland from Earliest Times to 1603* (2nd ed., Oxford, 1977), 285-6.

10. Cf. D. E. Meek and J. Kirk, 'John Carswell, superintendent of Argyll: a reassessment', *Recs. of Scottish Church History Soc.*, xix (1975), 2-3 and A. Ross, 'Reformation and repression', *Innes Review*, x (1959), 355.

11. *Reg. Privy Co.*, i, 582-4; iv, 533.

12. I owe this information to Ms Mary Verschuur, who is working on the Reformation in Perth. See also *CSP Foreign, Eliz.*, ii, no. 20.

13. See I. Flett, 'The Conflict of the Reformation and Democracy in the Geneva of Scotland, 1443-1610', unpublished St. Andrews M.Phil. (1981).

14. I owe much of this information to Fr. Allan White, o.p., who is working on the Reformation in Aberdeen. See B. McLennan, 'The Reformation in the burgh of Aberdeen', *Northern Scotland*, ii, 134, for details of these protests.

15. Lynch, *Edinburgh*, 77-9.

16. *Ibid.*, 97.

17. *Ibid.*, 265-6.

18. *Ibid.*, 31, 79.

19. *Ibid.*, 116, 183-4, 281-6.

20. *Ibid.*, 100-1.

21. *Ibid.*, 189, 284, 288; see J. Wormald, *Court, Kirk and Community: Scotland, 1470-1625* (London, 1981), 30.

22. Lynch, *Edinburgh*, 91, 96.

23. *Edin. Recs.*, 24 March 1560/61, iii, 101; Lynch, *Edinburgh*, 107-09.

24. See Ninian Winzet, *Certain Tractates* (Scottish Text Soc., 1888), i, 94-5; cf. Lynch, *Edinburgh*, 191-2, 196-7.

25. SRO, MS Acts and Decreets (CS 7/45), 16 Nov. 1569, ff. 36v-37v.

26. C. H. Haws, *Scottish Parish Clergy at the Reformation, 1540-1574* (Scottish Record Soc., 1972), 69, 214.

27. *Edinburgh, 1329-1929* (Edinburgh, 1929), 336.

28. See *RSS*, v, p. xiv, nos. 3334, 3342, 3368, 3374, 3417, 3419, 3425, 3452.

29. Knox, *Works*, iv, 528-9; Lynch, *Edinburgh*, 20-22, 33-4; *Edin. Recs.*, iii, 177-8.

30. Lynch, *Edinburgh*, 20. See SRO, MS Buik of the General Kirk of Edinburgh (CH 2/450/1).

31. *APS*, iii, 86-9; Lynch, *Edinburgh*, 20.

32. J. Wormald, *Court, Kirk and Community*, 167.

33. P. H. Ramsey, *Tudor Economic Problems* (London, 1966), 160-61.

34. See J. Kirk, '"The polities of the best reformed kirks": Scottish achievements and English aspirations in church government after the Reformation', *Scottish Historical Review*, lix (1980), 25-8.

35. P. Collinson, *The Elizabethan Puritan Movement* (London, 1967), 50-51, 141-2; C. Cross, *Church and People, 1450-1660* (London, 1976), 133-5; J. W. Sheils, 'Religion in provincial towns: innovation and tradition', in F. Heal and R. O'Day (eds.), *Church and Society in England: Henry VIII to James I* (London, 1977), 163.

36. I. B. Cowan, *Regional Aspects of the Scottish Reformation* (Hist. Assoc. pamp.,

1978), 6, 28-9; see *BUK*, i, 61, for an isolated example.

37. See W. K. Jordan, *Philanthropy in England, 1480-1660* (London, 1959), 253-63, 297-322.

38. Lynch, *Edinburgh*, 38-41, 269-71; Knox, *History*, ii, 277.

39. *Ibid.*, ii, 3.

40. *CSP Scot.*, i, no. 967.

41. Cowan, *Regional Aspects*, 27.

42. *Edin. Recs.*, iii, 38; see Wormald, *Court, Kirk and Community*, 34-5.

43. Cf. Kirk, 'Polities of the best reformed kirks', 43.

6

Covenant and Commonweal: the language of politics in Reformation Scotland

Roger Mason

I

THE Scottish Reformation — like many other aspects of Scottish history — is currently the subject of a good deal of revisionist discussion and interpretation. In recent years, a number of historians have made major contributions to our understanding of the nature of the complex and critical events of the two decades following 1550.[1] In the light of this research, facile assumptions regarding the irretrievable decay of the Catholic Church and the irresistible rise of Protestantism have at long last been consigned to oblivion. Instead, a more realistic picture has emerged in which the events of the 1550s and 1560s are set against and interpreted in terms of a variegated pattern of socio-political as well as religious pressures and aspirations. As other essays in this collection make clear, however, the revised picture is as yet far from complete, and there are many areas which still await detailed research. One such area — and by no means the least important of them — is the ideological context of the Reformation and in particular the role of political ideas in motivating and legitimating the conflicts of the period. Of course, if frequently misconstrued, the ideas of the prominent political theorists of these years — John Knox and George Buchanan — have nevertheless often received detailed commentary.[2] But little effort has been made to recover the beliefs and values of the political community at large and to consider the ways in which ideological assumptions and preconceptions may have affected the behaviour of those who participated — or chose not to participate — in the crucial events unfolding in their midst. Quite obviously, a short essay cannot do full justice to a topic which is not only potentially enormous in scope but which also confronts the daunting complexities of the relationship between political thought and action. Nevertheless, taking a limited empirical base and making some cautious methodological assumptions, the nature and importance of the ideological background to the Scottish Reformation may be tentatively explored. As this suggests, however, before going any further, it is necessary to describe briefly both the source material on which this essay is based and the type of approach adopted in analysing it.

A point easily lost sight of in discussions of the Scottish Reformation is that the rebellion which marked its crisis met with only limited public support. The rising of the Protestant Congregation in May 1559 was an enormous gamble, and that it eventually paid off was due, not to its overwhelming popularity, but to the timely intervention of the English government. That only a minority of Scots were actively engaged in the conflict, however, was not the fault of either the Congregation or their principal opponent, the Catholic Regent, Mary of Guise. On the contrary, throughout 1559 the two contending parties waged a propaganda war of unprecedented proportions in an effort to win adherents to their respective causes.[3] As a result there exists a substantial body of material — much of it preserved in Knox's own *History of the Reformation in Scotland* — through which it is possible to gain access to the ideological issues and divisions of the period. It is this material which forms the basis of the present study. Not surprisingly, given the nature of the crisis of 1559, much of it is concerned with the rights and wrongs of resisting established authority, and what follows is at one level simply an analysis of how the Congregation set about justifying armed rebellion. At the same time, however — and it is here that certain methodological assumptions are brought into play — an attempt is made to broaden the scope of discussion by inferring from the language in which the rebels chose to legitimate their actions something about how Scots in general perceived and reacted to what was happening around them. For the Congregation, like all politicians in search of support, were acutely sensitive to the expectations of their audience, and their propaganda came in consequence to be couched in the terms which they believed would win them the greatest sympathy and approval among their countrymen. An analysis of the language or languages in which the Congregation chose to address their compatriots, therefore, may yield valuable information regarding the political beliefs and expectations of the Scottish community at large. Furthermore, such an analysis may also reveal how ideological considerations had their effect both on the public behaviour of the Congregation and thereby on the course and resolution of the Reformation crisis itself.[4]

II

The most convenient point of departure for our inquiry is a letter written from Perth by 'The Faithfull Congregatioun of Christ Jesus in Scotland' on 22 May 1559 and addressed to the Regent, Mary of Guise. The letter is of importance not simply because it marks the Congregation's last formal defiance of the Regent before the outbreak of hostilities between them, but also because it gives a clear idea of the language in which they chose to legitimate their actions. As one might expect, that language was essentially religious in character. Stung by the Regent's telling jibe that they 'intended not religioun but the subversioun of authoritie',[5] the Congregation retorted that their 'revolt from our accustomed obedience' was prompted solely by reasons of faith and that they would at once revert to that obedience 'provided that our consciences may lyve in that peace and libertie which Christ Jesus hath purchassed till us by his bloode'. They sought only, they declared, to have God's Word 'trewlie preached' and His Holy Sacraments 'ryghtlie ministrat', in which regard they were firmly resolved 'never to be subject to mortall man'. Consequently, the Congregation asserted that, if the Regent persisted in her persecution of the faithful:

> we wilbe compelled to tak the sweard of just defence aganis all that persew us for the mater of religioun, and for our conscience saik; which awght not, nor may nott be subject to mortale creatures, farder than be God's worde man be able to prove that he hath power to command us.[6]

The Congregation insisted, in other words, that theirs was simply a revolt of conscience undertaken in defence of a religion which, prescribed by God and revealed in Scripture, was not amenable to the dictates of man. Signing themselves 'Your Grace's obedient subjectis in all thingis not repugnant to God', they defied the merely human authority of the Regent in the name of the higher and unchallengeable authority of the divine will. It was a stance of which their spiritual mentor, John Knox, would have wholeheartedly approved. Indeed, in declaring that they would rather expose their bodies to a 'thowsand deathis' than hazard eternal damnation 'by denying Christ Jesus and his manifest veritie', the Congregation spoke in an authentically Knoxian voice.

This, however, should come as no surprise, for Knox, returning from exile early in May 1559, was with the Congregation in Perth as they gathered both their military and their ideological resources in preparation for the Regent's expected onslaught. Whether or not he actually drafted the letter is impossible to determine, but its essentially Knoxian character will become immediately apparent when seen in the light of the preacher's own thinking. For, briefly stated, Knox's political thought stemmed from the theological premise that the elect had entered into a 'league and covenant' with God which bound them to the divine will as revealed in His Word irrespective of merely human laws and constitutions. Consequently, when the laws of men contradicted the law of God — when obedience to man meant rebellion against God — then the elect had in conscience no choice but to obey the binding imperative of the divine injunction and, sure in the knowledge of eternal felicity, suffer whatever infelicity they might in the meantime incur.[7] Patently, it was in accordance with just such an imperative that the Congregation felt obliged in conscience to defy the Regent. Moreover, if there is no explicit mention of a covenant in their letter, the idea is nonetheless latent in their commitment, on pain of damnation, to the laws of God rather than of men.

The concept is latent, in fact, throughout the early writings of the Congregation and not least in that 'Common Band' or covenant which signalled the emergence of Protestantism as an organised political force in

Scotland. The band is dated 3 December 1557 and in it the signatories confessed that they 'aught, according to our bonden deutie, to stryve in our Maisteris caus, evin unto the death', and promised 'befoir the Majestie of God . . . that we (be his grace) shall with all diligence continually apply our whole power, substance, and our verray lyves, to manteane, sett forward, and establish the most blessed word of God and his Congregation'.[8] The idea of banding together in loyalty to a common enterprise was familiar enough to sixteenth-century Scots, and there is evidence of its use in both social and political contexts in pre-Reformation times.[9] The band of 1557, however, by transferring it to a religious sphere, effectively transformed the traditional concept into a concrete expression of the league and covenant envisaged by Knox. For at the heart of the band lay a pledge to fulfil the law of God irrespective of the wishes of the temporal power and, although it remains unstated, it seems reasonable to suppose that, like Knox, its signatories viewed adherence to divine law as part of their 'contract' with God which promised them in return the assurance of eternal salvation.[10] It was this belief which lent Knox's covenanting ideology its apocalyptic urgency and which gave what may be called his covenanting language — the language of duty, conscience and necessity — its uncompromising character. Given their close ties with Knox, it is perhaps hardly surprising that at least initially it was in precisely these terms that the Congregation chose to construe their opposition to Mary of Guise.

Their use of the language of the covenant can, in fact, be readily illustrated from the many public documents issued by the Congregation in the course of 1558 and 1559. In 'the First Oratioun and Petitioun of the Protestantes of Scotland', for example, presented to the Regent in November 1558, they claimed in characteristic terms that they were 'of verray conscience and by the feare of our God, compelled to crave' remedy for the unjust tyranny of the ecclesiastical estate.[11] In similar vein, the imperatives stemming from their covenant with God are equally in evidence when, on 6 May 1559, in 'greif and troubill' of their minds, the Congregation felt 'constrainit' to write to the Regent, not only in the hope of relief, but also, 'according to our dewtye, to confess our Lord and God in the presens of princes, and nocht to be eschamit'. In this same letter, moreover, the Congregation vowed that, if the Regent commanded anything against the ordinance of God, they would 'of necessitie' disobey her, 'for God in vs aucht to hefe the first place'.[12] They continued to insist, however, that they were in arms only for conscience sake and that their aims were purely religious in character. When in July 1559, for example, the Regent proclaimed yet again that they were bent on usurping her authority, they replied that their 'mynd and purpose was and is to promote and sett furth the glorie of God', while 'in all civile and politick matteris, we ar and shalbe als obedient as ony uther your Gracis subjectis within the realme'.[13] It was this same stance which Lord James Stewart (the future Regent Moray) adopted when, after joining the Congregation, he was accused of fomenting sedition by his half-sister Mary, the absent Queen of Scots, and her husband Francis II of

France. In a letter of August 1559, Lord James declared that he had acted only 'for the advancement of Godis glorie . . . without ony maner derogatioun to your Majesteis dew obedience' and that, as the Congregation's proceedings were 'groundit upon the commandiment of the eternal God, we dar nocht leif the samyn unaccompleischeit'. He wished only, he added, that their Majesties 'did knaw the same, and the treuth thairof, as it is perswaidit to our conscience' and that God would illuminate their hearts and show them their duty towards their 'pure subjectis, Godis chosin pepill'.[14] Himself the signatory of a band made in the presence of God and binding him to the aims of the Congregation, Lord James was as aware as anyone of the obligations and imperatives stemming from a covenant with God.[15]

Yet however clear-cut this covenanting ideology may appear, it did not sanction resistance to constituted authority either lightly or easily. Even in matters of religion, it had long been a moot point among Protestants whether it was permissible to resist the 'powers' — including Catholic powers — by force. For Calvinists in particular, obedience to constituted authority was a cardinal principle of the 'discipline' essential to the right functioning of those 'godly commonwealths' which they sought to establish to the greater glory of God. Furthermore, they had to contend with that seemingly incontrovertible passage in Romans 13 where St. Paul had written that the powers that be were ordained by God and that whoever resisted them resisted the ordinance of God and would suffer damnation. St. Paul could hardly have been more explicit. Nor could he have envisaged the extraordinary ingenuity with which sixteenth-century Protestants would reinterpret his simple words in order to sanction resistance without negating this general and all-important principle of obedience. One such Protestant was, of course, John Knox, and it is worth briefly tracing the process by which he came to promulgate a resistance theory which was to figure also in the propaganda of the Congregation.[16] It was by no means an easy task, for in his earliest writings from exile the preacher was forced to concede that even Catholic powers were ordained by God —albeit merely as a punishment for the sins of the elect — and could not, therefore, as St. Paul had implied, be resisted. Neither, however, by the terms of their covenant with God, could the elect participate in idolatry, even if commanded to do so by the powers. Consequently, Knox was forced to the conclusion that the only option open to the elect was disobedience to constituted authority in all things repugnant to the law of God, but passive acceptance of, rather than active resistance to, any persecution that this stance might bring upon them.[17] It was only with difficulty (and perhaps only in response to the hideous suffering which such passivity inflicted on the martyrs of Marian England) that the preacher began to reinterpret what St. Paul had written in an attempt to accommodate a theory of resistance within the strict confines of the over-riding necessity of obedience.

What he came up with in the first instance was the perfectly simple idea that, as St. Paul had said that the 'powers' (plural) were ordained by God, then there must exist in each kingdom alternative, albeit inferior, magistrates whose office was, like a king's, of divine institution and whose duties were, again like a king's, to punish the wicked and protect the innocent. It followed from this that, even when a superior power commanded the contrary, the inferior magistrates were bound to fulfil the function assigned to them by God. In other words, put at its crudest, Knox could now argue that a virtuous and God-fearing (i.e. Protestant) magistrate was duty bound to protect the innocent elect from a wicked and God-less (i.e. Catholic) prince. It was this idea which the preacher was to develop at length in his *Appellation* of 1558, but in a letter written in October 1557 he had already assured the nobility of Scotland that they received 'honour, tribute and homage at Goddis Commandiment, not be reasson of your birth and progenye . . . but be reassoun of your office and dewtie'. The nobility were, in effect, the inferior magistrates of Scotland, and their 'office and duty' was, according to Knox, 'to vindicat and deliver your subjectes and brethrein from all violence and oppression, to the uttermost of your power' and even 'to hasard your awin lyvis (be it against Kingis or Empriouris) for thare deliverance'.[18] It may have been in response to this letter that, six weeks later, the Lords of the Congregation signed the Common Band.[19] Similarly, it was probably in accordance with this same conception of their role as inferior magistrates that, eighteen months later, they felt not only 'compelled' but also justified in taking up 'the sword of just defence'. Certainly, a few days after they used these words in their letter to the Regent of May 1559, the Congregation wrote an appeal to the whole nobility of Scotland in which, echoing Knox's phraseology, they addressed them as those 'whose dewetie is to defend innocentis, and to brydle the fury and raige of wicked men, wer it of Princes or Emperouris'.[20]

As with the letter to the Regent, it is unclear whether or not Knox had a hand in drafting this appeal to the nobility. It does, however, seem likely, for it employs a crucial ideological device which Knox was to defend at some length at a later stage in his career. The device must be considered crucial simply because, by itself, the idea of an inferior magistracy did not solve the conundrum posed by St. Paul in Romans 13. For while it created a magistracy ordained by God to defend the elect from persecution, it also created a plurality of powers to each and all of whom obedience was theoretically due. This was, of course, a palpable absurdity when divinely ordained magistrates were in arms against a divinely ordained prince and both were demanding obedience in accordance with the divine will. But how was this contradiction to be resolved without denying the Pauline maxim that *all* the powers were ordained by God and should not be resisted? Knox had, in fact, indicated the way out of this dilemma in his *Appellation* where, in arguing the necessity of obedience to a prince's just commands and of opposition to his 'blind rage', he had made an implicit distinction between a prince acting according to God's ordinance and a prince acting, as it were, *ultra vires*.[21] He had distinguished, in other words, between the power as ordained by God and the person who happened to wield that power and had argued that, if the latter failed to discharge his divinely appointed office, he might not only be disobeyed, but also resisted by force. It was this same distinction which the Congregation employed to advantage in their appeal to the nobility.[22] Admitting that any authority established by God must be 'good and perfyte' and was 'to be obeyed of all men, yea under the pane of damnation', they went on to point out that there was nevertheless 'a great difference betuix the authoritie quhiche is goddis ordinance, and the personis of those whiche ar placit in authoritie'. While the 'authoritie and Goddis ordinance' could, by definition, 'never do wrang', 'the corrupt person placed in this authoritie' could and often did prove wicked and unjust. At this point, however, the Congregation did not go on to infer (as Knox was to do in a debate in the General Assembly of 1564)[23] that the person of the prince might therefore be deposed without impugning the sanctity of the office he held. They merely warned those who hid behind the 'name and cloke of the Authoritie' that, if they continued to 'obey the iniust commandimentis of wicked rewlaris, ye sall suffer Goddis vengeance and just punishment with thame'. Nevertheless, it is clear from this that, by the end of May 1559, the Congregation were ideologically equipped, not only to resist the Regent, but also to carry out her deposition.

These revolutionary implications of the ideology now available to the Congregation were, in fact, made abundantly clear three months later when, on 28 August 1559, the Regent upbraided them for not showing 'debtful obedience' towards her and accused the preachers of encouraging disobedience to the 'hiear powers' in their irreverent and slanderous sermons.[24] The Congregation's response provides ample evidence that, whoever was the ideologue behind the rebel cause, whether it was Knox himself or some other preacher from among their ranks, he was quite familiar with the devices for circumventing Romans 13 outlined above.[25] He began conventionally enough, for example, by claiming that the preachers had always maintained 'the auctoratie of Princeis and Magistratis to be of God' and that they had always declared that 'they aucht to be honourit, feirit, obeyit, even for conscience saik; providit that they command nor requyre nathing expreslie repugning to Goddis commandiment and plane will, reveillit in his holy word'. He then went on, however, to argue that, if wicked princes commanded wicked things, then those who 'may and do brydill' them 'can not be accusit as resistaris of the aucthoratie, quhilk is Godis gud ordinance'. In other words, as God's ordinance was of necessity good, those who resisted an evil prince resisted, not the authority ordained by God, but only a corrupt person clad in that authority. As for the inferior magistrates enjoined by the divine will to 'brydill the fury and raige of Princeis', we are told that 'it appertenis to the Nobilitie, sworne and borne Counsallouris of the same, and allsua to the Barronis and Pepill, quhais voteis and consent ar to be requyreit in all greit and wechty materis of the communwelth'. Indeed, if these inferior magistrates were not to take action against a wicked prince, they would be considered as criminal as the prince himself and subject to the same vengeance of God. St. Paul would doubtless have stood amazed; and so too one suspects did Mary of Guise. For armed with this revolutionary ideology, the Congregation were not only

H

justified, but actually obliged by the imperative will of God to 'bridle' the Regent's 'rage and fury'.

It comes as no surprise, therefore, to find that on 21 October 1559 the Congregation formally deprived the Regent of her authority. What is slightly more surprising is that the Act of Suspension signed by 'The Nobility and Commouns of the Protestants of the Churche of Scotland' contains only the faintest traces of this covenanting theory of resistance.[26] Admittedly there is a passing reference to the 'debtful obedience' which subjects owe to sovereigns who proceed 'by Godis ordinance', and also a cursory aside to the effect that 'the Nobilitie, Barones, and Provest of Burrowes' are 'not onlie borne, but alswa sworne protectouris and defendaris' of the realm. Yet it is manifest from the Act as a whole that the Congregation were no longer acting solely in response to the imperative will of God and no longer, indeed, concerned solely with matters of conscience. Religion, in fact, is mentioned hardly at all in the Act, while self-righteous appeals to the divine will are notable only by their absence. Gone entirely, in short, is the covenanting language — the language of duty, conscience and necessity — with which we are now so familiar. Rather, the Act of Suspension is couched in a quite different language of rights, customs, laws and liberties. The Regent is accused, for example, of proceeding against her subjects without 'ony process or ordour of law'; of garrisoning the town of Perth and 'oppressing the liberties of the Quenis trew lieges'; of altering 'the auld law and consuetude of our realme'; of bringing in 'strangearis' (i.e. Frenchmen) with intent 'to suppress the commoun-weal, and libertie of our native countree'; and finally, of doing all this without consultation with those who 'be borne counsallouris to the same, be the ancient lawis of the realme'. Put briefly, the Congregation now claimed to be acting, not as servants of God, but as 'favoraris' of the 'commoun-weal', and they suspended the Regent, not as an offence before God, but as an 'ennemye to our commoun-weal'.

To say the least, this represents a major change of emphasis in the Congregation's propaganda which cries out for analysis and explanation. It is, however, only fair to admit that the change was neither as abrupt nor as unheralded as the foregoing account suggests. As will become clear in a moment, what may be called the language of the commonweal had figured prominently in the public discourse of the Congregation for some weeks before October 1559. Indeed, it is the very fact that during this period they appealed to both the covenant and the commonweal to legitimate their actions that lends such interest to the Congregation's public pronouncements of 1559. For it immediately raises the question of why, given that there were two languages available to them, they chose to adopt one mode of discourse rather than the other. Or, put more simply, why did they choose, when it came to the suspension of the Regent, to pose as defenders of the commonweal of Scotland rather than as signatories of a covenant with God? Leaving aside for the moment the possible implications of such a choice, we must first of all try and answer this question.

III

Broadly speaking, there were two sets of influences operating on the Congregation and affecting the way in which they couched their propaganda. The first of these was related to circumstances outwith Scotland and the second to internal events. Of the external influences we need at this stage say very little, as we will return to them later and view them in a rather different perspective. It is enough at this point simply to remember how dependent the Congregation were upon the resources and aid which England could supply; without them, indeed, the rebels would in the end almost certainly have been crushed. Equally, however, no reminder is needed of the fear and suspicion with which Elizabeth I regarded John Knox. His *First Blast of the Trumpet against the Monstrous Regiment of Women*, published in 1558 on the eve of the English Queen's unforeseen accession, was probably the least fortunately timed of all the preacher's blasts upon his favourite instrument. In such circumstances, it is hardly a coincidence that the lack of natural or Scriptural authority for female rule was not an argument which commended itself to the Congregation in their attempts to justify resistance to Mary of Guise. Elizabeth, however, was not just out of sympathy — to put it mildly — with the *First Blast*, she was also, on grounds of principle as well as of policy, out of sympathy with any show of resistance to constituted authority. Consequently, with little time for either religious fanatics or rebellious aristocrats (and probably still less if they hailed from Scotland), it was only with extreme reluctance that Elizabeth allowed William Cecil to shuffle her into open intervention on the Congregation's behalf.[27] Meanwhile, it was imperative that the Scottish rebels did not alienate the English Queen by justifying their revolt in terms with which Elizabeth's delicate digestion could not cope. The covenant, needless to say, was a morsel which she found as dangerous as it was distasteful. On these grounds alone, therefore, the Congregation would have had to think twice about the language in which they legitimated their actions. There were, however, other, purely Scottish grounds for doubting the advisability of confining themselves to an exclusively religious justification of their revolt, and it is on these that we ought first to concentrate.

Foremost among such native constraints must be ranked the plain fact that the Scots either did not understand or were not prepared to respond to the covenanting rhetoric initially employed by the Congregation. However effective it was in binding together the disparate — but nonetheless highly committed — elements of a revolutionary party, the stark imperatives of covenanting ideology had little appeal for those uncommitted souls whose faith — even if it *were* a Protestant faith — burned at somewhat less than the white heat of a John Knox.[28] We may reasonably assume that the Scottish governing class, whose support the Congregation so desperately needed, was no less religious than that of any other western European country. By the same token, however, neither was it any more likely to support a rebellion whose stated objectives were nothing more — or nothing less — than to have God's

Word 'truly preached' and His Holy Sacraments 'rightly ministered'. Perhaps contrary to received opinion, the Scots were not genetically prone to rebellion, and the ingrained habit of obedience, allied in equal doses with fear and apathy, characterised sixteenth-century political culture in a way that the Congregation found extremely hard to counter. As Lord James and the Earl of Argyll were forced to admit, it was far from easy 'to persuade a multitude to the revolt of an Authoritie established', [29] and such were the consequences of failure — imprisonment, forfeiture, exile, and ultimately execution — that even those most sympathetic to the Congregation's aims would naturally hesitate before committing themselves to such a risky and uncertain course of action. The Congregation, however, already in the field and already branded as a seditious rabble by an astute Regent, could not afford to wait upon the hesitant. For them the die was cast and, if they were to succeed in their enterprise, they needed converts quickly or even such support as they had would melt away in the face of the Regent's implacable hostility. Consequently, matters of faith alone being insufficient to move the uncommitted to rebel against the established authority, the Congregation had to provide them with greater incentives and more compelling grounds for joining their revolt.

That the Congregation were aware both of their weakness and of a possible means of compensating for it is intimated in the same letter, written late in May 1559, in which they appealed to the nobility to perform their role as divinely appointed magistrates. For, almost as a postscript, they requested those who opposed them to show moderation, if not 'for Godis cause', then for 'the preservatioun of our common cuntree, whiche we cannot sonnar betray in the handis of strangeris than that one of us distroy and murther ane uther'.[30] This oblique reference to Scotland's plight as a province of France, ruled by a French Regent and increasingly dominated by French officials, was to provide the Congregation with precisely the leverage they required to broaden the basis of their appeal. Events, moreover, played into their hands, for on 10 July 1559 Henry II of France was accidentally killed at a tournament and the Regent's daughter, Mary Stewart, the wife of the new King Francis II, became Queen of France as well as of Scots. This unlooked for eventuality — or, as Knox would have it, this 'wonderouse wark of God'[31] — was important not only because it lessened the chances of the Scottish Queen ever returning to her native realm, but also because it correspondingly increased the likelihood of Scotland becoming nothing more than an outlying and insignificant province of the French kingdom. The Scots had entertained just such forebodings ever since 1548 when, ironically enough, to save themselves from English domination, they had conveyed their infant Queen to France and to an eventual French marriage. Their fears had increased when a foreigner, Mary of Guise, obtained the Regency in 1554 and had increased still further in the wake of the mysterious goings-on which surrounded her daughter's marriage to the Dauphin in 1558. At the same time, the Regent's attempts to streamline the Scottish administration and, in particular, her intrusion of 'strangers' (Frenchmen) into key governmental posts had done little to reconcile the Scottish aristocracy to the prospect of rule from France.[32] Here, indeed, was a ripening harvest of political disaffection which the Congregation might reap simply by extending the scope of their appeal to include patriotism as well as Protestantism. For the Scottish ruling class, unwilling to revolt against 'an authority established' on the pretext of religion alone, might well respond to an opposition in the field if it posed also as the last bulwark of Scotland's — and, of course, their own — freedom and liberties.

The Congregation were not, as we have already seen, unaware of the potential benefits of such a stance, and they seem to have shared the belief of the Englishman Sir Henry Percy that many Scots would enlist in their ranks simply 'to keep owt the Frenche men'.[33] That conviction was doubtless increased after Mary's sudden elevation to the French throne and was assuredly not lessened by the arrival in August 1559 of a thousand French troops, intimating — or so the Congregation construed it — 'ane plane conqueist'.[34] Indeed, according to English observers, the Congregation actually welcomed this last development because they believed it would 'so stirre and irritate the herts of all Scottish men' and so increase their own power that they would be 'well able both to expell the French out of Scotlande, and also the better achieve the rest of their hole purpose'.[35] These were, however, private views and speculations, and publicly the Congregation continued to emphasise the purely religious motives for their revolt. It was not until the very end of August that they chose to pose openly as a patriotic as well as a Protestant organisation.[36] Interestingly, moreover, they did so in response to that same proclamation of the Regent, dated 28 August 1559, in which she had accused the preachers of encouraging disobedience to the 'higher powers' in their slanderous and irreverent sermons. As we have seen, this provoked the most complete statement of the covenanting theory of resistance that the Congregation had yet promulgated. It is noteworthy, however, that according to Knox this statement was composed only by 'sum men' (presumably the preachers themselves) and is no more than an addendum to the official 'publict letter' subscribed to by the Congregation as a whole.[37] It was this public letter, addressed 'To the Nobilitie, Burghis, and Communitie of this Realme of Scotland', which contained the Congregation's formal apology for their armed rebellion. It is significant, moreover, not only because it is undoubtedly the finest rhetorical exercise they ever penned, but also because it completely abandoned the religious justification for resistance they had hitherto employed.

In fact, the Congregation could hardly have been more explicit regarding the drastic rearrangement which their priorities had suddenly undergone. 'Giff religioun be not perswaidit unto yow', they declared (making significantly light of the obligations inherent in covenanting ideology),

> yit cast ye not away the cair ye aucht to have ower your commun-welth, quhilk ye se manifestlie and violentlie rewyneit befoir your eyis. Gif this will nott move you, remember your deir wyffis, children, and posteratie, your ancient heretagis and houssis . . .[38]

As Jenny Wormald has noted, these words have 'an eternal appeal', a nobility which transcends the context in which they were written, and it may even be true that the Congregation's newly professed patriotism was perfectly genuine and, as she puts it, 'not just propaganda'.[39] Whether motivated by conviction or expediency, however, there is no doubt that the Congregation now sought deliberately to arouse and exploit the most deep-seated of Scottish phobias: the fear, as their letter expressed it, of living 'under the perpetuall servitude of strangearis'. Nor is there any doubt that they did so in a language which (unlike their covenanting rhetoric) had for generations exerted a powerful influence over the Scottish political community. That language was dominated by the protean concept of the commonweal, and in order to grasp the full significance and implications of the patriotic stance now adopted by the Congregation, it is essential to look briefly at the history of this idea.

The term 'commonweal' was, in fact, a comparatively recent accession to the Scottish political vocabulary and had only begun to feature prominently in public discourse in the decades after 1520.[40] It had, however, rapidly acquired connotations of profound and lasting resonance. Without ever losing its primary, but unremarkable, meaning of the public or universal good, it had soon become endowed with a strongly patriotic inflection. Not least among the reasons for this was the fact that it was frequently used in conjunction with the vocabulary of freedom in which the medieval political community had so resoundingly protested its political autonomy. One need hardly dwell on the immense rhetorical power with which John Barbour and many other medieval writers had charged the Latin term *libertas* and its vernacular equivalents 'liberty' and 'freedom' — their impassioned pleas on behalf of an independent Scotland, free of the threat of English thraldom, are too well-known to require repetition.[41] It is sufficient here to point out that by the late 1530s the 'commonweal' had already become closely associated with this highly emotive vocabulary. In his version of the *History and Chronicles of Scotland*, for example, John Bellenden wrote of how Robert Bruce had such respect for 'the commoun weill and liberte of Scotland' that he could on no account surrender up 'his native cuntre, sen it bene fre to his dayis, to servitude of Inglismen'.[42] Stirring stuff, of which several further examples might be quoted. Of more importance to the present argument, however, is the fact that within a few years this suggestive coupling of the 'commonweal' with 'freedom' and 'liberty' was not confined to the literary world, but had entered the realm of workaday political discourse. In the 1540s, for example, the phrase 'the commonweal and liberty of this realm' was used almost as a refrain by those such as Cardinal David Beaton who led the opposition to a marriage alliance with England.[43] Furthermore, by the end of that decade, the 'commonweal' *by itself* was being employed in a manner which set off all the emotive resonances which in the Middle Ages had been triggered by the clarion-cry of 'freedom'. The author of the *Complaynt of Scotland*, for example, in imploring his countrymen to resist the English occupation of their native land, spoke quite simply, but with no apparent loss of rhetorical force, of the Scots' duty to their 'comont veil'.[44]

And so too, ten years later, did the Congregation. If the threat to Scotland's freedom now emanated from the old ally rather than the old enemy, this made no difference to the language in which Scottish fears of subjugation could best be aroused and articulated. In adopting the shibboleth of the commonweal, the Congregation picked up what had long been the password to the heartland of Scottish political consciousness. When, for example, they appealed in their public letter to all those 'as beir naturall lufe to thare cuntrey' to defend 'our derrest brethren, trew members of our commun-welth . . . most crewelie oppressit by strangearis', they merely echoed those who had led the opposition to England throughout the 1540s. Indeed, when they claimed in the same place that theirs was a righteous cause, undertaken in defence of 'your ancient rowmeis and heretageis, conquerit maist valiantlie, and defendit be your progenitouris against all strangearis, invaidaris of the same', they talked in terms which John Barbour's medieval audience would have readily understood. In other words, as the Congregation must themselves have calculated, in abandoning the language of the covenant and suggesting rather that anyone who opposed them was 'an ennemy to us, and to him self, and to his commun weill', they began to speak in a language which their compatriots not only understood, but to which they were accustomed to respond with vigour and alacrity.

If the commonweal was thus strongly associated with the idea of freedom, however, this by no means exhausts the wide-ranging connotations which it possessed for sixteenth-century Scots. As a brief look at Sir David Lindsay's *Satyre of the Thrie Estaitis* will show, the commonweal was also intimately connected with the exercise of kingship. Of course, according to the most elementary of contemporary political theories, one of a king's two main functions was the defence of the realm — or, in Scottish parlance, the maintenance of freedom — and in that sense there was already an implied relationship between kingship and the commonweal. In his *Satyre*, however, Lindsay was concerned rather with the second function attributed to contemporary monarchs — the administration of justice — and this too he brought into close association with the commonweal. He did so, moreover, in a manner as graphic as it is effective. For in the *Satyre* it is none other than John the Common Weill who, tattered and destitute as a result of royal negligence, confronts corrupt King Humanitie and begs him to renounce his vicious ways, take Gude Counsall back into his favour, and rule with justice for the common good of all. According to Lindsay, in other words, the commonweal of the realm, the well being and prosperity of the community, depends on the virtuous exercise of kingship. It is, therefore, only when the King agrees to reform his errant ways that John, newly appareled in resplendent finery, is able to resume his place in the parliament of the three estates and guide its subsequent deliberations in accordance with the public good.[45]

Lindsay was a skilled poet, but a conventional political thinker, and his *Satyre*, drawing on an essentially medieval conception of kingship, says nothing that his Scottish contemporaries would have found novel or unusual.

It comes as no surprise, therefore, to find the Congregation casting the Regent in the role, as it were, of corrupt King Humanitie and themselves in that of champions and defenders of an oppressed John the Common Weill. Certainly, when in the Act of Suspension they described Mary of Guise as an 'enemy to our commonweal' and themselves as its 'favourers', it was to these familiar ideas of kingship as well as to the freedom of the realm that they made reference. Similarly, in their public letter, when they scoffed derisively at the Regent's claim to be 'ane cairfull mothir ovir this commoun-wealth', they accused her not just of threatening its freedom, but also of imposing oppressive taxes, of debasing the coinage, of violating the ancient laws and liberties of the realm and, predictably enough, of refusing to heed the advice of her native-born counsellors. In short, like Lindsay's King Humanitie, Mary of Guise had failed adequately to perform her regal functions and was jeopardising the commonweal of the realm. Unlike King Humanitie, however, she showed no signs of heeding those who sought to remind her of her duties and obligations. Consequently, in order to protect the commonweal from any further tyrannical abuse, the Congregation felt justified in moving beyond remonstrance to open resistance.

This was obviously a quite critical step in their reasoning, but it was one which the Congregation tended to imply rather than openly to avow. In fact, neither in their public letter nor even in the Act of Suspension did they admit — far less attempt to justify — the fact that their actions represented an act of resistance to duly constituted authority. The only hint, for example, that they might be following established constitutional practice is an oblique and parenthetical reference to Thomas Cochrane, the evil (and probably fictional) counsellor of James III who was believed to have been hanged at Lauder Bridge in 1482.[46] The reign of James III culminating in his 'deposition' in 1488 was, of course, to become paradigmatic of aristocratic resistance to tyrannical rule and was to provide George Buchanan in particular with a useful precedent for the overthrow of a reigning monarch. The Congregation, however, could not afford to be as open in their acceptance of radical principles as was Buchanan. After all, whereas Buchanan was attempting to justify a revolution which had already occurred, they were seeking much needed support for a rebellion whose fate still hung in the balance. They were doing so, moreover, in terms of a language which made it both difficult and dangerous to construe their actions as positively anti-monarchical. For commonweal discourse stressed the supreme importance of the king as the symbol and guarantor of freedom and justice without explicitly sanctioning any corresponding mechanism for his removal should he fail to perform his allotted tasks. It was essentially a language of patriotic conservatism, a language to which the monarchy was central, but in which resistance to royal authority had no generally accepted status as a means of controlling or deposing a tyrannical ruler. Buchanan, in fact, exploiting the gap between the expectations and performance of royal government and endowing aristocratic resistance with both theoretical and prescriptive validity, was the first person fully to explore the possibility of adding a radical dimension to commonweal discourse.[47] As the reception of his work suggests, however, it was not a possibility which won immediate or overwhelming acceptance among the Scottish political community at large.

Clearly, therefore, although similar ideas to Buchanan's were certainly also available to the Congregation, they could be used only at the risk of challenging the highly conservative susceptibilities of those whose friendship they were actively courting. Consequently, the Congregation discussed them only in private,[48] while publicly they tried entirely to dissociate themselves from any attack on their lawful sovereigns, Mary Stewart and Francis II of France, by concentrating on the iniquitous rule of one who was 'bott a Regent'.[49] Suspending a regent was a far cry from deposing a sovereign, and the distinction gave the Congregation much more room to manoeuvre within the loyalist confines of commonweal discourse than was ever available to Buchanan. Thus in the Act of Suspension they were able to claim with quite breathtaking presumption, not only that Mary of Guise was governing 'plane contrarie' to the wishes of Mary Stewart and Francis II, but that they themselves were actually acting in their sovereigns' 'name and authoritie'.[50] With the aid of these transparent fictions, the Congregation neatly sidestepped the issue which Buchanan was forced to tackle head-on. The Regent's suspension, far from being an act of resistance of dubious legality, was in fact a perfectly justifiable step taken not only in defence of Mary Stewart and the freedom and liberties of her realm, but apparently also with her full knowledge and consent. This being the case, argued the Congregation, their cause was one from which no true lover of the commonweal could either withhold or withdraw his support.

Of course, defending the commonweal by no means precluded signing the covenant and, in emphasising the Regent's egregious tyranny, the Congregation did not entirely forget her manifest idolatry. Indeed, on several occasions in their propaganda, tyranny and idolatry are closely identified, while the defence of the 'true religion' is equated with the defence of the freedom and liberties of the realm.[51] But such attempts to protestantise the language of the commonweal were not pursued very far by the Congregation. On the contrary, throughout the autumn of 1559 they continued to appeal to their countrymen in terms which firmly subordinated Protestantism to patriotism rather than deliberately conflated them.[52] Having clearly decided, for example, that there was more to be gained from playing on the Scots' hatred of outsiders than on their sympathy for the reformers, the Congregation directed letters to all parts of the kingdom emphasising, as Knox tells us in his *History*, 'quhat dangear did hing ower all men, giff the Frensche sould be sufferit to plant in this cuntrey at thair plesour'.[53] The precise dangers which they dwelt upon are made clear in a letter which Archbishop Hamilton addressed to the Regent from Paisley at the end of September 1559. For he warned his mistress that the people of the west were being incited to rebel 'for the defence and weill of the realm' and that they were being told that the French would occupy their lands, do away with the native nobility and rule Scotland as a province after 'the exampill of Brytanny'.[54] Propaganda such as this was evidently designed to appeal both to the xenophobia of the Scots in general and, more particularly, to the self-interest of a governing elite which had much to lose should the reins — and profits — of government fall into the hands of foreigners. It was, moreover, a type of propaganda which, as J. H. Elliot has argued, found favour among rebel groups throughout early modern Europe.[55] Not surprisingly, therefore, when in October 1559 the Congregation addressed a Latin declaration to the princes of Christendom, they dwelt not on their religious grievances but on their role as defenders of Scotland's ancient laws and liberties.[56] In other words, both here and elsewhere in their propaganda, it was clearly in terms of the commonweal and not the covenant that the Congregation now chose to justify their actions. As they informed the Regent on 16 October 1559, if she persisted in her 'evyll mynd toward the common-weall and libertie of this realme', then 'according to the oath quhilk we have sworne for the maintenance of the commoun-weall . . . we will provide reamedy'.[57]

As we already know, the remedy prescribed by the Congregation was Mary of Guise's suspension from the authority. This apparently decisive move, however, far from marking the triumphant climax of the rebels' campaign, marked rather the beginnings of a sharp and rapid reversal in their fortunes. For in the months following her putative suspension, the Regent firmly seized the initiative, pushing the Congregation onto the defensive and leaving them in no position either to make her deposition effective or to drive out her French supporters. The former, indeed, would be accomplished only by Mary of Guise's death in June 1560 and the latter only by the intervention of England early in the same year.[58] The commonweal, it would seem, no more than the covenant, was capable of mobilising the Scots in numbers sufficient to overthrow the established authority. In fact, loudly and lengthily as the Congregation protested their own and their countrymen's patriotic duty, there is little evidence to suggest that their use of commonweal rhetoric secured the positive response they expected from the political community at large.[59] To anticipate an obvious doubt, however, this does not necessarily mean that the idea of the commonweal was much less important or influential than has been argued above. On the contrary, it may simply indicate that the generality of Scots remained unconvinced by the Congregation's protestations of allegiance to it. With this in mind, it is worth looking briefly at what reasons contemporary Scots had for doubting the plausibility of the Congregation's stance. For this will shed light, not only on why they gained so little support, but also on the more general implications of their use of commonweal discourse.

IV

If credibility be ranked among the most treasured assets of any political movement, then it was the Congregation's singular misfortune that from the very outset their motives were questioned and their professed aims scoffed at and derided. At the same time, however, one must pay tribute to the formidable political acumen which led Mary of Guise immediately to brand the Congregation as a pack of power-hungry opportunists bent simply on the overthrow of her own and her daughter's authority. As has already been suggested, the forces of inertia — fear, apathy, the habit of obedience — all worked to her advantage, and these were amply reinforced merely by the Regent's standing on her considerable dignity and anathematising the Congregation as a worldly and treacherous rabble. As early as May 1559, for example, she was pouring ridicule on the insurgents' claim to be in arms only for conscience sake, and throughout the subsequent campaign she continually and scornfully reiterated her belief that the Congregation 'mentt no religioun, but a plane rebellioun'.[60] Such charges gained credence when in July 1559 the rebels seized the coining-irons from the mint in order, as they said, to prevent further debasement of the coinage.[61] Such a blatantly political action seemed to substantiate the Regent's accusations, while making nonsense of the Congregation's much trumpeted distinction between obedience in temporal matters and disobedience only in things repugnant to God. The Congregation seem themselves to have realised as much, for according to Knox they then issued a 'publict proclamatioun' arguing that they 'did stay the printing irnes, in consideratioun that the commone wealth was greatlie hurt by corrupting of our money; and because that we war counsalouris of this realme, sworne to procure the proffite of the same . . .'[62] The full text of this proclamation has not survived, but this summary clearly intimates the dramatic change in the language of the Congregation's propaganda which was shortly to occur. Already the rebels were conscious that their covenanting ideology with all its sophisticated — or perhaps merely sophistical — devices for circumventing Romans 13 was no match for the Regent's vigorous condemnation of their activities as political blasphemy. Nor, indeed, by virtue of their own actions, was a purely religious justification of their revolt any longer credible. They had, in short, little choice but to suffer the indignity of shifting their ground and taking up a position both less exposed to the Regent's well-aimed barbs and more in keeping with their own behaviour.

It has already been argued that the stance the Congregation now chose to adopt — the defence of the commonweal — was by far the most advantageous available to them. Not only could it legitimate such actions as the seizure of the coining-irons, but it also allowed them to tap the sizeable reservoir of anti-French feeling among their compatriots. Nevertheless, it did not wholly shield them from the Regent's continued insistence that their real aim was the destruction of her own and particularly her daughter's power. The rebels were still ill-equipped to counter the extremely damaging accusation that their intention was neither religious reform nor the commonweal of the realm, but rather, as Mary Stewart herself opined, 'the subversioun of our authoritie, and usurpatioun of our Crown'.[63] In this regard, the emergence of the Duke of Châtelherault and his son the Earl of Arran as nominal leaders of the Congregation in September 1559 did nothing to enhance their credibility. For was it not these fickle and devious Hamiltons — heirs presumptive to the Scottish throne on the failure of the Stewart line — who stood to gain most should the Regent and her daughter be deposed? Their prominence in the Congregation's ranks simply lent additional credence to the Regent's assertion that the insurgents wished only 'to pervert the haill obedience' and accomplish 'ane plane usurpatioun of authoratie'.[64] Ample testimony to the effectiveness of this argument is provided by the Congregation's own reaction to it. For on the eve of the Regent's suspension they felt obliged to issue a declaration explicitly denying that the Hamiltons had any designs on the throne,[65] while in the Act of Suspension itself they claimed (as we have seen) that, far from acting against their true sovereigns, Mary Stewart and Francis II, they were actually acting in their name and authority. It is hard to imagine that the Scottish political community found such protestations of allegiance any more convincing than did Mary herself. The Scots' loyalty to the Stewart dynasty was doubtless based as much on pragmatism as on principle, but the spectre of a Hamilton succession can only have reinforced it.

As a threat to the Congregation's credibility, however, the Hamilton connection fades into comparative insignificance when set beside the rebels' dealings with England. For if, as the Congregation so clamorously insisted, the Regent and her French lackeys threatened the commonweal and liberty of the realm, what of themselves and their English paymasters? This represents a problem much larger than can be dealt with adequately here, but it is important to recognise that the Congregation's Anglophile policy was based on something more than their desperate need for financial and military assistance. As Arthur Williamson has amply documented, key figures in the Congregation were inspired by an apocalyptic vision of a reformed Britain uniting the realms of Scotland and England in a Protestant empire capable of withstanding even the Satanic powers of the papal Antichrist.[66] They were, in effect, the heirs of a unionist ideology developed by Protestants of the 1540s in support of the marriage of the infant Mary Stewart to Prince Edward of England. On that occasion, of course, to the accompaniment of a crescendo of commonweal rhetoric, the Scots had refused to take advantage of the providential opportunity to unite the realms. Yet God in His mercy — and through the agency of the Congregation — had seen fit to provide them with a means of redeeming their manifest sinfulness. As the Congregation wrote to Cecil in July 1559, they had once again been offered the chance to establish a 'confederacie, amitie, and leigue' between the realms which, being done 'for God's cause', would be quite unlike 'the pactions maid by warldlie men for warldlie proffeit'.[67] By no means every member of the Congregation shared these unionist sympathies, but hardly a letter passed between England and the rebels without some reference to the 'perpetual friendship' between the two realms which a successful rebellion would inaugurate. Nor does it seem unreasonable to suppose that the leadership — men such as Lord James and Knox himself — as well as pressing for a long-term dynastic union with England through the marriage of the Earl of Arran to Elizabeth Tudor, also seriously considered hastening the happy event by setting aside the claims of the Stewart line.[68] Whatever their precise intentions, however, the Congregation's attitude to England is clearly an element of their thinking which we cannot afford to ignore.

Certainly their Scottish contemporaries would not have ignored it. There was nothing, indeed, better calculated to arouse their suspicions than evidence of the Congregation trafficking with England. Even if there was, as seems likely, a growing body of opinion in Scotland favourable to closer and more amicable relations with the old enemy, the idea of union, and particularly one which passed over the ruling Scottish dynasty, would have appalled the majority of Scots. Moreover, even if the rebel leaders sincerely believed that union was in Scotland's best interests, such a belief was wholly inconsistent with the main thrust of commonweal rhetoric as both they and the Scottish political community at large employed it. Indeed, incorporating the vocabulary of freedom and predicating the exercise of justice within an in-dependent kingship, the language of the commonweal was quite antithetical to the unionist policy espoused by the Congregation's leadership. Consequently, openly to have avowed the nature of their dealings with England would have exposed the rebels' declared commitment to the commonweal as a hollow sham. Not surprisingly, therefore, the Congregation never publicly aired their Anglophile policy and conducted their negotiations with Elizabeth's ministers in the utmost secrecy. Nevertheless, the Regent did become aware that something was afoot, and in late June and again in early October 1559 she made pointed references in her public proclamations to 'messageis to and fra Ingland' and to the Congregation's 'seiking support of Ingland'.[69] The rebels were in no position to deny such accusations, but they could not afford to be completely honest about their intentions either. Consequently, they fell back on self-righteous obfuscation, declaring in October 1559 that the extent of their dealings with England would shortly be made 'manifest unto the warld, to the prayse of Godis haly name, and to the confusioun of all thame that sclander us for sa doing'.[70] In the meantime, the slander presumably continued apace; and presumably continued also to cast doubt on the Congregation's commitment to the commonweal and liberty of the realm. Nor, in fact, were the insurgents ever likely to be in a position to reveal the true nature of their dealings with England. For to have done so would not only have completely destroyed their credibility in Scotland, it would have completely alienated the Queen of England also.

Although it seems probable that William Cecil favoured the idea of union put forward by the Congregation, there is nothing to suggest that his mistress did. Elizabeth flirted with Arran as she flirted with so many other ardent suitors, but to marry him or, still worse, to ignore the legitimacy of the Stewart line's claim to the throne of Scotland were courses of action which she could not countenance. Matrimony and union aside, however, Cecil still faced a twofold problem with regard to Scotland: for not only did he have to con-vince his Queen of the wisdom of doing anything at all about the situation on her northern frontier, but having done so he had to provide her with plausible grounds for intervention in the affairs of an independent state. Religion was a non-starter with Elizabeth, and Cecil can only have been relieved when in late October 1559 Knox was replaced by Maitland of Lethington as the Congregation's go-between in the English negotiations. Equally, intervention on the basis of England's ancient claim to feudal superiority over Scotland, although considered by Cecil, would hardly have been welcome to Scots who could still recall Henry VIII's use of the same pretext.[71] In fact, the only grounds which were neither anathema to Elizabeth nor impolitic in Scotland were precisely those which the Congregation adopted after August 1559: namely, the defence of the freedom and liberties of the realm without in any way derogating from the authority of Mary Stewart, the lawful sovereign of Scotland. The rebels' initial adoption of this stance, however, does seem to have been a response to the Scottish pressures already discussed rather than to the importunities of their English allies. For it was not until November 1559 that Cecil finally instructed them to present their case to Elizabeth in terms which, ignoring the question of union and even that of religion, emphasised instead their loyalty to Mary Stewart and their desire only to free their realm from French tyranny and oppression.[72] Thereafter, however, the Congregation had a twofold reason for couching their propaganda in the language of the commonweal. Indeed, they were left with little choice, for to have done otherwise would have lost them the backing of England as surely as it would have diminished their support in Scotland.

Ironically enough, therefore, the two central planks of the Congregation's platform — religious reform and amity or union with England — are completely absent from their propaganda after November 1559. If their private correspondence remained preoccupied with these concerns, circumstances had conspired to force the Congregation into a public posture based exclusively on loyalty to Mary Stewart and the commonweal and liberty of her realm. Thus on 27 March 1560 they summoned the neutral lords of Scotland to join them in besieging Leith and, wholly ignoring the religious issue, urged them, on pain of being reputed 'playne enemyes to the common weile of this our native countrey', to help put the realm 'to lybertie and fredom'.[73] Similarly, a week or so later, they wrote to the Regent offering her a final chance to withdraw French troops peaceably from Scotland and insisting that they were driven to the extreme of armed resistance only in defence of the commonweal and liberty of the realm.[74] Predictably, moreover, it was precisely these secular concerns — and none other — which were adumbrated in the formal document by which Elizabeth agreed to intercede on the Congregation's behalf. In the Articles of Berwick, signed on 27 February 1560, the English Queen pledged to help the Scottish insurgents 'onlie . . . for the defence of the fredome of Scotland from conquiest', while the Congregation themselves were obliged to aver that they did not intend to 'wythdraw any dew obedience' from Mary Stewart provided that she neither subverted nor oppressed 'the just and ancient liberties' of the realm.[75] Elizabeth's intervention on these terms proved decisive. With an English navy in the Forth and an

English army in the Lowlands, many erstwhile neutral Scots found it expedient to admit the justice of the Congregation's cause. Perhaps crucially, however, it was a cause which had changed out of all recognition from that which, twelve months before, had aimed only to ensure that God's Word was 'truly preached' and His Holy Sacraments were 'rightly ministered'. Indeed, when the conflict was finally ended by the Treaty of Edinburgh in July 1560, the issue of religion was not even mentioned. By the terms of the treaty, the Scots were once again left free to enjoy their freedom and liberties and were once again to be governed by their native political elite, but their confessional allegiance was left wholly undetermined.[76]

Although the Congregation emerged victorious, then, they had ostensibly achieved only those objectives which they had been forced to espouse sometime after they had originally risen in revolt. Of course, over the next few months, they were to implement sweeping ecclesiastical reforms and to continue covertly to negotiate a dynastic union with England. Yet paradoxically the temporary abandonment of these aims — at least in public — had proved essential to the success of their rebellion. In order to win the support of Elizabeth and to gain at least the semblance of respectability in Scotland, the Congregation had been obliged to construe their actions, not as a Protestant crusade, but as a patriotic insurrection against the tyranny of France. They had had to do so, moreover, without impugning their allegiance to their lawful sovereign, Mary Queen of Scots. Given the effectiveness of the Regent's own propaganda, this last was the most difficult operation which the Congregation were called upon to perform. One may doubt, in fact, if they ever wholly allayed their countrymen's suspicions of their ultimate intentions. With the intervention of England, however, those who still doubted the sincerity of the Congregation's propaganda had to make do with whatever guarantees the rebels were prepared to offer. In this regard, one further document is worth consideration, for in the course of April and May 1560 the Congregation drew up and signed the third and last of their famous bands.[77] This final 'covenant' is of particular interest because, although (like its predecessors) it committed the signatories to 'the Reformatioun of Religioun, according to Goddes word', it did so in only the vaguest terms, while going on (unlike its predecessors) to concern itself primarily with the commonweal. Thus the principal undertaking entered into by the subscribers was that, aided by 'the Quene of Englandis armie', they would:

> effectuallie concur and joyne togidder . . . for expulsioun of the said strangeris [i.e., the French], oppressouris of oure libertie, furth of this Realme, and recovery of oure ancient fredomis and liberteis; to the end, that in tyme cuming, we may, under the obedience of the Kyng and Quene our Soveranis, be onlie rewllit be the lawis and customeis of the cuntrey, and borne men of the land.

Clearly, this was a covenant of a quite different type from those which the Congregation had entered upon in former days. So different, in fact, that it could be signed, as Knox put it, not only by those 'professing Chryst Jesus in

Scotland', but also by 'dyveris utheris' — including the conservative Earl of Huntly — 'that joynit with us, for expelling of the Frenche army'.[78] One can only surmise that the band's vague commitment to religious reform was far outweighed in the eyes of Huntly and his ilk by its firm commitment both to the freedom of the realm and to the reigning Stewart monarch. With the arrival in March of an English army, such an undertaking on the part of the Congregation — in the familiar form of a bond — may have tipped the balance in their favour, ensuring the quiescence of their opponents and paving the way for their eventual success.[79]

V

The Third Band provides an appropriate point at which to end our detailed analysis of the Congregation's propaganda and to begin rather to reflect on its more general significance. Perhaps the first and most obvious conclusion to be drawn from the content of the material and the manner in which it was deployed is that mid-sixteenth century Scots were highly conservative political thinkers. There seems no doubt, for example, that the rebels' abandonment of covenanting rhetoric and their adoption instead of the language of the commonweal was an attempt to redescribe their activities in the normative language of the political community at large and thus to legitimate their rebellion in the terms most likely to win widespread sympathy, approval and support. An analysis of that language reveals, moreover, that it was centred on an essentially medieval conception of kingship and was primarily concerned with the two fundamental functions — the maintenance of the freedom of the realm and the equitable administration of justice within it — which a king was conventionally expected to perform. Many sources other than the Congregation's propaganda suggest that it was in these relatively unsophisticated terms that Reformation Scots habitually described and discussed the political world they inhabited. It is, therefore, perfectly understandable that the insurgents should have abandoned the alien and unattractive imperatives of the covenant in favour of this more familiar mode of discourse. In so doing, however, they fell subject to certain important constraints. For in order to maintain the plausibility of their commitment to the commonweal, the Congregation were obliged — at least in public — to subordinate their Protestantism to their patriotism, to suppress their desire for a dynastic union with England, and to proclaim their allegiance to their lawful sovereign, Mary Stewart. If the majority of Scots remained sceptical about the motives behind these ideological manoeuvres, a combination of factors — not least the intercession of Elizabeth — saw the Congregation emerge nevertheless as victors over the Regent. In a sense, however, although they went on to initiate some of the ecclesiastical reforms they desired, it was not the Congregation who benefited most from the widespread use of commonweal discourse in Reformation Scotland. Arguably, in fact, the real beneficiary was none other than Mary Queen of Scots.

Fortuitous deaths play a disproportionately important role in the history of
the Scottish Reformation, and that of Mary Stewart's husband, Francis II of
France, is by no means the least significant of them. He died in December 1560
after a reign of only eighteen months and, just as his premature accession had
altered the state of affairs in Scotland, so too did his premature demise. For it
suddenly and quite unexpectedly freed his widow to return to her native realm
as an adult monarch with an incontestable right to the Scottish throne. Given
all that has been said and implied here about the language of the commonweal
and hence about the conservative susceptibilities of the Scottish political community, one would expect the prospect of a return to a traditional style of
kingship — albeit under a woman — to have been warmly anticipated in
Scotland. After all, the commonweal depended on the freedom of the realm
and the equitable administration of justice within it, while an independent
monarch was seen as the symbol and guarantor of both. Consequently, as
Mary was now free of her French ties, had no obligations towards England,
and was returning to her native realm to govern it in person, Scots who valued
the commonweal should have rejoiced as they had not done since the death of
Mary's father, James V, in 1542. Perhaps, then, old Sir Richard Maitland
(Lethington's father) spoke for many of his compatriots when he wrote:

> Now sen thow art arryvit in this land,
> Our native princes and Illustir quene,
> I traist to god this regioun sall stand
> Ane auld fre realme as it lang tyme hes bein;
> Quhairin richt sone thair sall be hard and sein
> Grit Ioy, Iustice, gude peax and policie,
> All cair and cummar banist quyt and clein,
> And ilk man leif in gude tranquillitie.[80]

Certainly, we could ask for no more succinct statement of the values and
expectations embodied in commonweal discourse and, Knox's baleful
comments apart, there is little to suggest that the Scots viewed their Queen's
return — regardless of her religion — in anything other than hopeful, albeit
apprehensive, terms.[81] Moreover, there was little that the Congregation could
do about it. Throughout their revolt they had publicly insisted on their loyalty
to Mary, while during much of it they had posed as selfless defenders of
precisely those things which her return now seemed to promise. They had been
trapped by the logic of their own propaganda: if they could claim credit for a
successful defence of the commonweal, it was Mary Stewart who reaped the
benefit of the patriotic conservatism which they had sought to arouse and
exploit.[82]

Finally, then, if political debate in Reformation Scotland was conducted
largely in the secular and inherently conservative language of the
commonweal, where does this leave the religious issues which ostensibly
sparked the crisis? Recent scholarship — the work, for example, of Ian Cowan
and Michael Lynch — has made clear that the Protestant tide, if rising in the

1550s, was far from irresistible in 1559 and that both then and for some time thereafter the confessional allegiance of the majority of Scots showed no marked preference for the reformed faith.[83] This certainly helps to explain the apparent lack of enthusiasm for the Congregation's cause, but it would be rash to conclude from it that the Scots were unmoved by matters of religion. Jenny Wormald is surely right to stress the genuine spiritual perplexity felt by many people at this time, while the unprecedented demand by a hundred or so lairds for admission to the 'Reformation Parliament' of August 1560 is perhaps indicative of the extent of this underlying desire for religious reform.[84] It is conceivable, indeed, that had Scotland been subjected to a magisterial reformation, initiated by a 'godly prince' and conducted in somewhat milder terms than those advocated by John Knox, it would have met with very little resistance. For under such circumstances it would have been possible to protestantise the language of the commonweal in a manner capable of legitimating reform without doing violence to the community's conservative political instincts.[85] As it was, however, the Congregation's rebellion placed many of their countrymen in an acute ideological dilemma: that of reconciling loyalty to a Catholic sovereign with a desire for Protestant reform. It was a dilemma which would persist at least until the accession of that 'godly king' James VI and which would contribute conspicuously to the instability of his mother's reign. In 1559-60, however, it is clear that the majority of Scots chose to subordinate the claims of conscience to the commands of the civil power. Ultimately, the conclusion is unavoidable that the Congregation owed the success of their rebellion, not to the support of the Scottish political community, but to the latter's acquiescence in the face of English intervention.

NOTES

1. The most important of these works are I. B. Cowan, *Regional Aspects of the Scottish Reformation* (Historical Association Pamphlet, London, 1978); Michael Lynch, *Edinburgh and the Reformation* (Edinburgh, 1981); and Jenny Wormald, *Court, Kirk and Community: Scotland 1470-1625* (London, 1981). In addition, two older works made significant contributions to the current revisionist climate: Gordon Donaldson, *The Scottish Reformation* (Cambridge, 1960) and *Essays on the Scottish Reformation*, ed. David McRoberts (Glasgow, 1962).

2. The best analysis of the formal political theory of the period is J. H. Burns, 'The Political Ideas of the Scottish Reformation', *Aberdeen University Review*, xxxvi (1955-6), 251-68.

3. Gordon Donaldson, *Scotland: James V-James VII* (Edinburgh, 1971), 100-2, writes that the Scots fought the battles of 1559 'less by weapons than by propaganda' and, after briefly reviewing the latter, concludes that the 'outstanding fact is the novel appeal of both sides to a public opinion'.

4. Those familiar with recent literature on the history of political ideas will recognise this approach as a pragmatic adaptation of the type of linguistic analysis

advocated by J. G. A. Pocock and Quentin Skinner. The following of their works were of particular help in formulating the methodological guidelines on which this essay is based: Pocock, *Politics, Language and Time: Essays on Political Thought and History* (London, 1972); Skinner, 'Some Problems in the Analysis of Political Thought and Action', *Political Theory*, ii (1974), 277-303; and Skinner, 'The Principles and Practice of Opposition: The case of Bolingbroke versus Walpole', in *Historical Perspectives: Studies in English Thought and Society in Honour of J. H. Plumb*, ed. Neil McKendrick (London, 1974), 93-128. In addition, I am grateful to N. T. Phillipson, E. E. Steiner and J. M. Wormald for their helpful comments on the methodological as well as other aspects of this paper.

5. D. Calderwood, *The History of the Kirk of Scotland*, ed. T. Thomson (Wodrow Society, 1842-9), i, 433.

6. *The Works of John Knox*, ed. D. Laing (Wodrow Society, 1846-64), i, 326-7.

7. For a fuller discussion of this interpretation of Knox's political views, see Roger A. Mason, 'Knox, Resistance and the Moral Imperative', *History of Political Thought*, i (1980-1), 411-36. His use of the covenant idea and some of his possible sources are also discussed in R. L. Greaves, 'John Knox and the Covenant Tradition', *Journal of Ecclesiastical History*, xxiv (1973), 23-32.

8. Knox, *Works*, i, 273-4.

9. On the background and significance of banding, see J. M. Brown, 'Bonds of Manrent in Scotland before 1603' (unpublished PhD thesis, University of Glasgow, 1974).

10. The fullest statement of Knox's understanding of the covenant and its implications occurs in *Works*, iii, 190ff.

11. *Ibid.*, i, 302; cf. the 'Protestatioun' laid before parliament the following month (*ibid.*, i, 312-4).

12. This letter was probably written by Erskine of Dun and is printed as an appendix to the Dun papers in *Miscellany of the Spalding Club* (Spalding Club, 1841-52), iv, 88-92.

13. Knox, *Works*, i, 365-6.

14. *Ibid.*, i, 387.

15. *Ibid.*, i, 344-5; this second band, dated 31 May 1559, was made immediately after Argyll and Lord James defected to the rebel camp and was presumably aimed at binding them (and the other noblemen who signed it) more securely to the Congregation's aims.

16. Knox was by no means unique among Protestants in attempting to fashion a resistance theory under these circumstances, and both he and his colleagues drew on a considerable reservoir of ideas developed in pre-Reformation times. For a discussion of the European context in which Knox operated and from which he derived many of the ideas analysed below, see in particular Quentin Skinner, *The Foundations of Modern Political Thought* (Cambridge, 1978), ii, Ch.7. See also Esther Hildebrandt, 'The Magdeburg Bekenntnis as a Possible Link Between German and English Resistance Theory in the Sixteenth Century', *Archiv für Reformationsgeschichte*, lxxi (1980), 227-53. It should be mentioned at this point that an alternative resistance theory promulgated by Knox and based on the justifiability of women's forcible exclusion from power is not discussed here. Although Knox is infamous for his statement of this theory in the *First Blast*, it does not figure in the thinking of the Congregation — presumably because they were so dependent on Elizabeth I of England for support.

17. This is the basic position set out by Knox in the several admonitory epistles he

wrote to his erstwhile congregations in England during the course of 1554 (printed in *Works*, iii, 157-216, 227-49, 251-330).

18. *Ibid.*, i, 272.

19. Knox's letter was written from Dieppe and dated 27 October 1557 and could therefore have been in the hands of the Congregation before the first band was signed on 3 December.

20. Knox, *Works*, i, 330.

21. *Ibid.*, iv, 496.

22. *Ibid.*, i, 331-2.

23. See *ibid.*, ii, 435-8, where Knox assured Maitland of Lethington 'that the Prince may be resistit, and yit the ordinance of God nocht violatit'.

24. *Ibid.*, i, 397-9.

25. *Ibid.*, i, 410-11. One obviously suspects Knox's influence, but as suggested above (note 16), the ideas discussed here were of European currency and it is quite conceivable that Scots other than Knox were aware of them.

26. For the full text of the Act of Suspension, see *ibid.*, i, 444-9.

27. The process is chronicled in Conyers Read, *Mr. Secretary Cecil and Queen Elizabeth* (New York, 1955), Ch. 7.

28. See H. G. Koenigsberger, 'The Organization of Revolutionary Parties in France and the Netherlands during the Sixteenth Century', in his *Estates and Revolutions: Essays in Early Modern European History* (Ithaca & London, 1971), 224-52. In this influential article, Koenigsberger argued (pp. 225-6) that: 'Religious belief alone, no matter whether it was held with fanatic conviction or for political expediency, could bring together the divergent interests of nobles, burghers, and peasants . . .' This was probably as true of the Scottish Congregation as it was of Protestant parties in France and the Netherlands. Nevertheless, the success of religious ideology in binding together those already committed (for whatever reason) to revolutionary action was hardly matched by its success in persuading the *uncommitted* of either the necessity or the legitimacy of that action.

29. *Calendar of the State Papers relating to Scotland and Mary, Queen of Scots 1547-1603*, edd. J. Bain and others (Edinburgh, 1898-), i, no. 516.

30. Knox, *Works*, i, 334.

31. *Ibid.*, i, 371.

32. For a more detailed analysis of the grievances arising out of French rule, see Donaldson, *Scotland: James V-James VII*, 86f.

33. See Knox, *Works*, vi, 35.

34. *Ibid.*, i, 396-7; cf. *CSP Scot.*, i, no. 492, where Kirkcaldy of Grange reported, a week after Henry II's death, that the barons and commons of Scotland were 'inflambed' against France.

35. Knox, *Works*, vi, 72.

36. Although in a proclamation issued in mid-July the Congregation had justified their seizure of the coining-irons in terms which anticipate the patriotic rhetoric they were later to exploit more fully (see below, p. 113).

37. Differentiating between the two responses to the Regent's proclamation, Knox says only: 'Besydis this, our publict letter, sum men answerit certane heidis of hir proclamatioun on this maner' (*Works*, i, 409). Its defence of the Knoxian attitude to the civil power suggests that the second response was the work of the preachers, but it should be pointed out that it also talks at some length of 'the tyrannie of strangeris' and the oppression of 'our commun-wealth' — the main preoccupations of the 'publict letter'.

38. For the full text of the letter from which this and subsequent quotations are taken, see *ibid.*, i, 400-8.

39. Wormald, *Court, Kirk and Community*, 118-9.

40. This conclusion is based on a study of government records (such as acts of parliament) where the term occurs only rarely before 1520, but with increasing frequency thereafter. The same timing is suggested by literary evidence: the first Scottish poet to use the term with any frequency was Sir David Lindsay writing his early works *circa* 1530. The term is probably a borrowing from English usage, but (as will become clear) it developed distinctive connotations in Scottish discourse. For interesting sidelights on its use in England and the key role it came to play there in the thinking of the 'Commonwealth Men', see Arthur B. Ferguson, *The Articulate Citizen and the English Renaissance* (Durham, N. C., 1965).

41. For an interesting discussion of the connotations acquired by the word during the Middle Ages, see G. W. S. Barrow, 'The Idea of Freedom in Late Medieval Scotland', *Innes Review*, xxx (1979), 16-34.

42. *The History and Chronicles of Scotland: written in Latin by Hector Boece . . . and translated by John Bellenden*, ed. Thomas Maitland (Edinburgh, 1821), ii, 363; for similar examples, see *ibid.*, i, 237 and ii, 440.

43. According to Sir Ralph Sadler, the English ambassador in Scotland, Beaton and his supporters constantly talked in terms of 'thonour, lybertie and commoune wealthe' of the realm; see *The Hamilton Papers*, ed. J. Bain (Edinburgh, 1890-2), ii, no. 38. This is borne out by the 'Secret Band' they signed in July 1543 pledging their loyalty to 'the common wele and lybertie of this realme' (*ibid.*, i, no. 446). Over the next few years, it was in similar terms that many Scots swore loyalty to Mary of Guise and her daughter; for several examples of this, see *The Scottish Correspondence of Mary of Lorraine*, ed. A. I. Cameron (Scottish History Society, 1927), 50, 79-80, 84, 85, 86-7.

44. *The Complaynt of Scotland*, ed. A. M. Stewart (Scottish Text Society, 1979), 57, 88, 234. As some of these quotations suggest, the 'commonweal' might be used to denote, not simply the welfare of a particular community, but the actual community whose welfare was at stake. This is true also of the Congregation's propaganda where both 'commonweal' and 'commonwealth' are occasionally used in the same sense — although with greater rhetorical weight — as terms such as realm, nation and kingdom.

45. The full text of the *Satyre* is printed in *The Works of Sir David Lindsay of the Mount 1490-1555*, ed. D. Hamer (Scottish Text Society, 1930-6), ii, *passim*.

46. See Knox, *Works*, i, 402-3. The political significance of the myths surrounding James III's relationships with his nobility and his favourites is discussed more fully in Norman Macdougall, *James III: A Political Study* (Edinburgh, 1982), Ch. 12. See also the same author's 'The Sources: A Reappraisal of the Legend', in *Scottish Society in the Fifteenth Century*, ed. J. M. Brown (London, 1977), 11-32.

47. For a discussion of Buchanan's political writings which emphasises the centrality of a conventional ideal of kingship to his thought, see Roger A. Mason, '*Rex Stoicus*: George Buchanan, James VI and the Scottish Polity', in *New Perspectives on the Politics and Culture of Early Modern Scotland*, edd. John Dwyer, Roger A. Mason and Alexander Murdoch (Edinburgh, 1982), 9-33.

48. For example, in a debate among the Congregation preceding the passing of the Act of Suspension, the preacher John Willock put forward an argument which, stripped of its religious garb, is not too far removed from that advocated by Buchanan and which was applicable, not just to the Regent, but to any sovereign authority.

Perhaps significantly, however, when asked for his judgment on Willock's discourse, Knox concurred only with the proviso that 'the iniquitie of the Quene Regent' should 'withdraw neather our heartis, neather yitt the heartis of other subjectis, from the obedience dew unto our Soveranis' (Knox, *Works*, i, 441-3).

49. *Ibid.*, i, 441.

50. *Ibid.*, i, 444, 448. Similarly, in a letter to the Regent written immediately after her suspension, the Congregation accused her of acting 'direct contrair our Soveranes Lord and Ladyis will, which we ever esteame to be for the weall, and nott for the hurt of this our commoun-wealth'. They then went on to say that 'any auctoritie ye have be reassone of our Soveranis commissioun . . ., the same, for maist wechtie reassones, is worthelie suspendit be us, in the name and authoritie of our Soveranis, whais counsall we ar of in the effares of this our commoun-weall' (*ibid.*, i, 449-50).

51. The best example is probably the Congregation's declaration of 3 October 1559 (*ibid.*, i, 424-33).

52. See, for example, the letter from Arran to Lord Semple asking him to support the Congregation, if not because he favoured their religion, 'yit nevertheles for the commoun wealth and libertie of this youre native countrey' (*Mary of Lorraine Corresp.*, 428-9). In similar vein, Lord Erskine, the keeper of Edinburgh castle, was urged to support the Congregation as 'our tender freynd, brother, and a member of the same communwealth with us' (Knox, *Works*, i, 415-7).

53. *Ibid.*, i, 417-8.

54. *Mary of Lorraine Corresp.*, 427-8.

55. J. H. Elliot, 'Revolution and Continuity in Early Modern Europe', *Past and Present*, xlii (1969), 35-56, esp. 47f.

56. A. Teulet, *Papiers d'Etat relatifs à l'Histoire de l'Ecosse au 16e Siècle* (Bannatyne Club, 1852), i, 414-28.

57. Knox, *Works*, i, 437-8.

58. For a succinct account of the course of events following the Regent's suspension, see Donaldson, *Scotland: James V-James VII*, 97-99.

59. Commenting, for example, on the Congregation's enforced withdrawal from Edinburgh early in November 1559, Knox wrote that they were openly called 'traytouris and heretiques' by the native inhabitants, leading him to conclude sourly that 'we wald never have belevit that our naturall countrey men and women could have wisshed our destructioun so unmercifullie, and have so rejosed in our adversitie' (*Works*, i, 465).

60. *Ibid.*, i, 338.

61. *Ibid.*, i, 364, 371-3.

62. *Ibid.*, i, 372.

63. *Ibid.*, i, 364.

64. *Ibid.*, i, 423.

65. *Ibid.*, i, 439-40.

66. Arthur H. Williamson, *Scottish National Consciousness in the Age of James VI: The Apocalypse, the Union and the Shaping of Scotland's Public Culture* (Edinburgh, 1979), 13-16; see also the same author's 'Scotland, Antichrist and the Invention of Great Britain', in *New Perspectives*, edd. Dwyer, Mason and Murdoch, 34-58.

67. Knox, *Works*, ii, 25.

68. Of course, the Congregation could not afford to be explicit, even in private correspondence, about their ultimate intentions vis-à-vis the Stewarts, and it may be that they would have been content simply to accept Mary's *de jure* sovereignty so long as

she remained in France and left them with *de facto* control of affairs in Scotland. It seems unlikely, however, that they would have wholly ignored the possibility of deposing Mary in the interests of a more rapid settlement of their relations with England. Their desire both for amity with England and a long-term dynastic union is amply documented in Book III of Knox's *History* (*Works*, ii, lff) and in the Congregation's correspondence with England as collected by Knox's editor (*ibid.*, vi, llff). Some of this material is discussed by Arthur Williamson (see note 66 above).

69. *Ibid.*, i, 364, 422-3.

70. *Ibid.*, i, 427.

71. On Cecil's consideration of the English claim to superiority, see Read, *Secretary Cecil and Queen Elizabeth*, 150-1. The claim had been pressed hard by Henry VIII, most notably in *A Declaratioun, Conteyning the Iust Causes and Consyderatiouns of this present warre with the Scottis, wherein alsoo appereth the trew and right title, that the kinges most royall maiesty hath to the soverayntie of Scotland* [1542], reprinted as an appendix to *The Complaynt of Scotlande*, ed. J. A. H. Murray (Early English Text Society, 1872), 191-206.

72. The instructions were passed on to the Congregation by Sir Ralph Sadler and are printed in *The State Papers and Letters of Sir Ralph Sadler*, ed. A. Clifford (Edinburgh, 1809), i, 566-73. That they followed them to the letter is evident from the instructions the Congregation gave to Maitland of Lethington before he left Scotland to continue the negotiations at the English court (see *ibid.*, i, 604-8).

73. *Ibid.*, i, 713-4.

74. *CSP Scot.*, i, no. 712 (see also *ibid.*, i, nos. 755, 806, 831).

75. Knox, *Works*, ii, 51; cf. *CSP Scot.*, i, nos. 702, 786.

76. An abridged version of the treaty is printed in *A Source Book of Scottish History*, edd. W. C. Dickinson, G. Donaldson and I. A. Milne (London & Edinburgh, 1952-4), ii, 171-5.

77. For the full text of the band, see Knox, *Works*, ii, 61-3.

78. *Ibid.*, ii, 61.

79. For a similar view, see Donaldson, *Scotland: James V-James VII*, 101-2.

80. 'Off the Quenis Arryvale in Scotland', ll. 9-16, printed in *The Maitland Folio Manuscript*, ed. W. A. Craigie (Scottish Text Society, 1919), 32-4.

81. For Knox's characteristic comments on Mary's arrival in Scotland, see *Works*, ii, 268-9. A more objective contemporary assessment of the likely impact of the Queen's homecoming is provided by Maitland of Lethington in a letter to Cecil of August 1561. Acknowledging the considerable support Mary would win amongst both Catholics and Protestants, he went on to emphasise the dangers to the Congregation if she returned and the dangers to the country if she did not: 'I assure you this whole Realm is in a miserable case. If the Queen our Sovereign come shortly home, the dangers be evident and many; and if she shall not come, it is not without great peril; yea, what is not to be feared in a Realm lacking lawful government?' The whole letter is of interest and is printed in Robert Keith, *History of the Affairs of Church and State in Scotland* (Edinburgh, 1844-50), iii, 211-6.

82. The point at which Mary herself began to antagonise the political community falls outside the scope of this essay, while the extent to which the debate surrounding the later years of her short reign was conducted in commonweal discourse must await future research. Certainly, however, the widespread support she continued to command in the years immediately following her deposition indicates that the conservatism apparent in 1559 was still a potent force in 1567.

83. Cowan, *Regional Aspects*, 26-36; Lynch, *Edinburgh and the Reformation*, esp. Chs. 5 and 6.

84. Wormald, *Court, Kirk and Community*, 117-21.

85. The later writings of Sir David Lindsay indicate both the manner in which commonweal discourse could be protestantised and the limitations imposed by the absence of a 'godly prince'. In his *Dialog betuix Experience and ane Courteour*, for example, he looked forward to the 'gude reformatione' which 'ane faithful prudent king' might inaugurate, but added resignedly: 'Tyll that kyng cum we mon tak paciens' (see Lindsay, *Works*, i, 276).

7

Royal and lay patronage in the Jacobean kirk, 1572-1600

James Kirk

THE ancient system of ecclesiastical patronage survived the Reformation intact despite the intention of reformers to subvert the old financial structure of benefices and to extinguish the rights of patrons in favour of the election, with congregational consent, of ministers to parish churches. As reformers in 1560 saw no sound reason to modify their ambitious plans, far less to press, for the integration of the benefices of the old church within the new structure of the reformed church as it took shape, a curious duality prevailed in the years immediately after 1560. Thus Protestant ministers were elected to parochial charges but not to the benefices attached which, in any event, were already occupied and unavailable, except in instances where the existing benefice holders happened to conform to the new regime and undertook service in the kirk.[1]

At the same time, during Mary's reign, the traditional machinery for presentation, followed by episcopal collation and finally institution continued to operate in the admission to benefices of candidates who need not undertake active service of any kind but who were nonetheless recipients of a legal title permitting them to enjoy the fruits of their benefices.[2] Not only did clergy of the old order continue after the Reformation to administer this machinery for conveying a legal title to benefices, but, in their capacity as patrons, they were also responsible for exercising an extensive patronage in appointments to parochial benefices. After all, only 148 out of 1,028 parishes remained unappropriated at the Reformation, so that the patronage of a majority of parsonages and vicarages had come to be engrossed by the appropriating institutions — by the religious houses, cathedrals, collegiate kirks, university colleges and independent hospitals. Even the patronage of the 148 unattached parishes was not entirely in the possession of laymen. At least 28 independent parsonages lay within episcopal patronage; the patronage of three further unappropriated parsonages belonged to religious houses; and of the remainder a proportion pertained to the crown, particularly after the annexation of the lordship of the Isles; all of which amply illustrates how little scope existed before 1560 for laymen to influence parochial appointments by presenting candidates of their own choice.[3]

The inability of the reformed church after 1560 to persuade successive governments to accept its plans for dissolving the structure of benefices, for eliminating patronage and for reallocating ecclesiastical finances on a radically different basis forced the kirk not to abandon its ultimate objectives but to temporise, first, by obtaining from the crown in 1562 a share in the thirds of revenues of the benefices, and then by accepting Mary's offer in 1566 that ministers should succeed to the lesser benefices, as they fell vacant. Thereafter, with the accession of James VI, the traditional machinery for episcopal collation was transferred by act of parliament in 1567 not to any of the conforming bishops as such (from whose role in the kirk statutory recognition was evidently withheld) but to the superintendents and 'utheris havand commissioun of the Kirk'.[4] The way was therefore open for ministers to gain access to the lesser benefices, as they became vacant.

Not only was the Catholic church finally excluded from administering the traditional ecclesiastical machinery in presentations to parochial benefices, but, as patrons of appropriated churches, prelates and others found their rights and powers undermined by the inroads of the crown, which increasingly advanced and extended its claims to a say in the disposal of benefices in ecclesiastical patronage. Even before 1560, the crown had asserted its control over some monastic patronage by making presentations to a number of appropriated churches. It is clear that out of some 120 presentations made by the crown in the decade preceding 1560, more than 15 presentations pertained to churches annexed to monasteries and whose patronage lay with the religious communities.[5] In each case, the presentation was made by the crown during an episcopal vacancy, which may or may not have been coincidental, and further investigation is required to establish whether, at that point, the crown continued merely to claim its traditional right to present *sede vacante* to benefices of which the bishop himself was patron or whether it sought to extend its powers during episcopal vacancies to include all benefices in ecclesiastical, and not just episcopal, patronage.

During Mary's personal rule, the crown, unlike some other patrons,[6] made few presentations to parochial benefices after October 1561, preferring instead to bestow the benefices by simple gift, thus obviating the need for ecclesiastical collation.[7] Yet not only did Mary now claim to have at her disposal the common kirks of cathedrals held by canons and chaplains,[8] she also proceeded to bestow by simple gift the vicarages of Inverkip, annexed to Paisley abbey, and Bourtie, belonging to St. Andrews priory.[9] In each case, the action seemed to threaten the existing commendator's rights of patronage. Though imprisoned by Mary in 1563 for saying mass, John Hamilton, the archbishop of St. Andrews and commendator of Paisley, had not then been forfeited and denounced as a rebel. Again, despite his escheat in 1565 for his part in the Chaseabout Raid, Lord James Stewart, the Earl of Moray and commendator of St. Andrews priory, had nonetheless received a remission in March 1566 and was thus restored in the month preceding Mary's grant of Bourtie in April 1566.[10] Why, indeed, the crown should have proceeded so is less than clear, for there was not even the slender pretext of a vacancy existing in either the bishopric of Glasgow or Aberdeen, in whose dioceses the respective benefices lay, where the nonconformist bishops — James Betoun of Glasgow (though absent in France) and William Gordon of Aberdeen — still retained effective title to the temporalities of their sees.[11] The assumption of such increased powers by the crown is again apparent in Mary's claim, advanced in 1562, that 'the haill patronage of the kirk landis and benefices pertening to the abbacie of Haliruidhous pertenit and pertenis to hir hienes as patrimonye of hir croune', regardless, or so it would seem, of the rights of the existing commendator, her half brother, Robert Stewart.[12] Even so, when it came to appointing titulars to the bishoprics, Mary explicitly recognised in her grants the right of candidates, so promoted, to dispose of vacant benefices in episcopal patronage.[13]

After the accession of James VI, however, the crown assumed greater, more comprehensive powers over monastic and episcopal property. Following Mary's precedent in making direct appointments to the prelacies, the crown retained its right to promote its own candidates to abbacies and bishoprics, and to enjoy the fruits of the emporalities during vacancies, but it also laid claim to the patronage of churches formerly in the possession of prelates.[14] Such an unprecedented control of monastic and episcopal patronage, which the crown assumed during the first decade of the new reign, cannot be traced to any surviving legislation, but it would not have been hard to justify the change on the purely practical ground that it would have been less than prudent for the new Protestant regime to permit prelates, many of whom remained suspect in religion, a continued say in selecting and presenting to so many parochial benefices candidates who were now expected to serve in the reformed church.

At the same time, while benefiting from the arrangement which permitted its ministers access to the lesser benefices, the reformed church continued its unrelenting campaign for the dissolution of the prelacies. Such a policy had been reiterated by the general assembly in December 1567, was acknowledged in July 1569, and, again, was defended by Superintendent Erskine of Dun in November 1571.[15] All this helps to illustrate how the kirk's ideals of 1560 were by no means to be lightly cast aside, even after the accession of a 'godly prince'. Evidently, an acceptance of financial endowment from the parochial benefices still brought no nearer the integration of the prelacies within the structure of the reformed church.

When King James' government forfeited the leading papalist and Marian bishops and began in 1571 to fill several of the vacant bishoprics with its own nominees without consulting the church (as it was legally entitled to do, especially so since the kirk had never claimed a say in such appointments), a storm of protest ensued, for the government had made no pretence of its real reason for filling the sees. Its main aim was not simply to secure the service of bishops in the reformed church or even to provide the church with a new, and additional, source of finance, but to allow leading supporters of the king's party access to episcopal temporalities on a lavish scale. This was amply recognised by contemporary opinion; hence the barons' criticism in 1571 that the government's action was corrupt and unjust on the grounds that:

> what can be a more readie way to banishe Christ Jesus from us and our posteritie than to famishe the ministers present, and tyrannicallie so to impyre above the poore flocke that the kirk sall be compelled to admitt dumbe dogges to the office, dignitie and rents appointed for sustentatioun of preaching pastors, and for other godlie uses?

In attacking 'suche a corruptioun begunne, and appearing to proceed', the petitioners complained to the Regent Lennox that 'erles and lords become bishops and abbots, gentlemen, courteours' babes, and persons unable to guide themselves, are promoted by you to suche benefices as require learned preachers. When such enormiteis are fostered, we say, what face of a kirk sall we look for ere it be long within this realme?' And they concluded their appeal on a constitutional note by threatening to decline their continued service to the crown, 'for we are not ignorant of the mutuall contract that God hath placed betwixt the supreme power and the subjects'.[16] Another contemporary commentator explained, no less vigorously, how 'everie erle lord and barroun tuik up all the landis abbasies bischopries to thame sellffis quhilk sould have sustenit the puir peopill'; and even the superintendent of Fife took action by threatening the titular archbishop of St. Andrews with excommunication if he dared to vote in name of the kirk in parliament.[17] Amid the furore caused by the government's unilateral appointments, Erskine of Dun added his protest.

In his letter, in November 1571, to the Earl of Mar, who had succeeded Lennox as Regent, Erskine argued that all benefices possessing tithes had a spiritual office annexed which belonged to the kirk, whose superintendents had a scriptural duty to examine all candidates promoted; and he warned that 'a greater offence or contempt of God and his kirk can no prince doe, than to sett up by his authoritie men in spirituall offices, as to creat bishops and pastors of the kirk; for so to doe, is to conclude no kirk of God to be; for the kirk can not be, without it have its owne proper jurisdictioun and libertie'. The existing superintendents, therefore, must withstand the intruded bishops who 'have no office nor jurisdictioun in the kirk of God'; and 'that great misorder used in Stirline at the last parliament, in creating bishops, placing them and giving them vote in parliament as bishops, in despite of the kirk and high contempt of God' must be reformed without delay, 'for if that misordered creation of bishops be not reformed, the kirk will first compleane unto God, and also unto all their brethrein, members of the kirk within this realme, and to all reformed kirks within Europe'. Such resolution, however, was tempered by a recognition that if the church's programme for 'dismembring (as they call it) of great benefices' could not be immediately secured 'in respect of this confused troublous time', then a compromise, acceptable to crown and kirk, might be achieved, at least 'whill further order may be tane'. This compromise, it was expected, would confirm 'the king or others in their patronages' and recognise 'their priviledges of presentatioun according to the lawes', on condition that 'the examinatioun and admissioun perteane onlie to the kirk, of all benefices having cure of soules'. In reply, the Regent showed himself ready to achieve an agreement 'by all possible meanes for quietting of suche things as were in controversie' and especially 'to procure the reforming of things disordered in all sorts, als farre as may be, reteaning the priviledge of the king, crown and patronage'.[18]

The compromise finally effected at the Convention of Leith in January 1571/2 identified the bishoprics with the work of the reformed church. Yet such a solution, as circumstances show, was achieved by government and church almost in spite of their policies and intentions. It was far from being the inevitable sequel to any great strategy by the government, far less the church, for merging the whole financial structure of benefices with the machinery of the reformed church. The settlement, so achieved at Leith, was certainly a solution which neither side had predicted: it required the government to abandon its plans to utilise the bishoprics simply as an extension of its system of political patronage and to recognise that candidates so promoted should undergo examination by the church and should exercise the spiritual office attached to the benefice; and the scheme, in turn, obliged the church to place in abeyance its plans for subverting the bishoprics and to acknowledge the utility in having placed at its disposal the financial and administrative structure of the bishoprics until a more comprehensive solution acceptable to the crown, parliament and church was devised when the king came of age.

In what was reported to be 'a quiet conference' at Leith, a financial settlement was accordingly negotiated by no more than eight commissioners on either side from the government and church. Since the estates had deferred discussion on the dissolution of the prelacies until such time as the king came of age, it became clear that any temporary solution on ecclesiastical endowment could be achieved only within the existing financial structure of benefices. From the outset, the Regent Mar had recognised that the settlement, so devised, should operate until 'his Highness perfect age; or while the same be altered and abolished be the three Estates in Parliament', and the general assembly, in turn, regarded the financial compromise devised at Leith not as a comprehensive and lasting settlement on ecclesiastical endowment, but as a temporary expedient to 'be only receivit as ane interim, untill farder and more perfyte ordour be obtainit at the handis of the Kings Majesties Regent and Nobilitie'.[19] Evidently, the church was not even prepared to adhere to the Leith settlement until the king's majority, for the expectation now was that agreement on the 'more perfyte ordour', which the assembly demanded, would be achieved rather more speedily after further negotiations with the new Regent, the Earl of Morton, who, as chancellor, had been one of the main architects of the Leith agreement.

Though subjected to severe criticism almost before it had begun to operate, the concordat of Leith was by no means unstatesmanlike. It offered a practical and practicable solution to the vexed question of the church's endowment, and it appeared to reconcile the needs of the church with the interests of crown and nobility. 'In consideratioun of the present state', it was decided not to alter the diocesan structure which existed 'befoir the reformation of religioun; at leist, to the Kingis Majesties majoritie, or consent of Parliament'. As vacancies arose, qualified candidates, of at least thirty years of age, were to be nominated by the crown within a year and a day, and thereafter examined by 'a certane assembly or cheptoure of learnit ministeris', who had power to elect or reject the candidates presented. The bishops, so elected, were to be subject to the general assembly in spiritual matters as they were to the crown in temporal affairs; they were to enjoy no greater jurisdiction in the church than that exercised by the superintendents, until 'the same be agreit upoun'; and they were to act with 'the advise of the best learnit of the Cheptour' in admitting candidates to the ministry.

This, then, was the machinery now provided so that the church might gain proper access to the finances of the bishoprics. But the settlement also extended to the abbacies and priories, from whose finances (other than the thirds) the church had been largely excluded. It was agreed that where vacancies occurred no further disposition of monastic property should be made until consideration was given to separating the teinds from the lands and rents of the appropriated churches, so that sufficient stipends might be allocated to the ministers serving at the annexed churches. Thereafter, suitable candidates promoted by the crown, to enjoy 'the remanent proffite and title of the benefice', were to represent the abbatial element, and sit with the bishops in parliament. On the extinction of the old monastic chapters, the ministers who served the annexed churches were to act in a capitular capacity in such matters as the disposition of monastic property; but, in the main, the revenues of the religious houses were not allocated to finance the work of the church, but were assigned, instead, to sustain senators of the college of justice and others employed in royal service who were considered eligible by the ordinary for promotion by the crown as titular abbots or commendators. It was certainly not envisaged that the title and office of abbot should be given to ministers. Such a step was evidently considered to be inappropriate or even improper. At any rate, it would obviously not have been easy, so shortly after the Reformation, to permit the appearance within the church of abbots and priors, whose suppression the reformers so strenuously had demanded in 1560. Besides, there was not even the slender prospect anyway that the crown and nobles, already in effective control of monastic revenues, would be persuaded to surrender their claims to the benefit of the church. If the church looked like acquiring at least a share of episcopal revenues, the crown and nobility seemed intent on maintaining their grip on monastic temporalities.

In the disposal of benefices having the cure of souls, which were attached to prelacies, the principle applied was that all such livings should be bestowed only on candidates for the ministry, of at least twenty-three years of age, who had been examined and found qualified by a bishop or superintendent 'of the true reformit Kirk'. Smaller vicarages, under £40 in yearly rental, were to be assigned not to trained ministers but to readers; and chaplainries were allocated to support bursars at the schools and universities. Common kirks attached to cathedrals were to be given to ministers as benefices; and prebends belonging to cathedrals and collegiate kirks were to be filled only after proper provision had been made for stipends by distinguishing the spirituality from the temporality. Even the poor were not ignored, for a tenth of the teinds was to be set aside for their needs. All in all, however, by identifying the old financial structure with the work of the new church, the negotiators at Leith provided the machinery whereby most of the revenues, with the exception of the monastic temporalities, could be inherited by the kirk; and alongside this machinery for endowment stood the ancient system of patronage, which, though modified by the persistent inroads of the crown, was still retained in its entirety.[20]

Insofar as a settlement was achieved, time was obviously necessary before the machinery provided could produce the expected results. At the same time, however, criticism was voiced in the assembly in August 1572 of certain aspects of the agreement which were 'found slanderous and offensive to the ears of many of the brethren, appeirand to sound to papistrie'. Nor was this all. Concern over further dynastic appointments to sees, sometimes of an un-reformed variety, over the failure of chapters to prevent scandalous promotions or to curb further dilapidation of episcopal revenues through nobles milking the bishoprics, and over the inability of bishops on their own admission adequately to administer their dioceses led the assembly by 1575 to consider the question 'whither if the Bischops, as they are now in the Kirk of Scotland, hes thair function of the word of God or not, or if the Chapiter appointit for creating of them aucht to be tollerated in this reformed Kirk'.[21] In any event, popular opinion, somewhat harshly, had already stigmatised the new bishops in 1572 as 'the lordis counterfett bischopis and nocht men of the kirk of God nor guid religioun';[22] and by 1576 the assembly itself had resolved to eliminate bishops, as such, from ecclesiastical administration.[23] The assembly's dissatisfaction with the Leith settlement was said to be such that even the Regent was obliged to recognise that the church ought to devise an alternative solution if it were not prepared to stand by the concordat of 1572.[24] This was done in the Second Book of Discipline of 1578 which reasserted the First Book of Discipline's intention of dissolving the benefices and of abolishing patronage.[25] This programme, after all, had never fully been abandoned by the church; and it wholly accorded with John Knox's farewell advice to the church: before his death in 1572 Knox had urged the replacement of the Leith episcopacy by the system devised in 1560, and he was prepared only to acquiesce in further appointments to benefices in the belief that the assembly's policy was to regard the Leith settlement as a temporary expedient pending its supersession by a more perfect order.[26]

Nonetheless, the operation of the Leith arrangements had at least enabled new appointments to be made with little delay to the sees of St. Andrews, Glasgow, Dunkeld, the Isles, Dunblane, Moray, Ross and ultimately, in 1577, to Aberdeen, where vacancies had arisen either through the forfeiture or death of the previous incumbents. In Galloway, it seems to have been impossible to extinguish the rights and claims of the family of Alexander Gordon; while in Orkney there was no serious intention of dispossessing Adam Bothwell from the title or Lord Robert Stewart from the property of the bishopric. Argyll continued to be held by the ineffective James Hamilton till his death in 1580; and in Ross, Alexander Hepburn, who died in 1578, had no immediate successor until the provision of David Lindsay in 1600. Among the existing bishops who continued to act, Robert Stewart in Caithness, though ageing, seems to have been fairly respectable; and, in 1575, Alexander Campbell, who had received a gift of Brechin from Mary in 1566, had finally to be instructed in the work of a bishop by superintendent Erskine of Dun.[27]

Some of the bishops experienced great difficulty in obtaining, and then retaining, possession of their property and revenues. Ross was perhaps the worst example. There, the chancellor discovered by 1573 that one of the Mackenzies of Kintail had not only taken up residence in the steeple at the Chanonry, 'quhilk now is becum ane filthie sty and den of thevis', but had 'maisterfully reft' the tenants of the whole fruits of the benefice, and had suppressed the preaching of the Word. By 1579, matters had scarcely improved, for the bishop's widow recalled how Colin Mackenzie had denied even 'a plaid or blankat' to protect her 'bairnis fra cauld', and how he had prevented the bishop from obtaining fuel, 'meit, drink or lugeing' by 'usand sic inhumane and cruell dealing aganis him that for displesour thairof he fell seik and nevir recoverit quhill he depairtit this life'. Nor could Lord Methven, who had received the temporality of the vacant bishopric, obtain peaceful possession of his gift. One of the bishop of Moray's houses was robbed in December 1573; the bishop of the Isles had some of his rents withheld by the McLeans and others; and James Boyd, the archbishop of Glasgow, had his troubles as well, when he found that his kinsman, Robert Boyd of Badinheath, who was earlier in receipt of a pension from the vacant archbishopric, had begun to demolish the archbishop's fortalice at Lochwood.[28]

Even when they gained effective access to their revenues, the bishops, as a whole, lost little time in rewarding kinsmen, friends and nobles with local interests by granting them feus, tacks and pensions on a generous scale. In Glasgow, where Porterfield's candidature for the archbishopric had been superseded in 1573 by that of James Boyd, the nephew of Lord Boyd, there was substance in the claim that the new bishop had been 'inducit be his Cheiff to tak the bischoprie, the gift wharof the said Lord Boid, being a grait counsallour to the Regent, haid purchassit for his commoditie'.[29] Certainly, the Regent Morton and the Boyds were prominent among the recipients of grants from the bishopric.[30] As Regent, Morton also advanced fellow Douglases to the sees of St. Andrews and Moray; and when the St. Andrews see again fell vacant, the Regent's former chaplain, Patrick Adamson, was appointed as successor, despite earlier opposition from the electoral chapter.[31] Once installed, Adamson showed his gratitude to the Regent by assigning pensions from the fruits of the bishopric to Morton's retainers and servitors,[32] while in the north, at least one royal confirmation survives of a charter granted by George Douglas, natural son of the Earl of Angus, as bishop of Moray to yet another Douglas.[33]

The Earl of Argyll evidently had an interest in the appointment to Dunkeld of James Paton, whom the assembly suspected of having made a simoniacal pact with Argyll. The earl and other Campbells, at any rate, were prominent beneficiaries of Paton's financial transactions and, by 1576, the assembly had dismissed Paton from office for dilapidating the resources of his see.[34] Successive earls of Argyll were influential in securing the appointment of Campbells, first, to the sees of Brechin and the Isles, and, then, to Argyll, with the death in 1580 of James Hamilton, the previous bishop, who had rewarded both the Earl of Argyll and at least one fellow Hamilton from the fruits of the bishopric of Argyll.[35] All the Campbells, so promoted, were active in making grants of episcopal property, frequently to other Campbells including the Argylls; and Brechin showed particular generosity to the 5th earl and his servitors.[36] The Earl of Caithness was among the recipients of pensions from Robert Stewart, as bishop of Caithness, and Gordon of Lochinvar and Laurence Gordon were two of the beneficiaries of the dynasty of Gordons appointed to the bishopric of Galloway.[37] In Orkney, Adam Bothwell gained a not undeserved reputation as a dilapidator; he exchanged the fruits of the bishopric for the commend of Holyrood in 1568; and he was charged with simony, though not so convicted, by the assembly in 1570.[38] A succession of Grahams replaced the former dynasty of Chisholms in Dunblane, where the family of the Earls of Montrose, who already had a financial interest in the bishopric, secured the appointment of their own kinsmen — first Andrew and then George Graham — as bishops.[39] The smaller number of charters granted by Andrew Graham is no indication that he intended to behave as a model bishop. The truth is he set the entire lands of the bishopric in feu to one individual — the Earl of Montrose — whereby (so the petitioners complained to parliament in 1578) 'ane thousand of our soverane Lordis commonis and pure people wilbe put to uter heirschip and extreme beggartie . . . quhen as sa grite rowmes quhairupon so mony ar sustenit salbe reducit in the handis of ane particular man'. When later 'accusit for wasting and delapidatioun of the patrimony of the kirk and setting of takis thairof againis the actis of the generall assemblie', the bold bishop 'desyrit to knaw quhat was dilapidatioun of the patrimony' and was promptly reminded 'that setting of fewis or takis of landis or teindis with diminutioun of the auld dewatty, setting of victuell for small pricis of silvir, geving of pentionis, namelie, to unqualefiet personis, and siclyk, was delapidatioun'. But there were parties besides the courts of the church who continued to complain of Graham's financial transactions. The spokesman for the 'possessuris and tennentis of the kirk landis of the bischoprik' protested in 1582 that Graham had:[40]

K

nocht onelie to the grit hurt, damnage and skayth of his successuris bot alswa to
the extreim hurt of us, possessuris and tennentis of the saidis kirk landis, sauld,
delapidat and put away the haill leving of the said bischoprie, or at the lest ane
gret part thairof in gret menis handis . . .

In Aberdeen, David Cunningham, the former dean of faculty at Glasgow
University, had little opportunity to offer financial rewards. His Catholic
predecessor, William Gordon, had already exhausted the patrimony of the
bishopric, effected by means of the 'lait conventioun' concluded between the
bishop and Queen Mary whereby 'the haill thrids of the said bischoprik wes
disponit in tak and assedatioun' to Gordon for life, in return for the payment
of 1,000 merks. The outcome was that 'the haill patrimony' had become:

> delapidat and exhausit . . ., the temporall landis and teindis gevin in fewis and
> assedationis, the haill victuallis and customes convertit in small pryces of silver
> and the silver maillis consumet by mony and grit pensionis, quhilk prodigall dis-
> positioun hes bene ratefeit and conservit be his hienes said umquhile moder in hir
> majoritie, be his gracis regentis, and his majesties self, quhairby the said
> bischoprik in thrid and twa pairt was altogedder waistit and dilapidat befoir the
> successioun and entres of the said Mr David thairto . . .

Cunningham therefore found that he had merely gained 'naikit titill and
enteres to the propertie', which yielded only £400 a year; yet he was still
obliged to pay 800 merks 'in satisfactioun of his thriddis, quhilk soume
exceidis far the rait of his present patrimony'.[41] There were difficulties, too, at
Glasgow, where Robert Montgomery was promoted to the see in 1581 by an
arrangement which gave the Duke of Lennox a lease of the bishopric for £1,000
a year, though there was still opportunity for Montgomeries, and others, to
benefit from episcopal gifts.[42]

Any expectation that the church might sufficiently augment its depleted
resources by operating the Leith agreement was soon to be disappointed. The
continued milking of the bishoprics by noble families had merely led to a
diminution in the revenues available for the work of the church. As it was, the
resources of the bishoprics at the time of the Reformation (it has been
estimated) ranged from a mere £1,300 in annual returns for Caithness, £1,350
for Orkney, £1,400 for Galloway, £1,500 for Dunblane, £1,800 for Brechin and
up to £6,500 for St. Andrews.[43] Episcopal resources were not inexhaustible;
the property was subject to taxation; and the financial dealings of the Leith
bishops, along with the heritage of earlier gifts from episcopal property,
ensured that the church received far less than its fair share of finance. All this
goes far towards explaining the assembly's hostile reaction to the operation of
the Leith arrangements and its determination to replace the Leith episcopacy
by a 'more perfyte ordour'.

The arrangements devised at Leith, however, were also applicable to the
abbacies; but even if the proposals had been consistently applied, it would
have taken a generation or so to clear out the existing commendators over
whose appointment there had been no ecclesiastical control whatsoever.

Besides, the retention of the monastic dignities (the offices of abbot and prior) as legal and financial entities spelt an end, in the foreseeable future at least, to the prospect of dissolving the prelacies, as the assembly had argued. This, in turn, was fatal to the likelihood of satisfactory stipends being assigned to the ministers of the appropriated churches, until at least such time as abbacies fell vacant; and it was contrary to the claim that the teinds were the proper patrimony of the kirk. When a vacancy in an abbacy did occur, however, the proposals at Leith did at least provide for an assessment of 'quhat portioun of the rentis consistis in kirkis and teinds, and quhat portioun in temporall landes', so that ministers serving at the annexed churches might be 'sustenit of the fruits belanging to the same kirkis, gif it be possible, be speciall assignatioun of samekle yeirlie stipend as salbe found reasonable', to be decided by the bishop or superintendent of the diocese and privy councillors deputed to that effect. Nor were the provisions for the appointment to abbacies of men of ability and repute entirely inoperative. Only 'well learnit and qualifeit' candidates examined and approved by the bishop of the province, it had been established in 1572, should be promoted to the abbacies, for they were expected to undertake service in the commonwealth and to vote as part of the ecclesiastical estate in parliament. Recognition of the church's newly acquired right to examine the crown's nominees to abbacies is apparent, not least, in the terms of the gift of Beauly to John Fraser in January 1572/3, which specified that Fraser, found sufficiently qualified by the ordinary, was to receive institution from the superintendent (or commissioner) of Ross. This went further than the earlier gift to Henry Kinneir *in expectationem* of the abbacy of Balmerino in 1569 which had merely recognised that Kinneir was 'sufficientlie qualifeit in lettiris, science and gude behaviour' to hold the office, but significantly enough the charter which finally secured for Kinneir effective possession in 1574 acknowledged the archbishop's testimony of Kinneir's suitability and directed the archbishop to give him institution. Similarly, the gift to Alexander Forbes of the priory of Balmerino in August 1574 recognised Forbes' academic qualifications and his suitability for the post, attested by the commissioner of the diocese of Aberdeen, to whom a mandate was directed to give him institution.[44]

At a convention of estates, however, which met on 5 March 1574/5, the decision was taken that no further dispositions of vacant abbacies, priories or nunneries should be made by the crown until such time as a constitution for the church had been determined and established, not later than Easter 1576. The enactment evidently came too late to prevent the gift of Eccles to James Hume from passing the privy seal on 26 March 1576; but when appointments resumed, the whole trend was for the crown to disregard the provisions reached at Leith for the promotion of suitably qualified candidates duly examined by the church. There was certainly no hint in the preferment to Pluscarden of James Douglas, the Regent's illegitimate son, that he had undergone examination by the church; and Thomas Fraser, who was 'nocht of perfyte age', was promoted to Beauly while still a minor in November 1579, though his tenure was short-lived, and in February 1580/1 the priory was gifted to Adam Cuming.[45]

If the principles of 1572, applicable to the abbacies, had evidently fallen into desuetude, the machinery which once more operated looked like safeguarding the proprietary rights established by leading noble families over the disposal of monastic property. The proposals of 1572, intent as they were on promoting men of ability and repute, threatened to undermine the quasi-hereditary rights enjoyed by successive lay commendators of a particular noble family, for the intention had evidently been to make service and ability, rather than birth, the criteria for advancement to the abbacies. That a principle of heredity continued to operate in the control of monastic property well after the Reformation is all too evident in the succession of Hamiltons at Paisley and at Arbroath, though with interruptions through forfeiture, in the succession of Leslies at Lindores, of Campbells at Iona and Ardchattan, Colvilles at Culross, Keiths at Deer, Kers at Newbattle, the Ruthvens at Scone, Frasers at Beauly, and Erskines at Cambuskenneth, Dryburgh and Inchmahome. The Stewarts also came to be well entrenched in St. Andrews, Pittenweem, Inchcolm and Arbroath, and, for a spell, at Crossraguel and Whithorn. This being so, the dilapidation of monastic property continued unabated on a scale which no doubt surpassed even that of the bishoprics, for the checks on alienation were purely minimal; and there was substance in the Second Book of Discipline's complaint in 1578 that the continued existence of conventual chapters 'servis for nathing now bot to set fewis and takis (gif ony thing be left) of kirk landis and teindis in hurt and prejudice thairof, as daylie experience teached'. The assembly, which registered the Second Book of Discipline among its acts in April 1581, also took the step of summoning all commendators suspected of 'devoreing the patrimonie . . . and daylie diminisching the rents of thair benefices', and it reiterated the old claim that the 'Prelacies be dissolvit'.[46]

The evident failure to secure satisfactory stipends for ministers of the annexed churches, even on the appointment of new commendators, led to parliament's intervention in November 1581. All promotions to prelacies were declared to be null, unless provision were made for ministers' stipends; but in spite of the act, the assembly continued to lament in 1583 that 'abbacies are disponed, without any provisioun made for the Ministers serving in the kirks annexed therto, directlie against the act of Parliament'. The abbacy of Arbroath granted to Esmé Stewart, Duke of Lennox (and subsequently gifted to Ludovic Stewart in July 1583) was cited by the assembly as one conspicuous example where no provision had been made for ministers' stipends. Nor was this all. Criticism was also voiced at how 'spirituall livings are givin to bairnes and translatit in temporal lordschips'. Holyrood had been gifted to the abbot's 'yong sone', John Bothwell, in February 1581/2; Newbattle had been bestowed on the existing commendator's son, under an arrangement whereby Mark Ker had been presented to the abbacy during his father's lifetime; and Scone had been erected into a temporal or secular lordship in favour of William, Lord Ruthven, the Earl of Gowrie, in October 1581.[47]

A temporary dislocation in the landholding pattern which had permitted the abbacies virtually to remain the preserves of particular noble houses is apparent with the onset of the Arran regime's conservative reaction against the ultra-protestant policies pursued by the preceding regime of the Ruthven lords, who, by 1584, had fled for safety to England, along with the leading presbyterian ministers.[48] As was to be expected in the circumstances, Gowrie lost Scone with his forfeiture in 1584, though the property was later restored to the family, after the collapse of Arran's rule, in 1586.[49] The ultra-protestant Erskines temporarily lost Cambuskenneth, Dryburgh and Inchmahome: Cambuskenneth was gifted in August 1584 to the Master of Livingston, an opponent of the Ruthven raiders; Inchmahome, in the same month, went to Henry Stewart, the son of Lord Doun, a supporter of Arran; and Dryburgh was granted at the same time to William Stewart of Caverstoun.[50] The Pitcairns were dislodged from Dunfermline in favour of the Master of Gray, a former Marian and promoter of the 'Association' (a scheme of joint rule by James and his mother), who became commendator in September 1585, though his tenure was indeed brief and by May 1587 the Earl of Huntly had secured the property. Kilwinning, somewhat surprisingly, was retained by the Cunninghams: James Cunningham obtained a gift of the abbacy in March 1584/5 in succession to Alexander Cunningham, despite Glencairn's support for the Ruthven raid in August 1582; but there was no surprise in the confirmation in October 1585 of Arran's own rights to the commend of St. Andrews priory, after the resignation of the Earl of March.[51]

The Arran regime (like preceding and, indeed, succeeding administrations) did little to impede the complete secularisation of monastic property, which looked like being achieved either by direct annexation to the crown or by the erection of this not inconsiderable property into heritable, temporal lordships. Either solution, however, completely disregarded any claim for the restitution of this property as patrimony of the church. Scone may have been one of the earliest erections of abbatial property into secular lordships, but others soon followed. By July 1587, Newbattle, Deer and Paisley were all converted into hereditary lordships in favour of the existing commendators, namely, Mark Ker, Claud Hamilton and Robert Keith; and in each case firm provision was made for the ministry either by specifying the stipends or by reserving parochial teinds for the support of the ministry.[52]

July 1587 was also the month in which the act of annexation was approved by parliament. Insofar as it contributed to the eclipse of episcopacy by appropriating to the crown the temporalities of benefices, the act was clearly a victory for the presbyterians, who were once more in the ascendancy, but it by no means satisfied presbyterian principles, which required nothing less than a comprehensive restitution of ecclesiastical property. Following the precedent established by James II's annexation of certain lands in 1455, and on the understanding that the crown had been 'greitly hurte' by the dispositions 'of auld to abbayis, Monasteries and utheris personis of the clergy', parliament sanctioned the annexation to the crown of the ecclesiastical temporalities with the exception of certain specified ecclesiastical properties already erected into temporal lordships: the earldoms of Gowrie, the lordship of Deer or Altrie, the baronies of Newbattle, Broughton and Kerse, the burgh of Canongate and part of Leith, the barony of Whitekirk, formerly belonging to Holyrood, the lordship of Musselburgh, hitherto pertaining to Dunfermline, and the temporalities of Paisley, Pluscarden, Coldingham, Kelso and Lesmahagow, as well as certain lands of North Berwick priory, were all exempted from the terms of the act; another category of exemptions favoured John Hamilton, commendator of Arbroath, John Bothwell, commendator of Holyrood, and Robert Douglas, provost of Lincluden, who were expressly confirmed in their livings. Benefices in lay patronage were also excepted from the terms of the act; but, at best, all that the church was entitled to receive from this measure was the teinds which, as spirituality, were expressly reserved along with manses and glebes for the support of the ministry.[53]

Designed to augment royal finances, the act considerably extended royal patronage in the sense that James was better placed to reward loyal supporters from this profitable new source of property now at the crown's disposal; but any dislocation which may have been anticipated was not pronounced in practice, for many properties were merely regranted to their previous possessors, the former commendators, who benefited by having their lands converted into hereditary lordships. Indeed, by the end of the reign, at least twenty-one out of thirty abbeys had been transferred into secular lordships. At the same time, the act did nothing to increase the crown's rights of patronage in the sense of presenting candidates to the annexed benefices; rather the reverse was true. After all, the crown already enjoyed, and had exercised for at least two decades, the right of presenting ministers to the majority of churches appropriated to religious houses and to many prebends attached to cathedrals. There were, of course, exceptions, for certain commendators retained, or were granted, rights of presentation to annexed churches. Andrew Moncrieff, on acquiring the commend of Elcho in 1570, had been authorised 'to dispoun ony inferiour benefices, chaiplanreis or alteragis quhen thai happin to vaik', but, in truth, the only parochial benefice annexed to Elcho was Dun, and the crown proceeded to present its own candidates to Dun on at least five occasions between 1570 and 1583. At Glenluce, Laurence Gordon as commendator in 1582 received the right to present to the appropriated churches of the abbacy, a right which indeed had been enjoyed by his immediate predecessors, but the only church was that of Glenluce itself, and the same circumstances applied at Pittenweem, with its two appropriated churches, when William Stewart was chosen as commendator in 1583. Although Coldingham had been gifted in 1571 to Alexander Hume, who obtained a confirmation of the patronage of the annexed churches in February 1573/4, the crown later assumed the right to make presentations from 1586; and despite gifts of the commend of Paisley, first, to William Erskine in November 1579 and, then, to Claud Hamilton in May 1586, with the patronage of the appropriated churches, the crown continued its practice of making appointments to benefices attached to the abbey.[54] Nonetheless, the policy which ensued of creating temporal lordships from monastic properties threatened to fragment the rights of patronage to parochial benefices which had come to be consolidated, so substantially, in the possession of the crown.

Hitherto the coexistence, with a minimum of friction, of a system of ecclesiastical patronage with a polity designed to protect congregational rights might best be explained by the concentration of so much patronage in the hands of the crown, which, for the most part, conscientiously discharged its duties in accordance with the legislation of 1567 governing presentations to the lesser benefices. In sharp contrast to the crown's extensive ecclesiastical patronage, the nobility had relatively little control over presentations to parochial benefices. In 1559 David Lindsay, Earl of Crawford, had the patronage of numerous chaplainries, but the only parochial benefices mentioned were the parsonage and vicarage of Inverarity. A charter in favour of Andrew, Earl of Rothes in 1564 specified the patronage of four parish churches; the Earl of Eglinton was recognised to hold the patronage of two parish churches in 1565; and the Earl Marischal's patronage increased from at least five parishes in 1587 to eight in 1592. Even Esmé Stewart, as Earl of Lennox, was merely assigned in 1580 the patronage of Dumbarton collegiate kirk and, more vaguely, 'ceterarum ecclesiarum et capellaniarum dicti comitatus'.[55] In England, a puritan patron like the 3rd earl of Huntingdon had the patronage of seven benefices in 1560, only to have acquired another seven by 1570.[56] A study of the influence of the nobility's patronage in the reformed church, which does exist for the Elizabethan church,[57] has yet to be undertaken for Scotland, but if a Scottish parallel is to be sought for the Earl of Bedford or for the Earl of Leicester, as a patron of 'godly' preachers, it might be found in Lord James Stewart, the Earl of Moray, who was probably responsible more than any individual for securing key appointments of Protestant ministers at the Reformation.

As a leader of the lords of the Congregation and commendator of the Augustinian priory in St. Andrews, Stewart had been well placed to foster the growth of Protestantism in the primatial city, which had an organised kirk session as early as October 1559, with Adam Heriot, an Augustinian canon, as minister; by 1560 another Augustinian from St. Andrews, John Duncanson, was placed as minister of Stirling (a parish annexed to the Benedictine house of Dunfermline); and a third, Patrick Kinloquhy, served at Linlithgow, which was appropriated to St. Andrews priory. Stewart was also one of the nobles who had earlier invited John Knox to return from Geneva in 1557; Christopher Goodman, who served for a spell as minister in St. Andrews, was considered to be his 'greyt freynd'; and he was instrumental in winning over to Protestantism John Winram, the sub-prior, who became superintendent of Fife, and John Row, from the papal curia, who entered the ministry at Kennoway, another parish annexed to St. Andrews priory, in April 1560 before moving to Perth. Also associated with Stewart's circle was the group from St. Andrews — twenty-one individuals in all — considered by the assembly in December

1560 to be qualified 'for ministreing and teaching'. Another protégé, commended to the English government in 1560, was Patrick Cockburn, a teacher of theology in St. Leonard's college, which had particularly close ties with the priory. Cockburn had earlier accompanied Stewart to Paris in 1548; he received an annual pension from Stewart in 1552 of £50 from the parish of Leuchars, annexed to the priory; he became a prebendary of Dunbar collegiate kirk, and, finally, served as minister at Haddington, yet another parish appropriated to the priory. Indeed, Augustinian canons serving the vast majority of parishes annexed to the priory followed Stewart's lead and conformed, undertaking service as ministers and readers in the reformed church.[58]

The principles which operated in early appointments and the degree of congregational initiative asserted in selecting ministers are not readily to be discerned, but once the initial phase of uncertainty and expediency had lapsed, it is probable that the views of congregations and kirk sessions were widely respected, regardless of the attitudes of patrons to the Reformation. That this proved possible is attributable to the essential moderation of the Scottish Reformation which permitted existing holders of benefices to retain their titles and property irrespective of their religious persuasion. This meant that a majority of benefices were already occupied and therefore unavailable for Protestant ministers not already in possession of a benefice under the old regime. This being so, patrons could, and did, continue to present to benefices, and, by a different process, ministers were admitted to serve congregations, a distinction which has constantly to be kept in view. Even where a minister secured a benefice, the likelihood was that the benefice which he held was geographically far removed from the parish at which he had undertaken service. This curious situation, which prevailed in many parishes, survived long after the act of 1567, permitting ministers access to the lesser benefices, and even after the act of 1573, depriving nonconformist benefice-holders. Only in instances where a minister was presented simultaneously to the benefice and to the church of the parish where he was selected to serve had the rights of patron and congregation to be reconciled. The tendency in royal presentations from 1567, however, was to assign to ministers the benefices (at first the vicarages) belonging to the parishes where the ministers served, so that the parallel systems of presentation to benefices, as financial entities, and of admissions to congregations ultimately coalesced.

At the same time, the First Book of Discipline had insisted that 'it appertaineth to the people and to everie severall Congregation to elect their Minister', and it even considered that 'the presentation of the people to whom he should be appointed Pastor must be preferred to the presentation of the counsell or greater church'. The superintendents and commissioners appointed by the assembly to admit ministers were accordingly obliged to respect congregational views; one presentation in 1568 explicitly sought to safeguard congregational rights by specifying that the superintendent should give collation to the presentee 'if he finds him sufficientlie qualifit in the premissis and having the benevolence and electioun of the parochinnaris of the . . . parroche kirk of

Moneydie'; and in 1567 parliament acceded to the request that patrons should be empowered to make new presentations to benefices which had been granted contrary to the 'ordoure' of the Book of Discipline, so that the church might be delivered from 'unproffitable pastoris'.[59] All in all, it was probably at least as true for Scotland as it was for England that 'godly' patrons took the wishes of their congregations into account. In England, archdeacon Lever's demand that the congregation should join with the patron in assenting to the presentation was wholly applicable to Scotland, where a candidate was normally required to preach for three successive Sundays in the church of the parish where he was presented, and only if the congregation was satisfied with the choice would the ecclesiastical authorities proceed to grant collation to the benefice and give admission to the church. Local pressures and family connections no doubt had a bearing on the selection of candidates. A patron's desire to provide a living for a kinsman, friend or servitor, or to advance the cause of a particular preacher were obvious enough motives; and even though a congregation possessed the negative right of objecting to the patron's choice, the initiative still lay with the patron to select a second candidate, within six months, to fill the vacancy. At the same time, however, the patron was no longer able to disregard the valid objections of the people, and the rejection of the patron's candidate either by the examining ecclesiastical authorities or by the congregation was a serious blow to the patron's prestige and influence in the community. It was therefore in the patron's own interest to secure a choice satisfactory to all. Consequently, in the decades after 1567 — at a time when the patronage of parochial benefices was still, in effect, concentrated in the possession of the crown — a majority of presentations went forward without noticeable friction or controversy.

By the late 1580s, the assumption by presbyteries of powers to supervise admissions and to grant collation, which had won the assembly's approval in 1581 but which was belatedly recognised by parliament in 1592, strengthened the ecclesiastical machinery and helped to check any recurrence of the old abuse, detected in the Second Book of Discipline of 1578, whereby a patron, presumably with the bishop's connivance, had intruded his nominee 'without lauchfull electioun and the assent of the peple ovir quhom the persone is placet'. Although the Second Book of Discipline had affirmed that the 'ordour quhilk Goddis word cravis can not stand with patronagis and presentationis to benefices usit in the papis kirk' and had therefore advocated their abolition, it was far from easy to resolve the inherent tensions between the two systems accentuated in the Book of Discipline. After all, patronage, which had originated in the assignment of land for the foundation of a church (*fundatio*), the erection of a church usually at a landowner's expense (*aedificatio*), and the granting of the means of support for the upkeep of the church and its minister (*donatio*), had long been recognised, and was jealously guarded by patrons, as a heritable property-right, normally conveyed with a barony or lands to which it was appendant. In short, the right of presentation, in the language of the lawyers, was an incorporeal hereditament, upheld by statute law; and the distinction observed in charters conveying property 'cum advocatione ecclesiarum et beneficiorum' and 'cum iure patronatus . . .' would seem to be explained on the basis that the more comprehensive *ius patronatus* also included a title to the patronage of the teinds, where a right of titularity was held to be incidental or accessory to a patron's rights over lands held 'cum decimis inclusis' — another important factor in explaining the refusal of patrons to accept the claims of the assembly and Second Book of Discipline; hence the assembly's patient acceptance in 1582 that the rights of patrons should continue to be respected 'unto the tyme the lawes be reformed according to the Word of God'.[60]

In an effort to introduce a measure of commonsense into the tenure of benefices and to resolve the confused situation still prevalent, the assembly had decreed in 1578, and again in 1580, that presentations to benefices should be restricted to the minister of the parish where the benefice lay.[61] The measure was not ineffective. Archibald Livingston, for example, on being presented to a benefice, indicated in 1583 that 'becaus he was laufullie provydit to the patronage of Cultir, he acknawlegit him self to be bund thairby of his dewatie to serve in the cuir of the ministrie at the kirk thairof'.[62] But the implementation of the assembly's enactment, which meant that sooner or later vacancies to benefices and parish churches would occur simultaneously, also had the effect of making explicit the tensions between the rights of patron and congregation; and the system itself to which presbyterianism was opposed was not without its weaknesses.

Presbyteries were often critical of the calibre of candidates presented by patrons. In 1594, Glasgow presbytery refused a presentation from the 'commendator' of Paisley 'as against the laws of God and man and good conscience'; it also required Stirling of Keir to present three candidates before it finally accepted one as minister of Baldernock.[63] Stirling presbytery also refused to admit a candidate presented by Blackadder of Tulliallan as patron; and Edinburgh presbytery upheld the complaints of the parishioners of St. Cuthbert's in 1586 that the candidate had sought the votes of the gentry in the parish contrary to the order observed, and it proceeded to condemn the admission as 'corrupt and not according to the ordour of a reformit kirk'.[64] It is significant, too, that the candidate promoted by a couple of lairds to Kemback in Fife should think it necessary to point out to the presbytery in 1596 that his 'contract wes bot subscryvit be the holl parochineris quhilk he cravit to be don befoir his admissioun'.[65] Yet there were also limits to the extent to which a presbytery was prepared to champion congregational rights. On a vacancy arising at St. Ninians near Stirling, a church annexed to Cambuskenneth abbey, the rights of the patron (be it commendator or crown) were eclipsed in 1587 when a powerful group of lairds on the kirk session presented their own leet of three prospective ministers to the presbytery for examination, so that all three, on being found qualified, might then be 'presentit to the particular assemblie of the said parroche kirk, thair to be voittit be thame quhome thai sould think maist meit to the said offeice'; but when it discovered that the 'particular assemblie of sum of the elderis and deacunis and utheris of the said parrochun' were about to elect and admit a minister without its consent, the presbytery promptly condemned the proceedings as 'plaine repugnant to Godis Word and gud ordur', since 'the admissione of all ministeris is onlie in the handis of the presbyteriis and utheris assembleis of ministeris'.[66] At Lenzie, where Lord Fleming had 'nominated' to the presbytery in January 1600 two successive candidates as minister, it was nonetheless the commendator of Cambuskenneth, as patron, who finally presented the second candidate, 'nominat be' Lord Fleming and approved by the parishioners, to the vicarage in April.[67] Sometimes a presbytery was persuaded to respect the wishes of a particularly influential patron. When the Earl of Morton presented his own candidate to the parsonage of Newlands in 1592, the presbytery initially declined collation on the grounds that another minister already served the parish, requiring that the earl present the minister of Newlands to the parsonage, but as soon as Morton threatened to retain for his own use the fruits of the parsonage, as he was legally entitled to do if the presbytery declined to admit a qualified candidate, the presbytery decided to give the earl's presentee collation to the benefice, provided the candidate, in turn, made financial provision for the minister who served the cure.[68] A particularly complicated dispute ensued at Eddleston where the parishioners in 1592 appealed for the provision of a minister to the synod, which granted Edinburgh presbytery full power to present a candidate to the benefice *iure devoluto*, if the patron failed to present, though the patronage itself was in dispute between Maitland of Thirlestane and Lord Yester; the parishioners declined Yester's kinsman as presentee; Yester was not disposed to accept the presbytery's nominee; and a third candidate nominated by the patron and approved by both congregation and presbytery was finally admitted a year later.[69]

Catholic patrons were also obliged to respect the legislation of 1567 and 1573 regulating the conditions of appointments to benefices; and the evidence suggests that, as the government of James VI stabilised, even nonconformist patrons were prepared to present candidates to serve in the reformed ministry. The replacement of the decrepit Alexander Livingston, minister at Kilsyth, by the presentation of William Livingston, a presbyterian minister of some repute, to the benefice of Kilsyth in 1599 looks like a dynastic appointment, for Lord Livingston was no archetypal 'godly' patron; but the choice was at least respectable and acceptable. Lord Fleming likewise showed a willingness to participate in the selection of a minister at Lenzie in 1600.[70] In the appointment, however, of Andrew Boyd as minister of Eaglesham, Glasgow presbytery seems to have usurped the Master of Eglinton's rights of presentation, but when Eglinton complained of Boyd's supposed intrusion in 1592, a majority of elders (whose names were suppressed for fear of reprisal or intimidation as Eglinton's tenants) testified in sworn statements that they had agreed to Boyd's admission.[71] In a possibly conservative analysis of the religious persuasion of the leading Scottish nobles and barons, prepared for the English government in 1592, four out of two dozen nobles were considered to be convinced Catholics, and nine out of thirty-three lords and barons were depicted as Roman Catholics.[72] But, at best, their patronage of parochial benefices was modest, and their influence, in this sphere at least, may be considered minimal.

What was potentially far more disruptive was the decided proliferation in the ranks of patrons, achieved largely at the expense of the crown. Increased activity in the land-market, the exchange of properties by purchase, grant or, occasionally, forfeiture, and most markedly the crown's transference of episcopal and abbatial estates, with full rights of patronage over the annexed churches, to numerous earls, lords and barons — the so-called lords of erection — following the act of annexation of 1587 led the assembly, in 1588 and again in 1591, to protest at this dispersal of crown patronage, and to urge an annulment of those rights already alienated. Such a fragmentation of patronage was held by the assembly to constitute an 'evident danger, hurt and prejudice to the haill Kirk', its discipline and patrimony; and so presbyteries were inhibited, in the meanwhile, from accepting presentations by the 'new patrons'.[73] The patronage of 29 churches annexed to Paisley, for example, fell to Claud Hamilton by 1592; Kelso with the right to present to more than 40 churches became the heritable property of Francis Stewart in 1588; Kilwinning, with 16 annexed churches, was assigned to William Melville in 1592; Arbroath, with 37 specified churches, was bestowed in 1608 on the Marquis of Hamilton; and Alexander Lindsay, created Lord Spynie with the erection of the lordship out of the temporality of the bishopric of Moray, came to possess the patronage of some 40 churches.[74] The dispersal of so much patronage complicated the church's task of exercising control and supervision of the system in an effort to reconcile divergent interests.

For the first time since the Middle Ages, the rights of presentation to the parochial benefices had come substantially into the possession of laymen other than the crown. The exercise of patronage had passed from prelate and crown to noble and laird. Changing patterns in the ownership of former ecclesiastical property made it difficult for either crown or church to recover what had been lost. The continued acquisition by laymen of ecclesiastical patronage in the reigns of James VI and Charles I, linked as it often was to the ownership of teinds, made it improbable that these rights would be readily recovered by either crown or parliament for the benefit of any churchman be he prelate or presbyter.

NOTES

1. For a discussion of the subject, see J. Kirk, 'The Exercise of Ecclesiastical Patronage by the Crown, 1560-1572', in *The Renaissance and Reformation in Scotland: Essays in Honour of Gordon Donaldson*, ed. I. B. Cowan and D. Shaw (Edinburgh, 1983), 93-113, at 94-5, 103ff.

2. *Register of the Privy Seal of Scotland* [RSS], ed. M. Livingstone, D. H. Fleming, J. Beveridge and G. Donaldson (Edinburgh, 1908-66), v, nos. 816, 827, 869, 876.

3. These figures are derived from the lists in I. B. Cowan, *The Parishes of Medieval Scotland* (Scottish Record Society, Edinburgh, 1967).

4. *Register of the Privy Council of Scotland* [*RPC*], lst ser., ed. J. H. Burton and D. Masson (Edinburgh, 1899-1908), i, 199-203, 487-8; *Acts of the Parliaments of Scotland* [*APS*], ed. T. Thomson and C. Innes, 12 vols. (Edinburgh, 1814-75), iii, 23.

5. This is based on an examination of the relevant entries from 1549 in *RSS*, iv and v.

6. Scottish Record Office [SRO], Register House Charters, RH6/1896 (presentation to Dunscore by commendator of Holywood, Nov. 1562); RH6/1975 (to Tullynessle by bishop of Aberdeen, Jan. 1564/5); RH6/2019 (to prebend of St. Dothan, Sandwick by by bishop of Orkney, Feb. 1565/6); cf. RH6/nos. 2196, 2313, 2830, 2933 (for later presentations, 1570-87). For royal confirmation of presentations by patrons other than the crown, see *RSS*, v, nos. 1638, 2064, 2148, 2531, 2563, 2607, 2653, 2663, 2721, 2722, 2836, 2840, 2852, 2859, 2942, 2946, 2998, 3042, 3308, 3383, 3433, 3469, 3498, 3533, 3541, 3551.

7. *RSS*, v, nos. 876, 1884, 2042, 2475, 2786, 2853, 3029, 3061, 3070 (presentations); nos. 856, 1159, 1302, 1321, 1368, 1416, 1445, 1469, 1490, 1513, 1551, 1635, 1660, 1733, 1785, 1894 etc. (gifts).

8. *Ibid.*, v, nos. 1709, 1751, 1998, 2092, 2192, 3173, 3286.

9. *Ibid.*, v, nos. 2029, 2761.

10. *Calendar of State Papers relating to Scotland and Mary, Queen of Scots* [*CSP Scot.*], ed. J. Bain *et al.*, 13 vols. (Edinburgh, 1898-1970), ii, nos. 7-9, 16; *RPC*, i, 349-50, 353-4, 409; *RSS*, v, nos. 2353, 2698.

11. D. E. R. Watt, *Fasti Ecclesiae Scoticanae Medii Aevi ad annum 1638* (Scottish Record Society, Edinburgh, 1969), 150; 4.

12. *RSS*, v, no. 965.

13. *Ibid.*, v, nos. 2066, 2806, 3373.

14. J. Kirk, 'The Exercise of Ecclesiastical Patronage by the Crown, 1560-1572', *Renaissance and Reformation in Scotland*, 97-8, 107-8.

15. *APS*, iii, 37; *The Booke of the Universall Kirk of Scotland: Acts and Proceedings of the General Assemblies of the Kirk of Scotland* [*BUK*], ed. T. Thomson, 3 vols. and appendix vol. (Maitland Club, Edinburgh, 1839-45), i, 151; D. Calderwood, *History of the Kirk of Scotland*, ed. T. Thomson and D. Laing, 8 vols. (Wodrow Society, Edinburgh, 1842-9), iii, 159-60.

16. Calderwood, *History*, iii, 144-6.

17. R. Lindsay of Pitscottie, *The Historie and Cronicles of Scotland* (Scottish Text Society, Edinburgh, 1889), ii, 260; R. Bannatyne, *Journal of the Transactions in Scotland* (Edinburgh, 1806), 246, 250-3, 255.

18. Calderwood, *History*, iii, 156-65.

19. *CSP Scot.*, iv, no. 149; *RPC*, ii, 106ff; *BUK*, i, 207-8, 246.

20. *BUK*, i, 209-36.

21. *Ibid.*, i, 243-4, 246, 249, 261, 269-70, 278, 286-8, 295, 297, 300, 301, 303, 308-9, 314-15, 317-18, 320-1, 323, 325, 326-7, 331-3, 335-6, 340-3.

22. Pitscottie, *Historie*, ii, 283; cf. 282.

23. *BUK*, i, 353-61.

24. J. Spottiswoode, *History of the Church of Scotland*, ed. M. Russell, 3 vols. (Spottiswoode Society, Edinburgh, 1851), ii, 202.

25. J. Kirk, ed., *The Second Book of Discipline* (Edinburgh, 1980), 234-8.

26. Bannatyne, *Journal*, 375; *BUK*, i, 248.

27. Watt, *Fasti*, 299; 150; 100; 206; 78; 217, 270; 4, 132-3, 254, 270-1; 61; 41; *BUK*, i, 318.

28. *RPC*, ii, 276-7; iii, 88-9, 90-1; *RSS*, vii, no. 2090; *RSS*, vi, no. 2469; *RPC*, iii, 124-5; 98-9.

29. *RSS*, vi, nos. 2142, 2175, 2192; *The Autobiography and Diary of Mr James Melvill*, ed. R. Pitcairn (Wodrow Society, Edinburgh, 1842), 47.

30. *RSS*, vii, nos. 180, 2075; SRO, CH4/1/2, Register of Presentations to Benefices, vol. 2, 83v., 84r. (Boyds); *Register of the Great Seal [RMS]*, ed. J. M. Thomson *et al.*, 11 vols. (Edinburgh, 1882-1914), iv, nos. 2199; 2382 (Boyd); 2407 (Boyd); 2727 and 2764 (Morton); 2881 (Boyd); 2937 (Lord Boyd); 2938; 2012; v, nos. 90, 451-2, 463-5, 469, 475, 491, 500, 509 (Lord Boyd); 520-22, 565, 581, 591, 603-9, 616, 618-21, 623-5, 646, 647, 657, 659, 670, 958, 986, 1018-22, 1131; 1900 (Boyd).

31. *RSS*, vi, nos. 1473-4, 1535; 2070, 2309, 2407; vii, nos. 789, 819; *CSP Scot.*, v, no. 187, p. 181.

32. *RSS*, vii, nos. 824, 862-4, 866-7, 869, 902, 916. For other grants of episcopal property by Adamson, see *RSS*, vii, nos. 827, 865, 868, 941, 1137, 1139, 1614, 1726, 1746, 2015, 2182, 2226, 2493, 2497; *RMS*, iv, nos. 2703-6, 2725, 2831, 2967, 3030; v, nos. 585, 632-3, 896, 1272, 1279, 1290, 2267; SRO, PS1/50, Register of the Privy Seal, fo. 49; PS1/51, fo. 86v; PS1/53, fos. 78, 86, 168; PS1/56, fo. 118.

33. *RMS*, vi, no. 1800. For other tacks and pensions, see also SRO, PS1/51, fo. 106; PS1/54, fo. 37v.

34. R. Keith, *An Historical Catalogue of the Scottish Bishops*, ed. M. Russel (Edinburgh, 1824), 97; *BUK*, i, 270, 300, 314, 332-3, 335-6, 340-1, 350-1; *RSS*, vi, nos. 2003, 2367, 2446; *RMS*, iv, nos. 2236-44, 2318, 2397, 2504, 2631, 2719, 2871, 2989; v, nos. 122, 205, 542; Argyll Transcripts, vi, 82, 214. Argyll retained his financial interest in the bishopric even with the restoration of Robert Crichton, the former Catholic bishop, by the conservative Arran regime in 1584 (SRO, PS1/52, Register of the Privy Seal, fos. 21v., 51; PS1/54, fo. 125; PS1/55, fo. 79).

35. Watt, *Fasti*, 41, 206; 28; *RSS*, vii, no. 341; Argyll Transcripts, vi, 222, 234; vii, 4, 23.

36. *RSS*, vii, no. 554; Argyll Transcripts, vi, 175, 209, 214; vii, 107, 208; SRO, PS1/63, Register of the Privy Seal, fo. 127v. (Isles); SRO, PS1/57, fo. 28v., 29; Argyll Transcripts, vii, 159, 176, 186, 193, 194, 262, 310 (Argyll); *RSS*, vii, nos. 978, 2355; SRO, CH4/1/2, Reg. Pres. Ben., 35v; *RMS*, iv, nos. 1745, 1746, 2228, 2443; v, nos. 138, 139, 242, 279, 786, 862, 890, 1059, 1271, 1278, 2006, 2808, 2833 (Brechin).

37. *RSS*, vi, nos. 1593, 1721, 2536; vii, nos. 987; 269 (earl); SRO, PS1/55, Register of the Privy Seal, fos. 53v., 220; PS1/63, fo. 124v; PS1/64, fo. 111 (Caithness); *RSS*, vi, no. 1746; vii, nos. 511; 832 (Lochinvar); 1699, 2222; PS1/50, fo. 9v. (Laurence Gordon); *RMS*, iv, no. 2694; v, nos. 174, 187, 271 (Galloway).

38. *RMS*, iv, nos. 1668, 1710; G. Donaldson, 'Bishop Adam Gordon and the Reformation in Orkney', *Records of the Scottish Church History Society [RSCHS]*, xiii, 100; *RSS*, vi. no. 506; *BUK*, i, 162-3, 165-8.

39. Watt, *Fasti*, 78; *RSS*, vi, nos. 590, 729.

40. *RSS*, vii, nos. 1795, 2008; SRO, PS1/58, Register of the Privy Seal, fos. 83, 110v; *RMS*, iv, no. 2912; *APS*, iii, 111-2; *Stirling Presbytery Records, 1581-1587*, ed. J. Kirk (Scottish History Society, Edinburgh, 1981), xxii-xxiii, 69-71.

41. Watt, *Fasti*, 4; J. Durkan and J. Kirk, *The University of Glasgow, 1451-1577* (Glasgow, 1977), 309, 338; SRO, PS1/61, Register of the Privy Seal, fo. 42; PS1/65, fo. 196. See further, PS1/47, fo. 113v; PS1/55, fo. 204; PS1/56, fos. 23v., 89; PS1/62,

fo. 5v; *RMS*, v, nos. 555, 876, 1124.

42. Spottiswoode, *History*, ii, 282; SRO, PS1/49, Register of the Privy Seal, fos. 133v., 138; PS1/50, fo. 9v; PS1/55, fo. 218; PS1/59, fo. 88; PS1/62, fo. 154v; PS1/63, fos. 50v., 150; PS1/64, fo. 80.

43. G. Donaldson, 'Leighton's Predecessors', *Journal of the Society of the Friends of Dunblane Cathedral*, xii, pt. ii (1975), 7-16, at 7.

44. *BUK*, i, 210; *RSS*, vi, nos. 1801; 635, 2467, 2807; *RMS*, iv, nos. 2232, 2290.

45. *APS*, iii, 90; *RSS*, vii, nos. 140, 885, 2113, 2133; SRO, CH4/1/2, Reg. Pres. Ben., fo. 49v.

46. J. Kirk, *The Second Book of Discipline*, 218; *BUK*, ii, 513, 514.

47. *APS*, iii, 211; *BUK*, ii, 632; SRO, CH4/1/2, Reg. Pres. Ben., fos. 91-2; *RMS*, v, no, 598; *BUK*, ii, 632, 634, 644; SRO, CH4/1/2, fo. 71; *RMS*, v, nos. 724; 258.

48. G. Donaldson, 'Scottish Presbyterian Exiles in England, 1584-1588', *RSCHS*, xiv (1963), 67-80.

49. *RMS*, v, no. 695; *APS*, iii, 479, 591.

50. SRO, CH4/1/2, Reg. Pres. Ben., fos. 105-6; *RMS*, iv, 720, 723.

51. SRO, CH4/1/2, Reg. Pres. Ben., fos. 82v.-83, 137-8, 173v; 125v-126; SRO, PS1/53, Register of the Privy Seal, fo. 58v.

52. *RMS*, v, nos. 1307, 1309, 1320.

53. *APS*, iii, 431-7.

54. *RSS*, vi, no. 911; Cowan, *Parishes*, 217; *RSS*, vi, 912; vii, 114, 266; SRO, CH4/1/2, Reg. Pres. Ben., fos. 89v., 94v; *RMS*, v, nos. 336; 78, 335; Cowan, *Parishes*, 219; *RMS*, v, no. 593; Cowan, *Parishes*, 223; *RSS*, vi, nos. 1163, 2318; *RMS*, iv, no. 2178; Cowan, *Parishes*, 215; SRO, CH4/1/2, Reg. Pres. Ben., 169v; 143v., 166r; SRO, PS1/62, 56r; CH4/1/2, fos. 147r., 171r; *RMS*, iv, no. 2922; v, no. 995; Cowan, *Parishes*, 223; *RSS*, vii, no. 2107; SRO, CH4/1/2, Reg. Pres. Ben., fos. 77r., 172r., 158v., 176v., 177r; SRO, PS1/59, Register of the Privy Seal, fo. 133r; PS1/60, fo. 129r; PS1/62, fos. 67v., 115r; PS1/63, fos. 119r., 267r.

55. *RMS*, iv, nos. 1353, 1564, 1674; v, nos. 1341, 2176; iv, no. 2972.

56. M. C. Cross, 'Noble Patronage in the Elizabethan Church', *The Historical Journal*, iii (1960), 1-16, at 3.

57. M. R. O'Day, 'Clerical Patronage and Recruitment in England in the Elizabethan and early Stuart periods, with special reference to the diocese of Coventry and Lichfield' (unpublished London Ph.D. thesis, 1972); cf. K. W. Shipps, 'Lay Patronage of East Anglian Puritan Clerics in Pre-Revolutionary England' (Yale Ph.D. dissertation, 1971).

58. *Register of the Minister, Elders and Deacons of the Christian Congregation of St. Andrews*, ed. D. H. Fleming, 2 vols. (Scottish History Society, Edinburgh, 1889-90), i, 3, 5; *Fasti Ecclesiae Scoticanae*, ed. H. Scott, 9 vols. (Edinburgh, 1915-61), v, 230; iv, 317; i, 214; *The Works of John Knox*, ed. D. Laing, 6 vols. (Wodrow Society, Edinburgh, 1846-64), i, 267-8; *CSP Scot.*, ii, no. 316; i, no. 902; *Fasti*, v, 91; *BUK*, i, 4; *Fasti*, i, 368; *RSS*, v, no. 1576. The annexed churches are listed in Cowan, *Parishes*, 224, and biographical details of the conforming Augustinian canons are provided in the *Fasti*.

59. J. K. Cameron, *The First Book of Discipline* (Edinburgh, 1972), 96, 99; *BUK*, i, 16; *RSS*, vi, no. 82; *APS*, iii, 37.

60. *BUK*, ii, 514, 568, 602; *APS*, iii, 542; J. Kirk, *The Second Book of Discipline*, 234; *BUK*, ii, 564-5, cf. 568.

61. *BUK*, ii, 409, 462.

62. *Stirling Presbytery Records, 177.*

63. Strathclyde Regional Archives, Glasgow Presbytery Records, i, fo. 21v., 26 Feb. 1593/4; fos. 8r.-v., 9v., 12v., 21v., 32v., 34r.-v., 24 April, 8 May, 15 May, 25 July 1593; 12 Feb. 1593/4; 16 July, 30 July 1594.

64. SRO, CH4/722/2, Stirling Presbytery Records, 6 June, 1 Aug., 12 Sept., 19 Sept. 1599; 16 Jan. 1600; SRO, CH4/121/1, Edinburgh Presbytery Records, 24 May, 31 May, 14 June 1586.

65. Holy Trinity Church, St. Andrews: St. Andrews Presbytery Records, 4 Nov. 1596.

66. *Stirling Presbytery Records, 267-70, 272-5.*

67. Strathclyde Regional Archives, Glasgow Presbytery Records, i, fos. 142v., 144r., 148r.-v., 149v., 150v., 152r.-153v., 154v.-155v., 8 January 1600-20 May 1600.

68. SRO, CH4/121/1, Edinburgh Presbytery Records, 2 May, 9 May, 13 June, 20 June 1592.

69. *The Records of the Synod of Lothian and Tweeddale, 1589-1596, 1640-1649,* ed. J. Kirk (Stair Society, Edinburgh, 1977), xxv and n. 53; 42, 44, 55.

70. See above, n. 67.

71. SRO, CH4/722/2, Stirling Presbytery Records, 4 July, 25 July, 10 Oct., 31 Oct., 5 Dec. 1592; cf. *BUK,* iii, 813-4.

72. *CSP Scot.,* x, no. 713.

73. *BUK,* ii, 733, 746, 784. (In 1600, the synod of Glasgow instructed its commissioners to the general assembly 'to lament that the donatioun of benefices quhilk of befoir be actis of parliament pertenit to his Majestie ar now devolvit in particular menis handis to the hurt of the ministerie, and to lament anent the new erectionis of benefices (*decimis inclusis*) in temporal lordshipes, specialie of the abbacie of Paslaye . . .' Strathclyde Regional Archives, Glasgow Presbytery Records, 16 Sept. 1600.)

74. *RMS,* v, nos. 2070 (patronage excepted from the earlier grant of 1587, *ibid.,* no. 1320); 1597, 2085; vi, no. 2075; v, no. 1727; *APS,* iii, 650-6; iv, 653-4.

8

Presbyterian and Canterburian in the Scottish Revolution

Walter Makey

SIR JAMES BALFOUR of Denmilne was an authority on heraldry and thus an admirer of aristocracy. He believed in a society of noblemen and lairds surmounted by a king whose main function was to hold it together. He found his ideal, or at least a close approximation to it, during the last two decades of James VI when the king, safely removed to the 'towardly riding horse' of the English throne, began to keep a factious kingdom in order; these were years of peace and gradual change which appealed to his conservative soul. The task of the church, at least in this world, was quite simply to assist the king in preserving the unity of the realm. He mistrusted ideology, and his admiration for Charles I was limited. He greeted the 1630s with apprehension and he would look back over the weary years of the 1640s with distaste and indeed despair. In 1649, his annals, normally brief, were interrupted by a long, and obviously personal, analysis of the troubles of his time. 'The chiefest bellows of this terrible fire' had, or so he felt, been 'the unhappy bishops of both kingdoms' and they were now — in 1649 — 'the preachers and ministers' who, in place of 'obedience and conformity', taught the people 'Christ's cause, religion, liberty and the priviledge of the subject' and 'quite poisoned [them] against their native sovereign and prince'. Churchmen who abandoned themselves to a 'spirit of faction' — that is of politics — were the 'most corroding cankers and the worst vipers in any commonwealth and most pernicious to the prince'. The conscience of the kingdom had been captured by idealists; war and revolution were the inevitable result. Balfour would have agreed that King James could be pope, but he would vehemently have denied that a bishop or a moderator — or, of course, the Pope of Rome — could claim such eminence.[1]

Balfour believed that Canterburian bishop and Presbyterian minister were equally guilty. They both appealed to divine right; they both derived their authority less from the king than from God. Eventually, or so they seemed to be saying, the magistrates would become the mere servant, if not of the Almighty at least of an almighty kirk. The elaborately structured society that

Balfour so obviously loved would simply wither away. Indeed this was already happening. Melville had called King James 'God's silly vassall' and, now as the revolution approached its climax, his successors on the Commission of the general assembly were reducing the remnants of the Parliament to abject submission. Laud had done much the same thing; he boasted that he did his preaching 'at a Council table where great men [were] gathered together to draw things to an issue'.[2] He and his bishops, English and Scottish alike, had used the high church preferences of a rather credulous king to lure him into a relationship which would eventually have compromised his authority. Both in their different ways were seeking to create a heaven on earth; both knew that they must change society to achieve it. They were revolutionaries in a strikingly similar cause. They both believed that their godly societies were beyond the understanding of mere amateurs, and both sought to exclude laymen from positions of ecclesiastical power. Each envisaged an indoctrinated, dedicated — and incidentally well paid — élite. Church property — its revenues and its power — was vital to both these great designs. This too was sacred.

The Second Book of Discipline defined the patrimony of the kirk, comprehensively enough, as everything that had ever been bestowed upon it since the beginning of time, and it went on to condemn the alienation of 'any of this patrimony' as 'detestable sacrilege before God'. If the old kirk had been well endowed, so too should the new. These revenues, vast as they once had been, were to be divided between the ministers, university teachers, the deserving poor and the officers who administered the kirk. These last were to include not only clerks and beadles but deacons and, above all, elders as well. Indeed the eldership was to be a spiritual office as was the ministry; the elder would be ordained as the minister was and, once ordained, he must, failing a formal dispensation from the kirk, serve for life. He was to be a full time, salaried churchman just as the minister was.[3] The Second Book of Discipline envisaged a church that would have been as bureaucratic as the Church of England or the Church of Rome — and its foundations would have been almost as ancient as Rome itself.

The collapse of this vast edifice of revolution is not difficult to explain. In 1641 George Gillespie, the radical thunderer of Edinburgh, would confess with obvious regret that the revenues of his church were too small 'to spare stipends for ruling elders'. The dreams of Samuel Rutherford, the theorist of the Covenant, were tormented by fantasies of teind and temporality; the kirk had been raped by a sacrilegious aristocracy; it had been left 'a poor naked Christ'.[4] The abolition of episcopacy brought back parts of the revenues from some of the bishoprics and gave them to the universities; but the church as a whole had — as we shall see — to rest content with an entitlement to a part, albeit a growing part, of the teinds. It would be wealthy enough to afford munificent stipends for its magnificent ministers; but the monastic temporalities, which might have sustained professional elders, were beyond its grasp. The elders of the Covenant remained unpaid and imperfectly indoctrinated amateurs; the godly society might still be betrayed by their inconstancy.

And yet it almost succeeded. The ministers, as Gilbert Burnet perceptively observed, worked up 'the inferior people to much zeal and, as they wrought any up to some measure of heat and knowledge, they brought them into their eldership'. The evidence strongly supports this conclusion. 'Disguised and histrionical men puffed up with titles' — to borrow George Gillespie's contemptuous description of the magnates — regularly deflowered the kirk at election time and, though outnumbered, they were a powerful force in most general assemblies.[5] They could influence legislation, and they were always strong enough to deflect a demand for the return of the patrimony. But the Assembly did not sit for long. For the rest of the year, these landed elders were preoccupied with commissions and committees, with Parliaments and armies. With a remarkable lack of perception, they abandoned the machinery of the kirk to their inferiors. The typical sessioner was a farmer or a feuar, often better educated than Burnet allowed, but easily overawed by the eloquence of the minister. And he seldom went — and perhaps was not encouraged to go — to presbytery meetings. The presbyteries in their turn were co-ordinated by the Commission of the general assembly, which met frequently and regularly, and this, as its records show, was the preserve of a relatively small group of leading ministers.[6] This was a professional church — and it almost won.

It is interesting that the ministers themselves usually came from a similar social background. The majority, insofar as their origins are known, were the sons of other and earlier ministers; but this merely pushes the question back into the previous generation. Most of the others were the sons of farmers or small landowners; only a handful were directly descended from magnates; hardly any had heritable jurisdiction of their own. A few came from the towns — and these were often influential — but most of them came from the outer fringes of their burgess communities or from just outside them. Alexander Henderson was almost certainly the son of a farmer who prospered and bought his farm; Samuel Rutherford was the son of a tenant farmer and James Guthrie of a small landowner. Robert Douglas, the perpetual moderator of the Commission, occasionally boasted of his descent from Mary — for his humour was as sarcastic as his manner — and, if this was true, he was the younger son of a natural son of Douglas of Lochleven. His background may have been landed, but it seems unlikely that his father had any land at all. Robert Baillie could trace his descent back to the Baillies of Lamington, but he had a long way to go and his father was a merchant — probably of little wealth or influence — from Glasgow. David Dickson was the son, and unusually the heir, of another Glasgow merchant who had prospered enough to buy a small estate in the locality. Robert Blair, more typically, was the ninth son of a merchant from the small port of Ayr. The two radical Gillespies were the sons of a minister of Kirkcaldy. Indeed the ministers' fathers, seen as a group, were neither a wealthy, a powerful nor even a distinguished collection of men. We know them only through the fame of some of their sons.[7]

The ministers and elders of the kirk were drawn from outside the feudal classes of the countryside and the burgh oligarchies of the towns, and it is scarcely surprising that some of them came to regard aristocracy almost as an evil in itself; 'better', as the ever quoteable Guthrie said, that they be 'of lower degree if godly than of higher degree if otherwise'.[8] It might be useful — though Guthrie himself had reservations about this — to retain a few tame noblemen in a powerless parliament — for somebody had to do the dirty work — but they could have no permanent place, still less an automatic voice, in the church itself. In a sense, all this was preposterous; a small band of articulate nobodies would challenge institutions with the prestige of the centuries behind them. And yet they almost won.

From 1625 to 1637, the bishops used the king to weaken the magnates; from 1637 to 1646 the ministers used the magnates to defeat the king; in 1647 and 1648 the ministers — and here they were lucky — used Oliver Cromwell to defeat the magnates. In 1649 and 1650, they ruled almost unchallenged. They always seemed to know that they would win. As Balfour said, they came to command the 'conscience' of the nation, the 'rudder that [steered] the actions, words and thoughts of the rational creature'. Scotland, or so it seemed, was ruled from the pulpit. Wodrow tells a revealing story — which may actually have happened — about an odd confrontation in the burgh kirk of Hamilton in 1648. The participants were James Nasmyth, the second minister of the parish, and the Duke himself. Nasyth was the son of a feuar and a notorious radical; Hamilton was a great nobleman about to lead the army of the Engagement into England. The minister told the general to his face — and in the face of the kirk — that he would never come back. Hamilton made his will and went; within the year he was dead — and James Nasmyth was first minister of Hamilton.[9] The Engagers seemed to have been beaten before they had started; the ministers seemed to have won because they always won. Cromwell, who actually fought the battle, was merely the instrument of Almighty God. He had come and they were sure that he would soon go away again. History was on their side.

In the end, history would cruelly betray them. By the 1660s, the state would command the church; Guthrie would have been executed; Rutherford and Baillie would be dead; Robert Douglas would live sarcastically on, covering his retreat into obscurity with boasts of the bishopric he could have had if he had wanted it; James Sharp, who had begun his rise to fame as a member of Douglas' Commission, would lead a largely passive kirk back to the crown. Scotland would be ruled by the ghost of James VI. But, in those heady years from Preston to Dunbar, all this was still in the future. The 'state opposite to a state', as Rutherford described it, was more than an idle dream.

Nor was it as preposterous as it may seem. During the sixteenth and the early seventeenth centuries, rural Scotland had experienced a series of social changes which added up to a revolution. Neither the bishops nor the ministers understood the causes, but the results were clear enough. Feuars and farmers were collectively wealthier and potentially stronger than the Lords who ruled them. Feudal society was crumbling and the church could only see — and seize — its chance.

These changes, mysterious as they were, were not universal in their impact; they affected the estates of the church differently from those of the civil magnates, uplands differently from lowlands, the east differently from the west. The pattern was complex — and doubly disruptive for its complexity — yet basically, it was simple enough. The Scots were a nation of mixed farmers, but the proportion of arable to pasture varied greatly from place to place. The relatively dry areas of the eastern seaboard formed a series of predominantly arable regions in which the farming community aimed to feed itself and to provide a small surplus to feed the towns. Here most of the rents were calculated in kind. But this was essentially a lowland pattern. Stow and Penicuik were only a few miles inland from Edinburgh, but they were both among the hills. Rainfall was higher and the agrarian economy had a definite pastoral bias. Here, as elsewhere in the Southern Uplands, rents were calculated entirely or almost entirely in money. Rather similarly, the moister climate of the west of Scotland yielded grass more readily than grain. Favoured enclaves apart, the emphasis was on grazing. In a good year, the farmers of the west might feed themselves, but poor seasons found them selling meat, butter or cheese in the more abundant grain markets of Lothian. They were accustomed to travel and to trade and, as the tax rolls show, they normally counted their rents in money. The Scottish economy had two quite distinct rent structures which reacted differently to the stresses of inflation.

It would be difficult to construct a cost of living index for sixteenth-century Scotland. It had been suggested, on the basis of controlled prices in burghs, that prices rose fourfold during the latter half of the century. The rather longer series available for the burgh of Edinburgh suggests that the price of ale rose sixfold and that of bread eightfold between the 1530s and the turn of the century and that the rise continued, though less steeply, into the seventeenth century. In Fife, where conversion prices happen to have survived well, barley seems to have sold at about 14/- per boll in the late 1530s and the early 1540s, at about 116/- per boll during the 1590s and at about 140/- per boll in the 1620s and 1630s when prices were no longer rising rapidly. Agricultural prices must have multiplied themselves about tenfold between the latter years of James V and the earlier years of Charles I.[10]

The exact multiplier varies with the commodity and with the chosen period of comparison; but it is obvious that the price rise — and thus its eventual impact — was much greater in Scotland that it was elsewhere. Nonetheless it was a slow and an insidious phenomenon. In the short run, it was concealed behind the ordinary fluctuations of dearth and abundance. Many people were vaguely aware that something was wrong; but they were not sure what it was and they had little idea of its meaning. There was a tendency for church and state to regard inflation as a moral problem. But the price revolution, misunderstood as it usually was, nibbled unobtrusively away at the foundations of the customary society. Charles I, Archbishop Laud and Samuel Rutherford would inherit a social structure that was ready to collapse.

The most obvious signs of decay were to be found on the estates of the old church. It is generally agreed that these were large and that quite possibly they accounted for about a third of the agricultural capacity of the kingdom. A high proportion of this huge accumulation of wealth was feued during the middle years of the sixteenth century. The meaning of this is vitally important. The superior — that is the church or its secular successors — retained the rights, mainly of jurisdiction, inherent in his superiority while alienating the produce of his land to a vassal. In return, the vassal paid an annual feu duty fixed in perpetuity and sometimes a capital sum representing a composition for part of the duty. On the arable lands of a church well endowed with good arable land, the rents were calculated in kind — and the superior had alienated these for an annual payment, fixed until the end of time and almost always expressed in money. The real value of his landed income diminished with each passing decade. The resulting transfers of wealth can only be regarded as spectacular.[11]

There is no reason to doubt that most of these transactions were concluded in ignorance of their consequences. A handful of sophisticates may have gambled on a rising trend in the price of corn, but the typical superior and the average vassal judged each deal on its contemporary merits. Ironically enough, the superior, who got either a capital sum or a small augmentation of the previous rent, must have thought that he was winning.. His eagerness flooded the market with some of the best agricultural land in Scotland. His vassals, who would eventually ride the price rise to something like affluence, may, no less ironically, have been more reluctant.

Whatever their motives may have been, we know with some certainty who the vassals were. They included a handful of noblemen, a fair number of lesser landowners, a few courtiers, a number of lawyers and the occasional burgess. Some of these must have got quite large estates, but they were less than half of the whole. The rest of the charters were granted to men who already possessed, and in many cases actually worked, the lands concerned. In addition, some of the wealthier vassals were merely middlemen who promptly sub-feued their acquisitions to the sitting tenants.[12] A very large number of husbandmen rather suddenly became the owners of their farms. At the same time, a smaller number of relatively obscure landowners added to their holdings. In one way or the other vast areas of land, and eventually most of the income from them, were transferred from the feudal classes to other social groups outside the privileged circle of the old order. This was revolution indeed.

The civil magnates seem to have resisted the temptations of wholesale feuing more successfully. Most of their lands seem still to have been farmed by tenants who, in the arable regions of the east, paid their rents in kind. The magnates of Lothian and lower Tweeddale, of Fife and lowland Perthshire, of Angus and of the coastal lowlands of the north-east and the Moray Firth held on to their wealth and thus justified their jurisdictions; wealth and power kept their balance. But, in the pastoral regions of Clydesdale, Ayrshire and

Galloway, it was otherwise. Here rents had traditionally been counted in money and they could only be raised if the landlord chose deliberately to increase them — and this was not too easy. Long centuries of relatively stable prices had produced a rather rigid rent structure with all the power of custom behind it. The magnate, the guardian of the customary society, was perhaps reluctant to betray his trust; indeed the official wisdom of the period, whether from parliament or pulpit, insisted on the virtue of constant rents; rackrenting was sin. It may be added that most tenants were difficult to dislodge. The rentaller enjoyed a complete security of tenure and thus a complete protection against rent rises. At the opposite extreme, the tenant at will could lawfully be evicted at any time. But the majority of sixteenth-century farmers seem to have held their lands on fairly long leases that were renewed, perhaps with the payment of a small grassum, at regular intervals. They were, as recent research has shown, reasonably secure.[13]

It need not be doubted that a determined landlord had the power — as he surely had the legal right — to raise rents when leases expired. In fact, it seldom seems to have occurred to him to do so. This was a rather conservative society in which change, even justifiable change, was suspect. This impression is confirmed by a marked scarcity of surviving sixteenth-century estate rentals; if rents never changed, there was no point in writing them down. And it may be significant that seventeenth-century rentals survive in some quantity, for then money rents were fluid; they were raised regularly — incidentally at a time when inflation was slowing down.

The estate records for the Hamilton empire in Clydesdale have lasted well, particularly those for the outlying pastoral barony of Avondale. Here a rental and some accounts of c.1540 precede a mass of seventeenth-century material including more rentals and an invaluable fragment from the baron court book of 1642.[14] The lands of the barony occupied the upper valley of the Water of Avon; they were disposed along a well-worn routeway leading from Clydesdale through the Irvine Gap into Cunningham and Kyle. The best lands of the barony, relatively low down around the tiny burgh of Strathaven, paid some of their rents in corn, but the rest were higher and wetter; they supported cattle and sheep and they counted their rents in money. The experience of Avondale, typical as it was of a multitude of estates round the fringes of the Southern Uplands, can only be revealing.

Some parts of the barony had already been alienated to gentlemen before 1540, and the rentals tell us little about these. Here the superior enjoyed the rights of jurisdiction and very little else. The fruits of the land were shared between the gentleman and his tenants. We do not know a great deal about the level of rents, but the scattered evidence of the testaments suggests that they were still low during the first two decades of the seventeenth century. They also suggest that the tenant farmers had almost total security of tenure; some of them passed on their 'rights', their 'titles' and their 'kindness' as well as their 'possession' of their lands to their heirs.[15] In practice, if not in theory, each damp acre had three owners — the superior, the gentleman and the farmer himself. The rent structure seems to have been rigid enough and, if it was, wealth was gradually passed down the social scale from the greatest to the least.

The rest of the barony was farmed by tenants who paid their rents directly to the superior. The testaments again suggest security of tenure and the rentals rigidity of rents — but only up to a point. In c.1630 most farms were paying the same money rent that they had paid nearly a century earlier; but, in a few cases, 'augmentations' were beginning to appear, and they were always large compared with the old rent. Thus, in Crookburn, one tenant was paying an augmented rent of nearly £27 per year, but his neighbour was still paying the old rent of only £10 for a farm that was nearly three times as large. They were certainly neighbours; they may not have been friends.

Rents were probably augmented when leases expired. The process was thus spread over a number of years — perhaps a couple of decades. It was still operating in 1642 when we find the great Lady Anna, mother of the Duke and the manager of his estates, offering the tenants a hard choice. They could pay either a vast augmentation of about ten times the old rent or a huge grassum which would allow them to pay the old rent for the rest of their lives after which their heirs would be enrolled as tenants at the new rent. The choice was an actuarial gamble which some farmers won and others lost. But all the tenants were confronted with a sudden demand for a huge sum of money enforced by the threat — the perfectly legal threat — of eviction. It is fair to add that very few tenants were actually evicted. Most of them paid and, in paying, showed that they could afford to pay. Lady Anna, whether she knew it or not, was merely compensating herself and her successors for a century of inflation. The real values of her augmented rents were about the same as they had been in the middle years of the previous century. But the new rents can only have seemed extortionate to the farmers who paid them — and who did not remember the values of the 1540s too clearly. And the dates are surely significant. Avondale, like the neighbouring parish of Glassford and indeed the whole of Clydesdale, was a stronghold of the coventicle. It formed part of a radical region which embraced the whole of the south-west with its moist Atlantic climate, its pastoral economy, its money rents — and its distinctive response to the great inflation.

We are not, of course, entitled to assume that Avondale was entirely typical; but the tax rolls of 1649, which distinguished income in money from income in kind, show a great preponderance of money rents in many western parishes, and this would scarcely have been possible if they had stayed at, or even near, their customary levels.[16] In some cases, they may have been raised in a series of steep steps rather than in a single upward leap. Either way, the effect can only have seemed oppressive. The connection with radical presbyterianism seems plausible enough. The parish of Mauchline, essentially the old ecclesiastical barony of Kylesmuir, had once belonged to Melrose Abbey. In the 1640s, it formed an outlying part of the inheritance of the Earl of Loudoun — a politician by preference and a Covenanter by coincidence — and his radical Countess, who was not entirely unlike Lady Anna. He was Lord Chancellor of Scotland; she understood the radical language of the ministers and her tenants. His debts were a legend; it may have been her job to repay them. The feued lands were beyond her reach, but it seems likely that the rents of the remainder were augmented during the 'twenties, the 'thirties and the 'forties. There were two kinds of farmer in Mauchline, the yeoman tenant and the yeoman feuar; they had once been the same; now the one must have paid ten times as much for his land as the other; the one was secure, the other was not. And they were neighbours still. The social structure of Kylesmuir had been torn to pieces. The local minister, Thomas Wylie, was a notorious radical who was one of the promoters of the Mauchline Rising against the Engagement. This was surely a peasants' revolt.[17]

All over lowland Scotland, the feudal system was in disarray. The feued lands of the temporalities were ruled by Lords of Erection who had the appearance of power without the wealth to give it substance. The pastoral baronies of the west were governed by superiors who were struggling to overcome their new-found poverty. In the east and the west, on hill and in valley, on civil land and church land, the superior was often an absentee. The baronial complex concentrated power in fewer hands; but, by removing the superior into the middle distance, it diminished his local impact. The little barony of Penicuik was owned by the Countess of Eglinton who seldom came near it. The baron court was run by a bailie who rented the largest farm on the estate and, perhaps symbolically, it met in the church. For the bailie was also an elder, while the rest of the session, or at least the active part of it, consisted of farmers only less prosperous than he was.[18] They had become the natural leaders of the local community. In many parishes, the kirk session reflected the realities of power more faithfully than did the civil power.

In this respect at least, the claims of the church were neither arrogant nor outrageous; but, in another sense, they were somewhat unrealistic. The inheritance of the Lords of Erection was also part of the patrimony of the kirk. If the one had been compromised by inflation, so too had the other. It might be argued that the church was claiming a divine right to very little. This was plainly half true, but it was not the whole of the truth. The patrimony included not only the lands but teinds as well. And these in their turn consisted of two elements. The parsonage had traditionally been paid in corn and it had thus maintained its original value. In a predominantly arable parish, like so many of those along the eastern seaboard, it was a lucrative asset; even in the west, where most parishes yielded at least some corn, it was still worth having. On the other hand, the pastoral teinds of the vicarage were almost worthless. These had once been paid in kind; but, like so many other pastoral revenues, they had, in some long forgotten past, been converted into fixed sums of money. The typical vicarage had decayed well before the Reformation — and this incidentally helps to explain the poor performance of the old church in rural areas. But inflation went on. By the end of the century, a vicarage was a pittance. The yield from the temporalities was similarly distorted. The feu duties had, as we have seen, been decimated; but the rents from the proper lands — that is from the lands still unfeued and thus farmed by tenants — were more flexible. In the arable east, where they were calculated in kind, they adjusted themselves to the price rise; in the pastoral west, where they were paid in money, they could be — and eventually would be — augmented. The proper lands were still valuable.

But these are generalities. In fact, the patrimony was divided up into a series of parcels, some once called abbacies and others still called bishoprics. Each parcel consisted of an estate or series of estates over which the holder had a civil jurisdiction and from which he drew the rents and feu duties; but it also included an assortment of appropriated teinds which belonged to the holder on the understanding that he would nonetheless provide for the minister of the parishes concerned. The parcels varied considerably in size and importance, but their character was uniform enough; they all had landed temporalities and they all had teinds. The ownership of these parcels was settled, with every appearance of permanence, soon after the Union of the Crowns. The bishoprics endowed bishops and thus became the property of the church. The abbacies, on the other hand, were granted, by charters confirmed in parliament, to lay Lords of Erection who were difficult to distinguish from civil magnates. If the bishoprics had been reunited with the church, the abbacies, subject only to the rather vague obligation to support the ministers of their appropriated kirks, were permanently secularised. This of course was sacrilege. The once proud patrimony of the church, inalienable though it may have been, was now reduced to the bishoprics and an entitlement to a part, often rather a small part, of the abbatial teinds. And this settlement seemed to be final.

The original charters of erection obliged the lord to use his newly acquired teinds to support a minister in the parishes to which they related. But these charters never defined an adequate stipend. Most rural stipends were thus the outcome of an unequal bargain between the titular of the teinds concerned, and an individual minister. This was recognised from the beginning and, in 1606, parliament established the first of a long series of commissions for the augmentation of stipends. This did not lay down a minimum, and yet it was only effective where the teinds were unusually large. But later parliaments were more forthcoming. King James, who made haste slowly, persuaded the parliament of 1617 to stipulate £333 or its equivalent in victual. The bishops' parliament of 1633 laid down £500; its aristocratic successors of 1641 and 1647 rather grudgingly agreed to the same figure; while the ministers' parliament of 1649 hoisted the minimum to £800.[19] These figures were not always achieved, particularly in small parishes; but it is obvious enough that the real advances were made by the Canterburians and by the radical Presbyterians. The intervening commissions of 1641 and 1647 were relatively, and perhaps significantly, inactive. In a sense this merely reflected the distractions of war; but it also illustrates the reluctance of an aristocracy which had suddenly been pushed back into power by the necessities of war. The battles of the Covenants were fought by an unhappy coalition of magnate and minister held together by a tacit understanding, nearly always honoured, that church property would not be mentioned at all. But the defeat of the Engagers changed the balance of power. The ministers of 1649, happy with their puppet parliament, were less reticent.

If the ministers of 1649 had a captive Marquis, the bishops of 1633 had had a captive king. The Canterburians had tempted Charles towards the comprehensive settlement of church property which his father had cautiously refused. In its original form, the Revocation of Charles I was consistent with the notion that the alienation of church property was sacrilege, that it would all be resumed by the crown and used to re-endow a powerful monolithic church. King James must surely have turned in his grave. The actual outcome, mildly diluted to ward off aristocratic discontent, was less catastrophic but radical enough. The teinds would not be confiscated as some had feared; but the heritor of the lands to which they related would be entitled to buy them at nine times their annual value if he wished. This was compulsory purchase, though the price was reasonable enough — especially as the heritor was buying an expanding obligation to support his local minister. The tithe reform was slow to mature, for many heritors already had tacks of their teinds, but the eventual impact was lasting and beneficial. The heritor now collected the teinds as well as the rents of his lands; the one was simply added to the other. The titular, often a distant absentee, was excluded from a process which he had frequently hindered; the rural economy was simplified and its efficiency enhanced.

The king, driven on by his bishops, tackled the temporalities too. The proper lands of the Lords of Erection were granted back to them for a money feu duty calculated in seventeenth-century terms; their rights of ownership were not seriously challenged, and this was therefore the least contentious part of the settlement. The fate of their feued lands was however much more controversial. The king reserved the right to buy out the feu duties at ten years purchase.[20] Once more this was reasonable in a narrowly financial sense; but the king, in buying the entitlement to the feu duties would be buying the superiority, and thus the jurisdiction, as well. He would be buying power at a price which had been reduced by inflation to a nominal level. And, if rumour did not lie, he was using English money to achieve his purpose. And, as if this was not enough, he was using the superiorities thus acquired to re-endow his bishops. The new bishopric of Edinburgh included part of the temporality and most of the teinds of the old abbey of Holyrood as well as the whole of the temporality of New Abbey in Galloway.[21] Similarly the estates of Arbroath Abbey and St. Andrews Priory were earmarked for the bishops of Brechin and St. Andrews. The trend of royal policy was plainly to buy, almost to confiscate, power from the magnates and then to transfer it to a highly centralised church. Seen in this light, the next rumour must have sounded plausible enough. This would have divided the lands of the remaining abbacies among forty-eight ministers who would thus have had a civil jurisdiction over them.

The act of 1633 abolishing ecclesiastical regalities cannot entirely have quieted these fears since the bishops had been specifically excluded from its scope. Churchmen, it seemed, could have regalities; magnates could not.[22]

These are of course questions rather than answers, but they are questions which the magnates themselves are bound to have asked. Above and beyond this, the Revocation of Charles I sought to diminish the power of titulars and Lords of Erection and to enhance the status of their vassals. Indeed, in one respect, it treated superior and vassal alike. Its central figure was the heritor, the man who held the property and drew the rents. Superiority was much less important. The revocation saw the ownership of land as a commercial rather than a jurisdictional function. It recognised the new realities of a society which had been tormented by a century of inflation. It provoked a revolution less because it was absurd than because it was real. The magnates opposed it less because it challenged their strength than because it exposed their weakness.

They were perhaps fortunate to find allies within the church itself. Most of the ministers — offended by Laud's Liturgy, bewildered by the Book of Canons and threatened by an alien ideology — were led by a talented minority of genuine presbyterians into a marriage with the magnates. This was an alliance of incompatibilities which would last as long as danger lasted — and not much longer. In 1649 the ministers, unshackled at last, went back to most of the policies of their Canterburian predecessors. They asked for the teinds — which now included the bishops' teinds — and they got much higher stipends. They welcomed, and indeed enacted, a petition from a committee of feuars from the kirklands which allowed the feuar to buy his own superiority while the crown, temporarily disabled, was unable to buy it for them — and the result was, of course, much the same. They extended the scope of the 1633 act against ecclesiastical regalities to include not only the jurisdictions that had once belonged to the bishops, but also those granted to magnates during the aristocratic years of the 'forties.[23] They brought back everything Laudian except his Liturgy — and, of course, his bishops.

Between them, the Canterburians and the Presbyterians got back most of the revenues of the old kirk which had survived the great inflation. Their most effective instruments were the augmentation commissioners of 1638 and 1649. Stipends rose so steeply that the teinds of many small parishes were totally exhausted; here at least, the aims of the First Book of Discipline were achieved. In some other much larger parishes their achievement would have been absurd. The teinds of St. Cuthbert's, the wealthy area surrounding the burgh of Edinburgh, were generous enough to supply two ministers and a fair proportion of the bishop's endowment as well.[24] In a sense, the ministers were in direct competition with the bishop. Indeed this sort of situation was not uncommon. The ministers of Edinburgh, whose numbers had grown as the burgh had grown, were expensive enough; they were usually paid at least twice as much as an ordinary parish minister. Part of their stipends came from the teinds of parishes, like Wemyss in Fife or Dunbarney in Perthshire, which had once sustained the collegiate churches of the burgh. Once again the ministers confronted themselves. The augmentation commissioners were presented with a difficult choice between a rural preacher of no great note and the mighty ministers of Edinburgh. It is interesting that they usually supported the parish against the city. Thus, for example, the stipend of Dunbarney was increased on three separate occasions between 1635 and 1649 from £308 to £707 — or about half the value of the teinds. The other half, reduced by the tacksman's profit to about £500, made a minor contribution to the mounting stipends of the capital.[25] These reasonably generous settlements confounded the Town Council, who had to make up the deficit, rather than the ministers; but rescue was at hand. In 1634 the bishops had produced the Annuity Tax levied on every householder in the City; a few years later, the abolition of episcopacy brought £6,000 from the bishopric of Orkney. The famous ministers of Edinburgh — Alexander Henderson, Robert Douglas, George Gillespie and the rest — did not starve.[26]

It is clear enough that the Canterburian and the Presbyterian succeeded in providing a stable and generous income for the ministers of the kirk and that, in doing so, they respected the social changes of the previous century. But the bishops were interrupted by the Government and the ministers by Oliver Cromwell. Each revolution was cut down well before its prime; we do not know the ultimate intentions of either of them. It is quite possible that one or the other would eventually have reclaimed the whole of the patrimony and the jurisdictions that would eventually have come with it. It is not impossible that the Melvillians would have used the bailies of the temporalities as the local hangmen of their local kirks; it is certain that the bishops used their civil jurisdictions during the 1630s. But the patrimony and its jurisdictions had already been devalued; it is equally possible that the church would have sought to create new systems of civil administration.

Indeed this was already happening. The great social problem of the period was represented by the army of the poor. It was generally agreed that the deserving poor — the aged, the sick and the wounded — 'who neither can nor may travail for their sustentation' — were the business of the church and that the rest — 'the stubborn and idle beggars who, moving from place to place, make a craft of their begging' — were criminals 'whom the civil magistrate ought to punish'.[27] If the unemployed were whipped enough, they would go away — at least as far as the next barony. It is obvious enough that this approach could not solve the problem. But the failure of the heritable juris-dictions drew attention to their impotence.

The first experiment, authorised by the famous poor law statute of 1579, seems to have failed. It allowed the crown to establish Justices of the Peace on the English model and it may have perished because too many barons were appointed as Justices. A much more interesting act of 1592 renewed the earlier statute and recognised the fact that it was useless; 'if the justices were negligent', the Crown would appoint new magistrates named by the kirk sessions.[28] 1592 was a good year for Melvillians, and this was surely a local manifestation of the theory of the two kingdoms. It is perhaps significant that such magistrates seem to have been operating in the radical years of 1649 and 1650.[29] Yet another act of 1600, when King James was stronger than he had been in 1592, turned the entire problem over to the kirk sessions.[30] Melville saw the magistrate as the servant of the kirk sessions; James saw the session as the servant of the Crown; both agreed that it was vital.

The next step belonged to the new highly centralised church of the Canterburian bishops. In 1635 the kirk session of Dundonald recorded an act against the entertainment of the sturdy beggar. The act was less unusual than the body which passed it. This included not only the ministers and the elders but the 'gentlemen' of the parish as well. In the spring of 1638 the same kirk session, similarly augmented, swore a little local Covenant to perform the same task.[31] Presbyterian and Canterburian alike were using the kirk session to deal with a problem which the First Book of Discipline had regarded as civil rather than ecclesiastical. In the meantime, during the early autumn of 1637, this same augmented session, like other kirk sessions elsewhere, sent in a petition against Laud's Liturgy. This indeed was an ecclesiastical matter, but it marked the beginning of a long process that would eventually defeat a king, overthrow his bishops, make war and eventually make peace again. The meaning of the word 'ecclesiastical' would stretch and snap. The civil parish grew out of the kirk session during the turmoil of a revolution. It repaired churches, paid schoolmasters, built bridges, failed to repel the plague and succeeded in raising rates; but, during the inspired informality of the bishops' wars, it levied taxes and recruited men; during the opposition to the Engagement, it presented political petitions and tried to hinder Hamilton's levy.

It did all these things and did most of them effectively because it respected the same social trends which had informed the Revocation of Charles I. It largely ignored the increasingly meaningless distinctions of medieval subinfeudation. It regarded a landed estate as a commercial enterprise rather than a unit of jurisdiction. Its hero was the heritor. In the feued lands of the temporalities and of the royal estates, he would be a landed vassal. In the proper lands or in a civil barony or regality, he would be a magnate with heritable jurisdiction. But the distinction would not be particularly important. A heritor was measured in real wealth rather than in pretended power.

The concept of the heritor represented the future. The revolutionaries seized eagerly upon it and turned it skilfully to their own purposes; but they were really interested in something else. They were seeking to create the godly society, that mysterious preparation for the kingdom of God which only a professional élite could achieve. Heritors might be useful at kirk session level, but they might be dangerous in the higher courts. The Commissioners of the general assembly, like the bishops of the 1630s, contrived to exclude most of the laymen from the inner citadels of the kirk. They constructed a 'state opposite to a state'; they claimed a monopoly of political power.[32] They groped for it, they half grasped it — and they lost it.

It is a truism that revolutions seldom achieve their real objectives and that they often achieve something else. The Scottish revolution failed in its own terms, but it deflected the course of history nonetheless. After a decade of war and insecurity, it was, as Rutherford confessed on his death bed, obsessed with power. The 'state opposite to a state' had become an end in itself; the godly society had receded and had eventually been lost. But Rutherford's revolution, with the help of Cromwell's army, had rattled the foundations of Scottish society. The feudal classes were driven into the arms of the crown; they accepted the centralised state and, with it, a church which would at least attempt to unify the state. Rebellion retreated romantically into the conventicle where it could fairly easily be contained. In the meantime the church itself found new assumptions; it would either support the state or it would, in separating itself from the state, disavow political power altogether. Either way, the 'state opposite to a state' was dead and it could never revive. Like the conventicle, it withdrew into the legend of the kirk.

Perhaps it had just been lucky. It had found feudal Scotland, tormented by inflation and pathetically conscious of the threat to its ancient jurisdictions, in temporary disarray. The magnates almost seemed to defeat themselves. But they too had a sense of history. They had adapted themselves to circumstances before and they would do so again. They had learned the arts and crafts of political survival. It was Lady Anna, a rackrenter by day and a radical by night, who showed the way. The seventeenth century would eventually belong to the landlord — superior or vassal — who augmented his rents and improved his estates. Heritable jurisdictions would continue a little longer — for the baron court was a convenient instrument of agricultural improvement — but it was no longer the bastion of feudal power. For now money was king and the church, no longer God, could worship God.

NOTES

1. *Historical Works of Sir James Balfour* (1824-5), iii, 426-7.

2. William Laud, *Works*, vi, 188.

3. *The Second Book of Discipline*, ed. J. Kirk (1980), 191-4, 209-12, 236. I should add that Dr. Kirk himself takes a different view of the meaning of these passages.

4. George Gillespie, *Assertion of the Government of the Church of Scotland in Points of Ruling Elders* (1641), 106; *The Letters of Samuel Rutherford*, ed. A. A. Bonar (1891), 56.

5. Gilbert Burnet, *History of My Own Time* (1897), i, 53-4; Gillespie, *op. cit.*, 10.

6. *Records of the Commission of the General Assembly*, SHS, xi, xxv, lviii *passim*; D. Stevenson, 'The General Assembly and the Commission of the Kirk, 1638-51', *RSCHS*, xix, Pt. I, 77-9.

7. W. Makey, *The Church of the Covenant* (Edinburgh 1979), Chapter 7.

8. James Guthrie, *Treatise of Ruling Elders and Deacons* (1690), 76.

9. *Historical Works of Sir James Balfour* (1824-5), iii, 426-7; Robert Wodrow, *Analecta* (Maitland Club, 1842), ii, 281.

10. Makey, *op. cit.*, 3.

11. Makey, *op. cit.*, 3-4.

12. M. Sanderson, *Scottish Rural Society in the 16th Century* (Edinburgh, 1982), Chapter 7.

13. *Ibid.*, Chapters 5 and 6; M. Sanderson, 'Kirkmen and their Tenants on the Eve of the Reformation', *RSCHS*, xviii, pt. I (1972), 41.

14. Rentals, Accounts, Court Books and Tacks for the barony of Avondale (from the Hamilton Papers unless otherwise stated) as follows: Accounts, 1535; Accounts, 1544-5 (*Exchequer Rolls*, xvii, 583-88; xviii, 59-64); Rental, c.1540; Rental, c.1630; Baron Court Book, 1642; Accounts, 1648-53; Rental, 1652-5; Rental, 1670-9; Tacks, 1642-1706.

15. I have examined the testaments, 1573-1658, of 72 Avondale farmers.

16. S.R.O., Exchequer Papers, Valuation Rolls, Parish Totals (E901) Ayrshire, Renfrewshire, Lanarkshire.

17. S.R.O., Exchequer Papers, Valuation Rolls, Parish Total and List of Heritors (E901), parish of Mauchline, Ayrshire.

18. T. I. Rae, *The Administration of the Scottish Frontier* (1966), 15, 17; J. J. Wilson, *Annals of Penicuik* (1891), 146-50; S.R.O., Clerk of Penicuik Papers, Rental of the barony of Penicuik, 1646.

19. *APS*, iv, 531, 605; v, 35-9, 401-3; vi, pt. I, 778-9, pt. II, 287-8.

20. *APS*, v, 197-204.

21. Charter of Mortification of the Bishopric of Edinburgh, 29.9.33. I have used the transcript and translation made by Professor Donaldson and kindly deposited by him in the Edinburgh City Archives.

22. *Letters and Journals of Robert Baillie, 1637-62*, ed. D. Laing (Bannatyne Club 73), i, 6-7.

23. Sir John Scott of Scotstarvet, *True Relation*, reproduced in *SHR*, xii, 77-80; *APS*, vi, pt. II, 244-6.

24. See above, n. 21.

25. Edinburgh City Archives: Town Council Minutes, 25.3.35, 26.10.49; Accounts of Collector of Kirk Rents, 1612-45, *passim*.

26. *RPCS, 1633-5*, 234-6; Edinburgh City Archives: Accounts of the Treasurer of Kirk Rents and Ministers' Stipends, 1657 (bound with the Kirk Treasurer's Accounts, 1648-63); *Extracts from the Records of the Burgh of Edinburgh, 1626-41*, 338-41.

27. John Knox, *History of the Reformation*, ii, 290.

28. *APS*, iii, 576.

29. Kirk Session Records, Rothiemay, 7.2.50; Mortlach, 29.6.50; Dyce, 14.10.49; Edzell, 6.12.49; Blairgowrie, 1649-50.

30. *APS*, iv, 232.

31. *The Kirk Session Record of Dundonald*, ed. H. Paton (1936), 398-400.

32. *Testimony left by Samuel Rutherford* (1726), 6-7.

9

Anti-clericalism in Scotland during the Restoration

Julia Buckroyd

WHY did the Restoration church settlement fail? For many Scottish historians in the past the question made no sense. It was evident to them that a regime which offended the sensibilities of what they took to be a popular Presbyterian majority would in the course of time be bound to fail, brought to the ground by a combination of anti-episcopal and pro-Presbyterian sympathies.

Wodrow and his heirs and successors did their best to document a catalogue of episcopal misdeeds whose obvious retribution was the downfall of the bishops, but this is hardly a sufficient explanation for the failure of the settlement. In the first place I am doubtful about the list of the bishops' cruelties and excesses. Where I can check up on Wodrow I very often find a rather different account of things. In the short-lived Church Commission, for example, so far as I can discover, Archbishop Sharp's influence was for moderation and leniency.[1]

Even laying aside the whole issue of Wodrow's accuracy and the question of numerical support for Presbyterianism, I am doubtful about Wodrow's argument, which seems to imply that the Scottish government responded to popular pressure, and is in some sense democratic. I am not certain how far the consent of the governed was thought necessary to Scottish seventeenth-century policy makers, but I am fairly certain that policy was not usually made in response to popular pressure. My impression of the post-Revolutionary church settlement, for example, is that it was, as much as the Restoration settlement, imposed from above, and likewise met with some resistance. It seems more likely that an explanation for the failure of the settlement is to be found by considering the relations between the Restoration church, principally in the persons of the bishops, and the politically active and significant rulers in Scotland, the political nation.

I should like to suggest that the Restoration church settlement failed because of the antipathy of the political nation to the episcopate. I am not here talking about personal antipathies (although they certainly existed) nor about the failings of the individual bishops, but about a general attitude that can perhaps most conveniently be labelled anti-clericalism. This anti-clericalism was so

167

widespread, so persistent and so deep-seated that it succeeded in undermining a settlement that had been effected with the apparent near-unanimous consent of the political nation. Almost nobody made a sustained objection to or protest against the initial decision to try to introduce legislation to bring in episcopacy, the drafting of the Act Rescissory in the Articles, the passage of the Act through parliament or the introduction of the various acts re-establishing episcopacy.[2] Yet the motives of the legislators and their refusal to co-operate with the bishops to make an episcopal system workable ensured without doubt its eventual failure.

Essentially what follows, therefore, is a documentation of the ways in which the anti-clericalism of the political nation denied the episcopal system the support that it required to survive the period of Lauderdale's ascendancy to 1679.

One of the general features of this anti-clericalism, and very possibly the background against which more specific cases of non-co-operation can be set, was a hostility to clerical pretensions of any kind. A legacy of antagonism to presbytery was undoubtedly one element behind the introduction and passing of the Act Rescissory. Middleton, who had personal experience of being made to do public penance by the Presbyterians, and whose royalist rising in 1654 had, at least in his estimation, not met with the support from the ministers that it deserved, asked the king to be allowed to introduce episcopal legislation 'for the humiliation of the preachers'.[3]

The reaction to the Protesters during 1660 by the Committee of Estates had been harsh.[4] Even the Resolutioners who had been at loggerheads with them for so long were taken aback by the treatment they received. Robert Douglas thought that the hostility to Guthrie had been inspired by revenge.[5] In February 1661 *Mercurius Caledonius*, the satirical paper begun in January of that year, was so offensive to the ministers that Sharp attempted to get it silenced, remarking grimly, 'One thing I am sure of, that the neglect and contempt of ministers is very visible'.[6] So visible was it that it became irresistible; Rothes excused his support of the Act Rescissory to Sharp on the grounds that he did not wish by opposing it to seem to support the Protesters, they, as he said, 'being still obnoxious to jealousy, and hated upon the account of their proceeding in the '48 and since'.[7]

The illusion, however, that this hostility was specially reserved for the Pro-testers and did not extend to Resolutioners, far less to the episcopate, proved to be that, an illusion. There was for example an attempt made to reduce the stipends of ministers in the parliament of 1661.[8] 'The drift of most of this parliament,' Sharp complained, 'is to bring the ministrie under beggary and the extremity of contempt.'[9] In 1662, when the Billeting Act was passed to exempt twelve Scots, to be named in secret ballots of Members of Parliament, from the royal pardon for the events since 1637, the story was told that the twelve bishops had been entered on one ballot as a joke.[10] If a joke, it was black humour. Again in 1667 Rothes wrote to Lauderdale protesting against the im-position of taxation on ministers, who had formerly been exempt, asserting that ministers were the butt of envy and malice.[11] Indeed in 1665 Sharp had written to Lauderdale asking him not to press for the exemption of bishops from taxation despite the poverty of most of the bishoprics, because of the hatred it was likely to provoke.[12]

This general atmosphere of contempt and hostility was the background against which much more serious opposition to the episcopate was conducted. The first sign of these policies was visible in the exclusion of churchmen from policy-making at the Restoration. If I may briefly recapitulate the events of the 1660s, the division in the church visible in the 1640s hardened after 1648 with the emergence of two opposing groups, the Protesters and the Resolutioners. The core of their disagreement lay in their respective attitudes towards the role of the king in society: the Protesters favoured a theocratic government while the Resolutioners were much more prepared to allow the king power to rule. During the interregnum the occupation forces in Scotland consistently favoured the Protesters and preferred them to posts in universities and parishes as well as using some of them — notably Johnston of Wariston — in the civil Government. Although the Resolutioners co-operated with the occupation forces, on the grounds 'that any government is to be preferred to anarchy and confusion', as David Dickson and his brethren later expressed it,[13] they maintained contact with the king in exile.

In late 1659 and early 1660, when it became obvious that 'a great revolution of affairs'[14] was afoot, the Protesters recognised that their only hope lay in trying to prevent the return of the king, but the Resolutioners were confident of the king's favourable disposition towards them. Accordingly they sent James Sharp to London as their agent to be responsible for promoting Resolutioner interests.[15]

In retrospect it is clear that the Resolutioners had a ludicrously inflated view of their value to the king and of the pressure they could bring to bear on him. During his six or eight months in London Sharp gradually became aware of this and tried to convey it to his brethren, but even he seemed sure that church affairs would be left to churchmen to resolve. As late as the end of May 1660 he wrote confidently to his brethren, 'I believe the king will not meddle with that which concerns the Kirk's interests, but will refer all to a General Assembly'.[16] Like his brethren, Sharp appeared to be able to sustain an entire confidence in the probity of the Resolutioners' behaviour and the king's goodwill to them, especially by contrast with the Protesters. Only later did Lauderdale express a secular view of the Resolutioners: 'they countenanced not those who did rise for the king, and treated with Cromwell'.[17]

The Resolutioners' trust in the king survived, however, even when in late June Sharp began to report from London that there were plans to destroy presbytery: 'I hear it is whispered by some noblemen here that it were fit it were done'.[18] He could still write with confidence:

> The king hath declared his resolution not to meddle with our church government which hath quieted the clamourings of some ranting men here, as if it were easy to set up episcopacy amongst us.[19]

The king's favour to the Resolutioners was manifested to Sharp's satisfaction in a draft of a proclamation for summoning a General Assembly,[20] and in the famous letter to Robert Douglas, presbytery of Edinburgh, assuring him of the royal favour:

> We do also resolve to protect and preserve the government of the church of Scotland as it is settled by law, without violation.[21]

With these documents secured, Sharp left London for Scotland, well pleased with what he had achieved[22] and apparently unconcerned that he, the lone representative of the Scottish church in London, had been sent home by the king with explicit instructions that he was not to be replaced.[23] The total trust of the Resolutioner leadership in the king may best be demonstrated by the fact that almost a year later, in June 1661, the ministers of Edinburgh wrote to Lauderdale with confidence only slightly dimmed:

> We doe still assure ourselves that his Sacred Majestie will not endeavour any change, at least without so much as hearing Ministers of the Gospel to speak for themselves.[24]

In December 1660, when the Scottish Council met in London to draw up Middleton's instructions as Commissioner for the coming parliament, in church affairs, there was no churchman present. The discussion focused not on religious issues, but whether in practice it would be politically possible for Middleton to introduce episcopacy. The opposition, such as it was, principally from Lauderdale, was expressed in exactly the same terms and asserted that to introduce episcopacy would politically be unwise.[25]

The significance of this meeting for an understanding of the fortunes of the Restoration church settlement can hardly be exaggerated. At a stroke the religious and theological considerations which had been rehearsed innumerable times over the previous one hundred years are reduced to the simple issue of political utility. The churchmen whose role in the formulation of policy had waxed and waned were now dismissed. Those who have supposed that Sharp was the malevolent evil genius behind the metamorphosis of church government in Scotland reckon without this intensely secular spirit. Sharp himself was well aware that policy-makers did not await his opinion. In April 1661 he remarked to Lauderdale:

> I am more acquainted with what passes here [in Edinburgh] by my own observations of persons and the wheels of their motions, than by anything they communicate to me, which they seldom do until they have fixed their resolution or have acted it.[26]

Indeed on numerous occasions during the spring of 1661 Sharp had occasion to remark on the changed status of ministers, and, it is hardly surprising, sometimes with a certain amount of bitterness:

> Now you see our statesmen will have the world know we are not a priestridden nation; we ministers must bear what we can not mend, we know nothing of their

making of acts, and when they are made we ought to put the best construction upon them.[27]

This secular control was manifested equally clearly in the actual process of re-establishment of the episcopate. In 1662 the estate of bishops was restored in terms that suggested a return to an episcopal church government where bishops were powerful figures, not only in political and material terms, but in terms of their control of church policies:

> Whatever shall be determined by his Majestie with advice of the Archbishops and bishops — in the externall Government and policie of the church — shall be valeid and effectuall.[28]

In fact the whole tenor of the Restoration church settlement ensured that the bishops would be subordinated to the civil power and prevented from exercising even those powers explicitly granted by the king. Take for example the question of nominations to bishoprics. It seems that until 1663 the practice was for the nomination to be made by the king but with advice from the Archbishop of St. Andrews, who in turn appears to have consulted Lauderdale.[29] In June 1663 the king gave Sharp the right of nomination to bishoprics.[30] In 1665 Sharp was made aware that Lauderdale was being approached directly and importuned to make nominations. He therefore reminded Lauderdale that the right of nomination belonged to him.[31] He was sent in return a blistering letter.[32] The effect was that in the future Sharp was obliged to continue to defer to Lauderdale's opinion. In 1669, for example, he wrote:

> Albeit by your favour I had a command and warrants from the king in the case of vacancies of bishoprics in this church, yet I shall be determined by your bishop's nomination. And if you will allow me to offer my humble opinion . . . [33]

In 1671, however, Robert Moray tried to reduce Sharp's influence even more. He wrote to Lauderdale:

> I have not yet had time to speak with Archbishop St. Andrews concerning the filling of the vacancy of the Isles, but I am told that he says that if you will recommend Mr. Ramsay, the Dean of Glasgow to him, that he will then be graciously pleased to recommend him. Now since I am told he pretends a right to those recommendations under the king's hand, I am of the opinion that his recommendation should be so little asked that I would rather put him out of all thoughts of having it considered.[34]

Later the same year Gilbert Burnet complained that Sharp was claiming credit for promoting his own bishops. He wrote to Lauderdale:

> The archbishop of St. Andrews sent for the bishop of Galloway to his house and made him abundantly sensible that he was to promote him; so that the civility of thanks is all must go to your share but the reality of the obligation is claimed entirely to himself.[35]

Any example of the bishops assuming any real political power or recognition met with undisguised hostility from the nobility even when those powers were granted by the king. In 1664, for example, Sharp was given precedence before the Chancellor, a development which Lauderdale notified to Primrose, the Lord Register, with unmistakable distaste:

> [here is] a letter which will be less welcome: it is a command to the Council that the archbishop of St. Andrews take place before the Chancellor in pursuance of the like command from the late king, dated July 1626, and accordingly his name is set first in all commissions.[36]

The death of Chancellor Glencairn in 1664 provoked a contest for the office in which Sharp was a competitor. The prospect that the primate might also be Chancellor aroused violent antipathy. Bellenden, the mouthpiece of Sharp's enemies, wrote to Lauderdale expressing their strong hostility to the whole idea:

> What esteeme he [Sharp] hath at Court I know not, but do conceive it fit that His Majesty may be tymelie informed how unacceptable a person he will be to fill the roume of Chancellar.[37]

Sharp's assumption of leadership in the crisis at the time of the Rullion Green Rising seems almost certainly the real reason behind his fall from power in 1667. He was accused, again by Bellenden, of 'usurping the direction of public affairs'[38] — a charge that clearly struck straight to Lauderdale's paranoid heart.

In many other ways the power of the bishops even within the church was limited and curtailed by the civil power. There was for example no meeting permitted of any national assembly of the church. The original desire for a general assembly voiced by the Resolutioners in 1660 had been frustrated in 1661 by the king. He had forbidden a meeting on the very erastian grounds that ministers might not meet in an assembly to give their views on church government because church assemblies must not be seen to challenge parliamentary authority.[39]

In 1663 an alternative was proposed in the form of a National Synod[40] and passed in the parliament of that year.[41] Although the act ensured effective royal supremacy in the synod by royal control of the agenda and the royal veto, nevertheless it allowed for an assembly which would have permitted a public display of support for the established church. In 1664 and 1665 there were plans for its meeting which the two archbishops and all the bishops supported.[42] In fact it never did meet and the whole project was dropped, probably at the king's command. After the events of 1659-71, however, the spirits of the establishment were so discouraged that it again began to be spoken of as a way of re-asserting the settlement.

In 1674 some of the most attractive and energetic figures in the church, Leighton, Gilbert Burnet, James Ramsay, bishop of Dunblane, and various ministers of the presbytery of Edinburgh, attempted to petition for the meeting of a National Synod. Gilbert Burnet was the most articulate among them and expressed his strong sense of the necessity of such a meeting to the Earl of

Tweeddale: 'It can be easily demonstrated that the want of it hath ruined our church'.[43] The Privy Council treated the request as the occasion for some cynical political infighting in which Lauderdale triumphed, using the opportunity to prevent a meeting of the Synod. By an unpleasant irony Lauderdale then used Sharp to bring the activists to book.[44] The remarkable feature of these events is that a meeting of the most enthusiastic supporters of the *established* church had been prevented, as an intolerable display of independence.

Indeed it seems that, in the opinion of the politicians, ecclesiastical policy should be made by politicians with or without the concurrence of the bishops. Sharp had consistently opposed the various modifications of church government suggested after 1666. This opposition was ignored, as was that of Alexander Burnet, archbishop of Glasgow. Sharp wrote to Lauderdale in May 1669 that the projected Indulgence was merely

> laying a foundation for encouraging and perpetuating a separation and schism in this church, which to my apprehension will be unavoidable if any considerable number of outed ministers be again put into charge and exempted wholly from the inspection and jurisdiction which the law and constitution of the church gives the bishops.[45]

When the Indulgence was made public in July 1669, Sharp wrote to Lauderdale indicating what he felt would be the likely effect on the orthodox clergy:

> Some of the bishops being in town and some ministers who have spoke with me are very surprised and affected with the apprehension they have of the consequences of this Indulgence which hath exceedingly raised the confidence of the opposing party and damped the hearts of those who own the settled government.[46]

He was prepared, however, to make the best of a bad job and to give his reluctant acquiescence. So, for example, he made a speech in the Privy Council on the same day indicating his public obedience:

> I have cause firmly to believe that the king is unalterably resolved to preserve the government of the church as now settled against all opposition and therefore [I] cannot have any jealousy that by these orders the weakening, much less the subverting that government is intended.[47]

Despite this, however, Tweeddale reacted with real fury to Sharp's desire to have some role in the formulation of policy:

> The grudge is still that these matters have been transacted without him, implying that whatsoever the king does order in church matters without the concurrence of the clergy is illegal. And I have heard he says that the King's Commissioner in an Assembly has not the like authority as in a Parliament, for the Supremacy is personal and cannot be delegated, but in the king's personal absence understands the primate to be his vicar. This I tell you that you may see what necessity there is of explaining acts of Parliament and asserting the king's authority more fully.[48]

The 'asserting of the king's authority more fully' resulted in the formulation of what became the Act of Supremacy. Its avowed aim was to reduce the influence of the clergy in the formulation of ecclesiastical law.[49] The point of it was to permit the evolution of ecclesiastical policy without the least necessity to consult the bishops. When Sharp attempted to retain some function for the bishops, arguing for example that bishops were essential for ordination,[50] Tweeddale again reacted in an astonishingly autocratic way, describing Sharp's resistance as 'presbyterian true blue'.[51]

These attitudes to episcopal power were reiterated in 1672 over Sharp's reaction to yet a further indulgence of which he disapproved. Sharp had written rather mildly to Lauderdale:

> I hope for pardon if I say that amidst all the apprehensions which go abroad of the great depression of the episcopal order by the late publications of his Majesty's pleasure in matters of religion, I retain my confidence of your lordship's entire affection to it and rely upon your patrociny and protection which will be sufficient for its support, notwithstanding of the high expectations of its adversaries.[52]

Moray's response to this was to write:

> [he] should as little have been consulted with there [in Scotland] as others of his coat were here [in England] . . . Either they need not be upon the knowledge of the designs suggested or if for decorum or other reason some of them must be, what they say should not be allowed great weight.[53]

By 1678 Sharp had been so cowed by this constant attrition of his power and his authority that his request to proclaim a fast day in thanksgiving for the king's survival of an assassination attempt was couched in the most craven and grovelling language:

> We [the Privy Council] should have first sent to know his Majesty's gracious pleasure, to whom by the constitution of this Church the appointing of public fasts doth belong but . . . presuming that it would not be unacceptable . . .[54]

The unmistakable cumulative effect of these attacks on episcopal authority was a general disbelief among the political nation and in the country at large that there was any fixed resolution to maintain an episcopal system. The confidence among the Resolutioners in 1660 that Charles at least would not betray presbytery was symptomatic of an ineradicable suspicion that, whatever might be said to the contrary, the king was not unalterably committed to episcopacy.

Charles did what he could to counteract the recurring rumours on this theme. He was prepared to assert that monarchical power and the episcopal settlement were inextricably related. In 1663, for example, he wrote in response to Sharp's complaints of Chancellor Glencairn's passive dissent:

> I cannot choose but tell you that the Crown can have no other sure foundation but upon the church's being well settled.[55]

Similarly in 1665 Sharp had been encouraged to be told

that our royal master in his princely judgement does take his honour and true interest to be so much concerned in the countenancing and maintaining of our legal settlement.[56]

These assertions were however obviously inadequate to still the rumours. The king, it was being said, was only a puppet in the hands of his courtiers. Accordingly in 1667, when the letter from the king countenancing the orthodox clergy was being discussed at court, additional measures were suggested to bolster the statement of the king's resolution to support episcopacy as Lauderdale reported:

My Lord Chancellor [of England] complimented me upon that letter . . . but wished that the archbishop of Glasgow and Bellenden might tell when they came to Scotland, and Lord Lauderdale might write to his friends, how perfectly it was the king's sense, lest it should be said in Scotland that my Lord Glasgow had desired, and Lord Lauderdale had written that letter, but the king concerned not himself in that letter.[57]

When changes in church government took place without Sharp's consent, it was inevitable that he should have doubts of the king's commitment and depended heavily on the king's repeated assurances of his resolution.[58] It is hard to believe Charles was not speaking for public consumption when in 1668 he received the news of the attempt on Sharp's life with the words:

'Well' said the king 'what can they say. A villain will attempt a murder everywhere. This was a fool, for he might kill Dr. Sharp, but the archbishop can never be killed, for I shall still make more'.[59]

It was felt necessary at every official opportunity for Charles to reiterate his support for the settlement, whether in letters to the Privy Council[60] or at the beginning of each parliament. In 1669, for example, the king's speech to parliament read by Lauderdale stressed that the king 'with no less zeal and constancy . . . will maintain the ancient government by archbishops and bishops'.[61] In the instructions to the parliament of 1672 Lauderdale was commanded:

You shall assure our Parliament of our constant continuing in our resolution to maintain the true reformed Protestant religion and the government of the church by archbishops and bishops, whatever seditious persons disaffected to our government may suggest to the contrary.[62]

In 1673 this message was repeated in the king's speech with even more emphasis:

And whereas the malicious tongues of the disaffected may still bespatter his Majesty and his government with base slanders and false suggestions, I am again particularly commanded to renew to you the fullest assurance of his Majesty's most constant continuance in his firm and unalterable resolutions to maintain the true reformed protestant religion and the government of this church by archbishops and bishops against popery and separation.[63]

In the same way Lauderdale found himself being required to reassert and reiterate his commitment to episcopacy in the face of considerable doubt as to his sincerity. His problem was the greater, of course, since no dispassionate observer could have detected an enthusiasm for presbytery in Charles at any stage, but Lauderdale had the reputation of a vigorous politician in the Presbyterian cause to live down, not to mention his role as pious youth and Resolutioner protégé. Of the important Scottish politicians at the Restoration, he was the one whose loyalty to presbytery lasted longest, borne down in the end, it seems, only by his political ambition. In 1663 Lauderdale tried to scotch persistent rumours of his presbyterian sympathies once and for all by a public assertion in parliament of his entire commitment to the episcopal settlement. He concluded his account of what he had said in parliament to the king with the words:

> if any shall hereafter slander me as an opposer of bishops, they must at the same time declare me a very fool.[64]

Not surprisingly the man who proved hardest to convince of Lauderdale's devotion to the new settlement was Sharp, whose estimate of Lauderdale's motivation for the change was extremely cynical. Nor was he above conveying these opinions to the king:

> [I said to the king that] for my part I trusted my Lord Lauderdale his protestations that he is right as to the government of the church seeing in point of gratitude to his master, prudence and regard to his own interest, he is obliged to it.[65]

But of course Sharp did not trust Lauderdale, and in view of his conduct probably had little reason to. As he remarked in 1667 when the control of church affairs had been taken out of his hands by Lauderdale:

> [this church] is now put into your hands to sink or swim as you shall be disposed towards the bishops of it.[66]

His attempts to ensure Lauderdale's continuing favour took the form of stressing how much Lauderdale was (and by implication would be held to be) responsible for the success of the settlement:

> No other thing can so much conduce for quieting the distempers of this church as the subjects knowing that the bishops do entirely rely upon your lordship's favour, advice and assistance.[67]

In 1669 the prospect of Indulgence and Act of Supremacy were drawing from Lauderdale assurances to Sharp 'to preserve inviolably the government of the church as now settled by law'[68] in the face of Sharp's disbelief. In other quarters, too, Lauderdale found it necessary to repeat his assertions of loyalty. He wrote to the Archbishop of Canterbury:

> You may indeed be assured (as you now profess you are) of the sincerity of my professed kindness and concernment for the ecclesiastical government as now settled.[69]

Tweeddale was another whose behaviour in the wake of the Rullion Green Rising had raised Sharp's apprehensions:

> I do confess I was upon some inducements tempted to a jealousy of the Earl of Tweeddale, his good affection to the settled government [of the church].[70]

These doubts about the commitment of the major politicians were however merely the tip of the iceberg; all kinds of rumours were constantly flying about tending to the same conclusion, that at any time the episcopal system might be dismantled. In 1664 Sharp wrote to Lauderdale commenting on the disastrous effect of the general suspicion that episcopacy would not last long:

> Whence that infusion is spread, God, he knoweth, but is of that operation with the most, bothe of our friends and adversaries that the design is laid and aworking, to render the bishops of this church insignificant and contemptible, to make their authority precarious, and then way is made for their inevitable ruin.[71]

In 1667 the fact that the two archbishops were out of favour did not go unnoticed, and all sorts of rumours began to circulate. Tweeddale reported to Robert Moray:

> There is great talk at Edinburgh of a change of [Privy] Council, and the archbishops should be left out. Bear down all you can such impudent lies.[72]

The various attempts at conciliation after 1666 produced a torrent of rumours. Tam Dalyell reported from the West:

> the lenity and liberty which is granted to the deposed ministers and Remonstrator crew makes most incline that way as if it were done of design one day to establish their presbytery.[73]

Lauderdale retailed other rumours:

> It seems there are reports that Crawford, Cassilis and Lothian are to be brought on the Council . . . Such reports do us much hurt for it gives fools occasion to talk as if the King would alter the government [of the church].[74]

The scheme for admitting of outed ministers on terms in 1668 induced Tweeddale to write to Robert Moray:

> the clergy must be raised a little in the esteem of the people or they shall be totally overthrown.[75]

Shortly afterwards he wrote again, making the point even more forcibly:

> All lookers on conclude a present change to be intended whereby order established by law should fall under absolute contempt.[76]

The plans for Indulgence and Supremacy produced a further surge of gossip. Tweeddale reported:

> much talking there is what shall be done this Parliament, the fanatics stretching their hopes of great things from it.[77]

The second Indulgence of 1671 had similar effects. Kincardine wrote to Lauderdale:

> I do not know anything [that] does our church affairs here more hurt than foolish hopes [of general indulgence] they are fed with and our unequal dealing with them, and slackness to execute either act of parliament or council in order to these affairs, which hath brought all acts in such contempt that they are no more cared for than gazettes.[78]

But it was not only those who hoped for the downfall of episcopacy who were affected by the policies of the administration; the orthodox clergy were extremely discouraged by it, particularly after 1669. Gilbert Burnet wrote to Tweeddale urging the strengthening of the establishment:

> 'For till that be,' he wrote, 'the discontented party here will never judge you design in earnest the preservation of episcopacy . . . hoping . . . they may force the king to the setting up of their so much idolised presbytery.[79]

It was probably not wholly in jest that it was reported to Lauderdale in 1669:

> The curates (as they call them) in the West, are at their last prayers, and one . . . said lately in his prayer 'And now lord if it be Thy will to shake and dissolve this church government, loose we pray the pins of it softly and grant us peace in our time.[80]

It is in this widespread conviction that episcopacy was not made to last that popular opinion responded to the anti-clericalism of the administration and assisted its ultimate downfall.

Nevertheless the ambiguous attitudes of the office-bearers and the persistent emasculating of episcopal power would not in themselves have created the environment in which the episcopal settlement was made to fail. Those two conditions, however, were the background against which a significant number, possibly the great majority, of the Scottish nobility simply failed to put the ecclesiastical legislation into effect. Any summary of the content of the letters of the two archbishops during the period would show this as their over-riding concern. By a simple policy of passive disobedience, a policy made possible by the ambivalent behaviour of the administration, the legislation putting the church settlement into effect was simply never systematically enacted.[81]

The Duke of Hamilton was the most important of those suspected of failing to put legislation into effect from early in the reign. Over the years he managed to find a vast range of excuses why that should be so, ranging from sciatica to inadequacies in the postal service. One of his most consistent excuses was that he lacked the money to carry out his duties and that if only the king would provide it, he would do what was expected of him.[82] It was typical, for example, that his troop in the militia had not taken the oath of allegiance by the required date in 1674.[83] Ultimately Hamilton made his protest public and used the failure of the church settlement as a way of attacking Lauderdale. In this he was exceptional; most of the nobility chose to make their protest by means of passive resistance.

Sharp was of course the one who repeatedly pointed out that the law was not being enacted, and that without the co-operation of the civil power it could not be. In 1664 he wrote to Lauderdale:

> I wish we had cause to say that all heer who profess to be convinced that it is high tym to guard against shism were carefull to suppress it; for our part who are church men we can but regrait the neglect.[84]

In 1667 the bishops as a whole wrote to Lauderdale making the same point in the wake of the Rullion Green Rising:

> Wee find our interest how wigorously soever imployed insufficient to prevaile over these [error, profainnes, schism, and sedition], without the reale assistance of the Ministers of State and justice of the kingdom.[85]

Nor was it simply the case that the hardline bishops constantly called for ever more rigorous enforcement of the laws. Gilbert Burnet reported that Leighton, a dove if there ever was one, found exactly the same situation as Archbishop of Glasgow:

> And tho' . . . he hath . . . done all [that] lay in his power for encouraging the regular clergy, yet without more vigorous assistance he will be too weak to resist a torrent which threatens to bear away the church as established.[86]

The inevitable effect was a further diminution of episcopal authority. Sharp repeatedly pointed out to Lauderdale how the settlement was undermined, and the effect of that on the population generally:

> It is the general expectation that if the lords [of Council] do not remit their care, but steadily pursue the methods laid for suppressing conventicles, so as the inferior magistrates and people be brought to believe they were in earnest, the work will not be so difficult as was imagined . . . The sorrows of our [the bishops'] condition [are seen] to be such that everybody may with impunity reproach and revile us, and those who should depend upon us, do thus lift up the heel against us.[87]

In 1675 and 1676 the situation had deteriorated to the point where known offenders were not apprehended, as Alexander Burnet wrote to Sharp:

> It is to little purpose to apprehend or punish inconsiderable persons while the ringleaders, who appeared most active in the last rebellion, and others that are since declared fugitives appeare publikely in contempt of all authority and cannot be (at least are not) seazed.[88]

What were the reasons for this widespread reluctance to enable the settlement to function, when after all it had been enacted by those same men who made its functioning impossible? It was clear to Sharp from the very beginning that the current of enthusiasm for episcopacy was not based upon religious or even theological considerations. As early as December 1660 he wrote to Patrick Drummond in London:

> Whatever may be the pretensions of some either with you or heir of introducing

episcopacy into this Church, I have cause to question ther reality, and doe think that when the matter is putt to the push it will be found that the setting up of Bishops is not at the bottom; I am not convinced that conscience or zeal as to the matters of Church Governement doeth sway much with some men, and I fear the most will unite in this one designe to treade upon the ministrie and render us wile and contemptible and am preesaging that this will be prosecuted to that extremity that in a short current of time it will open a door to bring in that with all disadvantages which most would avoyd.[89]

This general attitude of contempt for the ministry has been noted before, but it is perhaps possible to be more specific about the motivations of the nobility in establishing episcopacy, self-interested as these undoubtedly were. I think they can most nearly be expressed as a determination to be free of all direction and control by ecclesiastical persons of whatever kind. Since bishops were royal appointees, they could be used for other men's purposes but simultaneously denied any authority or power.

When it suited the administration, the bishops could be brought to heel. In 1667, after the Rullion Green Rising, for example, Sharp was publicly disgraced. Ostensibly he was brought down for the harshness of the punishment of nonconformity, which, it was said, had provoked the Rising. In fact he was punished for his intervention in public affairs as a politician in a time of crisis. Part of his disgrace was to be dismissed as President of the Convention of 1667 and to be replaced by the Duke of Hamilton, a known Presbyterian sympathiser.[90] Similarly from the time of Rullion Green to his eventual dismissal, a way was sought of snubbing Alexander Burnet, archbishop of Glasgow.[91] It is difficult not to hear a vindictive note in Robert Moray's comment to Lauderdale: 'You will certainly conclude it were not amiss he had some mortification given him'.[92]

The most remarkable example of this 'mortification' procedure is the case of the treatment meted out to Sharp over a complaint he made that found its way to the king, about the Earl of Kincardine. In 1665 the Earl, a known Presbyterian sympathiser, attended an irregularly conducted communion service. The king did not share the Scottish nobility's conviction that they were exempt from the operation of ecclesiastical law, so that Kincardine was in danger of political ruin. Lauderdale and Sir Robert Moray used their influence with the king to rescue Kincardine and then took revenge on Sharp. The primate was made to intercede for Kincardine with the king not only for a reprieve for him but for financial favours. Moray's indignation revealed his contempt for Sharp, bishops and ecclesiastical law:

It there be no greater restraint than he imagines as to reproving superiors, government and governors must be exposed to the foulest charges anybody can breathe out who satisfies himself with his own conscience and candour.[93]

On the other hand, although the bishops were to be kept in their places, they were also to be used. Their chief use was to ensure that the royal policies, whatever they might be, met with no opposition from the clergy. Never again were they to think that they might attempt to control the king, as Rothes wrote to Lauderdale with startling emphasis in March '61, when the fate of presbytery was in the balance:

> I am for the teacking auay the sivill sanxion from that act [giving legal status to presbyterian church government] that uie may leat our surthemen sie that they have a king relesid from thos fetirs hie uas formirlie tayd uith, uhich uill of nesesitie draue from them ther deou acnoulidgmint of him uhich uerie meanie of them ar shortcoming in, and uhen I consider uhen and hou this pour uas teacking from his majestie, and the bad yous mead of it and the sad afectis flouing from it, sum and tu meanie heaving the seam spirit in them nou as then, dus to me hould out the inuinsabill nesesitie of douing it.[94]

First of all, then, the function of the bishops was to keep the other clergy in order. In 1667 major modifications of ecclesiastical policy in the direction of compromise and toleration were initiated in the wake of the Rullion Green Rising and in face of the stated objections of the bishops. Nevertheless the task of the bishops was seen as orchestrating the acquiescence of the clergy as a whole. So, the Earl of Tweeddale wrote to Lauderdale commenting on the value of the two archbishops:

> The A[rch] B[ishhop of Glasgow] . . . will I hope upon this occasione give demonstratione of the usfulnes and nesescity of Bishops over such hot headid prag matike presbiters.[95]
>
> [Sharp] hes bein most useful at this time and without his presenc the inferiour clergy had flouen out to impertinencys.[96]

They themselves were on the whole ready to adopt this role, presumably in the hope that co-operation would bring its rewards:

> [Sharp] did assure me [Tweeddale] the clergy, not withstanding all endeavours to the contrary were well satisfied and did heartily close with and acquiesce to what was done and would so firmly continue.[97]

Additionally, however, the archbishops, and particularly Sharp, were to manage their fellow bishops in the interests of the administration. With reference to a change in political policy in 1667, Robert Moray remarked to Lauderdale, 'So, the two Archb[ishop]s not meddling, the others either will abstain or be insignificant.'[98]

The real measure of the weakness that this implied in the episcopate was the tone of contempt in which they were discussed. In 1667 the bishops sent a letter to Lauderdale signifying a dignified acquiescence in what they could not prevent and welcoming Lauderdale's public assertions, notwithstanding his policies, to maintain episcopacy. This letter found its way to Sir Robert Moray and Tweeddale who could not contain their derision:

> [Tweeddale] and I laughed till wee was weary at the letter of Bishops that was sent you . . . but in sum you will soon observe, as wee have done, what a silly company of people they are, and how usefull one of them [Sharp] is in mannaging of the rest.[99]

It is not surprising, then, given that the bishops performed these utilitarian functions for the administration, that the laws which maintained such an emasculated episcopacy should be widely flouted.

What are the wider implications of the anti-clericalism here described? There is undoubtedly nothing new about antipathy to clerical power in civil government. That is a very old song indeed, and one familiar in Scotland. What is different is the reluctance to permit churchmen to function at all. Whenever in the period since 1560 debates had been held on the role of the clergy, it had always been supposed that they had a role, other than simply carrying out the royal commands. Yet the logical conclusion of the activities of the Scottish politicians in the Restoration is that the clergy are there solely at the civil convenience. Middleton is said to have remarked tellingly:

> the Scottish lords beguiled themselves for they thought well to have brought in a sort of bishop to serve them by suppressing ministers freedom, which they called sauciness.[100]

It is certainly remarkable that any show of independence by the clergy was instantly labelled Presbyterian (and therefore completely unacceptable). The petition of the Synod of Glasgow in 1669, for example, was described by Tweeddale as 'somewhat like the presbyters and not unlike the beginning of the troubles'.[101] It was instantly christened the New Remonstrance. Similarly in 1671 Sharp's desire to control episcopal appointments was labelled by Robert Moray 'setting up of faction according to his old presbyterian principles'.[102] Scottish politicians were now completely unwilling to allow any independence of action in any sphere to churchmen.

Since 1560 the politics of church and state in Scotland had been inextricably intertwined. The language of theology had frequently expressed secular and political aims and motives. After 1660, however, these two elements in Scottish society are again separating out. The fierce desire of the Scottish nobility once again to fill their traditional political role, exiled from it as they had been during the Interregnum, made their ordinary desires for dominance even keener. The memory of their subordination to churchmen was an even sharper goad to seize all authority than their natural inclinations and expectations. These developments coincided with an increasing sophistication in political thought so that it was no longer so necessary to borrow theory from theology, and an increasing personal scepticism and secularism. Churchmen were being put in their places by newly confident politicians.

At least one contemporary was prepared to admit to all this, although he gave it a rather older name. William Douglas wrote to Lauderdale in August 1669, commenting on the passing of the Indulgence and the Act of Supremacy:

> It is debated now what sort of church government we have, whether Episcopal, Presbyterian or Erastian. For my own part I have read Erastus, but to speak with this Earl of Morton his grandfather, when they told him what Erastus' tenets were 'As I shall answer to God' (said he) 'I have ever been an Erastian all my days and I never knew it till now'. So be it for me.[103]

NOTES

1. J. M. Buckroyd, *Church and State in Scotland 1660-1681* (Edinburgh, 1980), 59.
2. *Ibid.*, 28-47.
3. *Ibid.*, 20-1, 27.
4. BM Add MS 23114; Minutes of Committee of Estates 1660, SRO PA 11/12.
5. HMC 72, Laing, i, 319.
6. J. M. Buckroyd, 'Mercurius Caledonius and its immediate successors', *SHR*, liv (April 1975), 11-21.
7. Sharp to Lauderdale, 15 April 1661, NLS 2512 f. 6.
8. *Lauderdale Papers*, 3 vols, ed. O. Airy (London 1884-5), hereafter *LP*, i, 72.
9. *Ibid.*, 69.
10. Edinburgh University Library MS. Dc5. 71, 141.
11. Rothes to Lauderdale, 3 Jan. 1667, BM Add MS 23216 f. 3.
12. Sharp to Lauderdale, 20 July 1665, NLS MS 2512 f. 80.
13. David Dickson etc. to Sharp, 17 March 1660, Glasgow University Library MS Gen. 210.
14. *Ibid.*, contemporary endorsement on the first page.
15. David Dickson etc. to Monck, 10 Jan. 1660, GUL MS Gen 210.
16. Sharp to ministers of Edinburgh, May 1660, GUL MS Gen 210.
17. Lauderdale to Tweeddale, 23 Feb. 1669, NLS MS 3136 f. 97.
18. Sharp to Douglas, 28 June 1660, GUL MS Gen 210.
19. *Ibid.*
20. *Ibid.*, 154-6.
21. King to Robert Douglas, 10 August 1660, GUL MS Gen 210.
22. Sharp to Douglas, 2 August 1660, GUL MS Gen 210.
23. Sharp to Douglas, 14 June 1660, GUL MS Gen 210.
24. *LP*, i, 294-5.
25. J. M. Buckroyd, *Church and State*, 27-8.
26. Sharp to Lauderdale, 15 April 1661, NLS MS 2512 f. 6.
27. *LP*, i, 73; see also *Ibid.*, 66, 87, 88.
28. *APS.*, vii, 254.
29. Sharp to Lauderdale, 20 Feb. 1663, NLS MS 2512 f. 17; same to the same, 23 Nov. 1663, *Ibid.*, f. 19.
30. Sharp to Lauderdale, 15 May 1665; *Ibid.*, f. 74.
31. *Ibid.*
32. *Ibid.*, ff. 76, 78.
33. Sharp to Lauderdale, 17 June 1669, *Ibid.*, f. 129; see also same to the same, 5 Jan. 1666, BM Add MS 35125 f. 130.
34. Robert Moray to Lauderdale, 23 Feb. 1671, BM Add MS 23134 f. 216.
35. Gilbert Burnet to Lauderdale, 20 Oct. 1671, NLS MS 3648 f. 9.
36. Lauderdale to Primrose, 16 Jan. 1664, NLS Acc. 7228/74, 13.
37. *LP*, i, 260; see also *Ibid.*, 223-4, 228, 242-3.
38. *Ibid.*, 253; see also *Ibid.*, 259.
39. Lauderdale to the ministers of Edinburgh, 26 Aug. 1661, NLS MS 3922 f. 17.
40. Draft of the Act for a National Synod, 1663, NLS MS 597 f. 114.
41. *APS*, vii, 465.
42. Tweeddale to Lauderdale, 6 Jan. 1664, NLS MS 7024 f. 4; Sharp to Lauderdale, 13 March 1665, NLS MS 2512 f. 68; Alexander Burnet to Lauderdale, 14 March 1665,

N

NLS MS 2512 f. 70.

43. Gilbert Burnet to Tweeddale, 25 May 1674, NLS MS 7121 f. 12.

44. J. M. Buckroyd, *Church and State*, 108-113.

45. Sharp to Lauderdale, 10 May 1669, NLS MS 2512 f. 126.

46. Sharp to Lauderdale, 20 July 1669, NLS MS 2512 f. 130.

47. *Ibid.*

48. HMC Laing, i, 372-3.

49. Passages of and notes upon Acts of Parliament relating to the King's Supremacy [July 1669], NLS Yester Box 130, folder 3.

50. Tweeddale to Robert Moray, 6 Nov. 1669, NLS MS 7024 f. 189.

51. Tweeddale to Robert Moray, 18 Nov. 1669, NLS MS 7024 f. 192.

52. Sharp to Lauderdale, 6 April 1672, NLS MS 2512 f. 148.

53. Robert Moray to Tweeddale, 13 April 1672, NLS MS 7005 f. 130.

54. Sharp to Lauderdale, 16 Nov. 1678, NLS MS 2512 f. 213.

55. King to Glencairn, 5 June 1663, NLS MS 573 f. 77.

56. Sharp to Lauderdale, 29 March 1665, NLS MS 2512 f. 72.

57. Lauderdale to Tweeddale, 16 May, 1667, NLS MS 7023 f. 34.

58. King to Sharp, December 1667, NLS Yester Box 130, folder 3.

59. Lauderdale to Tweeddale, 18 July 1668, NLS MS 7023 f. 182.

60. *RPC*, third series, 1668, ii, 541.

61. NLS MS 597 f. 212; see also f. 214.

62. Instructions to Lauderdale, 20 May 1672, BM Add MS 23135 f. 168; repeated *verbatim* in Parliament, *Ibid.*, f. 175.

63. Lauderdale's speech in Parliament, 1673, BM Add MS 23136 f. 16.

64. *LP*, i, 154-5; see also *Ibid.*, 157, 162; Gilbert Burnet, *History of My Own Time*, ed. O. Airy (Oxford, 1897) i, 366; Lauderdale to King, 13 July 1663, BM Add MS 23119 f. 86.

65. Sharp to Rothes, 28 May [1666], NLS Acc 7228/75.

66. Sharp to Lauderdale, 6 Nov. 1667, NLS MS 2512 f. 108.

67. Sharp to Lauderdale, 28 Oct. 1667, NLS MS 2512 f. 106.

68. Sharp to Lauderdale, 29 July 1669, BM Add MS 35125 f. 214.

69. Lauderdale to Sheldon, 2 Sept. 1667, NLS Yester Box 5, folder 5.

70. Sharp to Lauderdale, 15 Oct. 1667, NLS MS 2512 f. 104.

71. Sharp to Lauderdale, 21 July 1664, NLS MS 2512 f. 52.

72. Tweeddale to Robert Moray, 31 Oct. 1667, NLS MS 7024 f. 52.

73. Tam Dalyell to Lauderdale, 2 May 1667, BM Add MS 23126 f. 205.

74. Lauderdale to Robert Moray, 12 Oct. 1667, NLS MS 7023 f. 102.

75. Tweeddale to Robert Moray, 6 August 1668, NLS MS 7024 f. 107.

76. Tweeddale to Robert Moray, 19 August 1668, NLS MS 7024 f. 110.

77. Tweeddale to Robert Moray, 6 July 1669, NLS MS 7024 f. 166; see also Robert Moray to Tweeddale, 6 May 1669, NLS Yester Box 5, folder 4.

78. Kincardine to Lauderdale, [30 Nov.] 1671, BM Add MS 23135 f. 109.

79. Gilbert Burnet to Tweeddale, 29 Nov. 1669, NLS MS 7121, folder 5.

80. HMC 72, Laing, i, 375.

81. This subject is discussed at much greater length in J. M. Buckroyd, *Church and State*, *passim*. What follows is merely an outline of some features of the situation.

82. *Ibid.*, *passim* and *LP*, i, 202.

83. HMC 21, Hamilton Supplement, 87.

84. *LP*, i, 198; see also Sharp to [Lauderdale], 9 March 1676, NLS MS 2512 f. 197.

85. *LP*, ii, 60.

86. HMC xi (vi), Hamilton, 148.

87. Sharp to Lauderdale, June 1674, NLS MS 2512 f. 159.

88. HMC 72, Laing, i, 406; see also Alexander Burnet to Lauderdale, 15 August 1676, NLS MS 2512 f. 203; Sharp to Lauderdale, 13 May 1674, NLS MS 2512 f. 157.

89. *LP*, i, 49.

90. *Ibid.*, 209.

91. J. M. Buckroyd, 'The dismissal of Archbishop Alexander Burnet, 1669' (*Records of the Scottish Church History Society*, xviii (ii) 1973, 149-155).

92. *LP*, ii, 65.

93. Robert Moray to Kincardine, 20 April 1666, NLS MS 5050 f. 146; see also *Ibid.* f. 144, *LP*, ii, 228-33.

94. *LP*, i, 91.

95. *Ibid.*, ii, 9.

96. *Ibid.*, 32; see also *Ibid.*, 8, 31, 34.

97. *Ibid.*, 23.

98. *Ibid.*, 13.

99. *Ibid.*, 70. For the letter, see *Ibid.*, 59-61.

100. EUL MS Dc 5. 71, 199.

101. Tweeddale to Robert Moray, 30 Sept. 1669, NLS MS 7024 f. 180.

102. Robert Moray to Lauderdale, 23 Feb. 1671, BM Add MS 23134 f. 216.

103. HMC 72, Laing, i, 375.

10

'Neu-lights and Preachers Legall': some observations on the beginnings of Moderatism in the Church of Scotland

Henry Sefton

FEW Churchmen have been so roundly and so frequently abused as the Moderate divines of the Church of Scotland. Many Scottish historians have assumed that a Moderate is not only a highly objectionable ecclesiastic but also a readily recognisable one. It is therefore somewhat surprising to find that there is a wide diversity of opinion among historians of the Scottish church about the origins of Moderatism.

W. M. Hetherington, a most abusive opponent of the Moderates during the Ten Years Conflict preceding the Disruption of 1843, traces 'that ill-omened designation' to the Declaration of Indulgence issued in 1687 by James VII:

> In the first place we allow and tolerate the *moderate* Presbyterians to meet in their private houses and there to hear all such ministers as either have or are willing to accept of our Indulgence and none other.[1]

A. J. Campbell, writing just after the union of the Churches in 1929, finds the origin of the term in King William's message to the General Assembly of 1690: 'Moderation is what religion requires, neighbouring churches expect from you, and we recommend to you'.[2]

Hetherington traces the origin of Moderatism as a movement to the admission by the General Assembly of those who had previously conformed to the Episcopalian regime. He describes this as 'the most fatal event which ever occurred in the history of the Church of Scotland':

> It infused a baneful poison into her very heart, whence, ere long, flowed forth a lethal stream, corrupting and paralyzing her whole frame. It sowed the noxious seed which gradually sprang up and expanded into the deadly upas-tree[3] of Moderatism.[4]

William Law Mathieson, an Episcopalian layman writing in 1905, rejects this view but in its place puts forward a theory which is not dissimilar. He too finds the origins of Moderatism in the seventeenth century, but he discerns its early growth in the writings of Robert Leighton, Henry Scougal and Sir George Mackenzie, and he draws a parallel between the moderatism of the eighteenth century and those 'moderates' who were prepared to accept the episcopal regime imposed by James VI.[5] Dean Stanley takes this theory still farther when he traces 'the Moderation of the Church of Scotland' right back to George Buchanan.[6] Stanley put forward his views at a public lecture in Edinburgh and provoked a sharp reply from Robert Rainy of the Free Church New College, who dismissed Stanley's opinion as inaccurate and tendentious.[7]

Gavin Struthers, the historian of the Relief Church, also finds the origins of Moderatism in the seventeenth century but in the Netherlands. He asserts that while importing a Dutch king in William of Orange, the country also imported the Dutch theology of Arminianism. Exiled Scots preachers studying in Holland had become tinged with the doctrines of 'this heresy so flattering to the proud heart of man', and he goes on to say:

> These were by far the most learned and cultivated preachers. Elegance was thus unfortunately associated with defective views of salvation by grace. Error put on the appearance of an angel of light and under a chaste form of speech, which did not necessarily belong to it, corrupted the rising taste and genius which began to reappear in the pulpits of Scotland.[8]

Struthers gives no authority for this theory of the origins of Moderatism but he is to some extent supported by L. W. Sharp, editor of the early letters of Robert Wodrow, writing in 1937.[9] On the other hand such a view finds no support from G. D. Henderson, who was well qualified to trace Dutch influences in Scottish theology: 'The Moderates were sometimes called Arminians but in fact they were not interested in taking sides in this controversy'.[10]

In striking contrast to Struthers' view, C. G. McCrie regards the stoutly Calvinist James Hadow, Principal of St. Mary's College, St. Andrews as the forerunner of the Moderates. In an article published in 1884, McCrie very skilfully argues that it was an easy transition from preaching thoroughgoing predestinarian theology to inculcating duty, the moralities, the honest, the true, the good, the beautiful; but he fails to show that this indeed happened as a result of Hadow's teaching.[11]

A commonly held view[12] of Moderatism is that its origins are to be found in various heretical views of certain English Dissenters mediated by John Simson and in the writings of the third Earl of Shaftesbury which were promoted in Scotland by Francis Hutcheson. This view takes no account of the facts that both Simson and Hutcheson taught at Glasgow University and that most of the leading Moderate divines received their university education at Edinburgh. There is, moreover, a wide difference between the teaching of Simson and the teaching of Hutcheson. The contemporary minister of Eastwood, Robert Wodrow the historian, heartily opposed the former and cordially approved the latter. Simson lectured in Latin, and his students were unable to give satisfactory accounts of his teaching when he was accused of Arminianism in 1717 and of Arianism in 1726-9. Hutcheson was appointed Professor of Moral Philosophy at Glasgow in 1729 and was one of the first professors in Scotland to lecture in English. He attracted huge audiences of students and outsiders and undoubtedly exercised a considerable influence on the rising generation of students. An oblique tribute to this is paid in the ironical 'Athenian Creed' in John Witherspoon's 'Ecclesiastical Characteristics':

> I believe in the divinity of L. S————, the saintship of Marcus Aurelius, the perspicuity and sublimity of A————e, and the perpetual duration of Mr. H————n's works.[13]

Nevertheless it is clear that the writings of Shaftesbury were read and admired in Scotland long before Hutcheson settled there. In the Laing Manuscript Collection in Edinburgh University there exists 'A little treatise on Virtue and Merit in the spirit of the Earl of Shaftesbury'[14] which was written at least ten years earlier according to an endorsement by its author, Robert Wallace, to whom we shall return.

Hutcheson's influence is contrasted by Mathieson with that of William Hamilton, Professor of Divinity at Edinburgh from 1709 to 1732. Mathieson regards Hamilton as a representative of the moderation of the seventeenth century and Hutcheson as a typical eighteenth-century Moderate.[15] It might be more appropriate to regard Hamilton as typifying the transition between the religious warfare of the seventeenth century and the ecclesiastical controversies of the eighteenth. He had been baptised at an impressionable age at a Covenanting conventicle, his elder brother had fought at the battle of Bothwell Bridge and his family was renowned for its Covenanting sympathies.[16] But this same man has been described as 'a zealous moderate who contrived to train up a race of heterodox ministers by maintaining an ominous silence in reference to various doctrines of the Gospel'.[17] On the other hand it is clear that Hamilton retained his respect for the Covenanters. We are told on the authority of his son that he 'was in the use of recommending to his students at the conclusion of their course to maintain a tender and charitable respect towards their fathers in the Church who had not enjoyed the means of acquiring the literature and liberality of sentiment so amply provided in the more happy times in which their own lot had been cast'.[18]

It seems that a vast number of students sat under Hamilton during his teaching career, and at one point during his tenure of the Divinity chair he had two hundred students under his care.[19] The potential influence of a man in his position was clearly considerable, and tributes are not lacking from his former students. Principal William Leechman of Glasgow assured his friend and biographer, James Wodrow, 'that he was under great obligations to Professor Hamilton'.[20] James Oswald, minister at Methven and philosopher of the 'Common-sense' school, claimed that many of the leaders of the Church had 'been directed by the sentiments and spirit of Principal Hamilton whose scholars many of us were'.[21]

A generous tribute to Hamilton's abilities as a teacher is paid by one who was not one of his students but who was keenly interested in the affairs of Church and universities. John Ramsay of Ochtertyre writes:

> If the report of the aged may be believed none was ever better qualified to discharge the important trust of a professor of divinity. There was a sincerity, a kindness and a vein of liberality in all that he did and said that gained him the hearts of his students and made them enter with warmth into his views and sentiments. He certainly had the merit of breeding a number of eminent and amiable ministers who kept equally clear of fanaticism and laxity.[22]

The historian Robert Wodrow is not so sure whether Hamilton's students were keeping clear of laxity. In his *Analecta* he notes:

> The complaints of the wildnesses of the students at Edinburgh continou: their haunting dancing-schools and publick dancing; their night revells; and the sermons of some of the younger preachers against the Spirit's work, under the notion of enthusiasme, and making their auditorys laugh by mocking seriouse religion in the pulpit and smiling themselves. These give a very ill impression of their master if he indulge such things in them.[23]

Wodrow does hint that Hamilton may not have approved of such conduct. Oswald, his student, assures us that he did not:

> His friends and favourites were — not the flimsy superficial gentlemen who having picked up somewhat of the English language can read another's sermons with a becoming grace — but such as had drawn their knowledge from the sources of ancient learning and the Scriptures in their original languages and who by a gravity and decorum of behaviour did commend the religion they taught.[24]

In view of these comments about the influence of William Hamilton it is unfortunate that the evidence on which to assess his teaching is so meagre. His literary remains consist of a manuscript history of the Reformation in Scotland and one published sermon. To a large extent we are dependent on the diaries and reminiscences of his contemporaries[25] to gain any impression of the man and his views.

Robert Wodrow frequently speculates on Hamilton's views: 'its thought he is departed from the Calvinisticall doctrine, and the ordinary doctrine taught in this Church, though he hath the wisdom to keep himself in his clouds'.[26] The reticence of the Professor apparently made a great impression on at least one of his students. The biographer of Leechman records that not only did he learn much from his professor on points on which Hamilton spoke openly but that 'young as he was he learned something also in other points about which the Professor said nothing. The silence of such a man struck him it should seem and led him to investigate the causes of it'.[27] Robert Wodrow reports an incident where the Professor's caution seemed rather sinister. It seems that one of Hamilton's students had in a discourse insisted upon the absolute necessity of believing the doctrine of the Trinity. The Professor had commended the discourse but 'cautioned against too much positiveness in that matter since good and great men could not satisfy themselves in that matter as to its fundamentality'.[28]

Against this must be balanced two sermons delivered by Hamilton before the General Assemblies of 1728 and 1731. Wodrow heard both these sermons and has to admit that the preacher's comments on the doctrine of the Trinity and Christ's divinity were unexceptionable. But what is more significant is that on both occasions the Professor declared his dislike of ecclesiastical persecution. He told the Assembly in 1728 that 'God's service could not possibly be promoted by personal real injuries',[29] and his sermon in 1731 contained 'some hints against a spirit of persecution which were variously applyed'.[30] This aversion to persecution is reflected in practice, for Hamilton showed no enthusiasm for the prosecution of either the Glasites or of Professor John Simson of Glasgow. In both instances he urged leniency and incurred unpopularity and suspicion about his own opinions as a result of his efforts.[31]

Hamilton's teaching is important not because of its matter but because of its manner. It seems unlikely that his teaching was heretical, and his silence on certain topics may have had no more significance than a desire to set his students thinking. James Oswald claims that he taught his students 'a liberal manner of thinking on all subjects',[32] and this is borne out by the vigorous intellectual activities of the clubs set up by those who had sat under him.

In a particularly gloomy passage in his *Analecta* Wodrow describes the former students of William Hamilton as 'Neu-lights and Preachers-Legall'. He regards them as one of the many causes for concern in the Church and in the nation at large:

> We have the Marrou people on the one hand who print and scatter papers and sermons very cheap through the country, and are popular, and spreading and gaining ground in some places. In the North we have Popery not born doun, and very much encreasing. In the West we have Mr. Simson's unhappy affair. To say nothing of Mr. Glass and Archibald in Angus; and the Neu-Lights and Preachers-Legall shall I call them or Arminian? Too much has been given as an occasion, last year and formerly, to nottice Mr. Wisheart and his keepers. Of this kind are reconed Mr. Telfair; the two Armstrongs, in the Merse; Mr. P. Cumming, Lochmaben; Mr. Wallace, Maffet; and Mr. Taylor and Gybson in Dumblain and Alloway wer once numbered among them.[33]

Mr. Wishart and his friends had indeed been the subject of Wodrow's disapproving comments ever since Wishart's induction to the Tron Parish of Glasgow in September 1724. Wishart was the son of Principal William Wishart of Edinburgh and bore the same Christian name.

At the March Communion season in 1725 Wodrow had noted that three of the helpers at the Tron parish 'were spoken of as members of a club at Edinburgh where creeds etc. were not much defended'.[34] The early decades of the eighteenth century saw the establishment of many clubs in both Edinburgh and Glasgow,[35] and it is probable that the club to which Wodrow here refers is the Rankenian Club[36] which was founded in 1717 and included Wishart and others of the 'Neu-lights' among its members. Another member, Robert

Wallace, describes the activities of this or some other similar club: 'He and his companions att the University of Edinburgh studied all the controversies of that time and indeed all which were of real importance with great care during a course of 6 years before and after 1720'. These words were written by Wallace when he was going through his papers in December 1767 and form part of a comment on 'A Little Treatise against imposing Creeds or Confessions of Faith as a necessary term of Laick or Ministeriall Communion' which he describes as having been written by him before the year 1720. The treatise was never published and seems to have been prepared only for submission to a meeting of the club. Wallace's keen interest in philosophical and scientific enquiry is reflected in his argument that progress in both of these would be impossible if assent to particular propositions were made binding on their practitioners. He considers that theology should have the same liberty.[37]

We have no similar early productions of any other of the 'Neu-lights'. Despite their dislike of creeds and confessions, only one, Charles Telfer, seems to have made any difficulty about signing the Westminster Confession, but according to Wodrow, 'he came off his difficultys when he sau there was none there would license him without subscribing'.[38] Telfer was settled in Hawick; William Armstrong was inducted to Canonbie in succession to his father; Patrick Cuming went to Kirkmahoe in 1720 and thence to Lochmaben in 1725; Wallace was presented to Moffat in 1723. They were thus settled at no great distance from each other and they continued to meet as a club wherein, according to Wodrow, 'pretty odd notions, pretty much favouring Arminianisme wer vented'.[39]

William Wishart's settlement at Glasgow meant that he was separated from his friends by a considerable distance, but he was still able to indulge his fondness for clubs. There were several clubs in Glasgow which discussed theological questions and one of them, the Triumpherian Club, was renamed the Sophocardian in Wishart's honour. Wodrow regarded these clubs with great disfavour because, as he said, there was no 'solid grave person to moderat' and the members gave a 'loose to their fancy and enquirys without any stated rule of them or any solid principles'.[40]

Wishart also kept in touch with his friends, and for the first year or two after his induction to the Tron parish he asked one or more of them to assist him at the Communion seasons. For his first Communion in October 1724 he invited both Telfer and Wallace to preach, apparently as an experiment to see how notions of liberty and searching would go down.[41] Only Wallace was able to come but his two discourses created a sensation. His first sermon was from the text 'Faith without works is dead', and in it he asserted that evil works were worse than evil opinions and condemned those who prosecuted those who differed from them in opinion and overlooked those who were loose in practice. He also insisted at some length on the necessity of impartial enquiry in matters of religion. This sermon created such a stir that the Professor of Medicine in the University, a notable 'free-liver and free-thinker', according to Ramsay of Ochtertyre,[42] came to hear the second. Professor Johnston's verdict, doubtless a facetious one, was that the man ought not to be tolerated as a minister in any Protestant Church.[43]

At the Communion in October the following year Telfer made as great a sensation with a sermon on religious wisdom, in which he called upon his hearers to examine their knowledge and principles and exhorted them not to tie themselves down to favourite systems and creeds.[44] Telfer's Communion sermons gave great offence to many, and while Wishart tried to smooth things over he did not desert his friend. On subsequent Sundays he took as his ordinary[45] the text 'Prove all things' in which he tried to commend what his helper had been saying. One of the petitions he used at public worship was 'Lord rebuke or bear down a spirit of imposition and persecution not only in Papists but in Christians of whatever denomination'.[46]

Similar sentiments were expressed by Patrick Cuming in his sermon before the Synod of Dumfries in April 1726: 'We should suffer others to differ from us as freely as we would be allowed to do from them . . . Our own Faults and Errors should surely suggest Gentleness and Moderation to others'. Cuming goes on to claim this excellent virtue of moderation for the Church of Scotland and compares her attitude with the uncharitable attitude of the Church of Rome and some Protestants 'who doom all others who are not under their particular Form of Government'. Strife and division had always been fatal to the Church and could accomplish from within what her foes wished to do from without.[47]

Robert Wallace was even more exercised about the foes of the Church than Cuming was, and this influenced his choice of subject when in 1730 he was called upon to deliver the Dumfries Synod Sermon. Whereas Cuming had been concerned to represent the moderation of the Church of Scotland and 'to reason against the uncharitable Principle of those who exclude from Salvation all such as are not under Prelatical Government',[48] Wallace considered that the great controversy of the time was not about 'Rites and Ceremonies, or the Constitution and Model of a Church'. The debates of the time were about the foundation of Christianity and whether the Christian Church ought to have a being at all.[49] For this reason he chooses as his subject 'The Regard due to Divine Revelation' and seeks to prove that revelation is not unnecessary and irrelevant as the Deists alleged.

The text of the sermon is I Thessalonians 5:20,21, 'Despise not prophesyings. Prove all things. Hold fast that which is good'. Wallace paraphrases the text as enjoining 'not to despise all pretences to divine Revelation without tryal but to examine the different pretences, embracing such as they found good, and rejecting the spurious and false'. He pleads for due regard to be paid to Divine Revelation but at the same time he advocates 'Free-thinking' which 'in the true sense of the word is very noble and generous'. Free-thinking is defined as 'the hearkening to the voice of sound reason, the examining impartially both sides of the question, with a disposition to adhere to the strongest side and to imbrace the Truth wherever it appears, in spite of all prejudices, of all the opposition and authority of men'. In his opinion 'it's only an impartial inquiry and free search that according to the ordinary course of things can preserve Religion in any measure of purity'. He suggests to his hearers that they ought not to deal with their people merely by way of authority and to instruct them to believe so and so but also to offer them reasons according to their ability to understand them. The sermon ends with a prayer for preservation 'from a deluge of Scepticism and Deism on the one hand; and implicit faith and blind obedience on the other'.[50]

Between the time of the delivery of the sermon and its appearance in print in 1731 there was published in London a book entitled *Christianity as Old as the Creation, or The Gospel as a Republication of Nature*. This did not bear the author's name but is now known to be the work of Matthew Tindal, a Fellow of All Souls' College, Oxford. It marks the culmination of the Deistic movement. While he does not directly attack historical Christianity, Tindal's argument tends to show that the notion of revelation is superfluous. The topic was so closely related to the subject of his Synod sermon that when he published it Wallace prefaced it with some remarks on Tindal's arguments on the Perfection of the Law of Nature. Later that year an attack on Wallace's Preface was published anonymously in London. This pamphlet favours the Deists and may be the work of a Berwickshire gentleman, William Dudgeon. Wallace published a reply to this the following year.

Wallace's Synod Sermon earned him high favour, but his defence of it involved him in further controversy. Queen Caroline was apparently so impressed by the sermon that she commended Wallace to the notice of the Earl of Islay, then supreme in Scottish affairs. In consequence Wallace was called to be one of the ministers of Edinburgh[51] on the occasion of the vacancy caused by the death of one of his old teachers, Professor Hamilton. The 'Reply', however, earned Wallace the censure of those who, according to Ramsay, 'were very dexterous at spying heresy where none was meant'.[52] A pamphleteer accused Wallace of openly proclaiming 'that we want not a Divine Revelation to tell us that God will pardon the penitent . . . but only to fix the Time when the Pardon will be granted. And hence the necessity of Revelation is gloriously evinced'. There is however no record of a formal libel against Wallace in the minutes of the Presbytery of Edinburgh, and he was appointed to exercise his office in New Greyfriars Church in 1733.[53]

When William Wishart was called four years later to minister in Edinburgh, he was confronted with a formal charge of heresy by the Presbytery of Edinburgh. Wishart had left Glasgow in 1730 to become minister of one of the Scots churches in London, and the charge of heresy was founded on two sermons which he preached and published there. The case gave rise to an abundant crop of pamphlets on both sides. The writer of one of them accused Wishart of being better acquainted with Lord Shaftesbury's *Characteristics* than with his Bible. This is doubtless the reason why Wishart does not employ his rhetoric 'in denouncing the Judgments of God against Sinners and setting in Array the Terrors of the Lord before their Eyes'. This is what Wishart should have done in the sermon which he had preached before the Societies for the

Reformation of Manners. This would have been much more effective than his subtle and metaphysical reasoning. Liberty, Charity and Moderation were very fine things, but they were deeply suspect when spoken of by a man like Wishart — *Timeo Danaos et dona ferentes*.[54] The case eventually came before the General Assembly of 1738 which dismissed the charges and ordered Wishart's admission as one of the ministers of Edinburgh.[55] He had been elected Principal of the University of Edinburgh in 1736.

Wallace was the last of the 'Neu-lights' to be settled in Edinburgh. Patrick Cuming had been admitted as one of the ministers of Edinburgh in 1732 and in 1737 had been appointed Professor of Church History in the University. Two others of the 'Neu-lights' listed by Wodrow were called to minister in Edinburgh but died shortly after their translation.[56] Charles Telfer of Hawick and William Armstrong of Canonbie also died young. But Wishart, Wallace and Cuming all achieved positions of considerable influence during their ministries in Edinburgh. None of them, however, attempted to have altered the terms of subscription to the Westminster Confession of Faith.

NOTES

1. W. M. Hetherington, *History of the Church of Scotland* (Edinburgh, 1841), 518.

2. A. J. Campbell, *Two Centuries of the Church of Scotland 1707-1929* (Paisley, 1930), 34f.

3. 'Antiaris toxicaria' is the botanical name of this poisonous tree found in Java.

4. Hetherington, *op. cit.*, 556f.

5. W. L. Mathieson, *Scotland and the Union* (Glasgow, 1905), 250f.

6. A. P. Stanley, *The Church of Scotland* (London, 1872), 98.

7. R. Rainy, *Three Lectures on the Church of Scotland* (Edinburgh, 1872), 64-85.

8. G. Struthers, *History of the Relief Church* (Glasgow, 1843), 54.

9. L. W. Sharp (ed.), *Early Letters of Robert Wodrow* (S.H.S., Edinburgh, 1937), xliii.

10. G. D. Henderson, 'Dutch Influences in Scottish Theology', in *Evangelical Quarterly*, 5 (1933), 37f.

11. C. G. McCrie, 'Rev. James Hog of Carnock and Principal Hadow of St. Andrews', in *British and Foreign Evangelical Review*, 33 (1884), 716f; see also S. Mechie, 'The Theological Climate in Early Eighteenth Century Scotland', in D. Shaw (ed.), *Reformation and Revolution* (Edinburgh, 1967), 258-72.

12. E.g. H. G. Graham, *Scottish Men of Letters in the Eighteenth Century* (London, 1901), 32-4; J. S. H. Burleigh, *A Church History of Scotland* (London, 1960), 295. For detailed modern surveys of Moderatism, see Andrew L. Drummond and James Bulloch, *The Scottish Church 1688-1843* (Edinburgh, 1973), esp. 64-81; and James K. Cameron, 'Theological Controversy: A Factor in the Origins of the Scottish Enlightenment', in *The Origins and Nature of the Scottish Enlightenment*, ed. R. H. Campbell and Andrew S. Skinner (Edinburgh, 1982), 116-130.

13. *The Works of John Witherspoon*, Vol. VI (Edinburgh, 1805), 185f.

14. Laing MSS II 620[19], University of Edinburgh.

15. W. L. Mathieson, *The Awakening of Scotland* (Glasgow, 1910), 196.

16. J. Warrick, *Moderators of the Church of Scotland* (Edinburgh, 1913), 240f.

17. J. S. Reid, *Presbyterian Church in Ireland* (2nd edn., London, 1853), III, 405.

18. T. Somerville, *My own Life and Times* (Edinburgh, 1861), 64.

19. R. Wodrow, *Correspondence*, Vol. III (Wodrow Society, Edinburgh, 1843), 259.

20. J. Wodrow, *Life of Leechman*, 4 (prefixed to *Sermons* (London, 1789)).

21. J. Oswald, *Letters concerning the Church of Scotland* (Edinburgh, 1767), 23.

22. J. Ramsay, *Scotland and Scotsmen in the Eighteenth Century* (Edinburgh, 1888), I, 227f.

23. Robert Wodrow, *Analecta*, 1701-31 (Maitland Club, Glasgow, 1842), IV, 213.

24. J. Ramsay, *op. cit.*, 23.

25. These include Robert Wodrow, John Ramsay, William Mitchell, Thomas Boston, William Leechman and James Oswald.

26. R. Wodrow, *Analecta*, IV, 139f.

27. J. Wodrow, *Life of Leechman*, 4.

28. R. Wodrow, *Analecta*, III, 302.

29. R. Wodrow, *Correspondence*, III, 338.

30. R. Wodrow, *Analecta*, IV, 237.

31. *Ibid.*, IV, 135, 188, 261f; R. Wodrow, *Correspondence*, III, 348, 370, 378, 438f.

32. J. Ramsay, *op. cit.*, 23.

33. R. Wodrow, *Analecta*, III, 360.

34. R. Wodrow, *Correspondence*, III, 190.

35. Cf. D. D. McElroy, 'The Literary Clubs and Societies of 18th Century Scotland' (unpublished Ph.D. Thesis, Edinburgh, 1952).

36. So called because it met in Ranken's tavern. A list of the members is given in Lord Woodhouselee, *Life of Kames* (Edinburgh, 1807), I, app., viii.

37. Laing MSS. II 620[18].

38. Wodrow, *Analecta*, III, 174.

39. *Ibid.*, IV, 165.

40. *Ibid.*, III, 183. Sophocardian was the adjective from the Latinised form of Wishart, first used by George Buchanan of the martyr, George Wishart.

41. *Ibid.*, III, 175, 238.

42. Ramsay, *op. cit.*, I, 277.

43. Wodrow, *Analecta*, III, 167-9.

44. *Ibid.*, III, 239f.

45. A text on which a series of sermons was preached in order to extract the full meaning.

46. Wodrow, *Analecta*, III, 246f.

47. P. Cuming, *A Sermon Preach'd at the Opening of the Synod of Dumfreis, April 12th 1726* (London, 1727), 20, 37.

48. *Ibid.*, Preface.

49. R. Wallace, *The Regard due to Divine Revelation* (London, 1731), iii.

50. *Ibid.*, 3f, 58, 68, 70.

51. *Scots Magazine*, Vol. 33, 341.

52. Ramsay, *op. cit.*, I, 242.

53. 'Observations upon Church Affairs addressed to Principal Smith' (London, 1734), 13f. For Wallace's subsequent involvement in Church politics, see Richard B. Sher, 'Moderates, Managers and Popular Politics in Mid-Eighteenth Century Edinburgh: The Drysdale "Bustle" of the 1760s', in *New Perspectives on the Politics*

and Culture of Early Modern Scotland, ed. John Dwyer, Roger A. Mason, and Alexander Murdoch (Edinburgh, 1982), esp. 191-5.

54. 'Some Observations on these Two Sermons of Dr. Wishart's which have given offence to the Presbytery of Edinburgh' (Edinburgh, 1737), 3f.

55. Acts of the General Assembly, 1738.

56. Archibald Gibson (Dunblane) trans. Edinburgh (Lady Yesters) 1732, died 1733. John Taylor (Alloa) trans. Edinburgh (Tolbooth) 1735, died 1736.

11

Patronage and Party in the Church of Scotland, 1750-1800

Richard Sher and Alexander Murdoch

Lang, *Patronage*, wi' rod o' airn,
Has shor'd the Kirk's undoin.[1]

WHEN Robert Burns penned these lines in the mid-1780s, the church patronage controversy that seemed to threaten 'the Kirk's undoin' had reached a sort of impasse. After decades of intense conflict, the Moderate and Popular parties in the Church of Scotland stopped fighting about patronage. That they did so may come as a surprise to those who are accustomed to read Scottish history backwards by interpreting ecclesiastical developments of the eighteenth and early nineteenth centuries as one long prelude to the Disruption of 1843. This 'Whig' interpretation of Scottish ecclesiastical history can explain neither the lack of serious opposition to patronage in the General Assembly between the mid-1780s and the late 1820s nor the sense of resignation and serenity that one finds in the writings of churchmen at that period. Thus, Sir Henry Moncreiff Wellwood, the universally respected leader of the Popular party, was willing to accept patronage as a fact of life in the influential 'Brief Account of the Constitution of the Established Church of Scotland' that he appended to his biography of John Erskine in 1818.[2] Writing his memoirs at about the same time, the Moderate minister Thomas Somerville doubted if many of his countrymen could 'form any conception' of the extent and vehemence of 'party spirit' about the patronage question fifty or sixty years before.[3] If the steady accumulation of grievances over patronage was leading the kirk down the path to ruin, these clergymen from rival parties apparently had no idea that this was the case. Nor did Henry Dundas, who remarked privately in 1811 that the patronage question which had so divided the church since the Union 'was now very much at rest'.[4]

The reduction of conflict over the patronage question was not simply the 'lull before the storm' that ecclesiastical historians telling the tale of the Disruption have made it out to be.[5] A period of more than forty years, after all, is a rather long lull. It is important to keep in mind that the political and socio-economic conditions of the Disruption era were entirely different from those of the period with which we shall be chiefly concerned in this essay: the 'classical' age of hostilities over the patronage question during the 1750s, 1760s, 1770s, and early 1780s. Since Scotland at that time was a far less industrial-ised, far less urbanised, and far less populous place than it would be in the 1830s and 1840s, it naturally lacked the strong urban-bourgeois element that played such an important role in the Disruption. It also lacked the political hopes and expectations which accompanied the Reform Bill of 1832 and, coming after a century of political and ecclesiastical turmoil rather than after decades of Tory repression, placed a much higher premium on the need for maintaining order. For these reasons we must be wary of attributing the same motives, meanings, and objectives to the eighteenth-century and nineteenth-century participants in the Scottish patronage wars. Continuity undoubtedly existed, but too often the extent of that continuity has been exaggerated.

As soon as the patronage struggles of the eighteenth century are treated on their own terms, it becomes apparent that they were considerably more complex than is usually thought. Our aim in this essay is to recapture some of that complexity. Looking first at general patterns of confrontation over the patronage question, we shall attempt to show that such confrontation took different forms, manifested itself sporadically rather than continuously, and came to a halt around 1785 for a variety of reasons that were not exclusively ecclesiastical in nature. We shall then investigate the spectrum of opinion on the patronage issue within the Church of Scotland. Our chief concern in this regard will be to examine the critical differences that divided factions within the anti-patronage or Popular party during the second half of the eighteenth century, particularly as to the problem of finding a more desirable alternative to patronage. While we certainly are not the first historians to take notice of these internal differences among eighteenth-century opponents of patronage, we hope to place them in sharper focus, and to relate them, where possible, to the broader social, political, and ideological contexts that lay outside the limits of the kirk. Finally, it will be necessary to consider the various arguments put forward in support of patronage by its chief defenders, the Moderate party, for here, too, matters seem to us somewhat more complicated than the stan-dard ecclesiastical histories of Scotland would suggest.

Patterns of Confrontation

Two principal sorts of evidence correspond to the two principal sorts of con-frontation over patronage during the second half of the eighteenth century. First, there are the records of disputed presentations that reached the highest court of ecclesiastical appeal, the General Assembly, and subsequently were described in the Scots Magazine and in the lengthy report of the parliamentary committee on church patronage in Scotland in 1834.[6] While hardly scratching the surface of such sources, our investigation of these records and supporting materials has raised two points of interest:

  1. If intensity of popular opposition to a patron's nominee or 'presentee' is

used as a criterion, it appears that members of the gentry and nobility were far more likely than the crown to make an unpopular presentation. Conflict like that at Eaglesham in Renfrewshire in 1767, when the carriages of ministers arriving to induct an unpopular presentee were driven out of the parish by a stone-throwing mob that 'hooted with the most bitter execrations',[7] usually involved a stubborn member of the aristocracy and an equally stubborn kirk session or congregation. Another well-known case of the 1760s, that of St. Ninians in Stirlingshire, was particularly bitter because many of the local landowners or 'heritors' were Episcopalian and the patron himself unusually obnoxious.[8] Though there is ample evidence to show that government managers like James Stuart Mackenzie and Henry Dundas often deferred to prominent local landowners when filling vacant Scottish churches controlled by the crown, it seems that they rarely were foolish enough to permit controversial presentations that might stir up popular resentment.[9] Moreover, according to the most reliable estimate that we have found, the crown was the patron of scarcely one quarter of Scotland's more than 900 parish livings during the eighteenth century (see Table 1, Estimate 1). Why, then, did anti-patronage literature of this period tend to exaggerate the powers and evils of the crown? As we shall see, the answer to this question seems to us to have more to do with political ideology and rhetoric than with the narrow issue of church patronage.

2. Ecclesiastical reports in the *Scots Magazine* indicate that General Assemblies in the third quarter of the eighteenth century heard almost two and a half times as many presentation disputes as did assemblies in the last quarter of the century. In fact, the number of disputed presentations that reached the Assembly increased steadily in every half-decade from 1751 to 1775, after which it dropped sharply and remained low for the rest of the century, excepting the early 1780s (see Table 2). This quantitative decline in presentations brought before the General Assembly was accompanied by a significant qualitative change: after 1784 the point at issue in such cases shifted increasingly from the institution and implementation of patronage itself to the personal character or qualifications of the presentee — a form of protest recognised as legitimate, at least in theory, even by proponents of patronage.[10] To be sure, local opposition to unpopular presentations did not disappear in the late eighteenth and early nineteenth centuries, as readers of Dr. Kenneth J. Logue's recent study of popular disturbances in that period will appreciate.[11] But most of the violent settlements or 'intrusions' that Logue discusses, such as those at Newburgh (Fife) in 1785 and at Assynt (Sutherland) in 1813, were isolated and largely symbolic incidents, quite different from the St. Ninians case, which in the early 1770s provoked a General Assembly debate sufficiently warm, controversial, and national in scope to warrant publication by James Boswell in the *London Magazine*.[12]

Besides disputes over particular presentations, confrontation over church patronage took the form of periodic crises involving general issues or policies that were ultimately resolved in the General Assembly. For convenience, these

Table 1. Scottish Church Patronage in the Eighteenth Century

Type of Patron	Number of Parishes and Percentage of Whole	
	Estimate 1	Estimate 2
Crown	255 (27%)	334 (36%)
Crown and another party (joint patrons)	33 (3%)	—
Two parties other than crown (joint patrons)	21 (2%)	—
Nobility	297 (32%)	309 (33%)
Baronets and Gentlemen	263 (28%)	233 (25%)
Town Councils (royal burghs)	46 (5%)	45 (5%)
Burghs of Barony	—	2 (less than 1%)
Heritors and Elders	8 (1%)	3 (less than 1%)
Universities	8 (1%)	10 (1%)
Uncertain	7 (1%)	—
	938 (100%)	936 (100%)

Estimate 1: *An Exact List of all the Synods and Presbyteries in Scotland; the Parishes in each Presbytery; and, the Names of the Present Minister and Patron of each Parish* (n.p., c.1775), as corrected by James Stuart Mackenzie in the copy at Mount Stuart, Bute. We are grateful to the Marquess of Bute for permission to cite this source and to his archivist, Miss Catherine Armet, for making it available to us.

Estimate 2: Andrew Crosbie, *Thoughts of a Layman concerning Patronage and Presentations* (Edinburgh, 1769), 35-36.

Table 2. Presentation Disputes in the General Assembly, 1751-1800

Inclusive Dates	Number of Disputed Presentations
1751-1755	9
1756-1760	13
1761-1765	13
1766-1770	17
1771-1775	21
1776-1780	3
1781-1785	12
1786-1790	5
1791-1795	5
1796-1800	6

Source: Reports of the proceedings of the General Assembly of the Church of Scotland in the *Scots Magazine*, 1751-1800.

Note: Cases brought before the Assembly in two or more years have been counted more than once.

crises may be grouped into four major periods: (1) the crisis of the 1730s that produced the original secession; (2) the church polity crisis of 1751-1753, involving the Torphichen and Inverkeithing settlement disputes of 1751 and 1752, respectively, the suspension of Rev. Thomas Gillespie in 1752, and the unsuccessful counter-offensive to have Gillespie reinstated or 'reponed' in 1753; (3) the continuous crisis of the 1760s, involving three separate episodes: the conflict over the right of the town councils of Edinburgh and Glasgow to present ministers to vacant churches in those towns (1762-1764), the Schism Overture affair of 1765-1766, and the anti-patronage campaign of 1768-1769; (4) the anti-patronage offensive and pro-patronage counter-offensive of 1782-1785.[13] While these crises occasionally originated over a particular presentation or settlement dispute, they soon went beyond it to a consideration of broader issues, such as the nature of Presbyterian church polity in the crisis generated by the Torphichen and Inverkeithing controversies of 1751-1752 and the relationship between ecclesiastical and municipal authority in the Edinburgh and Glasgow presentation disputes of 1762-1764. It was because they transcended the narrow particulars and local character of ordinary presentation and settlement disputes that these general crises produced a mode of warfare that one rarely finds in connection with even the most virulent parish dispute: the patronage pamphlet. On the basis of our examination of scores of these pamphlets from the eighteenth century, we offer the following observations:

1. Nearly all of the patronage pamphlets that we have located were published during or immediately after the general crises mentioned above. Thus, we have found seventeen such pamphlets from the tumultuous 1730s but just one from the 1740s, nineteen from the years 1752-1754 but only one from the years 1755-1761, dozens from the decade 1762-1772 but only three from the years 1773 to 1780, fifteen from the early 1780s but virtually none from the latter part of that decade.[14] Like disputed presentations, then, general patronage crises and the pamphlets they generated tended to run in cycles. In the second quarter of the eighteenth century those cycles were not always in harmony — the 1740s, for example, were a 'hot' decade for presentation disputes[15] but an extremely 'cold' one for general crises and pamphlets about patronage. In the period 1751-1785, however, the correspondence between presentation disputes and patronage pamphlets and crises becomes quite close. The years of the most intense crises and pamphlet wars over patronage, such as the 1760s and the early 1780s, were also years in which an unusually large number of presentation disputes came before the General Assembly. Conversely, the late 1770s and the period after 1785 were noticeably quiet on all fronts. How can we explain this oscillating rhythm of interest in the patronage issue? In particular, how can we explain the dramatic reduction in conflict over all aspects of the patronage question after the mid-1780s?

A variety of traditional explanations go far towards answering the latter question. First, the rapid growth of the secession churches — from 45 congregations in 1750 to 202 congregations in 1785 to 302 congregations in 1800[16] —

rid the established church of the most vigorous foes of patronage, leaving behind a residue that was more willing to accept patronage as the law of the land. Secondly, decades of pro-patronage decisions in the General Assembly eventually produced feelings of frustration, hopelessness, and apathy among the opponents of patronage, whose only alternatives were secession or resignation.[17] Finally, resignation turned to repression during the French Revolutionary era, when the clergy in the Church of Scotland closed ranks in defence of order, and anything that smacked of democracy or dissent was considered dangerous.[18] These explanations seem true to some extent, but more work is needed to substantiate them. We know that foundations of secession congregations often mirrored local disputed presentations, where an unpopular presentee would spur the irreconcilable element in the parish to secede and call its own minister.[19] But nationally there is no indication of a mass exodus from the established church after the mid-1780s.[20] The argument for growing frustration and apathy also sounds plausible, but there is no hard evidence for it besides the testimony of Henry Moncreiff Wellwood, and it tends to beg the question of why such frustration and apathy took effect in the mid-1780s rather than at some other time. The argument stressing the role of the French Revolution, or rather the reaction to it, is likewise valid to a point but must not be over-emphasised; when the Revolution began, after all, the church patronage question was already moribund, and all that remained was to nail the coffin shut. Finally, none of these traditional explanations can tell us much about why party conflict over the patronage question rose and fell as it did in the several decades before 1785.

Two additional explanations seem to us to be worthy of consideration. First, it should be noted that times of low interest in the patronage question were usually times in which Scottish churchmen were distracted by other issues. Just before the patronage crisis of 1751-1753 the main issues were the 'Forty-Five and the agitation to augment ministers' stipends. In the mid and late 1750s the ecclesiastical parties were preoccupied with the famous infidelity cases of Lord Kames and David Hume and with the controversy concerning John Home's tragedy *Douglas*. During the late 1770s confrontation centred on the American War of Independence and the issue of Roman Catholic relief.

Secondly, it seems to us that the connection between party conflict over church patronage in Scotland and the general political situation in Great Britain goes much deeper than the matter of the French Revolution. Crises in which the defenders of patronage were on the offensive, such as those of 1751-1753 and 1762-1764, occurred when political power was in the hands of men sympathetic to the policies of the Moderate party, such as the third Duke of Argyll and the Earl of Bute. By contrast, the ministries of politicians whose policies on such questions were not clear, or who were widely considered friendly to 'popular' causes, such as the Marquis of Rockingham in the mid-1760s and Rockingham, Charles James Fox, and the Earl of Shelburne in the early 1780s, coincided with significant increases in both disputed presentations and broader attacks on patronage in the ecclesiastical courts. In the 1760s the

Duke of Grafton, Rockingham's secretary of state for the Northern Department, almost certainly fuelled such agitation by publicly proclaiming that the government intended to show greater concern for the preferences of the people when filling vacant churches in its care.[21] In 1782 secular and ecclesiastical politics became closely intertwined as Scottish Whigs like Henry Erskine joined forces with sympathetic members of the Popular party in attempting to have the General Assembly congratulate the king on the recent change of ministries (from North to Rockingham) and in reviving anti-patronage agitation.[22] The hopes of opponents of patronage rose still higher in 1783, when the Fox-North coalition ministry appointed Henry Erskine to the office of lord advocate and caused the resignation of the leading friend of the Moderates and church patronage in government, Henry Dundas. By the end of the year, however, Dundas was back in power as Scottish manager for the younger William Pitt, whose resounding triumph in the general election of April 1784 set the stage for the decisive victory of pro-patronage forces in the General Assembly the following month.[23] In the parishes, similarly, it is quite plausible that congregations and kirk sessions saw no point in challenging unpopular presentations in such an unfavourable political climate. Only in the second quarter of the nineteenth century did that climate change significantly, and the remarkable upsurge of patronage hostilities in the decade preceding the Disruption, though precipitated in large measure by religious, economic, and social factors, cannot be understood apart from the hopes for ecclesiastical reform that were raised — and soon dashed — following the ascension of the Whigs and passage of the great Reform Bill.[24]

2. Turning from the chronology of patronage pamphlets to their content, we find that only a small minority of such pamphlets took positions that were directly or indirectly pro-patronage. Of more than two dozen patronage pamphlets that we examined from the period 1766-1772, for example, only five favoured patronage. Similarly small proportions of pro-patronage pamphlets were found in the early 1750s and early 1780s. These figures came as no surprise, since we would expect agitators for reform to rely more heavily upon polemical pamphleteering than those defending the established order. Somewhat more surprising, however, is the fact that relatively few of the non-seceder anti-patronage pamphlets which we studied advocated the ecclesiastical sovereignty of the people. This is not to deny the existence of a strong radical undercurrent in the Popular party, especially during the 1760s and early 1780s. But it does suggest that the dominant ideology of the Popular party was not radical in a democratic sense. What, then, was it?

The Patronage Debate: History and Typology

Answering this question requires a deeper understanding of the historical background of the eighteenth-century patronage controversy. The patronage question was part of the delicate issue of the relationship of church and state dating back to the sixteenth century. The Reformation had actually increased rather than diminished the wealth and power of the crown and great landowners by allowing them to assume many of the temporal possessions of the old church. As makers of civil legislation and traditional patrons of most clerical benefices, they had both law and custom on their side. Yet the institution of patronage was never agreeable to the cutting edge of the Presbyterian kirk, which continually registered protests against it.

Protests against patronage, however, remained just that until the latter stages of the Wars of the Covenant, when the Parliament of 1649 abolished lay patronage in favour of selection by presbytery and kirk session, much as Andrew Melville had recommended in the *Second Book of Discipline* nearly a century earlier.[25] The radical Presbyterian clergy carried the change through in the General Assembly of 1649. These developments marked the temporary triumph of a theocratic, clerical strain of Scots Presbyterian thought that was a good deal more conservative than is usually thought. According to the parliamentary act of 1649, the local presbytery, which was certain to be dominated by clergymen,[26] would take the initiative in filling a vacant church by directing the names of suitable candidates to the elders of the kirk session, who would then meet to choose their minister under the chairmanship of a clergyman designated by the presbytery. It is true that the elders had the right to name candidates in addition to those recommended by the presbytery and that the congregation could reject a minister — yet the presbytery was granted the authority to deny a congregation's objection. Thus, the act of 1649 favoured clergy-dominated presbyteries over local kirk sessions and paid little more than lip-service to the rights of congregations.

Nor was the act of 1649 so hostile to the landed interest as one might at first suppose. Patrons of course did lose the right to present ministers, as well as the right to control the sometimes lucrative teinds (tithes) from which ministers' stipends were paid, but, as Dr. Walter Makey has observed, transferring the teinds from the patrons to the landed interest as a whole made good economic sense for a feudal Parliament in which 'barons were many, but patrons were few'.[27] This cleavage between the patrons and the landed interest as a whole is an important point which is usually overlooked in discussions of the patronage question. Since church patronage was controlled overwhelmingly by the crown and the great landowners (particularly the latter), there was, as we shall see, room in the eighteenth century for an anti-patronage movement that claimed to represent the interests not of the 'people' or the clergy but of the small and middle-sized landowners who comprised the majority of Scottish heritors, together with the elders of the kirk session, who also tended to be men with at least some property.[28]

The work of the Scots Parliament of 1649 was undone in 1660, when lay patronage was reinstituted along with the monarchy and Episcopalianism — though the teinds were not returned to the patrons at this time. After the Revolution the wheel turned once more: in 1690 the Scots Parliament and a reluctant William III restored Presbyterianism and granted the right to 'name and propose' a minister to a vacant church in a 'landward or country parish' to the elders and Protestant heritors of that parish acting together, subject to the approval of the congregation.[29] This arrangement represented a compromise of considerable subtlety. Patrons were compensated for their loss of power — bought off, as it were — by once again gaining the right to collect teinds. Congregations were given a voice of sorts, either indirectly through their kirk sessions or directly through their qualified veto power. Presbyteries received the right to arbitrate cases of congregational opposition to the nominee and the right to select the minister in the event the heritors and elders did not exercise the right of nomination within six months. Above all, the landed interest, in the form of the heritors, gained the upper hand in the process of selecting ministers for vacant churches outside the burghs.[30] The most controversial aspect of the act was the decision to include all Protestant heritors in that process, thereby giving Episcopalian landowners an active role in the re-established Presbyterian church. Land, it seems, was now deemed more important than doctrine.

Insofar as it made the greatest concessions to the landed interest, in the broadest sense of that term, the act of 1690 may be seen as a gesture towards the Whig ideology of 1688 and the 'commonwealthman' ideal. Landowners as heritors were already expected to take the lead in local affairs by maintaining the church and the school; now their importance would be enhanced by the additional right of helping to choose the minister. The landed gentry in the 'commonwealthman' tradition were expected to participate actively in national affairs, to undertake the responsibility of local government, and to be independent of great magnates and their factions, as well as of the crown. Perhaps in a country where the gentry had little opportunity for political involvement there were hopes that ecclesiastical affairs would constitute a forum for the exercise of civic virtue.

The final turn of the wheel occurred in 1712, when a Tory government that cared neither for Whig ideology nor for the assurances in the Treaty of Union about Scottish ecclesiastical autonomy pushed through the Parliament of the United Kingdom an act restoring patronage in Scotland. The patronage act of 1712 was of course a blow to the 'people', since the kirk session and congregation were deprived of their active parts in the ministerial selection process, but it was an even more damaging blow to the heritors. This was true, first of all, because the heritors lost their primary role in the nomination of new ministers to vacant churches, and it was true, secondly, because the right to collect teinds, which had reverted to patrons in 1690 as compensation for their loss of the right to present ministers, remained with the patrons after 1712. The latter point would be aired as a grievance at the height of anti-patronage activity in 1769 as unfair to the 'landed interest', meaning the heritors.[31]

Throughout the eighteenth century opponents of patronage were united in their opposition to the act of 1712, but they were divided into three major schools of thought concerning the best alternative to it, each with many subdivisions and variations and each with sound precedents drawn from Scots Presbyterian theory and, in some cases, practice. The first and most radical position drew its primary inspiration from the Bible as interpreted by John

Knox in the *First Book of Discipline* (1560-1561), which called for the selection of a minister by all male heads of households in a congregation.[32] Here piety served as the chief qualification for voting rights: selection was a function of election. Though this radical scheme for filling vacant churches was never adopted by the Church of Scotland, let alone the government, it lived on in the hearts of sizeable numbers of devout Presbyterians. In the seventeenth century it was represented by the idea of congregations of the elect meeting outwith the normal framework of the church. The famous Covenanting divine Samuel Rutherford, for instance, argued that the right of electing a minister should reside in 'the body of the people'.[33] The conventicles of the late seventeenth century, with their emphasis on preaching by popular ministers, were also part of this radical Calvinist tradition. So were Ebenezer Erskine and those who followed him out of the Church of Scotland in the original secession of the 1730s, as well as most seceders in subsequent decades.

The second half of the eighteenth century witnessed the emergence of another, more secular version of this radical position. It first surfaced on a large scale during the controversy over the presentation of Rev. John Drysdale to an Edinburgh church in the early 1760s, when agitation for relatively democratic elections of new ministers was linked to demands for burgh government reform.[34] For the next twenty years the connection between ecclesiastical and secular radicalism remained strong within certain segments of the established church. We find it in a figure like John Maclaurin, later Lord Dreghorn of the Court of Session, who combined support for the rights of parishioners in the selection of their minister with advocacy of radical political causes such as American independence and parliamentary reform.[35] And we find it particularly in the anti-patronage campaign of the early 1780s, when radical Whigs like Henry Erskine embraced the anti-patronage cause, and anonymous pamphleteers used the language of political radicalism in an ecclesiastical context.[36] This alliance between ecclesiastical and secular radicalism was mutually advantageous: one side could exploit the popular rhetoric of Wilkes and 'real' Whiggism on behalf of an ecclesiastical cause that might otherwise seem old-fashioned, while the other side could exploit the deep-seated religious sentiments of the Scots Presbyterians on behalf of a political cause that might otherwise seem distant and remote. Thus, a memorial sent to the secretary of state for home affairs in 1783 described ecclesiastical patronage as 'the point on which the Common People of Scotland are maddest' and added that 'the ministers who command them always touch this *Key*, and liberty-mad people touch it too because they say that it is the only key on which they can be touched'.[37]

While the radical undercurrent in the Church of Scotland unquestionably deserves further attention from scholars, we must be careful not to exaggerate its importance during the eighteenth century. For one thing, it was apparently a minority position among the articulate opponents of patronage within the kirk. For another, we cannot automatically assume that the use of radical-sounding rhetoric or the support of progressive political causes such as

American independence signifies a truly popular or democratic position on the question of the best alternative to patronage. Finally, we have seen that this radical undercurrent actually was composed of two separate strains that happened to reach a similar conclusion by totally different means. The older, Calvinist tradition represented 'democracy' amongst the elect only, with emphasis on the right of male heads of households to select a minister of sufficient Godliness for the spiritual needs of their congregation. While the newer, radical Whig tradition drew on the heritage and appeal of its pious brother, the extent to which these two radical strains merged is still far from clear.[38] What is clear is that during the French Revolution the popular party dissociated itself from radical activity. The church patronage issue continued to be raised by Scots radicals of that era, but if a meaningful connection is to be found between those radicals and Presbyterianism, it will have to be sought amongst the seceders rather than amongst churchmen in the Popular party of the kirk.

The second major alternative to patronage that was advocated was that ministers should be selected by presbytery and kirk session, with the role of heads of households restricted to a qualified veto power. This view had its roots in Melville's *Second Book of Discipline* (1578) and in the parliamentary act and General Assembly directory of 1649. We have seen that the latter gave the greatest share of authority to the presbytery, and that they represented an essentially theocratic or clerical point of view. Though this alternative was definitely on the decline during the eighteenth century, it should be noted that ministers dominated the anti-patronage movement and that presbyteries were frequently the greatest strongholds of anti-patronage sentiment in the church. There is reason to believe that some clergymen viewed the law of patronage as part of a general attempt by the landed élite 'to humble and depress the clergy'.[39] The pro-patronage majority in the General Assembly often had to deal with a recalcitrant presbytery, as in the case of Inverkeithing in 1752, rather than an angry congregation, and it is sometimes difficult to tell if the members of such a presbytery were refusing to induct a presentee because of their own opinions or because the congregation could not be brought to accept him.[40] These observations serve as a reminder that the spirit of 1649 remained current in the eighteenth-century kirk, though its full impact was once again felt amongst the seceders, usually in combination with the more radical tradition of John Knox.

We now turn to the third and, we believe, most important of the alternatives to patronage in the Church of Scotland during the second half of the eighteenth century. Advocates of this alternative could on occasion make concessions to the people or even to the patrons, and they were not averse to assigning a respectable role to kirk sessions and presbyteries. Their chief concern, however, was to restore the primacy of local men of landed property in the process of filling vacant churches in 'landward' parishes. Scanning the Presbyterian past for suitable precedents, they settled not upon the two *Books of Discipline* or the achievements of 1649 but upon the act of 1690. If their rhetoric sometimes was filled with radical-sounding references to 'liberty', its intention was not democratic, and its source was not John Calvin, John Knox, or John Wilkes but the Whig ideology of 1688-1690 and the 'commonwealth-man' tradition.

The first major manifestation of this view was the General Assembly's act of 1732, which basically restated the law of 1690 as the mode of procedure for the filling of vacant parishes where the patron failed to present a minister within the legal time limit of six months. It is worth noting that Ebenezer Erskine's wrath was directed originally not against the patronage act of 1712, which was not yet widely enforced, but against this act passed by the General Assembly twenty years later. While Erskine's outcry may have been provoked in part by the high-handed manner in which the act was enacted by the 'prevailing party' in the assembly despite strong opposition from the presbyteries, and in part by the act's subtle change of wording — giving heritors and elders the right to 'elect' rather than merely 'name and propose' a minister — the heart of his position was opposition to the compromise of 1690 itself for entrusting so much ecclesiastical authority to the heritor — a non-ecclesiastical person who might be an Episcopalian and whose sole qualification for such authority was the possession of wealth in land, symbolised in Erskine's terms by a 'gold ring' and 'gay clothing'.[41] The churchmen responsible for the act of 1732, such as Principal William Hamilton of Edinburgh University and his disciples, could justly claim to represent the 'moderate' element in the church at this time,[42] but it was their misfortune to be trapped between a radical Calvinist faction led by Erskine and, at the opposite extreme, Walpole's Scottish manager Archibald Campbell, Earl of Islay (later third Duke of Argyll), who was determined to enforce the law of patronage at all costs. If the fury of the former sometimes drove them into the arms of the latter, it was chiefly because there was nowhere else to turn. Within another twenty years time would play a semantic trick that would continue to confuse ecclesiastical historians for two centuries: the secession of Erskine's faction and the emergence after 1750 of a party that gave unequivocal support to the law of patronage would shift the entire spectrum of opinion within the established church to the 'right', so that the term 'Moderate' would come to be applied as a party label to the friends of patronage, just as the term 'Popular' would be applied to the party favouring selection of ministers by heritors and elders rather than by the 'people'.[43]

A clear expression of the principles of 1690 and 1732 may be found in the anti-patronage pamphlet published in 1735 by the celebrated Glasgow professor of moral philosophy, Francis Hutcheson: *Considerations on Patron-ages, Addressed to the Gentlemen of Scotland*. Probably because the need to resist monarchical despotism was an essential feature of the Whig ideals to which he subscribed, Hutcheson grossly inflated the number of parishes where the minister was appointed by crown patronage.[44] He proceeded to argue that unless the gentry, along with other concerned members of the local élite such as elders, regained the power to choose the ministers of their parish, the clergy of Scotland would become venal lackeys of the government and a handful of lords. At the same time he gave short shrift to the idea of popular election of ministers, stating that 'the populace are by no means the fittest and best judges of ministerial qualifications'.[45] Hutcheson's position was consistent with the Revolution Whig and 'commonwealthman' principles that he articulated elsewhere.[46] His pamphlet on patronage was not, in our opinion, the 'manifesto of the Scottish Enlightenment' and of Scottish nationalism that Dr. Davie has found it to be;[47] rather, it was a manifesto of the Whig-Presbyterian principles of 1688-1690 and an attempt to apply the ideology of 'commonwealthman' civic virtue to the Scottish ecclesiastical context of the eighteenth century.

Though Francis Hutcheson died before the classic age of patronage confrontation that stretched from 1751 to 1785, the views that he represented lived on to become the principal doctrine of the Popular party during that period. In the patronage controversy of the early 1780s, for example, a return to the principles of 1690 was the primary objective of a majority of anti-patronage agitators, and Rev. John Gillies, a prominent Popular party leader, took pains to differentiate his 'Old Constitutional Society in Glasgow', which stood for those principles, from the more democratic 'New Constitutional Society' that he feared would give his party a bad name.[48] A similar point of view was expressed in the mid-1760s by Patrick Cuming's faction of clergymen — misleadingly dubbed 'Old' or 'Early' Moderates by nineteenth-century ecclesiastical historians. As the spokesman for Cuming's circle, Rev. James Oswald of Methven, the 'common sense' philosopher, attacked unlimited patronage and its Moderate party supporters on the ground of corruption, defended his faction's earlier pro-patronage stance in alliance with the Argyll interest and the government as a temporary, albeit necessary, expedient for 'repelling the usurpations of the people', invoked the civil act of 1690 and the ecclesiastical act of 1732 as his group's ultimate standards, and made a special appeal to the right of the Scottish gentry to check the power of patrons.[49]

The same faith in the principles of 1690 and the primacy of the 'landed interest' appears, with variations, in perhaps the most famous of all anti-patronage pamphlets from the period we are treating: *Thoughts of a Layman concerning Patronage and Presentations,* published anonymously in 1769 by Andrew Crosbie, a lawyer, landowner, and lay leader of the Popular Party in the church. Like Hutcheson, Crosbie exaggerated the power of the crown in the disposal of Scottish church patronage, though his exaggeration was less extreme and his main point about the dominance of the crown and nobility together was true enough.[50] In an apparent effort to appease all concerned parties, and in reaction to the corruption which had already overtaken the unreformed Scottish electoral system, Crosbie suggested that the best way to select parish ministers was by instituting an elaborate method of election by delegates from the heritors, elders, parishioners, and perhaps even the patron. His primary purpose, however, was to increase the authority of the heritors and other members of the 'middle rank of people', whom he considered 'best qualified of any to judge of the talents of pastors'.[51] Crosbie adopted this position not only because he was concerned for the welfare of the kirk but because he believed that the 'middle rank' in Scotland had no other outlet for the exercise of 'liberty'.[52] Though his rhetoric was sometimes radical in tone, his conception of ecclesiastical and political liberty was generally closer to that of a Revolution Whig or Presbyterian 'commonwealthman' from earlier in the century, such as Francis Hutcheson, than to that of the most radical proponents of 'Wilkes and Liberty' in his own day.

This point will become clearer if we take a moment to consider the context of Crosbie's pamphlet. It was written as part of the campaign of 1768-1769 to secure support for an application to Parliament by the General Assembly calling for repeal of the act of 1712. Taking advantage of the absence from Edinburgh of the Moderate party leader William Robertson, who had gone to London to arrange publication of his history of Charles V, Crosbie and his supporters in the Popular party persuaded a majority in the General Assembly of 1768 to appoint a committee to 'correspond with the landed interest and royal boroughs of Scotland, and the several presbyteries' as to the most desirable alternative to patronage. Crosbie himself served on this committee, which sent six copies of his pamphlet to the moderator of every presbytery in the country along with a request that each minister in the presbytery consult the heritors in his parish about this matter.[53] Here was an opportunity for the 'landed interest' of Scotland to assert itself by proclaiming patronage a grievance and declaring its right to participate in the process of filling vacant churches. The county meeting of landed gentry on issues of concern to them was already a feature of Scottish political life in the 1760s. Whether as commissioners of supply, justices of the peace, or heritors (three overlapping categories), they had not hesitated to meet on issues as diverse as a Scots militia, the spread of paper currency, vails, poaching, and the instability of a monetary tax for the upkeep of the roads.[54] On this occasion, however, no such activism was aroused. Not only were there apparently no county meetings to consider this issue; there was not even a single reply to Crosbie's committee from any presbytery in Scotland! Perhaps because many of them already served as patrons or were consulted by patrons about the choice of a new minister, perhaps because they were frightened to put themselves in opposition to the nobility and government, or perhaps because they simply did not care enough about ecclesiastical affairs, the gentry and smaller landowners evidently did not consider it to be in their best interest to speak out against the law of patronage. For Crosbie and his associates, this turn of events was disastrous; their star witness had been called and remained silent. After Crosbie's committee reported the embarrassing results of its activities to the General Assembly of 1769, William Robertson and the Moderates had no difficulty quashing an attempt to reappoint a committee of correspondence with the landed interest and the presbyteries on the patronage question.[55] The only recourse of Crosbie and his party was to submit a protest which spoke of 'religious and civil liberty' and attempted, *inter alia*, to drive a wedge between great and small landowners over the question of teinds.[56]

Though Andrew Crosbie's anti-patronage campaign was dead by 1770, it is significant for our argument that in that year Rev. Thomas Randall of Stirling, a well-respected figure of the Popular party, published a collection of *Tracts Concerning Patronage* which praised Crosbie's pamphlet and included a reprint of Francis Hutcheson's *Considerations on Patronages.*[57] Hutcheson and Crosbie's belief that lay patronage dominated by the crown and the nobility should be replaced by a system that vested the lion's share of authority in local heritors and elders was the dominant view of the Popular party throughout the second half of the eighteenth century. The Popular party in the Church of Scotland was therefore not fundamentally 'popular' at all in the usual sense of that term; rather, it represented an élitist Whig view based on the ideology of 1688-1690 and the 'commonwealthman' tradition.[58] This helps to explain why a prominent advocate and landowner like Andrew Crosbie or high-born clergymen like John Erskine and Sir Henry Moncreiff Wellwood could serve as its leaders, why the two ecclesiastical parties in the Church of Scotland were about equally conservative during the turbulent 1790s, and why the bitter patronage struggles of the period 1751-1785 never came close to producing a major schism like the one that tore the kirk asunder in 1843. It also helps to explain the consistent failure of the Popular party to win any victories on the patronage question. Outflanked on the 'left' by seceders and those still within the established church who favoured popular elections or the primacy of presbyteries and kirk sessions, and outflanked on the 'right' by the Moderate party, the government, and a landed interest that refused to identify with it, the Popular party was never able to have its way.

The divisions amongst the opponents of lay patronage demonstrate the problems of the opposition. What of the Moderates who defended patronage under the leadership of William Robertson? Why did they support it? Were they hacks or stooges for the government of the day and its Scottish managers? Were they lackeys of the 'ruling class'?[59] Were they simply being expedient in avoiding an issue which the church was bound to lose? Or did they have some kind of commitment to the principle of patronage itself? In order to suggest answers to these questions, it will be useful to examine the four arguments that the Moderates themselves most commonly employed when addressing the patronage issue.

The first two arguments deftly circumvented the matter of patronage as such by emphasising instead the importance of law and order. First, the Moderates admitted that patronage was a hard law but insisted that it was a law nevertheless and therefore had to be obeyed. Sometimes this argument took the form of a strong and positive commitment to the laws of the realm — law as the bedrock of society and the bulwark against 'anarchy and confusion' — while other times it manifested itself as mere expediency — a reluctant resignation to forces that the church was powerless to control. Either way, the issue was not whether one approved of patronage but whether one was prepared to obey the law. Exploiting this approach to the fullest, William Robertson sometimes implied that he was no lover of patronage and adopted a conciliatory attitude towards the sizeable portion of the kirk that was dead set against it. It was this attitude that Sir Henry Moncreiff Wellwood had in mind when he conceded that Robertson tried 'never wantonly to offend the prejudices of the people, and rather to endeavour to manage them, than directly to combat them'.[60] A good example is the well-known fact that throughout the Robertson era the General Assembly continued to include a clause against the 'grievance' of patronage in its annual instructions to its quarterly commission.[61] This conciliatory, law-of-the-land argument for accepting patronage appears frequently in Moderate pamphlets, sermons, and speeches, such as Alexander Gerard's speech as moderator of the General Assembly of 1764 and Thomas Hardy's popular pamphlet, *Principles of Moderation*.[62]

The second of the Moderates' defences of patronage shifted the issue from civil to ecclesiastical law and order. Here emphasis was placed on the importance of church discipline in general and of the authority of the General Assembly in a Presbyterian system of church government in particular. This argument was put forward most forcefully by the Moderates in the second and third points in their famous 'Reasons of Dissent' of March 1752, which brilliantly turned the tables on presbyters who refused to settle an unpopular presentee to the parish of Inverkeithing by charging them with violating the essential principles of Presbyterianism.[63] Once again the critical issue was not patronage *per se* but law and order, in this instance the law of the General Assembly and the order that came from submission to it. The foremost authority on the Moderates, Dr. Ian D. L. Clark, has stressed the significance of the law-and-order principle in explaining the Moderates' commitment to enforcing the patronage act of 1712.[64] A key point in this reading of the Moderates is their independence of the government ministry in London. Simply put, they were not government hacks, but they were willing to co-operate with the government in the management of a strong, unified, and orderly national church. There is much evidence to support this interpretation, though how far ecclesiastical independence was simply the result of the exceptional weakness of governments in London during the Robertson years is still open to question. However, much as we admire Dr. Clark's path-breaking work, we believe it has overemphasised the principle of civil and ecclesiastical law and order in accounting for the Moderates' support of patronage. That principle was certainly important, and one of the present authors has stressed its usefulness in helping to explain the social and political conservatism of Moderate ideology as a whole.[65] Yet it was far from being the only ground on which the Moderates based their pro-patronage arguments.

We now come to the third such argument. Despite the fact that patronage had Episcopalian and Roman Catholic associations, or perhaps because of it, Moderates were sometimes at pains to show that patronage was not fundamentally un-Presbyterian. This was done, for example, by repeatedly pointing out that the act of 1592 which originally established Presbyterian church government in Scotland had not abolished patronage.[66] A particularly important instance of this approach concerns the brief biography of William Carstares which Rev. Joseph McCormick prefixed to the collection of

Carstares' state papers and correspondence that he published in 1774. McCormick was a strong party Moderate and a descendant of Carstares, who was revered amongst all members of the Church of Scotland as the man who did most to re-establish Presbyterianism in 1690. This reference helps to explain why Thomas Randall included the representations against patronage given in by Carstares and other commissioners of the General Assembly to the House of Lords in 1712 in his anti-patronage tracts of 1770.[67] McCormick, on the other hand, portrayed Carstares as a kind of proto-Moderate. He did so with the full support of William Robertson and other Moderates, who did all they could to get the book published and appreciated.[68]

At times McCormick's biography reads more like a life of William Robertson than of Carstares, as when it asserts that Carstares' appointment as principal of Edinburgh University permitted him to exert influence 'in promoting the interest of literature in the university, and of moderation in the church'[69] — this about a man who as late as 1714 was still justifying the notorious execution of Thomas Aikenhead for blasphemy in 1697.[70] According to McCormick, Carstares 'knew, that, from the reformation down to the revolution, in all the vicissitudes of church government, patronage had been the law of the land. He knew, that by the act of 1592, which has always been considered as the grand charter of presbyterian government, patronages were incorporated with its very constitution'.[71] And, like a good Moderate of the 1770s, he feared that freedom to choose their ministers would give the Presbyterian populace and clergy more power 'than they knew how to use with moderation'.[72] These questionable claims suggest that McCormick and his Moderate friends were using Carstares to justify their own party programme by giving patronage respectability and legitimacy as part of the Scots Presbyterian heritage.

The last and most direct argument that the Moderates utilised on behalf of patronage was that it was good in itself, or rather a necessary means to a desirable end. No Moderate dared to use this argument in the 1750s, but in the debate in the General Assembly of 1766 over the 'Schism Overture' we find William Robertson espousing it, contending that the institution of patronage by enlightened members of the upper classes and representatives of the government had helped to improve the quality of the Scottish clergy.[73] We find the same sort of view expressed in two of the pamphlets published by Moderates in 1769 in reply to Andrew Crosbie's *Thoughts of a Layman*.[74] A cynic might interpret this argument in narrowly political terms, by claiming that the Moderates really meant that patronage was the best way to build up the strength and stature of their party. But this interpretation would not be entirely fair. For the Moderates the key issue was the creation and maintenance of a polite, enlightened Scottish clergy leading their nation out of the abyss of seventeenth-century fanaticism. Patronage was therefore esteemed for its partiality to ministers who were moderate in their values as well as Moderate in their ecclesiastical politics. Either way, government and the landed élite were being used by the Moderates to achieve their ends rather than vice versa. Though perhaps less frequently employed than some of their other reasons for supporting patronage, this enlightened élitist argument was in our opinion common enough, and important enough, to cast doubt upon Dr. Clark's contention that the Robertson Moderates 'were not committed to the view that patronage was inherently desirable or justified'.[75]

Conclusion

Our intention in this essay has been to suggest some reasons for regarding the Scottish church patronage confrontations of the second half of the eighteenth century as considerably more complicated and interesting than has traditionally been thought. We have tried to show that the sporadic nature of those confrontations, whether in the form of local presentation disputes or broader crises of the sort that touched off pamphlet wars, reflected 'external' factors, such as political changes at Westminster, as well as 'internal' or ecclesiastical ones; that the long period of relative peace over the patronage issue between the mid-1780s and the late 1820s raises serious questions about the true extent of the continuity of anti-patronage agitation from the eighteenth to the nineteenth century; and that the church patronage struggles of the eighteenth century were in no sense mere dress rehearsals for the tragedy of 1843.

We have also tried to show that the so-called Popular party, while unified in its opposition to the law of patronage, was in fact fragmented into various elements that favoured quite different alternatives to that law. Amongst those elements were radicals — who were themselves divided according to whether their democratic inspiration derived from the old Calvinist spirit of John Knox or the new Whig spirit of John Wilkes — and an apparently larger number of more moderate churchmen who had no desire to see the right of filling vacant churches placed in the hands of the 'people'. Churchmen of the latter variety put their faith in the eldership of the kirk sessions, in the clergy-dominated presbyteries, and above all in the 'landed interest' as represented by heritors, who seemed to constitute the happy medium between the crown and nobility on the one hand and the people on the other. Their rhetorical ammunition came not only from their Presbyterian heritage but also from their political one; it was the heritage of the 'commonwealthman', the 'Glorious' Revolution, and the Scottish Revolution Settlement of 1690. From Francis Hutcheson to Sir Henry Moncreiff Wellwood, this was the dominant outlook in what came to be called the Popular party during the second half of the eighteenth century. As Andrew Crosbie learned the hard way in 1769, however, this programme had a fatal flaw: the heritors, the key element in the amorphous 'middle rank' to which Crosbie and his party appealed, remained unmoved. Militia schemes and improving societies could still ignite their sense of civic virtue, but matters of ecclesiastical polity apparently could not. Thus, the Popular party never secured the solid social and economic foundation that the urban bourgeoisie would eventually provide for the resurgent Evangelicals of the nineteenth century.[76]

As for the Moderates of William Robertson's day, we have seen that their reasons for supporting the law of patronage varied greatly. Some may indeed have been lackeys of the nobility and government, as their detractors have maintained for two hundred years, but most appear to have viewed lay patronage as a legitimate Presbyterian option, a critical test of ecclesiastical as well as civil law and order, and a useful means of getting the nobility and government to serve *their* interests, and those of Scotland generally, by giving preferment to 'enlightened' clergymen. On this topic, as on virtually every other topic raised in this essay, a great deal of additional research remains to be done. Yet this much may be said about the two ecclesiastical parties in the Church of Scotland during the Robertson era: to view the Moderates as the party of the aristocracy and their opponents as the party of the people makes about as much sense as the analogous claims that used to be made about Tories and Whigs in the political realm. No doubt the Popular party was more sensitive to the preferences of parishioners and more inclined to employ the inflammatory rhetoric of 'liberty'. Nevertheless, the Moderate and Popular parties were both predominantly élitist during this period, and to deny or ignore this fact is to risk seriously misunderstanding the nature of eighteenth-century Scottish ecclesiastical politics.

NOTES

The authors wish to thank Dr. Stewart J. Brown and Dr. Roger Emerson for helpful criticisms of an earlier draft of this paper.

1. Robert Burns, 'The Ordination' (1786), in *Poems and Songs*, ed. James Kinsley (London, 1971), 172. 'Shor'd' in this context means threatened.
2. Sir Henry Moncreiff Wellwood, *Account of the Life and Writings of John Erskine* (Edinburgh, 1818), appendix 1. All references in this essay are to the edition of the 'Brief Account' published separately in Edinburgh by the author's nephew Sir James Wellwood Moncreiff in 1833.
3. Thomas Somerville, *My Life and Times, 1741-1814* (Edinburgh, 1861), 73-74.
4. William L. Clements Library, University of Michigan, Melville Papers, Henry Dundas (then Viscount Melville) to his son Robert Saunders Dundas, 11 March 1811. We are grateful to David Brown of the University of Edinburgh for this reference.
5. A. L. Drummond and J. Bulloch, *The Scottish Church, 1688-1843: The Age of the Moderates* (Edinburgh, 1973), 212.
6. Report of the Select Committee on Church Patronage, Scotland, *Parliamentary Papers*, 1834, vol. v, especially appendix 2.
7. *Scots Magazine*, XXIX (June 1767), 329-30.
8. *Ibid.*, XXXI (May 1769), 275-6 and 226. See also *ibid.*, XLIX (May 1787), 256, where it is reported that the creditors of the patron of the parish of St. Ninians had advertised the right of patronage for sale upon the parish becoming vacant by the death of the late incumbent. We would not wish to leave the impression, however, that this sort of behaviour was typical of most Scottish patrons.

9. I. D. L. Clark, 'Moderatism and the Moderate Party in the Church of Scotland' (Cambridge University Ph.D., 1963), 57-58; James Stuart Mackenzie's church patronage notebook, Mount Stuart, Isle of Bute; correspondence of Henry Dundas cited in note 4 above, where Dundas boasts of the success of his policy of ensuring the 'moderation of the Crown in the exercise of the presentations' in its care by paying 'discreet attention to local circumstances' — meaning chiefly the wishes of the 'landed interest of the parish' as represented by the county Member of Parliament, subject to close supervision by government managers.

10. See, for example, *A Friendly Address to the Laity of the Church of Scotland, in Relation to the Laws of Patronage* (Edinburgh, 1772). The accounts of disputed presentations printed in the *Scots Magazine* reveal the shift in protests over presentations at the end of the century.

11. K. J. Logue, *Popular Disturbances in Scotland, 1780-1815* (Edinburgh, 1979), chap. 7.

12. [James Boswell], 'Debates in the General Assembly of the Church of Scotland', *London Magazine*, XLII (April-August 1773), 188-91, 227, 296-9, 340-4, 396.

13. The best sources for the details of these crises are contemporary newspaper and magazine accounts of the proceedings of the General Assembly, many of which are compiled in N. Morren (ed.), *Annals of the General Assembly of the Church of Scotland, 1739-1766* (Edinburgh, 1838-40). See also J. Cunningham, *The Church History of Scotland* (Edinburgh, 1859), ii, and other standard histories of the established church and the seceders.

14. These figures are based on church patronage pamphlets in the libraries of Edinburgh and in the New York Public Library.

15. Morren lists no fewer than thirty-eight disputed presentations that reached the General Assembly during the 1740s. *Annals*, i, 345-67.

16. W. MacKelvie, *Annals and Statistics of the United Presbyterian Church*, ed. W. Blair (Edinburgh, 1873), 31-37.

17. Moncreiff Wellwood, *Brief Account*, 86; *Parliamentary Papers*, 1834, v, 336, Appendices, 156.

18. Moncreiff Wellwood, *Brief Account*, 86; Clark, 'Moderatism and the Moderate Party', 115, 124, 159-160.

19. MacKelvie, *Annals*, 11-12.

20. There was an increase in the number of new secession congregations after 1785, but it was relatively slight: from an average of 5.8 new congregations per year in the period 1750-1785 to an average of 6.7 per year in the period 1786-1800, according to the data presented in MacKelvie, *Annals*, 31-37.

21. Morren, *Annals*, ii, vi-vii.

22. H. W. Meikle, *Scotland and the French Revolution* (Glasgow 1912, reprinted London, 1969), 2, 34.

23. The day after the General Assembly of 1784 rejected the anti-patronage overtures under consideration, supporters of patronage went on the offensive and enacted, without a formal vote, a resolution expunging from the Assembly's annual instructions to its quarterly Commission a clause calling for vigilance against the 'grievance' of patronage. Significantly, young Robert Dundas, Henry's nephew and Scottish sub-minister, played a conspicuous part in these proceedings. *Ibid.*, 38-39.

24. The formation of a parliamentary committee on church patronage in Scotland and the publication of that committee's massive report in 1834 seemed to promise government reforms which never materialised. On the general role of national politics

in the 'ten years' conflict' leading up to the Disruption, see G. I. T. Machin, 'The Disruption and British Politics, 1834-43', *Scottish Historical Review*, LI (April 1972), 20-51.

25. *The Second Book of Discipline*, ed. J. Kirk (Edinburgh, 1980). The following discussion of the act of 1649 owes much to W. Makey, *The Church of the Covenant, 1637-1651* (Edinburgh, 1979), 78-80.

26. Though in theory ministers and elders were equally represented in presbyteries, in practice the former were usually far more plentiful. In the mid-eighteenth century Rev. John Maclaurin of Glasgow asserted that ministers normally outnumbered elders attending presbytery meetings by more than two to one. *A Loud Cry for Help to the Struggling Church of Scotland* (Glasgow, 1753), 31.

27. Makey, *Church of the Covenant*, 80. Dr. Makey speculates that Johnston of Wariston used this argument to persuade the Parliament to abolish patronage.

28. Although more work needs to be done on the social composition of the eldership, it seems safe to assume that elders in rural parishes were usually men of property and were virtually never landless labourers or other members of the lower classes. Even in a populous burgh like Edinburgh, where a somewhat more democratic spirit prevailed, elders who were merchants or shopkeepers, and other men of relatively substantial rank and property, outnumbered elders who were tradesmen by almost three to one in 1762 — and some of the latter were also quite well off. The elders who sat in the General Assembly during the eighteenth century — though admittedly men of higher social standing than the eldership as a whole — were predominantly members of the propertied classes, including baronets and other landed gentlemen, lawyers, judges, merchants, professors, and a smattering of peers. Cf. the evidence on early nineteenth-century assembly membership in Iain F. Maciver, 'The Evangelical Party and the Eldership in the General Assembly, 1820-1843', *Records of the Scottish Church History Society*, XX (1978), 1-13.

29. T. Maxwell, 'William III and the Scots Presbyterians', *Records of the Scottish Church History Society*, XV (1966), 169-91. The act of 1690 is reprinted in W. C. Dickinson and G. Donaldson (eds.), *A Source Book of Scottish History*, iii (Edinburgh and London, 1954), 214-16. In the burghs responsibility for calling ministers remained with the 'magistrats, toune counsell and kirke sessione'.

30. The pre-eminent position of the heritors in the process of nominating ministers is here assumed on the basis of three factors, any or all of which may have been operative in a given parish: (1) numerical superiority of heritors over elders; (2) inclusion of heritors or their representatives amongst the eldership; (3) deference of elders to the wishes of heritors.

31. *Scots Magazine*, XXXI (May 1769), 227.

32. *The First Book of Discipline*, ed. J. K. Cameron (Edinburgh, 1972). Cf. John Calvin, *Institutes of the Christian Religion*, ed. John T. McNeill (Philadelphia, 1960), 4.3.13-15. But Calvin qualified his advocacy of popular election of ministers by charging the clergy with responsibility for presiding over such elections 'in order that the multitude may not go wrong'. In this sense, his position was also compatible with the second, Melvillian alternative to patronage discussed below.

33. Quoted in Makey, *Church of the Covenant*, 79.

34. See R. B. Sher, 'Moderates, Managers and Popular Politics in Mid-Eighteenth Century Edinburgh: The Drysdale "Bustle" of the 1760s', in J. Dwyer *et al* (eds.), *New Perspectives on the Politics and Culture of Early Modern Scotland* (Edinburgh, 1982), 179-209.

35. In *Considerations on Patronage* (Edinburgh, 1766) Maclaurin wrote: 'The Presbyterian religion . . . plainly suppose[s] and declare[s] that the minister to be settled is the choice of the people in the parish, for whose benefit he is intended'. On Maclaurin's radicalism, see the sketch in T. Murray, *Biographical Annals of the Parish of Colinton* (Edinburgh, 1863), 53.

36. See especially [Patrick Bannerman], *An Address to the People of Scotland, on Ecclesiastical and Civil Liberty* (Edinburgh, 1782) and *An Address on Civil and Ecclesiastical Liberty* (Edinburgh, 1783). The latter pamphlet, not seen by us, is discussed in Meikle, *Scotland and the French Revolution*, 36.

37. *Ibid.*, 38.

38. We look forward to the completion of John Brims' Ph.D. thesis at the University of Edinburgh to shed some light on this question.

39. See the speech of Agelaus in *Philopatris; or, the Committee of Overtures. A Dialogue* (Edinburgh, 1766), 12.

40. In regard to the Inverkeithing case, it is perhaps significant that the presentee whom a majority of the ministers in the Presbytery of Dunfermline refused to settle soon became popular with the people of that pious parish. Drummond and Bulloch, *Scottish Church*, 69.

41. Andrew J. Campbell, *Two Centuries of the Church of Scotland, 1707-1929* (Paisley, 1930), 48-55.

42. See Henry R. Sefton, 'The Early Development of Moderatism in the Church of Scotland' (Glasgow University Ph.D., 1962), esp. chap. iii. Also see Dr. Sefton's contribution to this volume.

43. Thomas Randall remarked upon this change of terminology in *A Candid Inquiry into the Constitution of the Church of Scotland in Relation to the Settlement of Ministers* (1770), 53, in Randall (ed.), *Tracts Concerning Patronage, by some Eminent Hands* (Edinburgh, 1770).

44. Hutcheson's claim of 'above 550 churches' where the crown was patron (*Considerations on Patronages* [London, 1735], 24) was approximately twice the true figure. Absurd as Hutcheson's claim now seems, it apparently had great rhetorical appeal for the opponents of patronage and was repeated without qualification as late as 1783 in *A Collection of Letters on Patronage and Popular Election*, 56.

45. Hutcheson, *Considerations on Patronages*, 34.

46. See especially P. Jones, 'The Triumph of the Professors: Civic Moralism at the Scottish Universities, 1720-1770', in I. Hont and M. Ignatieff (eds.), *Wealth and Virtue: The Shaping of Political Economy in the Scottish Enlightenment* (Cambridge, 1983), as well as C. Robbins, *The Eighteenth-Century Commonwealthman* (Cambridge, Mass., 1961), 185-195.

47. G. E. Davie, 'Hume, Reid, and the Passion for Ideas', in D. Young *et al,* *Edinburgh in the Age of Reason* (Edinburgh, 1967), 25-28.

48. John Gillies, *Letter of the Old Constitutional Society in Glasgow* (16 September 1783), in *A Speech addressed to the Provincial Synod of Glasgow and Ayr* (Edinburgh, 1784).

49. James Oswald, *Letters concerning the Present State of the Church of Scotland, and the consequent Danger to Religion and Learning, from the arbitrary and unconstitutional Exercise of the Law of Patronage* (Edinburgh, 1767), especially letters v, vi, and vii.

50. See Table I above.

51. Andrew Crosbie, *Thoughts of a Layman concerning Patronage and Presen-*

tations (Edinburgh, 1769), 34.

52. *Ibid.*, 28.

53. *Scots Magazine*, XXX (May 1768), 277 and (May 1769), 274.

54. J. Dwyer and A. Murdoch, 'Paradigms and Politics: Manners, Morals and the Rise of Henry Dundas, 1770-1784', in Dwyer *et al*, *New Perspectives*, 210-248.

55. *Scots Magazine*, XXXI (May 1769), 274. The vote was 115 to 87. It was at this point that Robert Wallace, a Presbyterian minister and 'commonwealthman' of Francis Hutcheson's generation, stopped writing 'Thoughts upon the application by the General Assembly of 1768 to the Gentlemen of the landed Interest in Scotland about Patronages' (Edinburgh University Library, La.II.620[27]), which would have served the Popular party cause if Wallace had managed to complete it. A note that Wallace later appended to the portion of this pamphlet that he did complete implies that the presbyteries did not solicit the opinions of the landed interest as actively as Crosbie and his supporters would have wished, but this circumstance cannot explain fully why the landed interest remained silent.

56. *Ibid.*, 227, especially point no. 5. Originally submitted by Crosbie and three others, the protest was later signed by an additional forty-five members of the General Assembly.

57. See note 43 above. Hutcheson's pamphlet was also reprinted separately at Glasgow in 1774.

58. If our view is correct, it makes little sense to say that 'the Popular Party contended for the rights of the parishioners at large, or at least heads of families', as Drummond and Bulloch argue in *The Scottish Church*, 62 — unless (as is not clear) the statement is meant to apply only to the 1730s and 1740s, in which case the use of the term 'Popular Party' as a formal party label is anachronistic and quite misleading. On the latter point, see Clark, 'Moderatism and the Moderate Party', 49-54.

59. See, for example, David Craig, *Scottish Literature and the Scottish People, 1680-1830* (London, 1961), chap. ii.

60. Moncreiff Wellwood, *Brief Account*, 85.

61. See note 23 above.

62. Morren, *Annals*, ii, 405-410; Thomas Hardy, *The Principles of Moderation, addressed to the Clergy of the Popular Interest in the Church of Scotland* (Edinburgh, 1782), 11.

63. Morren, *Annals*, i, 231-242.

64. Clark, 'Moderatism and the Moderate Party', pt. i, and 'From Protest to Reaction: The Moderate Regime in the Church of Scotland, 1752-1805', in N. T. Phillipson and R. Mitchison (eds.), *Scotland in the Age of Improvement: Essays in Scottish History in the Eighteenth Century* (Edinburgh, 1970), 200-224.

65. See R. B. Sher's forthcoming book on the William Robertson circle of 'Moderate literati'.

66. The act of 1592 is printed in Dickinson and Donaldson, *Source Book*, iii, 48-49. Eighteenth-century opponents of patronage could reply that this act would have abolished patronage if the Presbyterian party of the time had had its way.

67. Randall, *Tracts Concerning Patronage*, no. 1.

68. British Library, Egerton MS 2182, fos. 39-40, William Robertson to John Douglas, Bishop of Carlisle, 19 March 1773, and MS 2185, fos. 90-91, Alexander Carlyle to Bishop Douglas, 11 March 1773.

69. Joseph McCormick, 'The Life of Mr William Carstares', in *The State Papers and Letters addressed to William Carstares* (Edinburgh, 1774), 69.

70. G. E. Davie, *The Scottish Enlightenment* (London, Historical Association pamphlet, 1981), 9.

71. McCormick, 'Life of Carstares', 48.

72. *Ibid.*, 48-49.

73. Morren, *Annals*, ii, 331-332.

74. Henry Grieve, *Observations on the Overture Concerning Patronage* (Edinburgh, 1769), 14; *A Letter to the Author of a Pamphlet on Patronage and Presentations* (Edinburgh, 1769), 14-15.

75. Clark, 'From Protest to Reaction', in Phillipson and Mitchison, *Scotland in the Age of Improvement*, 206. Dr. Clark briefly acknowledges the Moderates' use of this mode of argument but seems to regard it as mere window-dressing. On the other hand, in his article 'The Making of Principal Robertson in 1762: Politics and the University of Edinburgh in the Second Half of the Eighteenth Century', *Scottish Historical Review*, XLIX (April 1970), 60-84, Jeremy J. Cater fully appreciates its importance but gives the impression that Robertson and his friends never employed it openly.

76. See A. A. McLaren, *Religion and Social Class: The Disruption Years in Aberdeen* (London, 1974), 209.

12

Voluntaryism and Reunion, 1874-1929

Ian Machin

IN the late nineteenth and early twentieth centuries disestablishment and Presbyterian reunion were the rival leading questions in Scottish Church-State relations. Reunion was seen from one standpoint as an alternative to disestablishment, from another as something which could only come after disestablishment. Of the three Kirks — the main divisions of Scottish Presbyterianism since the 1840s — the Church of Scotland was a State establishment, the United Presbyterian (U.P.) Church was Voluntary in both practice and principle, and the Free Church was Voluntary in practice but not decidedly in principle. The Free Church supposedly adhered to Chalmers' ideal of a spiritually independent establishment, so was free to reunite with the Church of Scotland when the latter was spiritually liberated from the State. But in fact the Free Church, being Voluntary in practice, had drawn closer to the United Presbyterian Church. Negotiations for a union of the Free and U.P. Churches lasted from 1863 to 1873, and foundered on the firm objections of a Free Church minority to the principle of Voluntaryism. The establishment ideal still commanded considerable support in the Free Church.

Soon after this defeat, however, the frustrated majority in the Free Church received new strength from an unlikely quarter, the removal of patronage in the Church of Scotland. The Conservative Government's Patronage Act of 1874 was intended to aid the established Church by abolishing patronage, the main ostensible cause of the Disruption of 1843, and hence promoting reunion of the seceders with the establishment. But hopes that the lost sheep would be regained were not realised. Free Churchmen were proud of their independent achievement since 1843 and were not to be tempted back to a body which they still regarded as spiritually subordinate to the secular State.[1] Indeed, most Free Churchmen proceeded to emphasise their separation by supporting a disestablishment campaign which lasted for many years. Until the end of the century, Voluntaryism was stronger than hopes of reunion.

Disestablishment was not only a Scottish movement but a British one. Stimulated by the achievement of Irish disestablishment in 1869, it was quite a powerful movement in England and Wales in the 1870s and early 1880s —

stronger in England than it was later, and weaker in Wales. In Scotland it was strongest of all at this stage, and Scottish Voluntaries drew additional support from south of the border.[2]

Within Scotland the movement was developing vigorously before 1874, especially among the United Presbyterians. Their Voluntary commitment was championed by Principal John Cairns and Dr. G. C. Hutton, and had then the support of the great majority of U.P. ministers and members. The United Presbyterian presbyteries and Synod adopted motions for disestablishment and appointed committees on the subject with very little dissent.[3] The Free Church was more divided. Dr. Robert Rainy and his followers were ardent Voluntaries in their attitude to the existing establishment though they continued to pay respect to Chalmers' establishment ideal. The Free Church minority led by Dr. James Begg, who had opposed union with the United Presbyterians, clearly upheld the establishment principle. Begg thought the Patronage Act was a promising opening for reunion with the Church of Scotland. But the growth of religious liberalism in that Church was another obstacle for the Free Church minority. John Kennedy of Dingwall, a leading Free Kirk minister, zealously defended Calvinist orthodoxy and scriptural inspiration; and these theological views increasingly distinguished the Begg-Kennedy group from many not only in the Church of Scotland and United Presbyterian Church but also in their own Free Church.[4] These differences meant that the Free Kirk presbyteries and General Assemblies were often divided in their debates and resolutions on disestablishment.[5] But Voluntary opinions seemed to obtain the support of most Free Churchmen except in the northern and western Highlands, where the views of Kennedy and Begg prevailed.

Outside the courts of the three Kirks, Voluntaryism attracted wide public attention. Meetings on the subject were attended by thousands.[6] The Press gave much space and argument to the topic, elections were affected by it, and rival pamphlets and articles poured out even more relentlessly than during the 'ten years' conflict' of 1834-43.[7] A Scottish Disestablishment Association provided a central source of propaganda, and a Scottish Council of the Liberation Society (the most widespread Voluntary organisation, centred in London) was formed in 1877. Disestablishment had become the leading Scottish question of the time.

The Voluntary argument was a powerful one in an age moving towards democracy, based as this argument was on the ideals of spiritual freedom from State control, of religious equality and financial equity. But the 'Church defence' side of the debate, preaching the virtues of a State-recognised national religion with an assured territorial organisation, was by no means lacking in resilience. Neither side would have wished to regard mere numbers as the decisive element in a spiritual conflict, and the figures produced by one side were of course disputed by the other. But statistics were a real concern in the contest, and might even have provided welcome relief from intellectual distinctions which reached an almost medieval subtlety. It was estimated in 1874 that the Free and United Presbyterian Churches combined had a clear numerical lead over the Church of Scotland.[8] But in 1882 Principal John Tulloch (of St. Mary's College, St. Andrews) said that the establishment had considerably more communicants than the other two Churches together, and that communicants in the Church of Scotland were increasing at a much faster rate.[9]

The consciousness of quicker expansion boosted establishment morale, but the need for anti-Voluntary propaganda was nonetheless pressing. In this matter Tulloch took a lead, urging the raising of funds, the formation of a Church Defence Association, the production of literature, and inducements to Begg and his followers to rejoin the Church — 'I wish the bosom of the Church to be as broad and ample as possible,' said Tulloch, 'and so to find room for even a Begg'.[10] He wanted 'a good pull and a pull altogether, to increase the majority against disestablishment'.[11] Whether there was a majority of Scotsmen against disestablishment was a matter of contention, but certainly the current success of the established Church was an important hindrance to Voluntary hopes. The revival taking place in the establishment made it difficult for Voluntaries to insist that they fulfilled the democratic criterion of possessing a clear majority.

Argument from numbers naturally affected politicians, whose parliamentary careers might depend on satisfying a majority of electors in their constituencies. The Voluntaries sought political success for their aims, as only Parliament could decide whether or not an established Church should continue. A political solution had already been applied to the Church of Ireland in 1869. Scottish Voluntaries urged similar action in their own country, looking to the Liberal party to carry it out as Conservatives were firm defenders of the establishment. But Voluntary claims were embarrassing to a party in which there were many 'Church Liberals', such as Tulloch, and party unity would be weakened by the adoption of voluntaryism. Liberal leaders therefore tried to avoid committing themselves, and said that a solution must emerge from the matured opinions of the Scottish people — an admirably liberal sentiment which also had the merit of helping to maintain Liberal party unity.

Lord Hartington, then the recognised leader of the party (Gladstone being in temporary retirement), was due to visit Scotland in November 1877. He realised, as he told Gladstone, that he would have to be 'extremely careful' over disestablishment.[12] Consequently he said in Edinburgh that, if ever Scottish opinion was 'fully formed' on the subject, the Liberals would deal with the matter 'on its merits'.[13] Similarly opaque pronouncements were made in the next few years by Gladstone, who told Rainy in 1879 that he adhered to Hartington's declaration.[14] For the time being the different views within the party, reflecting the growing conflict between Whigs and radicals, did not realistically permit any other attitude to be taken. Scottish disestablishment was a sectional interest. As such it could not be ignored without risking the loss of some supporters, but neither could it be promoted without risking the loss of others.

The return of a Liberal Government in 1880 did little to assist the Voluntary cause. Gladstone, in his Midlothian campaign of November 1879, tried to soothe establishment fears and accused the Conservatives of stirring up the dispute in order to divide Liberals.[15] Conservative candidates in the 1880 election did indeed raise disestablishment for the sake of opposing it, while few Liberal candidates referred to the subject. Those Liberals who did mention it usually said it was not yet a question of practical politics.[16] One candidate happily stated it was a matter 'which the Liberal party have agreed to sink'.[17] The new Government was faced with other problems, especially Ireland and the Bradlaugh case, and when Gladstone did express opinions on Scottish disestablishment they were still non-commital.[18] He told the Queen in 1883 that he did not think this question had made much progress in recent years.[19]

Despite Gladstone's wishful thinking the controversy remained lively. In 1881 there was much propaganda activity by the Scottish Council of the Liberation Society in support of J. Dick Peddie (president of this Council, M.P. for Kilmarnock Burghs and a United Presbyterian elder), who tried to raise the question in Parliament.[20] Eventually he introduced a detailed bill of Scottish disestablishment in October 1884, but this did not receive a debate.[21] The non-established Presbyterian Churches were active in discussing the matter, and public meetings in favour of disestablishment continued to be held.[22] Against such efforts the Church of Scotland General Assembly formed in 1882 a Church Interests Committee, of which the Conservative politician Lord Balfour of Burleigh was a convener. This committee sponsored many petitions against Peddie's bill, containing 688,195 signatures.[23] This was impressive support for the establishment claim that Church defence was no less popular than disestablishment. Church defence meetings were held, local bodies formed, and an elaborate National Church Society was founded.[24] Lord Salisbury, when visiting Scotland, took defence of the establishment as one of his leading aims, and later told a Conservative colleague that he ought to 'work the question of the Scottish Church Establishment' as it was a 'telling factor' in many parts of Scotland.[25] Clearly the efforts of each side were only stimulating its opponents, and both were building up so much support that only stalemate was likely to ensue.

Church reunion was not forgotten amidst the controversy. It was seen not merely in efforts by the Church of Scotland to strengthen its hand by gaining Free Church allies,[26] but in the broader aim of removing the current hostility. An Edinburgh public meeting held in November 1884 to promote reunion did not attract a large audience, but did appoint a small committee. A Union Association was formed, and met with 'slow but substantial sympathy and encouragement'. However, by June 1885 the committee decided not to hold further meetings for the time being, as there was no probability of reunion 'in the present state of ecclesiastical relations in Scotland'.[27] Clearly the time for fruitful attempts at reunion had not yet come.

Fervent support for the rival and mutually sustaining causes of disestablishment and Church defence reached its height in 1885. A Voluntary pamphlet told new working-class voters that Church disestablishment would release funds for free education; a counter-publication reminded them that Church endowments existed to provide religious services for the poor who could scarcely afford voluntary contributions.[28] Early in 1885 Peddie introduced another disestablishment bill, but this was again opposed by a great many petitioners and was deprived of a second reading by pressure of government business. The Liberals were embarrassed by the growing importance of the disestablishment question in Scotland and England as the autumn general election approached; and especially by the Church defence assault of the Conservatives, probing the weaknesses of Liberal division in order to strengthen themselves.[29] 'The Church would be stripped and bare', declared Lord Salisbury; 'in every part of the land the machinery by which God's Word has been preached . . . would be put an end to.'[30]

In Scotland the presbyteries of rival Churches urged diverse electoral action upon members. A new radical organisation, the National Liberal Federation of Scotland, voted to make disestablishment a test question for Liberal candidates. Some of these were pressed to declare Voluntary opinions against their own judgement, and disputing Liberal candidates challenged each other in thirteen constituencies over the issue.[31] The question was thus threatening to disrupt the Liberal party, to the dismay of the party leaders. In face of this threat even the decidedly radical Joseph Chamberlain was driven to make contradictory statements, veering from a committed Voluntary position to a conciliatory and neutral one. Gladstone began with pronouncements of studied ambiguity, but took to discouraging disestablishment in accordance with advice from Lord Rosebery and other Scottish Liberals and against the plea of 1475 Scottish dissenting ministers.[32] By November, when he launched another Midlothian campaign, Gladstone had decided that hopes of disestablishment must be quashed in the interests of party unity. Accordingly, on 11 November at the Free Church Assembly Hall he said that disestablishment could not be a test question in the elections, and relegated any prospect of achieving it to 'the end of a long vista'.[33] Despite angry Voluntary protests, the leader's word prevailed. Disestablishment was not, after all, a vital issue in the elections. It was not adopted as a test of Liberalism. The Liberals were to split not over disestablishment but Home Rule, and the prominence of this question temporarily diminished the prominence of Voluntaryism.

Liberal division over Irish Home Rule brought the Conservatives into power for most of the next twenty years. The seceders from Gladstone were proportionally more numerous among Scottish M.Ps., and Scotland returned a higher proportion of Liberal Unionist M.Ps. in 1886 than any other part of the United Kingdom.[34] Voluntaries could not hope to succeed while Unionists ruled, but they could at least hope to exert more pressure on Liberal politicians who had lost many of their 'pro-Church' followers in the Home Rule split. Some Voluntaries, however, also became Unionists, and this weakened their Voluntaryism because they were now allied to an erastian Conservative party.[35] Some 'Church' Liberals, moreover, remained Gladstonians, so a restrictive influence over Voluntaryism remained amongst Liberals. The prospects for Voluntaryism, therefore, had not markedly changed, but they did seem brighter within the Liberal ranks. Because of the increased influence of Voluntaries in his party, Gladstone's 'long vista' became shorter; and within three years he gave his blessing, if rather unwillingly, to the cause he had indefinitely postponed in 1885.

The anti-climax for Voluntaryism caused by Gladstone's speech in November 1885 was sustained for a while by his adoption of Home Rule. In 1886 Scottish disestablishment made no headway, in spite of the decision of various Voluntary societies to form a federal Disestablishment Council for Scotland. Dr. Charles Cameron, a Glasgow Liberal M.P., brought forward the first of a series of parliamentary motions for disestablishment, but was easily defeated by 239 votes to 127; and Voluntaryism made little impact in the election of July 1886 which was fought over Home Rule.

But those who aimed at Presbyterian reunion on the basis of a modified Establishment had no greater success. Robert Finlay, a Liberal M.P. for Inverness Burghs who became a Liberal Unionist, introduced a bill early in 1886 to facilitate the reunion of Free Churchmen with the Church of Scotland by declaring that Church's complete spiritual independence. But the bill, although it could be claimed that its principle was successful thirty-five years later, won little support among the parties it was meant to reunite, and was lost in the House of Commons with few Scottish members supporting it.[36]

During the next few years, however, sentiment in favour of reunion became stronger, and discussion of the question was more active.[37] In July 1890 a Laymen's League was formed, consisting of Presbyterians from different Churches (including some United Presbyterians) in order to oppose disestablishment and promote union. In the same year a resolution in favour of disestablishment met with opposition for the first time in the U.P. Synod, and opposition was also voiced in some of the presbyteries and congregations of that Church.[38] But in spite of these developments and the political changes which had partly caused them, it was clear that neither disestablishment nor reunion could yet succeed, and that the argument between them would have to continue.

Radical influence in Scottish Liberalism caused the passage of Voluntary resolutions at party conferences in the later 1880s and the urging of Scottish disestablishment at the annual meetings of the National Liberal Federation. Charles Cameron introduced another motion in the Commons in June 1888; the majority against it dropped from the 112 votes of two years previously to only 52, and no Scottish Liberal voted against it. Moreover, Gladstone was now being won round. Addressing the National Liberal Federation in October 1887, he said that the questions of Scottish and Welsh disestablishment were 'ripe for decision', but only when more of a solution had been reached on Irish Home Rule.[39] He finally declared his support for Scottish and Welsh disestablishment (but not English) in a speech in Cornwall on 12 June 1889.[40] He even seemed to have mustered some zeal for the cause, for he told Rosebery: 'In argument I think the Scotch Church has not the rag of a case'.[41] Scottish

Voluntaries naturally exulted in his belated enlightenment. But an eminent Conservative was disgusted with this latest escapade of 'the dishonest old man', and asked: 'if he lives, how low will he go?'[42]

Following his declared conversion, 'the most respected politician in Scotland' acted on his word by voting for another disestablishment motion of Dr. Cameron in May 1890, which was lost by a further reduced margin of only 38 votes.[43] Church defenders counter-attacked by disseminating propaganda, forming new committees and holding public meetings.[44] But after these events came another anti-climax for Scottish Voluntaries. Scottish disestablishment now seemed weaker than the more aggressively urged and impressively supported Welsh case, and only Welsh disestablishment was adopted as a Liberal policy in the Newcastle Programme of 1891. Moreover, under the impact of the Parnell divorce case Liberal expectations of marked electoral success were decreased, and the general election of July 1892 brought them quite a slender majority for which they depended entirely on divided and demoralised Irish Home Rule M.P.s.

The prominence of Home Rule in this election could not disguise the importance of the disestablishment issue in Scottish contests. Particular efforts were made by opponents of Voluntaryism to weaken electoral support for it. The Laymen's League, the Church Interests Committee of the Church of Scotland, presbytery committees, and other bodies such as the Dundee Church Establishment Association, called on electors to vote against candidates who favoured disestablishment.[45] Asquith, standing in East Fife, said he would vote for disestablishment and found 'the Kirk [of Scotland], who is a vigorous old lady, scratching and kicking at me like a muscular virago'.[46] A Liberal newspaper asserted: 'The Kirk has exerted at this election every ounce of strength it possesses. Every parish manse has been a Tory Committee room; very many pulpits have been turned into Conservative platforms; collections at the church doors have been taken practically on behalf of Tory candidates'.[47] The national Kirk's campaign had a degree of success. In some county constituencies, especially in the east, Liberal support declined, and Gladstone's majority in Midlothian sank to only a sixth of its level at the last contest in 1885[48] — though perhaps reaction against Parnell was more responsible for this than support for the established Church. Even so, the number of Scottish Liberal M.P.s increased, and it was claimed that Scotland returned 46 members pledged to disestablishment and only 19 against.[49] Optimistic Voluntaries might have thought their chance for success had come.

Once in office, however, the Liberals again did not play the part for which the Voluntaries had cast them. The Governments of 1892 to 1895 failed to achieve not only Irish Home Rule but Welsh and Scottish disestablishment. Although the Government made some demonstration of assisting Welsh disestablishment, they showed very little enthusiasm for Scottish — for which indeed there was now decidedly less pressure than for Welsh. A disestablishment bill introduced by Dr. Cameron handsomely passed its first reading in May 1893, with Gladstone praising it and voting in its favour.[50] But this was as far as the bill went in a session largely taken up by Home Rule, and in any case the Voluntaries thought their aim important enough to warrant a government bill rather than a mere private one. They campaigned for more positive government action. Church defenders showed at least an equal disposition to resist, and tried to make their organisation more widespread and efficient.[51]

In March 1894 Gladstone resigned and was succeeded by Rosebery. A premier who was by no means zealous for Scottish disestablishment was thus replaced by one who was even less so. Rosebery was under some pressure from the Queen, who was strongly opposed to Voluntaryism.[52] Speaking in Edinburgh on 17 March, Rosebery defended the principle of an established Church and supported the Voluntaries on grounds of party political expediency alone: 'He held that the State had as much right to maintain an Established Church, for its own purposes and its own interests, as it had to establish a standing army . . . But seeing that nearly every manse of the Established Church had become an agency for the Tory party, he was compelled to own that the continuance of the Establishment and of the Liberal party in Scotland, side by side, was coming to be inconsistent'.[53] During 1894 Cameron's bill was again brought in, but as fruitlessly as before. In 1895 a similar pattern recurred, some prominent Scottish Liberals having pleaded unsuccessfully that the Government should adopt the bill.[54] In June 1895 Rosebery resigned, and disestablishment was an issue once more in the election that followed.[55] The results showed a marked swing to Unionism, not least in Scotland; and the Liberals then commenced a decade in opposition, having done nothing to satisfy the disheartened ranks of Scottish Voluntaryism: 1895 seemed an appropriate anniversary for 1885.

The familar counterpoint of disestablishment and reunion had continued, and much attention had been given during the Liberal ministry to reunion through modification of the existing establishment. The principle of national religion might be maintained by means of a compromise leading to reunion between the established Church and other Presbyterian Churches. In the spring of 1894 private meetings commenced between representatives of the 'three Kirks', and continued for many months. The spirit of the discussions was reported to be most conciliatory, but nothing tangible resulted because differences over the establishment question were still too entrenched.[56] Efforts by the Laymen's League to gain support for reunion continued, but as yet remained barren of result.

Prospective union of another kind, however, became much more likely at this period — union of the Free Church and the United Presbyterians, which might have the effect of advancing Voluntaryism rather than weakening it. There were similar theological tendencies in these Churches — the relaxation of strict Calvinism and the growth of Arminianism, shown by the adoption of appropriate declarations in the U.P. Church in 1879 and the Free Church in 1892. Growing rejection of scriptural inerrancy was also taking place in the two bodies. Such developments helped to provide a common background for progress towards union, but they were resisted by a Free Church minority. A small secession from the Free Church occurred in 1893 in reaction to the declaration of the previous year. Free Church opponents of Voluntaryism emphasised their religious conservatism as another reason for resisting union.[57] It was being shown, as in the previous negotiations of 1863-73, that union of the two Churches would not have unanimous agreement.

Practical moves to unite the two denominations seem to have begun at a meeting of the Dundee Free Church Office-bearers' Union on 6 March 1894. The chairman said that lay officials ought to lead the way, and 'should there and then take the first step in a movement having for its object the ultimate Union of the two Churches'. A committee was appointed to take action, and a similar move took place in Glasgow.[58] In 1895 and later the union was discussed, and resolutions in its favour were passed, in the presbyteries and higher courts of the two Churches. The Free Church General Assembly was less unanimous than the United Presbyterian Synod because of the minority who insisted that union would contravene the establishment principle of the Free Church. In 1897, however, the Free Church assembly passed by a large majority a motion of Principal Rainy to negotiate on the practical questions of union; and thence the two Churches advanced, through joint meetings of their committees, towards a conjunction.[59] The Free Assembly of May 1900 adopted a Uniting Act by 557 votes to 29. This was sent down to presbyteries and accepted by all except four (Dingwall, Lochcarron, Skye and Inveraray). All the presbyteries of the U.P. Church had already approved of the Act, though 15 out of 539 kirk sessions had disapproved.[60]

The union formally took place on 31 October, and the United Free Church came into being. A small but significant minority of Free Churchmen stayed out and declared themselves the Free Church Continuing. Though they had not prevented the formation of the United Church, they soon did much, for a time, to take the wind out of its sails. Moreover, while the union might have seemed to promise a revival of Voluntaryism, this was scarcely the result. The new Church left this matter as an open question and did not regard it with much urgency. Consequently, if rather surprisingly, a more confident Voluntary movement did not materialise.

Despite the appearance in 1900 that Voluntaryism had been strengthened, in the next twenty years the disestablishment claim was overwhelmed by arguments preferring reunion on the basis of a reformed establishment. Before these arguments took root, the political situation remained discouraging to Voluntaryism until 1906; and the United Free Church was subjected in its first years to a strong legal challenge which caused it to concentrate on internal defence rather than an external scheme like disestablishment.

The little Free Church Continuing set out to attack the new Goliath over property rights, as they had threatened to do before the union took place. They claimed the entire property of the large pre-1900 Free Church on the ground that they alone represented the original doctrines and principles of that body, especially the principle of establishment and the doctrine of predestination. In the course of the bitter conflict a remarkable legal victory was gained by the 'Wee Frees' in 1904, when the House of Lords overturned the judgement of the Court of Session and assigned the whole property of the former Free Church to the much reduced continuation.[61] But the magnitude of the victory was embarrassing to the Free Church. If their twenty-eight ministers kept all the buildings, they would have to manage seven hundred churches and numerous overseas missions, maintain three divinity colleges and produce fifteen professors to teach, as yet, no students. In fact the Free Churchmen did not intend to keep the whole property but only to provide comfortably for their needs out of it.[62] The problem was resolved, though to the dissatisfaction of many of the contenders, by the Churches (Scotland) Act of 1905, which appointed an executive commission to share out the temporalities between the two Churches. The Free Church secured an allocation which was too generous in the view of many United Free Churchmen.

The absorption of energies in this dispute doubtless acted as a brake on those who still wished to urge the Voluntary cause. Support given to the U.F. Church by members of the establishment in the crisis perhaps promoted ideas of a Presbyterian union larger than that of 1900. Moreover, the addition of a clause to the 1905 Act, giving the Church of Scotland power to alter the terms of subscription to its Confession of Faith independently of the State, assisted the prospect of reunion with a Church which already possessed relaxed terms of subscription. It did this largely by demonstrating the loosening of the State bond: the *United Free Church Magazine* said that the clause 'alters the whole relation of the Church to the State'.[63] The Church of Scotland adopted a new relaxed formula in 1910.

Wider social, religious and political developments were also lowering denominational barriers and relegating contentious issues like Voluntaryism to a less prominent place. There was increasing worry, common to most denominations, about the large number of people who had no link with the Churches. It was stated in 1900 that over 1,600,000 people in Scotland, or 37.5 per cent of the population, had no Church connection.[64] The percentage of churchless was growing because the increase of church members was well below the rise in population. In 1908, for instance, the Church of Scotland gained 4,500 members, the U.F. Church fewer than 500; to keep pace with the rise in population that year, both Churches together needed an increase of 12,000.[65] Another shared concern of the Churches was widespread social deprivation. This prompted common participation in reform bodies such as the Scottish Christian Social Union. Such developments assisted ecumenicalism, which emphasised ideas held in common and suggested routes to compromise and unity in the search for greater religious effectiveness.[66] Moreover, the demand for social reform was beginning to change the face of politics. The aims of the new Labour party, for example, were very largely social and economic. This party tended (except in Wales and in some individual cases) to regard the battle for religious equality as practically won and the Voluntary cry as irrelevant to their main concerns.

These developments helped to provide a decisive challenge to longstanding ecclesiastical causes. By 1910, even the resistance of English and Welsh Nonconformists to rate-supported Anglican or Catholic denominational schools — so powerful a cry a few years before — had greatly declined in active support. Only Welsh disestablishment, with its strong combination of religious, social and nationalist motives, continued to flourish and went on to succeed. Scottish and English disestablishment, which had not the same array of resources to draw on, were becoming pale reflections of their former selves.

The United Free Assembly continued for some years to pass resolutions advocating disestablishment, but these began to seem a formality. Even the advent of a Liberal Government at the end of 1905 failed to cause a significant revival of Scottish Voluntaryism, though in 1907 the U.F. Assembly did send a manifesto to the prime minister, Campbell-Bannerman, in favour of disestablishment.[67] In the election campaign which gave the Liberals a huge majority in 1906, disestablishment, though not ignored, was generally a minor topic.[68]

Instead of Voluntaryism and Church defence, projects for the union of the two large Presbyterian Churches were about to become the major ecclesiastical interest. Such proposals did not rest on a precondition of disestablishment but on the possibility of accepting establishment status provided this was accompanied by guarantees of spiritual independence from the State. Even some formerly strong campaigners for Voluntaryism now urged the new approach.[69] So it was that the prospect of reunion on non-Voluntary lines was coming, after many years of rivalry with Voluntaryism, to assume more importance than the latter; and the union of 1900 was eventually succeeded not by another strong attack on the establishment but by conciliation towards it.

The negotiations leading to union have received ample treatment in both detail and summary,[70] and it will suffice to trace the main stages. A formal move to open discussions on co-operation and union commenced in the Edinburgh presbytery of the Church of Scotland in 1907, and was continued in the General Assembly, where it was resolved in the following year to propose a conference with the United Free Church. The U.F. Church agreed to this in 1909. Each Church appointed a negotiating committee of a hundred members, and arrangements were made for joint discussions. In 1912 both General Assemblies had an important Memorandum to consider. This proposed a *via media*, a means of combining spiritual independence with a recognised national Church.[71]

But progress was not exactly smooth, for considerable objection to union was still being shown in both Churches. In the Church of Scotland there were some who wished to maintain the existing relationship with the State; in the U.F. Church there were Voluntaries who feared that their principle would be lost. The Scottish Disestablishment Council and the *Liberator* (the journal of the Liberation Society) lamented the declining support for Voluntaryism and called for its revival.[72] But Voluntary enthusiasm was shrinking in face of the

R

interest in reunion. There was little reference to Voluntaryism in the two general elections of 1910, and some Liberal candidates clearly wished to shelve the question while the union discussions were proceeding.[73] Both General Assemblies agreed in 1913 to proceed towards union on the basis of the Memorandum of 1912, and draft articles of a constitution for a united Church were prepared by a committee of the Church of Scotland Assembly.

Much had thus been achieved, but the war delayed further progress. At the same time, however, by its cathartic and combining effects, the war encouraged hopes of ecclesiastical reconstruction when it ended. It also hastened the decline of disestablishment, not least by dividing and weakening the Liberal party. After the war only a few M.P.s were prepared to support disestablishment.[74]

In 1915 it was decided to postpone the discussions on union until armed hostilities ceased. However, discussions recommenced in March 1918 while fighting was still at its height, to the irritation of at least one minister who complained that he could not 'give his mind to the important subjects to be debated'.[75]

Though there were still differences and delays, the matter moved on apace after 1918. In January 1919 a joint conference of the two Churches welcomed some 'articles declaratory of the constitution of the Church of Scotland'. In May a joint committee said of these articles: 'on the terms now proposed, the Church . . . would be both national and free. The continuity and identity of the Church of Scotland would be maintained, while at the same time the Church would bear the character of a purely spiritual institution, in no sense deriving powers from or controlled by the State, nor enjoying any privilege to the prejudice of other Churches'.[76] Wider approval for the articles was obtained, though opposition to them on establishment grounds was voiced by the National Church Defence Association.

Approach was then made to the Government for legislation to put the articles into effect. After a delay in 1920, the Government's Church of Scotland Bill was brought into Parliament in 1921. The bill passed without a great deal of opposition, though various objections were raised on Voluntary grounds. One M.P., Joseph Johnstone, an elder of the United Free Church and a former United Presbyterian, deplored 'this abject surrender . . . of the principle of a free Church in a free State, and of religious equality, by this great united democratic Free Church, abandoning all its past declarations in favour of disestablishment, and entering voluntarily into the establishment fold'.[77] The new Act acknowledged the spiritual independence of the Church of Scotland, the most important step to be taken if union with the U.F. Church was to be achieved.[78]

In Wales disestablishment came into effect in 1920, but Scotland's Church problems were being resolved in a different way. After the 1921 Act there was further debate over the transfer of the temporalities to the possession of the Church of Scotland independently of the State. A settlement of the question of endowments was reached by an Act of 1925. But its provisions satisfied by no means all of those interested in the union negotiations, on the ground that the Church of Scotland might still be left with a financial advantage over other Churches, and therefore might still be in a privileged position over them contrary to previous assurances. In 1926, eighteen per cent of the United Free Assembly was still opposed to union.[79] However, the large majority was clearly in favour, and during the next three years administrative arrangements for a united Church were drawn up and approved. The union of the entire Church of Scotland with most of the United Free Church was ceremonially attained in October 1929. Loyalty to absolute Voluntaryism still claimed the dissident minority of the U.F. Church, which kept the name of that Church and remained a separate body. Thus pure Voluntaryism, while much weakened, continued to receive support.

The settlements of the 1920s enabled the Church of Scotland to absorb most of the elements which had left her in the preceding two hundred years. This result confirmed that a lengthy era of religious division and strife had been replaced by one of conciliation and union. In the outcome it was not disestablishment which formed the basis of union, but an attenuated and nominal type of establishment providing real spiritual independence and self-government. Principles of spiritual freedom were wedded to national recognition of religion; hence Chalmers' ideal seemed to have attained success. Political, social and intellectual developments had all played their parts in reducing the pressure of Voluntaryism and opening paths of compromise. More fundamentally, the impressive revival of the Church of Scotland in the later nineteenth century and the very slender religious divisions which separated most Presbyterians from each other had left insufficient scope for a radical new departure on Voluntary lines. In Wales the differences between Churchmen and Nonconformists were great enough to end in disestablishment. But the much weaker divisions in Scotland between establishment and dissenting Presbyterians encouraged the different outcome of reunion. Ultimately, the Church of Scotland had emerged strengthened through change — it was not *semper eadem*, perhaps, but certainly *nec tamen consumebatur*.

NOTES

1. Cf. printed 'statement of objections to Church Patronage Bill, July 1874'; Gladstone Papers, British Library Add. MS. 44444, fo. 12.

2. E.g. Minutes of the Liberation Society, 13 Aug. 1874, A/LIB/5, p. 152 (Greater London Record Office); *Nonconformist*, 9 Sept. 1874; *Primitive Methodist Magazine*, Nov. 1874, n.s. xii (1874), 704. For the origins and justification of Scottish Voluntaryism, see G. I. T. Machin, *Politics and the Churches in Great Britain, 1832 to 1868* (Oxford, 1977), 25-6, 100-101, 113-14.

3. A. R. McEwen, *Life and Letters of John Cairns, D.D., LL.D.* (London, 1895), 603-25; A. Oliver, *Life of George Clark Hutton, D.D.* (Paisley, 1910), 231-5; *United Presbyterian Magazine*, n.s. xxii (1878), 183, 236-8, 263-4; Minutes of Edinburgh

United Presbyterian presbytery, 30 June 1874 (Scottish Record Office, CH3/111/34, pp. 442-8); Aberdeen U.P. presbytery, 13 Dec. 1881 (CH3/2/15, pp. 105-6); Dundee U.P. presbytery, 3 Apr. 1883 (CH3/91/9, p. 39, now in Archives of Dundee District Council).

4. J. Kennedy, *The disestablishment movement in the Free Church* (Edinburgh, 1882), 11-13, 26.

5. For example the Free Church Assembly of 1875 declared, with 397 votes in favour and 84 against, for the ending of 'the existing connection between Church and State' (P. Carnegie Simpson, *The Life of Principal Rainy*, 2 vols., London 1909, i. 277-8). Similar divisions of opinion, with minorities opposed to disestablishment, are also shown in the Minutes of Edinburgh Free presbytery, 28 Nov. 1875 (Scottish Record Office, CH3/111/29, pp. 457-8) and 27 Mar. 1878 (ibid., pp. 10-11); Glasgow Free presbytery, 21 Feb. 1877 (CH3/146/39, pp. 67-9) and 15 Apr. 1878 (ibid., pp. 208-10).

6. Minutes of Liberation Society, 17 Dec. 1874, A/LIB/5, p. 194.

7. E.g. A. Taylor Innes, *The Scotch Law of Establishment* (Edinburgh, 1875); Rev. James Begg, *The principles, position and prospects of the Free Church of Scotland* (Edinburgh, 1875); Rev. John Kennedy, *Letter to the members of the Free Church in the Highlands* (Edinburgh, 1876); Rev. John Tulloch, *Position and prospects of the Church of Scotland* (Edinburgh, 1878); Anon., *The National Church: an appeal against disestablishment* (London and Edinburgh, 1878); *Some facts about the Scottish Establishment* (Liberation Society tract, London, n.d.); Rev. R. Rainy, 'Disestablishment in Scotland', *Contemporary Review*, xli (1882), 431-44; Rev. J. Tulloch, 'Disestablishment in Scotland: a reply', *ibid.*, 749-67.

8. Rev. James Johnston, *The ecclesiastical and religious statistics of Scotland* (Glasgow, 1874), 28: Church of Scotland members and adherents 1,063,000, Free Church 790,000, United Presbyterian 474,000.

9. J. Tulloch, 'Disestablishment in Scotland: a reply', *Contemporary Review*, xli (1882), 756-7: Tulloch claimed that Church of Scotland communicants were about 550,000, Free Church and the U.P. communicants together only 407,000. But cf. the tables in R. Currie, A. Gilbert and L. Horsley, *Churches and Churchgoers: patterns of Church growth in the British Isles since 1700* (Oxford, 1977), 132-3.

10. Tulloch to Rev. Dr. Phin, 11 Feb. 1878; Mrs. M. Oliphant, *A Memoir of the Life of John Tulloch* (Edinburgh, 1888), 325-6.

11. *Ibid.*, 338; see also 345-7.

12. Hartington to Gladstone, 31 Oct. 1877; Gladstone Papers, 44144, fo. 244.

13. J. G. Kellas, 'The Liberal party and the Scottish Church disestablishment crisis', *English Historical Review*, lxxix (1964), 32-3.

14. Simpson, *Rainy*, ii. 6-8.

15. W. E. Gladstone, *Midlothian Speeches, 1879* (Leicester, 1971), 76-80; *Scotsman*, 23 Mar. 1880, p.4 (leading article).

16. Kellas, *op. cit.*, 33; *Scotsman*, 4 Mar. 1880 (p.1), 8 Mar. (p.6), 11 Mar. (p.1), 12 Mar. (p.1), 13 Mar. (p.1), 23 Mar. (p.1); *Dundee Advertiser*, 10 Mar. (p.6), 13 Mar. (pp.1, 5, 6), 19 Mar. (p.6), 20 Mar. (p.1), 1 Apr. (p.6).

17. *Scotsman*, 23 Mar. 1880, p.1.

18. D. A. Hamer, *Liberal Politics in the Age of Gladstone and Rosebery* (Oxford, 1972), 89-90; Simpson, *Rainy*, ii, 10-16.

19. J. Morley, *The Life of William Ewart Gladstone* (3 vols., London, 1903), iii, 102.

20. *Fourth annual report of the Scottish Council of the Liberation Society 1880-1* (Edinburgh, 1881), 9-14. Cf. Minutes of Edinburgh U.P. presbytery, 6 Dec. 1881

(CH3/111/36, pp. 246-7) and 4 Apr. 1882 (ibid., p. 279).

21. A. L. Drummond and J. Bulloch, *The Church in late Victorian Scotland, 1874-1900* (Edinburgh, 1978), 115-16; Kellas, *op. cit.*, 34.

22. *Fourth annual report of Scottish Council of Liberation Society*, 15; newspaper report of a meeting on 31 Jan. 1882 (Lamb collection, 176 (11), Dundee Local History Library, Central Library, Dundee).

23. Kellas, *op. cit.*, 35.

24. Newspaper report of a meeting on 28 Feb. 1882 (Lamb Collection, 176 (ll), Dundee Local History Library); Rev. A. H. Charteris to Lord Balfour of Burleigh, 7 Dec. 1882 (Balfour of Burleigh Papers, 53, in private hands).

25. Salisbury to R. A. Cross, 30 Oct. 1883 (Cross Papers, British Library Add. MS. 51263, fo. 76); *Congregationalist*, xii (1883), 10; *United Presbyterian Magazine*, n.s. xxvii, 62-3.

26. E.g. a resolution of the Church of Scotland presbytery of Abertarff (Lochaber) that an attempt should be made to unite with the numerous non-Voluntary Free Churchmen of the North and West Highlands; Minutes of this presbytery, 27 Dec. 1882 (CH2/7/8, pp. 424-5).

27. *Report of the proceedings of the Scottish Presbyterian Union Association during its first session, ending 10 June 1885* (Edinburgh, 1886), 3 ff.

28. Anon., *Disestablishment and free education: an address to the working men of Scotland, by a layman* (Glasgow, 1885); Anon., *Disestablishment: what will it put in my pocket?* (Glasgow, 1885).

29. See A. Simon, 'Church disestablishment as a factor in the general election of 1885', *Historical Journal*, xviii (1975), 791-820.

30. *Annual Register*, cxxvii (1885), 169.

31. Minutes of Dundee U.P. presbytery, 6 Oct. 1885 (CH3/19/9, p. 166, now in Archives of Dundee District Council); Aberdeen U.P. presbytery, 26 and 27 Oct. 1885 (CH3/2/15, pp. 209-10); Dundee Church of Scotland presbytery, 4 Nov. 1885 (CH2/103/23, pp. 307-14, now in Dundee District Council archives); Rev. J. Pringle to Hon. Arthur Elliot, M.P., 7 and 17 Sept. 1885 (Arthur Elliot Papers, National Library of Scotland); Rev. Robert Fordyce to Hon. Arthur Elliot, 3 Nov. 1885 (ibid.); *Scotsman*, 24 Oct. 1885 (pp. 11-12), 26 Oct. 1885 (p. 4); J. G. Kellas, 'The Liberal party and the Scottish Church disestablishment crisis', 35-7; J. G. Kellas, 'The Liberal party in Scotland, 1876-95', *Scottish Historical Review*, 44 (1965), 6; D. C. Savage, 'Scottish Politics, 1885-6', *ibid.*, 40 (1961), 118-24; J. F. McCaffrey, 'Political reactions in the Glasgow constituencies at the general elections of 1885 and 1886' (Ph.D. thesis, University of Glasgow, 1970), 99-106, 113-15.

32. Simon, *op. cit.*, 810; Kellas, 'The Liberal party and the Scottish Church disestablishment crisis', 37; Drummond and Bulloch, *op. cit.*, 119-21; Sheriff Mackintosh to Earl of Rosebery, 27 Oct. 1885 (Rosebery Papers, National Library of Scotland, 10084, fos. 68-73); D. Crawford to Rosebery, 1 Nov. 1885 (ibid., fos. 103-8).

33. Kellas, *op. cit.*, 37; Simpson, *Rainy*, ii. 36-9.

34. Kellas, 'The Liberal party in Scotland, 1876-95', 10.

35. W. L. Calderwood and D. Woodside, *The Life of Henry Calderwood* (London, 1900), 345.

36. R. B. Finlay to Rosebery, 21 Dec. 1885 (Rosebery Papers, 10084, fos. 275-7); Kellas, 'The Liberal party and the Scottish Church disestablishment crisis', 38-9; Simpson, *Rainy*, ii. 51-72; *United Presbyterian Magazine*, n.s. iii (1886), 89; Anon., *The Claim of Right, with the draft of Mr. Finlay's Bill, and report of the conference to*

promote it (Edinburgh, 1886); A. Taylor Innes, *Mr. Finlay's Bill and the Law of 1843* (Edinburgh, 1886); Prof. W. G. Blaikie, *Ought the Free Church to resume connection with the State?* (London and Edinburgh, 1886).

37. E.g. Minutes of Dundee Church of Scotland presbytery, 3 Mar. 1886 (CH2/103/23, pp. 335-6, Dundee District Council archives); *Dundee Advertiser*, 7 June 1886, p. 3; Prof. H. Calderwood, *Disestablishment and Union of the Presbyterians of Scotland* (Edinburgh, 1889); *United Presbyterian Magazine*, vi (1889), 545-9; Calderwood and Woodside, *op. cit.*, 345-7; R. Sjölinder, *Presbyterian Reunion in Scotland, 1907-21* (Edinburgh, 1962), 93-101.

38. A. L. Drummond and J. Bulloch, *The Church in late Victorian Scotland*, 124; Minutes of Edinburgh U.P. presbytery, 1 Apr. 1890, 7 Oct. 1890, 3 Mar. 1891, 7 Apr. 1891 (CH3/111/38, pp. 238-9, 280-1, 340-1).

39. *Annual Register*, cxxix (1887), 161-2.

40. *Ibid.*, cxxxi (1889), 135-6. Cf. Gladstone to Balfour of Burleigh, 15 Aug. 1889 (Balfour of Burleigh Papers, 9); Rev. David Mitchell to Gladstone, 7 Nov. 1889 (Rosebery Papers, 10023, fos. 274-5).

41. Gladstone to Rosebery, 10 Nov. 1889; Rosebery Papers 10023, fos. 276-7.

42. Earl of Cranbrook's diary, 14 June 1889; Nancy E. Johnson (ed.), *The Diary of Gathorne Hardy, later Lord Cranbrook* (Oxford, 1981), 737.

43. *The Disestablishment Banner* (journal of Disestablishment Council for Scotland), xvii (May and October 1890).

44. E.g. Minutes of Dundee Church of Scotland presbytery, 11 June 1890, 3 Sept. 1890, 4 Feb. 1891 (CH2/103/24, pp. 281-3, 292-5, 336-8).

45. *The Laymen's League and the General Election* (Laymen's League Office, Edinburgh, 1892); *To the People of Scotland: an address by the Committee on Church Interests of the General Assembly of the Church of Scotland* (Edinburgh , 1892); Minutes of Dundee District Church of Scotland presbytery, 27 June 1892 (CH2/103/24, pp. 505-9).

46. Asquith to Mrs. Horner, 12 July 1892 (J. Spender and C. Asquith, *Life of Herbert Henry Asquith*, 2 vols., London, 1932, i, 75); *Scotsman*, 1 July 1892 (pp. 1, 10), 2 July (pp. 8, 12); *Dundee Advertiser*, 4 July, p.6.

47. *The People's Journal* (Dundee), 16 July 1892.

48. Kellas, 'The Liberal party and the Scottish Church disestablishment crisis', 42-3; *Annual Register*, cxxxiv (1892), 179.

49. Simpson, *Rainy*, ii. 148.

50. *Annual Register*, cxxxv (1893), 237.

51. E.g. leaflets on a Dundee public meeting in favour of disestablishment, held on 21 Dec. 1893 (in Lamb Collection, Dundee Local History Library, 176); Minutes of Dundee Church of Scotland presbytery, 5 Apr., 1 Nov. 1893, 7 Feb., 14 Mar., 4 Apr., 2 May 1894 (CH2/103/24, pp. 13-14, 116-17, 142-3, 147, 163, 173).

52. Kellas, *op. cit.*, 45-6.

53. *Annual Register*, cxxxvi (1894), 77-9.

54. H. Campbell-Bannerman to Rosebery, 16 Jan. 1895 (Rosebery Papers, 10003, fos. 53-4); Lord Tweedmouth to Rosebery, 16 Jan. 1895 (ibid., 10101, fos. 125-7); Simpson, *Rainy*, ii. 150-3.

55. *Scotsman*, 1 July 1895 (p.8), 2 July (p.6), 3 July (p.6), 4 July (p.1).

56. Rev. Dr. James Robertson to A. J. Balfour, 5 June 1894 (A. J. Balfour Papers, British Library Add. MS. 49790, fos. 114-20); *Annual Register*, cxxxviii (1896), 215; R. Sjölinder, *Presbyterian Reunion in Scotland*, 101-2.

57. A. Stewart and J. Kennedy Cameron, *The Free Church of Scotland, 1843-1910: a vindication* (Edinburgh and Glasgow, n.d. [1910]), 66-75, 121-4; Simpson, *Rainy*, ii. 109-29.

58. *Dundee Advertiser*, 7 Mar. 1894. Cf. Simpson, *Rainy*, ii, 194; Minutes of Dundee Free presbytery, CH3/91/6, pp. 40-1; *A plea for union between the United Presbyterian Church and the Free Church of Scotland, addressed by the Dundee Free Church office-bearers to their brother office-bearers* (Dundee, 1895; in Lamb Collection, Dundee Local History Library, 177).

59. Simpson, *Rainy*, ii. 194-223; Stewart and Cameron, 87 ff.

60. *Annual Register*, cxlii (1900), 250; Minutes of Dundee U.P. presbytery, 8 Feb. 1899 (CH3/91/13, pp. 321-2).

61. Stewart and Cameron, *op cit.*, 151-240; Simpson, *Rainy*, ii. 300 ff; *Annual Register*, cxlvi (1904), 235-8; W. T. Stead, *Are there any Free Churches? An examination of the strange true story of the Free Church of Scotland in the light of the recent decision of the House of Lords* (London, 1904).

62. Stewart and Cameron, *op. cit.*, 268, 284.

63. *United Free Church Magazine*, Sept. 1905, p.2. Cf. Rev Dr. James Robertson to A. J. Balfour, 24 Sept. 1904 (Balfour Papers, 49790, fos. 141-3); D. Sommer, *Haldane of Cloan, his life and times, 1856-1928* (London, 1960), 379-80; Stewart and Cameron, *op. cit.*, 302-4.

64. Sjölinder, *op. cit.*, 57.

65. Augustus Muir, *John White, C.H., D.D., LL.D.* (London, 1958), 120.

66. Sjölinder, *op. cit.*, 69-90.

67. J. H. S. Burleigh, *A Church History of Scotland* (London, 1960), 399.

68. Prof J. A. Paterson to Campbell-Bannerman, 29 Nov. 1905 (Campbell-Bannerman Papers, British Library Add. MS. 41238, fos. 105-6); *Scotsman*, 3 Jan. 1906 (p. 10), 4 Jan 1906 (p.7); *Dundee Advertiser*, 19 Jan. 1906, p.8. (but also 22 Jan. 1906, p.9).

69. G. F. Barbour, *The Life of Alexander Whyte, D.D.* (London, 1924), 517.

70. Sjölinder, *op. cit.*, 163 ff; Muir, *John White*, 112 ff; Rev A. I. Dunlop, 'The paths to reunion in 1929', *Records of the Scottish Church History Society*, xx (1980), 163-78.

71. Rev. Dr. Archibald Henderson (U.F. Church) to Balfour of Burleigh, 19 Feb. and 8 Mar. 1912, copies (Lord Sands Papers, Scottish Record Office, CH1/10/2); Sheriff Christopher Johnston (later Lord Sands) to Balfour of Burleigh, 2 May 1912 (ibid., CH1/10/9); Henderson to Johnston, May 1912 (ibid.); Rev. John White to Keir Hardie, Apr. 1914 (A. Gammie, *Dr. John White, a biography and a study*, London 1929, 146-51).

72. *The Liberator*, Sept. 1911 (pp. 147-8), Mar. 1913 (pp. 41-2), June 1914 (p.88), Oct. 1918 (p.59). But the U.F. Church and the Church of Scotland respectively still supported and opposed Welsh disestablishment; Minutes of Edinburgh Church of Scotland presbytery, 26 June 1912 (CH2/121/34, p. 299), and of Edinburgh U.F. presbytery, 2 July 1912 (CH3/111/46, p.2).

73. *Dundee Advertiser*, 12 Jan. 1910, p.9 (A. F. Whyte, candidate for Perth), 1 Dec. 1910, p.3 (J. D. Miller, candidate for St. Andrews burghs).

74. Sjölinder, *op. cit.*, 312-13.

75. Rev. D. Macmillan to Rev. Dr. Williamson, 10 Apr. 1918; Sands Papers, CH1/10/16.

76. Printed statement in Sands Papers, CH1/10/20, fo. 40.

77. Hansard, *Parliamentary Debates*, 5th Series, vol. 144, col. 963. The debate on the second reading (22 June 1921) is reported in vol. 143, cols. 1397-1469, and on the third reading (11 July 1921) in vol. 144, cols. 951-69.

78. F. Lyall, *Of Presbyters and Kings — Church and State in the Law of Scotland* (Aberdeen, 1980), 66-84; A. I. Dunlop, *op. cit.*, 171; Muir, *White*, 200-13; Sjölinder, 309-56. The Church of Scotland Act is printed in J. T. Cox, ed., *Practice and Procedure in the Church of Scotland* (6th ed., Edinburgh, 1976), 470-2.

79. Muir, *White*, 238-40, 249.

Index